■ The Venturesome Economy

Amar Bhidé

The Venturesome Economy

How Innovation

Sustains Prosperity

in a More

Connected World

PRINCETON UNIVERSITY PRESS
Princeton and Oxford

Library of Congress Control Number: 2008933009

ISBN-13: 978-0-691-13517-5

British Library Cataloging-in-Publication Data is available

This book has been composed in Minion and Myriad
Printed on acid-free paper. ∞
press.princeton.edu
Printed in the United States of America

10 9 8 7 6 5 4 3 2 1

To the memory of my parents,

who long ago

ventured to lands afar

and brought the world home to us.

■ Contents

■ Preface

The growing integration of the world's economy in general, and the increased participation of China and India in international trade in particular, raise important questions: Will competition from more than a billion Chinese and Indians reduce wages and imperil the prosperity of the West? What, if anything, is to be done?

Classical economic theories of the eighteenth and nineteenth centuries provide limited guidance. These theories assume that trade takes place between countries with comparative advantages based in immutable natural advantages: It behooves Britain, where it rains a lot, to focus on rearing sheep and shearing wool and to let sunny Portugal grow grapes and make port. Because geographic conditions are fixed, in classical economic theory the wool-for-port trade continues forever.[1] But today the comparative advantage of poor countries derives from their historical failure to use the technological innovations that made the West rich. The impetus for trade between rich and poor countries arises from the differences in their accumulated technological capabilities rather than in their geographic endowments. As Edmund Phelps and I have noted, trade based on differences in technological capabilities can eventually extinguish itself: Openness to trade helps China become more technologically advanced and prosperous; increased prosperity causes wage differentials with the United States to shrink, ultimately making it unprofitable to import cotton from the United States and send back shirts and skirts.[2]

A large body of modern economic research does incorporate the dynamic interactions of trade and innovation. In the view of some, however, modern theories continue to exclude many crucial real-world features of the modern economy. As Phelps observed in his Nobel Prize lecture, the "distinctive character of the modern economy" involves "uncertainty, ambiguity [and] diversity of beliefs." Entrepreneurs "have to act on their 'animal spirits,'" often launching their innovations first and discovering the benefits and costs afterward.[3] But, Phelps writes elsewhere, instead of treating the modern economy as it really is ("an evolving, unruly, open-ended system"), the "established body of economic theory" implies a "deterministic future." Economists ignore disagreements about what might happen—uncertainty is instead watered down to well-defined probability distributions.[4]

All theories, of course, simplify, but the degree of simplification ought to depend on context and purpose. Boat builders can ignore the possibility of tidal waves and icebergs when they design recreational sailboats, but not when they design supertankers. Unfortunately, because tractable mathematical models cannot cope with a large number of variables, economists often have to simplify far more than is warranted by the context. Depending on the simplifying assumptions, different models can produce conflicting results; model A may show technological advances in backward economies to be good for advanced economies, while model B shows precisely the opposite. But with both models far removed from real-world conditions, we cannot identify which is the more likely result.

Fortunately, we do have a pragmatic, well-tested model for integrating a wide range of facts and theories when a situation so demands: the common-law trial.[5] Many witnesses provide testimony about various facets of the case. Some of it is qualitative, some of it is not. Lawyers offer theories to tie the facts together, using precedents or case law to inform their interpretations. In certain kinds of trials, criminologists, psychologists, pathologists, economists, and other such experts also testify. As both sides muster facts, precedents, and experts that favor their own theory, the sum of their arguments provides a comprehensive view.

To be sure, this combination of induction and deduction does not produce incontrovertible results. Unless one side makes a palpably unreasonable argument, judges and jurors face considerable ambiguity. Experts disagree. The same facts, depending on how they are weighted, suggest the application of different precedents and legal theories. Moreover, although common-law judges must respect precedent, they also have to keep in mind the distinctive circumstances of the case at hand as well as the fact that changes may make some precedents obsolete. Inevitably decisions turn on subjective judgments, not on objective deduction. And well-considered decisions rendered by an experienced judge may be reversed on appeal. Nevertheless, most of us wouldn't trade this judicial process for a more objective approach that excludes all but a few quantifiable variables. We wouldn't want cases decided using the kinds of scoring models employed to issue credit cards, for instance.*

Unlike a planned trial, my common-law type of inquiry about the nexus between globalization and innovation has evolved in a rather unexpected way.

Twenty years ago I started studying new and emerging businesses. Virtually all the businesses I examined operated entirely within the United States—they didn't buy or sell anything abroad. When the "offshoring" of services gained momentum, I wondered whether the "entrepreneurial" companies that my research had focused on were involved in this new form of international trade.

In 2002, I undertook a comprehensive study of the climate for entrepreneurship in Bangalore, which famously has been at the center of the offshoring boom in India.[6] In the course of this research I observed that large multinational companies were the main users of offshore services; small U.S. businesses lacked the scale needed to take advantage of the low-cost labor force. The experience piqued my curiosity: if entrepreneurial businesses weren't well suited for offshoring, did another facet of globalization matter to them?

Returning to the United States, I began studying the cross-border interactions of businesses financed by professional venture capitalists (VCs). I focused on VC-backed businesses because I believed (for reasons I discuss in chapter 1) that this genre was likely to have more international activity than other kinds of small or entrepreneurial businesses. Since my Bangalore experience suggested that offshoring was not important to most new and emerging businesses, I decided to examine, in the broadest possible way, how the world outside the United States affected U.S.-based, VC-backed businesses. My research associate and I asked the CEOs of 106 such

---

* Arguably the common-law trial reasoning and process is in fact what is used by such economists as the chairman of the Federal Reserve when they have to confront a complex and dynamic world. A less deliberate, more "seat of the pants," variant is often used to make business decisions.

businesses about all the possible ways they might engage in cross-border activities and transactions: To what degree, and why, did their businesses serve overseas customers and secure goods, services, intellectual property, and capital from abroad? Did they face competitors from abroad? What role did immigrants play in starting and staffing their companies?

I had few preconceptions about the form or extent of the globalization that I would observe—rather, I relied on interviewees telling us what kinds of cross-border interactions were important to their businesses. Similarly, I started with no hypotheses about why VC-backed businesses have cross-border engagements—I expected to formulate hypotheses while collecting the data.* This inductive approach does not always produce interesting results; I have more than once done fieldwork that failed the "So what?" test. With this project, I was fortunate. My fieldwork has not just illuminated the specific question of what VC-backed businesses do, but provided a revealing perspective on the interaction between innovation and globalization and its meaning for our long-run prosperity.[7]

My assessments aren't definitive, but to paraphrase Keynes, finally we have to decide. In an evolving, unruly world, we have to rely on provisional judgments, for we can't reach fixed conclusions. I hope that readers—even those who don't accept all my inferences—will find them useful in thinking about what policies should, and what policies should not, be pursued to cope with globalization.

---

* Many scholars in the social sciences regard the collection of data in the absence of well-formulated hypotheses as *verboten*. By contrast, natural scientists seem (like common-law jurists) more open to a two-way flow between facts and hypotheses: some researchers design experiments to test the predictions of a theory; others collect data that may subsequently be woven into a theory because they regard certain facts as prima facie useful and important. For instance, upon discovering a new planet, astronomers will try to measure its circumference and distance from its star. When biologists find a new species, they want to know what it eats, how much it weighs, and so on. I happen to believe that the study of the workings and dynamics of human society would benefit from a similarly evenhanded approach, in which theorizing doesn't always precede data-collection. I find it puzzling, for instance, that for all the many books and articles that have recently been written about multinational corporations, it is hard to find data on the proportion the overseas activities of these corporations represent of their total revenues, assets, or employment.

■ Introduction

Many manufacturing companies that once flourished in the United States have succumbed to overseas competition or have relocated much of their activity abroad. Domestic employees of U.S. companies make few of the ubiquitous objects of daily life—most of the clothes and shoes that Americans wear, their furnishings, children's toys, TV sets, phones, and computers are produced by foreign companies, typically in foreign factories. Even the ships and containers that carry these goods to the United States most often come out of overseas shipyards and factories.

Now services appear to be reprising the journey of manufacturing. Just as the manufacturing exodus started with the low-wage, relatively unskilled work of assembling trinkets or stitching clothes, the offshoring of services started with data entry, routine software programming and testing, and phone banks that answer customers' questions (with varying degrees of success) or make telemarketing calls. At a later stage, overseas manufacturing went high end, producing numerically controlled machine tools, robots, and high-performance automobiles, for example. In a similar way, the offshoring of services has expanded to include what Peter Drucker called "knowledge work." Companies such as Microsoft are offshoring software architecture, not just low-end programming.[1] Overseas workers with advanced degrees are analyzing financial statements, testing trading strategies, designing computer chips, and reading X-rays for U.S. clients.

Most significant, in the eyes of some, is the offshoring of R&D. According to a cover story in *BusinessWeek,* when Western companies farmed out manufacturing in the 1980s and 1990s, they promised to keep "all the important research and development" in-house. That pledge has now become "passé." Companies such as Dell and Motorola are buying "complete designs" from Asian manufacturers. While electronics is "furthest down the road," the "search for offshore help" is "spreading to nearly every corner of the economy" as U.S. companies find that their current R&D spending "isn't yielding enough bang for the buck." While outsourcing may reduce costs in the short run, *BusinessWeek* cautions, Western companies could "lose their technology edge" as their Asian contractors move up the "innovation ladder."[2]

■ The Fear of Flatness

Compared to imports of manufactured products, the offshoring of services, particularly of R&D, is still small in terms of dollar amounts and number of jobs. Nevertheless, the phenomenon has touched a nerve. Television programs such as the Lou Dobbs show, Thomas Friedman's best-seller *The World Is Flat*, the New Jersey State Legislature (which sought to keep government agencies from offshoring services), the presidential campaign of John Kerry, the Economic Report of the President in 2004, the National Science Foundation, and several distinguished academics have all weighed in on the issue.

The offshoring of services attracts attention because the media are sensitive to its consequences. To imagine their jobs threatened by offshore labor has been a shock to college-educated knowledge workers, including those in the media, who expect to avoid prolonged involuntary unemployment and to earn a good living.* Knowledge workers are also the consumers likely to watch news network channels and read high-toned books and newspaper columns. Naturally, TV shows, books, and columns cover the interests of their core audiences.

---

* Many of the manufacturing workers whose jobs migrated overseas didn't expect secure high-paying jobs. High-paying employment for the long haul offered by unionized steel and automobile companies was never the norm in industries such as apparel and footwear. Moreover, job losses (or wage cuts) in manufacturing aren't always newsworthy: employment and incomes have long been uncertain, with or without imports, because of productivity improvements and cyclical downturns.

Besides menacing an influential class, the rise of offshoring up the so-called value chain—from telemarketing, to tele-radiology, to cutting-edge R&D—has raised concerns about the long-term prosperity of the United States. Many worry that the country's lead in science and technology, which they believe mitigated its loss of low-end manufacturing jobs, will erode as R&D relocates to low-cost locations. Harvard economist Richard Freeman warns that "American technological competitiveness" could soon be threatened "as large developing countries like China and India harness their growing scientific and engineering expertise to their enormous, low-wage labor forces."[3]

How should the United States prepare for what the blue-ribbon Committee on Prospering in the Global Economy of the 21st Century calls a "gathering storm"? One answer, given by a group that includes Ross Perot, Pat Buchanan, Lou Dobbs, and members of the New Jersey and other state legislatures, is America-first protectionism. A historical populist response to threats from overseas has been to throw up barriers, but that reaction fell out of favor after the Smoot-Hawley Act of 1930—which squeezed trade by raising tariffs on imported goods—is thought to have helped turn what might have been a recession into the Great Depression. Protectionism has now made a comeback of sorts, sometimes in the guise of demands for level playing fields that unfair traders abroad have allegedly tilted. This neoprotectionism has resonated with unexpected groups: a September 2007 *Wall Street Journal*/NBC poll found that a majority of Republican voters believed free trade was bad for the U.S. economy.[4]

Another, apparently more progressive, answer is given by the Committee on Prospering in the Global Economy, formed by the National Academy of Sciences, the National Academy of Engineering, and the Institute of Medicine. Its prescription: more spending on science and technology. Specific recommendations include increasing federal outlays on long-term basic research by 10 percent a year for the next seven years; new research grants for outstanding early career researchers; a National Coordination Office for Research Infrastructure; 25,000 new undergraduate scholarships to U.S. citizens earning undergraduate degrees at U.S. institutions in the sciences, engineering, and math; 5,000 new graduate fellowships; the addition of 10,000 science and math school teachers; tax credits for employers who make available continuing education to practicing scientists and engineers; and automatic work permits for international students who receive doctorates in science and engineering in the United States.

Much of the establishment, Democratic and Republican, has embraced this "techno-fetishism and techno-nationalism" (to borrow terms from Ostry and Nelson).[5] Its advocates assert that prosperity requires continued leadership in cutting-edge science and technology. According to Thomas Friedman, in the "new era of globalization" people have the tools to "compete, connect and collaborate from anywhere." In such a world, the United States must "do whatever can be done first. It matters that Google was invented here." In language that might characterize predations in a high-security penitentiary, Friedman asserts: "What can be done will be done by someone, somewhere. The only question is whether it will be done by you or to you."[6]

Although their popularity in the mainstream is recent, techno-nationalist prognoses and prescriptions aren't new. Just as doomsday prophets rue the migration of services abroad today, a previous generation sounded similar calls about manufacturing and offered similar palliatives. In 1984, for instance, presidential candidate Walter Mondale said the United States was in danger of becoming a nation of burger flippers. A prize-winning article in the *Harvard Business Review* argued that the United States was "managing" its way to economic decline. A 1983 presidential commission declared: "Our Nation is at risk. Our once unchallenged preeminence in commerce, industry, science, and technological innovation is being overtaken by competitors throughout the world." The commission noted that the Japanese made automobiles more efficiently than did Americans, that the Koreans had recently built the world's most efficient steel mill, and that American machine tools, "once the pride of the world," were being displaced by German products. The commission's recommendations to counter the loss of this edge included a high school curriculum that included three years of math, three years of science, and one-half year of computer science. In a similar vein, some scholars in the 1980s attributed the lagging performance of the U.S. economy to the existence of too many lawyers and too few engineers and scientists, offering Japan and Germany as examples of better occupational ratios.*

As it happened, the United States prospered while the Japanese and German economies slackened. And it wasn't because the warnings were

---

* I was lucky to avoid the Japan-mania: in June 1981, I coauthored a *Wall Street Journal* op-ed titled "The Crucial Weaknesses of Japan Inc.," in which I pointed out that the much vaunted consensual Japanese system also limited the dynamism of its economy.

acted upon. There was no great improvement in math and science education in high schools. Enrollment in law schools remained robust, and managers continued to increase their share of overall employment. The U.S.
share of scientific articles, PhDs in science and engineering, and patents
continued to decline. The service sector (including hamburger chains) continued to expand, and manufacturing employment continued to stagnate.

All the while, new best-sellers continually "warn[ed] the American
public of dire consequences of losing the 'race' for the 21st century."[7] And
this was while the Japanese and the continental European economies were
slowing and *before* the takeoff of the Chinese economy entered the public
consciousness.

Of course the United States can't count on the same ending to every
episode of the Losing Our Lead serial. The integration of China and India
into the global economy is a seminal development, unprecedented in its
scale. Could it be different this time? Is the United States finally on the verge
of being pummeled by a technological hurricane? In my view, apprehen-
sions about the offshoring of R&D and the growth of scientific capabilities
in China and India arise from a failure to appreciate the complex nature of
the modern innovation system and its interactions with globalization.
Techno-nationalists, I argue, have a narrow conception of innovation and
its relationship to globalization. Less simplistic analyses of the complex
realities lead to a completely different prognosis.

■ A Complex, Multiplayer Game

Almost everyone agrees that technological innovation plays a crucial role
in sustaining prosperity. Similarly, few deny the significance of globalization or doubt that technological innovation affects globalization and vice
versa. But both technological innovation and globalization are complex,
and they interact in complex ways. This complexity makes their effects on
each other and on a nation's prosperity a challenge to understand. We must
be careful to formulate policies that sustain rather than undermine economic prosperity by, for instance, favoring one form of innovative activity
over another.

The difficulty of defining technological innovation reveals the great diversity of its forms.[8] To expose the nature of this diversity and understand
its implications, I first, paradoxically, need to simplify. Therefore, I divide

the many forms of innovation into two categories, new *products* and the new *know-how* upon which they are based,* and further stratify both know-how and products into three levels, as I explain in the following.

For any new product, the underlying know-how ranges from *high-level* general principles, to *mid-level* technologies, to *ground-level* context-specific heuristics or rules of thumb. In microprocessors, for instance, high-level know-how includes the laws of solid-state physics; mid-level, the circuit designs and chip layouts; and ground-level, the tweaking of conditions in a specific semiconductor fabrication plant to maximize the quality and yield of the microprocessors produced.

New products can similarly range from high-level building blocks or raw materials (microprocessors or the silicon used to make them), to mid-level intermediate goods (the motherboards that contain the microprocessor in laptop computers), to ground-level final products (laptop computers). As shown in figure I.1, each level of product is supported by multiple levels of know-how.[†9]

The figure shows a similar stratification of know-how for high-level coffee beans, mid-level coffee-roasting equipment, and the ground-level cup of espresso. Apparently multilevel technological innovation stirs up centuries-old beverages just as it does newfangled computers.

Individual forms of technological innovation, especially at the high level, usually have limited economic or commercial value unless they are complemented by lower-level innovations. A breakthrough in solid-state physics has value in the semiconductor industry only to the degree that it is accompanied by the development of new microprocessor designs; and the new designs may be useless without the development of plant-level tweaks for large-scale production of the microprocessor. Similarly, realizing the value of a new high-level microprocessor may require the development of

---

* This roughly corresponds to other commonly used taxonomies such as "ideas" and "objects"; "nonrival" and "rival" goods; and "bits" and "atoms." Note also that throughout this book, my usage of "products" includes services unless otherwise specified.

† Even these nine categories of know-how and three categories of products involve considerable simplification. First, there really aren't three distinct levels—know-how and products actually occupy a continuum from high level to ground level. Second, differences in level aren't the only way new know-how and products can be distinguished. Innovations can also vary in the degree to which they are novel, represent breakthroughs, have "general purpose" rather than "niche" applications, are proprietary or open source, and so on. In other words, the forms of innovation occupy a multidimensional space rather than a flat plane.

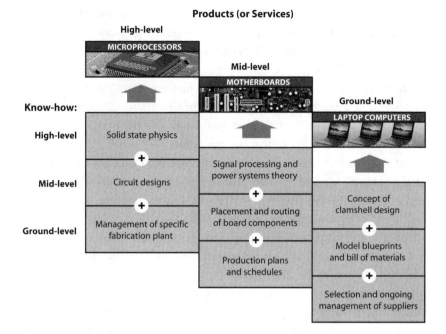

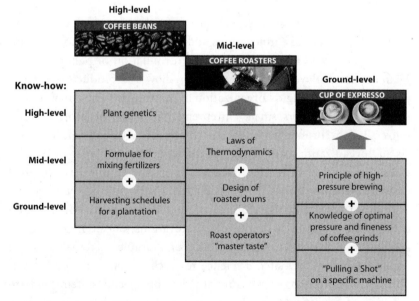

Figure I.1. Levels of innovation for know-how and products

new mid-level motherboards and ground-level computers. At the same time, high-level innovations often provide the building blocks, and a reason, for lower-level innovations. A breakthrough in solid-state physics may, for instance, provide the motive and the means for developing new microprocessor designs, and a new microprocessor may stimulate the development of new motherboards and computers. In other words, the different forms of innovation interact in complicated ways, and it is these interconnected, multilevel advances that create economic value.

Interconnected, multilevel innovations that aren't, in the usual sense, "technological" are also necessary for realizing the value of new know-how and products. A new "diskless" (or "thin client") computer, for instance, will generate revenue for its producer and value for its users only if it is effectively marketed by the former and properly deployed by the latter. Marketing and organizational innovations are usually required; for example, the producer of the diskless computer may have to develop new sales pitches and materials, and users may have to reorganize their IT departments. These marketing and organizational innovations can also be stratified into my scheme of three levels. On the marketing side, for instance, the vendor has to figure out a "unique selling proposition" (high level), a sales and marketing strategy (mid-level), and a plan for individual sales calls (ground-level).

The specialization and interrelationships of the individuals and organizations that undertake innovations add yet another dimension of complexity that should be factored into the formulation of public policies. Many different players develop new know-how and products—or complementary marketing or organizational innovations. They may be solo inventors and designers, small "entrepreneurial" firms, megacorporations, university labs, or independent research centers, with different individuals and organizations specializing in different levels or kinds of innovations. Some small firms, for instance, specialize in mid-level product design, others provide plant-level engineering services, and yet others develop advertising campaigns for new products. Large companies like IBM undertake a relatively wide range of innovations, but even here we see specialization at the level of subunits. For example, R&D labs at IBM undertake high-level material science research or semiconductor development. Other groups in the company develop specific systems and applications for particular market segments. This specialization in turn means that no individual, lab, small business, or subunit of a large business can on its own develop the full set of innovations necessary to create economic value.

In my view, it is futile to argue about which innovations or innovators make the most valuable contribution to economic prosperity. Rather, different kinds of innovations and innovators often play complementary roles. To state the proposition in the terminology of cyberspace, *innovations that sustain modern prosperity have a variety of forms and are developed and used through a massively multiplayer, multilevel, and multiperiod game.*

Consider, for instance, the transistor, the key active component in almost all modern electronics. A German physicist, Julius Edgar Lilienfeld, registered the first three patents for field-effect transistors in 1928. In 1934, another German physicist, Oskar Heil, patented another field-effect transistor. However, none of the patented designs were ever built. In 1947, William Shockley, John Bardeen, and Walter Brattain of Bell Labs in New Jersey built the first practical point-contact transistor. Bell used this transistor in limited quantities, and it remained largely a laboratory curiosity. In 1950, Shockley developed the radically different bipolar junction transistor that was licensed to companies such as Texas Instruments (which used it to produce a limited run of radios as a sales tool). The chemical instability of the early transistors limited them to low-power applications, but developments in design slowly overcame these problems. In about two decades, transistors replaced vacuum tubes in radios and televisions and then spawned new devices such as the personal computer.

The German physicists' discoveries, in other words, kicked off an extended process of developing know-how at multiple levels. Some steps involved high-level breakthroughs, such as the discovery of the "transistor effect," which earned Shockley, Bardeen, and Brattain a Nobel Prize in Physics. Other steps, such as improving the chemical stability of transistors, required the development of lower-level, context-specific knowledge rather than a general law or principle; some of this lower-level knowledge (e.g., getting high production "yields" in a semiconductor plant) was very difficult to codify and is still considered a black art.

Companies that incorporated transistors into lower-level products such as radios also played an important role in realizing the economic value of transistors. Their contribution, too, had different levels and facets. To switch from vacuum tubes to transistors, radio manufacturers had to solve engineering problems, create new designs, and figure out how to price, market, and distribute transistor radios.

A similar complexity characterizes the phenomenon of globalization. Cross-border interactions encompass a variety of flows that can be of importance to an innovator. These include licensing of know-how, the export and import of final products, the procurement of intermediate goods and services ("offshoring"), equity investments, and the use of immigrant labor. Each type of flow can be divided into further subcategories—for instance, the tasks performed offshore can be mundane, highly creative, or anything in between. The factors encouraging or impeding cross-border flows are also different for different types of flows. For example, licensing is affected by the security of intellectual property (IP) rights, exports and imports by transportation costs and customs duties, offshoring by differentials in the costs and quality of labor, equity investment by capital market structures, and the employment of immigrants by the availability of working permits. Whereas changes in these factors may have helped increase many kinds of cross-border flows, increases have not been uniform. For instance, international trade in manufactured goods has skyrocketed, but most service sectors remain "untraded"—services in retailing, real estate, and health care are almost entirely domestically produced and consumed.

The complexity of globalization spills over into its intersections with innovation. Some innovators can more easily export their products than others—but the extensive use of offshoring may not be a sensible choice for all heavy exporters. Developments such as plummeting communication costs have made the world smaller and the multiplayer innovation game more international in scope—but not to the same degree for all players and for all their cross-border engagements.

Techno-nationalist arguments based on sound-bites or parsimonious economic models cannot deal with the complexity of the multiplayer game. They rarely distinguish between different levels and kinds of know-how. Instead, they equate innovation with scientific publications or patents on cutting-edge technology produced in universities or in commercial research labs. They ignore the contributions of the other players in the innovation game that don't result in publications or patents.

Techno-nationalists also tend to oversimplify the phenomenon of globalization, often assuming that high-level know-how never crosses national borders—only the final products made using the know-how are traded.* This assumption, we will see, is pivotal in theoretical models of North-South trade that Richard Freeman invokes to predict the woeful consequences of the erosion of U.S. technological leadership. In fact, high-level ideas cross national borders rather easily, whereas a large proportion of "final" output, especially in the service sector, does not.

To embrace the complexity that is ignored by many pundits, policymakers, and theorists, I have chosen a style of inquiry patterned after a common-law trial. I examined in detail what individual players do—and why—taking into account many contextual factors. As I have mentioned, my primary research focused on businesses backed by venture capitalists (VCs), many of which, as we will see, play in the middle of the innovation game. Studying them provides a panoramic view and allows us to make informed inferences about what the other players do. Although I began with all the possible global interactions of VC-backed businesses, in this research project I focus on three: the pursuit of overseas customers, offshoring, and the role of immigrants. These factors most concern the companies I studied—and also provide insights about the more controversial features of globalization.

■ **Propositions**

My analyses of the multiplayer game and its cross-border interactions suggest outcomes that differ sharply from the dire predictions of the techno-nationalists. According to my assessment, the United States isn't locked into a winner-take-all race for scientific and technological leadership, and the growth of research capabilities in China and India—and thus their share of cutting-edge research—does not reduce U.S. prosperity. My analysis suggests the opposite outcome: advances abroad will *improve* living standards in the United States. Moreover, the benefits I identify aren't the usual ones, by which prosperity abroad increases opportunities for U.S. exporters. Instead, I show that cutting-edge research developed abroad benefits domestic production and consumption in the service sector.

The implications of my analysis for public policy are also contrary to techno-nationalist prescriptions: I suggest that the United States embrace

* Technology transfer is central to the Bhidé-Phelps (2007) analysis of China's trade.

the expansion of research capabilities abroad, not devote more resources to maintaining its lead in science and cutting-edge technology.* This fundamentally different general strategy implies different choices of policy in a wide range of specific areas, such as the funding of scientific research, R&D subsidies, immigration laws, promoting savings and investment by reducing consumption, and training of scientists and engineers.

My assessment and prescriptions differ so sharply from those of the techno-nationalists for reasons that I preview below.

The World is a long way from being Flat—China and India aren't anywhere close to catching up with the United States in their capacity to develop and use technological innovations. Starting afresh may allow China and India to leapfrog ahead in some fields, in building advanced mobile phone networks, for example. But excelling in the overall innovation game requires a great and diverse team, which, history suggests, takes a very long time to build.

Consider Japan, which began to "enter the world" after the Boshin War of 1868. In the subsequent Meiji Restoration, the country abolished its feudal system and instituted a Western legal system and a quasi-parliamentary constitutional government. In a few decades, Japan had modernized its industry, its military, and its educational system. Today Japan is a highly developed economy and makes important contributions to advancing the technological frontier. But nearly a century and a half after Japan started modernizing, its overall capacity to develop and use innovations, as evidenced by average productivity,[10] remains behind that of the United States.

Similarly, Korea and Taiwan started industrializing (as it happens, under Japanese rule) about a century ago and enjoyed miraculous rates of growth after the 1960s. In several sectors of the electronics industry, Korean and Taiwanese companies are technological leaders. Yet their overall productivity suggests they have less capacity to develop and use innovations than has Japan. Is it likely, then, that within any reader's lifetime China and India will attain the parity with the United States that has eluded Japan, Korea, and Taiwan?

The fear of offshoring of innovation is similarly exaggerated—don't expect to hear a giant sucking sound anytime soon. *The massive relocation*

---

* I am *not* arguing for reducing public spending on basic scientific research. My point is simply that the threatened loss of scientific "preeminence" should not influence the level of spending.

of innovation appears highly unlikely. The fact that U.S. companies have started R&D centers abroad that do high-level research doesn't mean that all lower-level know-how development will quickly follow. Of the many activities included in the innovation game, only some are performed well in remote, low-cost locations. Many mid-level activities, for instance, are best conducted close to potential customers.

Any catch-up, even if it takes place gradually and in the normal course of development, will to some degree reduce the U.S. "lead." Furthermore, the global influence of techno-nationalism could accelerate this process. As alarmists in the United States don't fail to remind us, governments in "emerging" countries such as China and India—also in the thrall of techno-nationalist thinking—are making a determined effort to leap ahead in cutting-edge science and technology. I am skeptical that these efforts are going to do any more good for China's and India's economy than did similar efforts in Europe and Japan in the 1970s and 1980s.[11] But put aside the issue of whether investing in cutting-edge research represents a good use of Chinese and Indian resources; does whatever erosion of U.S. primacy in developing high-level know-how that this might cause really threaten U.S. prosperity? Should the U.S. government respond in kind by putting even more money into research?

Princeton economist Paul Krugman, in a 1994 *Foreign Affairs* essay, decried a "dangerous obsession" with "national competitiveness." The tendency to think that "the United States and Japan are competitors in the same sense that Coca-Cola competes with Pepsi," Krugman pointed out, is widespread; he quoted President Clinton's claim that "each nation is like a big corporation competing in the global marketplace." This premise, which is at the heart of techno-nationalism, Krugman persuasively argues, is "flatly, completely and demonstrably wrong."[12] Although "competitive problems could arise in principle, as a practical, empirical matter, the major nations of the world are not to any significant degree in economic competition with each other."[13]

The techno-nationalist claim that U.S. prosperity requires that the country "maintain its scientific and technological lead" is particularly dubious: the argument fails to recognize that *the development of scientific knowledge or cutting-edge technology is not a zero-sum competition.* The results of scientific research are available at no charge to anyone anywhere in the world. Most arguments for the public funding of scientific research are in fact based on the unwillingness of private investors to undertake research that cannot yield a profit. Cutting-edge technology (as opposed to scientific research) has commercial value because it can be patented; but patent owners generally don't charge higher fees to foreign licensors. The then tiny Japanese company Sony was one of the first licensors of Bell Labs' transistor patent. It paid $50,000 for a license (after obtaining special permission from the Japanese Ministry of Finance) that started it on the road to becoming a household name in consumer electronics.

If patent holders choose to exploit their invention on their own (i.e., not grant licenses to anyone), this does not mean that the country of origin secures most of the benefit at the expense of other countries. Suppose IBM chooses to exploit internally, rather than freely license, a breakthrough from its China Research Laboratory (employing 150 research staff in Beijing). This does not help China and hurt everyone else. Rather, as I discuss at length later in this book, the benefits go to IBM's stockholders, to employees who make or market the product that embodies the invention, and—above all—to customers, who secure the lion's share of the benefit from most innovations. These stockholders, employees, and customers, who number in the tens of millions, are located all over the world.

In a world where breakthrough ideas easily cross national borders, the origin of ideas is inconsequential. Contrary to Thomas Friedman's assertion, it does not matter that Google's search algorithm was invented in California. After all, a Briton invented the protocols of the World Wide Web—in a lab in Switzerland. A Swede and a Dane in Tallinn, Estonia, started Skype, the leading provider of peer-to-peer Internet telephony. How did the foreign origins of these innovations harm the U.S. economy?

The techno-nationalist preoccupation with high-level research also obscures the importance of what happens at lower levels of the innovation game. High-level breakthroughs that originate in China or India can, in principle, be used to develop mid- and ground-level products of value to workers and consumers everywhere. But the benefits are not automatic: realizing the value of high-level innovation requires venturesome lower-level players who have the resourcefulness and gumption to solve challenging technical and business problems. Without venturesome radio manufacturers such as Sony, transistors might have remained lab curiosities.

Moreover, the benefits of lower-level venturesome consumption often remain in the country where it occurs, and all countries don't have the same capacity for such consumption. Therefore, I argue, because high-level ideas cross borders easily, a nation's *"venturesome consumption"—the willingness and ability of intermediate producers and individual consumers to take a chance on and effectively use new know-how and products—is at least as important as, if not more important than, its capacity to undertake high-level research.* Maryland has a higher per capita income than Mississippi, Norway has a higher per capita income than Nigeria, and Bosnia has a higher per capita income than Bangladesh; the richer places are not ahead because they are (or once were) significant developers of breakthrough technologies. Rather, they are wealthier because of their capacity to benefit from innovations that originated elsewhere. Conversely, the city of Rochester, New York (home to Xerox, Kodak, and the University of Rochester) is reputed to have one of the highest number of patents per capita of any city in the United States. It is far from the most economically vibrant.

The United States, according to my analysis, has more than just great scientists and research labs: it also hosts an innovation game with many players who can exploit high-level breakthroughs regardless of where they originate. Therefore, the erosion of the U.S. lead in cutting-edge research isn't just harmless: *an increase in the world's supply of high-level know-how provides more raw material for mid- and ground-level innovations that increase living standards in the United States.* The U.S. technological lead narrowed after World War II as Western Europe and Japan rebuilt their economies and research capabilities. This led not to a decrease, but to an *increase* in U.S. prosperity.* The United States likely enjoys a *higher* standard of living because Taiwan and Korea have started contributing to the world's supply of scientific and technological knowledge.

The venturesome consumption of information technology (IT) innovations by the service sector in the United States plays an especially important role in my argument. The service sector now accounts for a large share of economic activity in the United States—nearly 70 percent of GDP in 2004 (up from 54 percent in 1974).[14] The benefits of innovations that improve the performance of U.S. service providers accrue mainly to U.S. workers and consumers because, in contrast to manufacturing, most services are

---

* As we will see in chapter 7, Paul Samuelson makes the opposite suggestion, that European and Japanese reconstruction may have dampened growth in the United States.

not traded—they are both produced and consumed in the United States. For example, an electronic health records system improves the productivity of U.S. health-care workers and the quality of care enjoyed by U.S. patients. In contrast, even if a U.S. innovator develops a more efficient process for making shoes, it may have little impact on U.S. productivity (since most shoes sold in the United States are imported).

As we will see, the exceptional capacity of service businesses such as Wal-Mart to use new high-level technologies has been one of the main reasons that productivity and incomes have grown faster in the United States than in Europe and Japan since the mid-1990s. Suppose researchers in, say, Germany develop a technology that helps retailers reduce inventories. The exceptional capacity of companies such as Wal-Mart to use it will lead to greater increases in productivity and living standards in the United States than in countries—possibly including Germany—where regulations, custom, and other factors may discourage retailers from using the new technology.

How should the United States (and other advanced countries) respond to the inevitable growth in the share of high-level know-how that is developed in low-wage countries? I argue that *techno-nationalist prescriptions to protect the U.S. lead in high-level know-how may do more harm than good by impairing the performance of the other players in the innovation game who use high-level know-how.*

On the surface, the prescriptions seem benign: how could training more scientists and engineers, investing more in basic scientific research and R&D, or improving the quality of math and science education do harm? Beware the consequences of nostrums harvested from piecemeal analyses! Consider, for instance, the argument for subsidizing research in cutting-edge science and technology. Advocates cite research showing that such investments have produced higher "social" returns than "private" returns because they produce knowledge spillovers for other producers that cannot be captured by the firms undertaking the R&D. Obviously, profit-maximizing businesses will invest less in R&D than would be best for society as a whole. Everyone therefore benefits if R&D spending is promoted through subsidies or tax credits. Or so the advocates would have us believe.

Those outside the choir have reason to be skeptical about the sermon. Increasing the rewards for doing something does usually lead people to do more of it. But more effort doesn't always lead to more output. Einstein's research produced great knowledge spillovers: could they really have been increased if he had been given a tax break that induced him to spend more time doing research? Moreover, doing more of X may mean doing less of Y, reducing rather than increasing the public good. Suppose Einstein had spent more time doing theoretical physics and less giving thoughtful and influential speeches about world peace and the dangers of nuclear weapons. Would society have been better off?

Similarly, even if diverting resources from, say, marketing to R&D actually increases knowledge spillovers, the reduction in marketing activities can lead to a net loss to society. One reason is that spillovers of technical knowledge are not the only kind of value that innovations generate. Commercially successful innovations also produce what economists call a consumer surplus—the utility or value that buyers receive in excess of the price they pay. In many cases (e.g., a new drug while it remains under patent), the consumer surplus (the difference between the price of the drug and its value to the purchaser) can represent the primary source of the so-called social value of the innovation.[15]

But commercial success (which generates the consumer surplus) generally requires both technical effort (such as R&D) and marketing effort. Notwithstanding Ralph Waldo Emerson's claim about the world beating a path to the door of someone who builds a better mousetrap,[16] new products and processes, even great ones, don't sell themselves. Companies have sales and marketing departments for a reason. And doing more R&D and less marketing may reduce consumer surplus to a greater degree than it increases the spillovers of technical knowledge.

There is another reason diverting resources from marketing to R&D may be harmful: just as R&D can produce spillovers of technical knowledge, marketing can produce spillovers of "consumer knowledge," and reduced marketing tends to diminish the latter kind of spillovers. To take a concrete example, Dan Bricklin and Bob Frankston's invention of the spreadsheet created huge spillovers for Lotus Development Corporation (which later developed 1-2-3) and Microsoft (whose Excel spreadsheet now dominates the category). In fact Bricklin and Frankston's personal financial returns from the venture were negligible. But the spillovers that Bricklin and Frankston generated weren't just of the technical kind. Lotus and Microsoft profited enormously from pioneers' efforts to educate customers and create a market for spreadsheets. If Bricklin and Frankston had done more R&D and less marketing, the *total* spillover of technical and consumer knowledge could well have been less.

Consumer knowledge spillovers are nearly impossible to measure, whereas estimating the spillovers of technical knowledge is merely extraordinarily challenging. But the measurement problem should not lead to the conclusion that inducing businesses to undertake more R&D and less marketing would benefit society. Net of the costs, society could be better off—or it could be worse off. No one can actually know which, especially at the level of the economy as a whole.*

Businesses have long recognized the importance of multipronged investment in R&D, organizational capabilities, marketing, and so on, that is at least roughly balanced. Innovative products don't help companies that can't sell them,† and the capacity to sell innovative products is wasted if there are no products to sell. The importance of multipronged investment in the creation of the large modern corporation is a recurring theme in the work of the preeminent business historian Alfred Chandler.

It is certainly possible that the mix of investments that maximizes a firm's profits shortchanges the common good—a ratio of R&D to marketing ideal for stockholders may be too high or too low for society at large. But variations between firms make it virtually impossible to formulate public policies that will induce them to choose a mix of investments that is better aligned with society's interests. In a complex, dynamic economy, what constitutes a well-balanced portfolio of investments for IBM now— from the point of view of its stockholders *or* society at large—won't necessarily suit General Motors and may not be appropriate for IBM in the future. Given such variations across organizations and time, what justifies giving *all* firms tax credits for R&D but not for marketing? Why should the tax code assume that developing a new drug is always better for society than improving the effective use of existing treatments through more intensive marketing? The alternative approach of designing incentives for individual firms is, in a market-based economy, unworkable. Who, save for die-hard advocates of state control, would suggest the creation of a board

---

* I imagine most mainstream economists would not dispute the logic of this analysis. However, observing that the net effects of R&D subsidies are indeterminate is too obvious to merit publication in a scholarly journal and is of little interest to policymakers. Studies of knowledge spillovers from R&D are publishable and interesting; and the accumulation of many "peer-reviewed" published studies is used to assert a scientific justification for R&D subsidies.

† A reader recalls the example of how Xerox stumbled in the copier market: "Xerox thought it was all about R&D and erecting patent barriers to entry, while Canon and Minolta innovated with product size and user maintenance, originally with less good technology, and finally destroyed Xerox' dominance."

that would make a case-by-case determination of whether to subsidize R&D or marketing?

The same problem arises with schemes to train more engineers and scientists. Why should public policy encourage individuals to pursue careers in science and engineering instead of taking a liberal arts degree and becoming managers or entrepreneurs? Managers and entrepreneurs play important roles in the innovation game—how can we know that having fewer of them will improve the common good?

This is not an argument for a laissez-faire, benign neglect of technology. Indeed, I argue in chapter 16 that technological progress expands the minimal functions of government. For example, compared to an agrarian society, a technologically advanced economy requires a more sophisticated system for demarcating and enforcing intellectual property rights; and, as Jaffe and Lerner's critique of the U.S. patent system indicates, good systems do not always emerge spontaneously.[17] Similarly, the emergence of cyberspace engenders cyber-crime, which necessitates cyber-cops. But effective intervention also requires humility—an appreciation of how difficult it is to fathom the complexity of the modern economy—and alertness to the unintended consequences of policies based on a limited understanding.

In addition, although complacency is dangerous, fretting about imaginary threats impairs our ability to confront real problems. A pointless preoccupation with the growth of R&D in China and India distracts us from more significant issues that arise from their integration into the global economy: what will happen to energy prices and climate change if the per capita fossil fuel consumption of more than two billion people approaches that of the developed world? As Phelps and I have argued, China has increased its capacity to produce modern goods for international markets more quickly than it has increased its capacity to consume such goods.[18] The resulting savings glut has been channeled to U.S. borrowers through a financial system with serious defects, recently revealed by the subprime crisis. Reforming the financial system, it seems to me, is of critical importance in a global economy. There is also no shortage of serious domestic issues, ranging from the fiscal consequences of an aging population to the status of 12 million illegal immigrants.[19]

Globalization has important consequences for the distribution of incomes, and this has been the subject of an extensive and well-merited debate. I have nothing to add to this discourse except to note the following: even if cross-border flows (and innovation) aren't zero sum at an aggregated national level—that is, Americans don't suffer when the Chinese advance—they may increase disparities of income in both countries. Indeed, any kind of trade—internal or international—and technological innovation can increase income disparities: Robinson Crusoes working with rudimentary tools on isolated islands are more likely to enjoy similar standards of living than members of a specialized, technologically advanced society. Rapid changes in trading patterns and technology can also cause unsettling dislocations.

Even if trade and innovation lead to unpleasant consequences for some, societies can ameliorate these consequences without impeding trade or technological progress (for instance through "adjustment" programs, negative income tax rates, or low-wage subsidies). Indeed, the historical evidence suggests that societies that have blocked trade and hindered technological advances have typically dragged down overall living standards *and* concentrated wealth and power in the hands of a few individuals. How a country may ameliorate the unfortunate consequences of globalization and innovation without losing their benefits is a serious question, but it lies outside the scope of my book. My focus is on the overall wealth and prosperity of nations, and I focus on just one aspect of globalization, its intersection with technological innovation.*

■ An iConic Illustration

The iPod, the portable media player that Apple introduced in 2001, has been a runaway hit—by the end of 2006, Apple had sold nearly 70 million units. Its story illustrates many of the propositions I have just outlined.

Apple was cofounded and is tightly managed by a college dropout, and it did not develop cutting-edge technology or employ many PhDs in science or engineering to develop the iPod. The iPod wasn't the first music player of its

---

* The much larger aspect of globalization pertains to trade in seasoned goods and services. Many fine books about the causes, benefits, and losses have been written about this. The top 24 books (out of 46,288) as of this writing on Amazon under "globalization" include those (in order of appearance) by my Columbia colleagues Joseph Stiglitz and Jagdish Bhagwati (who sharply disagree), Martin Wolf, Dani Rodrick, Daniel Cohen, and Francis Cairncross. My thinking has of course been informed by reading some of these works, but their overlap with this book is limited.

kind: Singapore-based Creative Technology was selling the Nomad jukebox nearly two years before Apple introduced the iPod. Indeed, Creative later sued Apple for patent infringement and received a $100 million settlement. The attractiveness of Apple's products lies in their "simplicity, intelligence and whimsy" rather than in new technology.[20] The iPod and other Apple products are popular because they are "masterpieces of industrial design and enlightened human interfacing. They make competitors' products—even when they're better machines—seem plodding and prosaic."[21]

Susan Kevorkian, an analyst at IDC, points out that "Creative's original Nomad jukebox was designed to look like a CD player. Apple innovated on the hard-drive based portable media player form factor by making it smaller and rectangular—e.g. by embracing the form factor of the hard drive, rather than trying to disguise it." The iPod's subsequent evolution made it more than an "entertainment device." It became "a fashion accessory" that provided "hipness by association," a means to store and manage data and entertainment files, and way to "stay current on the go with audio books, news and information podcasts and video clips."[22]

Apple CEO Steve Jobs's talent for marketing is another not-so-secret weapon for the company. In spite of (or possibly because of) Jobs's disdain for market research, Michael Malone regards him as "the greatest marketer of our time, the most charismatic figure in electronics history."[23] Another industry observer jests that Jobs may have, beyond natural charisma, a supernatural "reality distortion field."[24] The company as a whole is credited with an outstanding marketing flair.

Other aspects of the iPod phenomenon are sometimes overlooked: Apple has been a skilled integrator—a deft orchestrator of a multiplayer game—not a go-it-alone innovator. Apple's iTunes Store provides a legal and convenient ("end to end") way for consumers to buy individual songs (for 99 cents in the United States) that can be played on an iPod. In order to establish the store, Jobs orchestrated: he had to overcome difficult contracting problems with the music companies that owned the copyrights to the songs. On the product development side, Apple started with software based on PortalPlayer's reference platform and contracted with a company called Pixo (founded by Paul Mercer, also a college dropout) to help design and implement the user interface.

Especially noteworthy are the high-level know-how and products used in the iPod mix that originated abroad. The English company ARM, for instance, developed the "intellectual property core" for the "brains," or the

CPU, of the player. The Fraunhofer Institute for Integrated Circuits in Germany licensed MP3 sound compression technology patents to Apple. Fraunhofer itself was not the sole inventor of MP3 technology; Phillips (Holland), Thomson (France), Sisvel (Italy), and Bell Labs (United States) also made important contributions. The 1.8-inch hard drives that put "1000 songs in your pocket" and were used in the first five generations of the iPod came from the Japanese company Toshiba. Later, the iPod Mini used 1-inch "microdrives" supplied by Hitachi (Japan) and Seagate (United States). Flash memories, which were used instead of hard drives in the iPod Nano, were supplied by Toshiba and Samsung (Korea). Wolfson Electronics, head-quartered in Edinburgh, Scotland, developed the audio codecs.[25]

The venturesome spirit of U.S. consumers has also played a crucial role in the success of the iPod—and several other Apple products. According to Malone, Steve Jobs can introduce "clumsy, overpriced 1.0 version[s] and trust that the army of several million Apple true believers will rush out and buy. That is the crucial, often overlooked, key to Apple's continuing success. Other wildcatters have to pray the market recognizes their brilliant new products quickly enough before they go bankrupt. Apple, by compar-ison, always knows that it will be able to finance versions 2.0, 3.0, etc., on sales to its captive market—and by then, it will have perfected a definitive product the whole world wants to own."[26]

Although Apple markets the iPod all over the world, its army of true be-lievers enrolls largely in the United States. In 2000, the year before the iPod was launched, the United States (which accounts for less than 5 percent of the world's population and about 30 percent of its GDP)[27] accounted for 85 percent of the global shipments of MP3 players.[28] As the market matured and prices fell to levels where consumers in less well-to-do countries could afford players, the U.S. share of the global market also declined—but not to levels commensurate with the U.S. share of world GDP. According to a Morgan Stanley estimate, in 2005, the United States accounted for about 70 percent of worldwide shipments of digital music devices. U.S. consumers have been particularly receptive to Apple's high-end, high-priced products: according to Morgan Stanley, Apple's share of the U.S. market is nearly two and a half times its share in other markets. In 2005, Apple sold 27.1 million iPods in the United States—more than five and a half times the 4.8 million it sold in the rest of the world.[29]

The bottom-line question, however, is how the iPod's success helps the U.S. economy.

The product has surely been profitable for the company—Apple is estimated to earn a gross margin of 20 percent to 30 percent on iPod sales, stellar in the consumer electronics industry. This growth in profits—and expectations of more to come—helped increase the stock price from about $10 a share in October 2001, when the iPod was introduced, to about $70 a share by the end of 2005. But who are the shareholders? Foreigners can buy Apple's stock as easily as U.S. investors, so the geographic distribution of Apple's shareholding is simply a matter of the preferences of investors. Similarly, a lot of labor has been employed in manufacturing the nearly 70 million iPods that were sold from 2001 to 2006. But where? The players are made, or more properly assembled, in China—using components that are also made in the Far East.

The iPod has affected U.S. jobs mainly in the "untradeable" service sector. It is difficult to estimate how many Americans have been employed in the distribution, marketing, and sales of the players, but the value added of these activities seems to be roughly equal to the value added of the production activities undertaken in the Far East.[30] An equally significant benefit is the value the iPod has created for its venturesome consumers. The tangible and intangible benefits it provides make it virtually impossible to estimate the magnitude of this consumer surplus, but the iPod would not have enjoyed runaway success unless it provided value significantly in excess of its purchase price. Therefore, just as the venturesomeness of U.S. buyers made a large contribution to the success of the iPod, U.S. buyers have reaped a large share of the value it created.*

It is also worth asking how things might have been different if the Finnish company Nokia had become the leading vendor of MP3 players. Asia would probably have remained the venue of choice for assembly and component manufacturing. Apple's (potentially global) shareholders would likely have been poorer and Nokia's (also potentially global) shareholders richer. A hundred or fewer product designers and engineers might have worked in Finland instead of California (although it should be noted that some of Nokia's designers are based in California). But in terms of the significant economy-wide effects on service sector employment and consumer surplus, the critical question pertains to the attractiveness of the U.S. market: if Nokia had also focused on U.S. consumers, little would have changed. In other words, in a world where the high-level innovations—MP3 standards,

---

* Note, however, that even if other economies may not have received the same benefits as the U.S. economy, they haven't suffered any harm either.

ARM microprocessor designs—are mobile, what happens at the lower levels of the innovation game is crucial.

■ Why Study VC-Backed Businesses?

Although the iPod provides a catchy illustration, my propositions derive from a detailed examination of businesses with much lower profiles— U.S.-based, VC-backed businesses that had not yet gone public at the time of my study.* VC-backed businesses are, of course, only one of the players of the innovation game; in fact, large public companies devote far more resources to innovative activity and develop significantly more new know-how and products. Large companies also account for a much larger share of cross-border activity. Nevertheless, for several reasons a study of VC-backed businesses provides a useful view of the economic drivers of the innovation game and its cross-border interactions.

First, *VC-backed businesses are relatively uncomplicated players.* To use an analogy: the fruit fly is among the most studied organisms in biological research, particularly in genetics, because it provides a simple model: it has only four pairs of chromosomes, three autosomes and one sex chromosome. Its genome is compact, having about half the number of genes as the human genome, and was almost completely sequenced in 2000. Analogously, VC-backed businesses offer a simple and clear model of technological innovation and its cross-border ramifications, especially in comparison to large corporations.

They concentrate on technological innovation. For reasons that I will discuss later, VCs tend to focus their investments in "high tech" sectors where innovation is vigorous. In 2005, for instance, 85 percent of VC investments in the United States were in information technology/telecom or life sciences—sectors that account for less than 20 percent of U.S. GDP, but are the loci of a great deal of innovative activity. VC-backed businesses are pure innovators: their business models are entirely predicated on commercializing new products or know-how.

The economic considerations that go into their choices about innovation and cross-border interactions are therefore easier to observe. VCs have the power and incentive to require businesses to try to maximize their financial

---

* I describe the details of my study in the next chapter.

returns—and to minimize the impact of emotion, empire-building, ego, and political jockeying. The economic rationale behind those businesses' technology investments, and the degree to which those businesses focus on overseas markets, use offshoring, and recruit immigrants are therefore fairly transparent.

In contrast, only a minority of large companies focuses on high-tech industries, and even the ones that do aren't pure innovators. They also attend to sizable businesses that have already matured. The interactions between the innovative and ongoing activities of large firms can obscure their moves and motivations. For instance, what does one make of the research centers that many large high-tech companies have set up in China? To what extent are the centers a quid pro quo for selling existing products to the Chinese government? How many actually undertake cutting-edge research, and how many are really facilities that adapt existing products for the Chinese market, dressed up for PR purposes as research centers? Factors such as intramural conflicts between divisions and the egos of CEOs of large companies can make it difficult to identify the economic factors behind their choices about globalization and innovation.

A second advantage of studying VC-backed businesses is that they provide *a window on the middle level of the innovation game* in terms of both product and know-how *and thus help us identify some of its distinguishing features* vis-à-vis other levels. Research on innovation tends to focus on high-level knowledge developed in labs or R&D centers that typically results in scientific publications and patents.* Most of the VC-backed businesses I studied, however, did not undertake high-level research or develop high-level products such as the transistor. Rather, their innovations combined or extended high-level know-how and products. According to one CEO, his company undertook integration projects, not science projects.†

---

* Freeman and Soete's (1997) *The Economics of Industrial Innovation* (third edition) is an instructive case in point. This encyclopedic, 470-page volume extensively reviews the literature on innovation. In defining their scope, however, the authors write: "This book is primarily concerned with the innovations arising from the professional R&D system and with the allocation of resources to that system." They admit that the system employs less than 2 percent of the working population but assert that it "originates a large proportion of the new and improved materials, products, processes and systems, which are the ultimate source of economic advance."

† As we will see in chapter 2, the core technical contribution of VC-backed businesses is often not "patentable," because what was not "obvious" about the combinatorial know-how was hard to codify (and at least in principle, a patentable invention must be both nonobvious and replicable by a practitioner who reads the patent).

VC-backed businesses didn't develop technical know-how only—they also developed "nontechnological" complements such as sales and marketing pitches and architectures and routines for their internal organizations.

My study also shows how mid-level players combine and extend higher-level innovations. The VC-backed businesses used different people and procedures than the typical lab doing high-level research: They employed a much smaller proportion of PhDs in their technical staff, and their overall workforces contained a larger proportion of managers and sales and marketing staff. In contrast to the physicists who developed the modern transistor inside the precincts of Bell Labs, the development teams of many of the VC-backed businesses I studied had a close, ongoing relationship with users. Communication and persuasion were as crucial as technical virtuosity, and the technical tasks themselves involved more ad hoc improvisation than classical scientific experimentation.*

Third, studying VC-backed businesses *provides insights about the use of "high tech" innovations by "low tech" service businesses.* The great majority of the VC-backed businesses I studied developed innovations used by other businesses—few targeted individual consumers. Many of the business customers weren't companies producing high-tech products; a large proportion were low-tech businesses providing services rather than tangible goods. Low-tech businesses providing services (such as Wal-Mart and the Prudential Insurance Company) account for a large share of economic activity. The value-added by the business sector as a whole accounted for about 77 percent of U.S. GDP in 2004,[31] and as has been mentioned, services accounted for nearly 70 percent of GDP; consequently, customers' effective use of the kinds of high-tech innovations developed by the businesses in my study matters a great deal to the performance of the U.S. economy.

Although VC-backed businesses provide a relatively easy-to-study model of innovation, especially at the mid-level, they aren't the only or even the dominant mid-level players. I do not subscribe to a common belief in their extraordinary capacity for innovation. A predisposition to believe different forms of organization have different capabilities and limitations induces skepticism: if VC-backed businesses are much more productive in generating

---

* A large proportion—but not all—of the VC-backed businesses I studied played at the middle level of the innovation game. Some developed higher- or lower-level innovations. These variations in my sample also highlighted differences in how the innovation game is played at different levels.

innovations than corporate R&D units, as some researchers have claimed,[32] why haven't we seen a significant redeployment of corporate R&D resources to the VC model?[33] And why are VCs and company founders so eager to adopt an inferior organizational form through an IPO or merger with publicly traded companies? To my way of thinking, research comparing innovation productivity based on patent counts and the like is misleading, because different kinds of organizations use different processes to produce different (and often complementary) innovations.* There are good and bad trumpet players and flautists; but to say that trumpet players as a class are more productive because they blow more wind through their instruments misses the point. Just as symphonies require many instruments—replacing flautists with trumpeters doesn't improve a performance—the multiplayer innovation game draws on the contributions of VC-backed businesses and large corporations, of scientific research and R&D, and of marketing and management.

Indeed, my study of what VC-backed businesses do—as well as what they rely on others to do—highlights the high degree of specialization of the individual players, both within and across organizations. For instance, VC-backed businesses often rely on other innovators to develop high-level know-how or products. Similarly, they depend on their early customers to provide ongoing feedback; more than one referred to such customers as "development partners." My study also suggests considerable variety in the nature of interactions. Some (as with early customers) can require a face-to-face dialogue, rich in nuance and information. Other, more terse interactions[34]—for example with licensors of technologies—can occur remotely. And although such observations do not add up to a comprehensive account of the multiplayer innovation game, this variety of organizations and interactions has important implications for assessing how the United States should respond to the emergence of new sources of cutting-edge research abroad.

Although I derived my propositions through an inductive process, from observations of mid- and ground-level innovations—a territory outside the field of vision of many scholars—my research is by no means sui generis. As in a common-law trial or judicial enquiry, it is crucial in inductive research to keep an open mind—but impossible to start with a tabula rasa, a clean slate. One cannot "just observe": a first-time visitor from London will see

---

* The comparisons also rely on assumptions that are, in my view, somewhat implausible, although they are commonly relied on in well-regarded research (see chapter 6).

New York very differently than will a visitor from Lagos. Although good investigators avoid looking only for data that confirms a theory, preconceptions and prior beliefs inevitably inform the questions researchers ask and the inferences they make.[35] The box titled "Prior Art" describes the theories and ideas that guided this inquiry and the framing of my inferences.

Prior Art

Just as a devout Hindu might begin a journey with a prayer to the Lord Ganesh, it is obligatory to start a discussion on modern innovation by invoking Joseph Schumpeter. The thousands of pages he wrote over more than four decades contained sharp, unequivocal claims as well as tangles of contradictions: Jon Elster describes Schumpeter as an elusive writer who could contradict himself in the course of a single paragraph.[36] Nevertheless, as Rosenberg puts it, "His model has become the accepted one for all innovative activity."[37]

I do not question Schumpeter's overall thesis—that innovation drives long-term growth. And like many others I applaud the highly textured and historical nature of his analysis. But I am otherwise not a devotee. More granular theories can provide superior insights—provided they get the details right. As far as I can tell, Schumpeter's eloquent and voluminous writings about innovation and entrepreneurship weren't informed by a systematic study of actual innovators or entrepreneurs. His model (or at least the common conceptions of it) has many elements that are, to put it politely, incongruent with a large body of empirical research as well as with my own observations of the modern innovation system. I believe that misconceptions in the Schumpeterian model are at the heart of many alarmist prognoses of the consequences of the erosion of the U.S. technological lead.

Mainstream economics does not make the extensive mistakes and exhibit the muddle that I find in Schumpeter. But as I mentioned in the preface, I share Phelps's view that it has limited utility in helping us understand the evolving, unruly processes of innovation.[38]

Rather, the two theorists whose views of entrepreneurship form the core of the "priors" that have informed my observations and interpretations are

Frank Knight and Friedrich Hayek. Other particularly noteworthy influences are Chandler's work on large industrial enterprise, Elster's book on technical change, Nelson and Winter's evolutionary theory, and Phelps's analysis of modern capitalism. This is of course only a partial list.

My metaphor of a multiperiod, multiplayer game is largely a contemporized amalgam of Nelson and Winter's evolutionary theory, Rosenberg's research on incremental innovation, and the idea of an innovation system popularized by Nelson and other scholars. The construct of "venturesome consumption" incorporates the ideas of many researchers, including work on technology diffusion by David, Griliches, Mansfield, and Nelson and Phelps; work on consumer-led innovation by Rosenberg and Von Hippel; and work on "absorptive capacity" by Cohen and Levinthal. Craft, Ghemawat, Leamer and many others have made the point that the world is far from flat. On the policy side, my critique of techno-nationalism is of a piece with Krugman's attack on the pursuit of "competitiveness" and with the argument that David has made for decades against public policies that emphasize the development of new technologies and neglect their diffusion.

As the preceding indicates, many of my individual propositions, especially about innovation, are not novel (although gaps in my knowledge of the prior research led to some "independent rediscoveries"). My contribution (aside from observations of VC-backed businesses, which I believe represents new field data) lies in combining propositions about innovation and cross-border interactions to provide a fresh assessment of an anxiety-inducing feature of globalization.

■ What Lies Ahead

To continue the analogy of a trial, I present the depositions and testimonies of my witnesses before I make my broader arguments and judgments. Specifically, book 1 focuses on the results of my interviews with the CEOs of VC-backed businesses. It explores the nexus between the role these businesses play in the innovation game and their cross-border interactions. The exploration reveals important features of the innovation game, including the extent of its globalization. Book 2 broadens and integrates the inferences from book 1 to rebut techno-nationalist alarmism about the erosion of the U.S. lead in cutting-edge science and technology. It also suggests an approach to formulating public policies that is more in sync with the way the technologically advanced world really works.

The depth and detail provided in book 1 make, I believe, the broader arguments of book 2 more persuasive in the following way: since we could not independently verify what the CEOs told us, the context, the circumstantial evidence, and the statements our "witnesses" gave during "cross-examination" will allow readers to assess the credibility of the "testimony." The details should also help readers evaluate the quality of my generalizations. For instance, because I focused on VC-backed businesses, I had to make judgments about what features of their innovative activity and cross-border engagements would apply to other players in the innovation game. Similarly, I had to make inferences about players, such as customers and outsourcing companies, that the companies in my sample did business with but whom we did not interview. My sharing of the background facts gives readers an opportunity to decide if they agree with my judgments and inferences.

I also believe that the detailed evidence is a necessary antidote to the sweeping pronouncements of popular gurus and to highly abstracted theories of growth and trade that are far removed from the reality of modern capitalist innovation. I can think of no way to apprehend this reality without the laborious, methodologically tricky process of talking to the people who shape it—or at least taking the time to peruse the results of such an enquiry.

Presenting the more detailed and special case first may not be to every reader's taste. Some may prefer to review the broader closing arguments and judgments first. I have therefore written the two books in the form of more or less independent modules. Some readers may choose to start with book 2 and then return to book 1 for the underlying evidence—or to learn more about VC-backed businesses.

Book 1

Cautious Voyagers ■

Why VC-Backed

Businesses

Still Favor Home

■ Has the world really become every business's oyster?

"No right-thinking businessman or woman, whether in El Paso or Detroit, thinks in terms of the U.S. only now," says Richard W. Fisher, president of the Federal Reserve Bank of Dallas. But how much does the world outside really matter to the more than twenty million small businesses in the United States? The barber in New York may have been born outside the United States and may trim the locks of numerous immigrants. But it would be a stretch to say that the barber participates in international trade. Similarly, the neighborhood florist who buys roses from a local wholesaler may care little whether the flowers were grown in Vermont or Venezuela.

Although many small businesses have little concern for what happens outside their neighborhoods, in this era of globalization, more ambitious ventures could in principle be active abroad.

One factor making the global playing field accessible to them, according to economist Hal Varian, is that "information technology is a great leveler. As computers get cheaper, more powerful, and more connected, technologies that were only available to the Wal-Marts of the world become available to the small fry." Varian describes how two Silicon Valley entrepreneurs use technology to do business abroad:

Rashmi Sinha told me her software company had six employees: two in the United States and four in New Delhi. [An]other [entrepreneur], Cosimo Spera, started a company to develop applications and services for mobile phones; his company has five employees in the United States, eight in Spain and two in Italy.

Both of these micro-multinational companies work pretty much the same way, using e-mail, Web pages, voice-over-Internet phone services and other Internet technology to coordinate their far-flung operations. "Just think," said Ms. Sinha, "my little six-person operation is now a global business."[1]*

How common and significant are such micro-multinationals? What factors, besides information technologies, encourage—or discourage—new and emerging companies from doing business abroad? To what degree do cross-border engagements fit with their basic business strategies? These were the sorts of questions that my interviews with the CEOs of VC-backed businesses were designed to answer (see box).

How This Study Was Conducted

In the early 1990s, I conducted research on high-growth start-ups, primarily using interviews of the founders of one hundred companies from the 1989 *Inc.* 500 list, a compilation of the fastest growing privately held companies in the United States. *Inc.* magazine compiles this list after soliciting applications and nominations for companies that have at least a five-year track record, with a minimum of $100,000 in revenues at the start of the five-year period (corroborated by their income-tax filings). Since appearance on the list has marketing cachet, *Inc.* receives between 10,000 and 20,000 applications or nominations; from these, it picks the top 500 as ranked by their five-year sales record. The *Inc.* list obviously excluded small, low-growth businesses. More subtly, the requirement of a five-year track record also screened out most "elite" VC-backed candidates, because successful businesses in this category often become publicly owned within five years.

---

* Thomas Friedman (2006) has similar stories.

The fieldwork that research associate Elizabeth Gordon and I have done for this current inquiry into VC-backed businesses is both similar to and different from the *Inc.* study.

- In the *Inc.* study, virtually everyone we interviewed was a founder-CEO. In the present study, about half of the CEOs we interviewed were not founders.

- As in the prior study, we sought in-depth, comprehensive information on each company. But the process of gathering this information was different. With the *Inc.* companies, we used only face-to-face interviews, some of which lasted up to three hours. In the recent study, we collected information in advance: before we interviewed CEOs, Elizabeth Gordon compiled a dossier on the company, relying on its website; databases such as Factiva, LexisNexis, and Dun & Bradstreet; web searches; and when available, investment memoranda provided by the VCs. Then she created a summary from the dossier describing a firm's current business, a brief historical profile including the backgrounds of the founders and data on its international involvement as evidenced by its overseas sales, competitors, investors, facilities, outsourcing, and so on. We started most interviews by asking the CEO to review and if necessary modify the summary. Next, we asked interviewees for their perspective about changes in globalization they had encountered in the course of their careers. We then discussed the choices they made about overseas activities and their future plans in their current companies. In the final segment of the interview the CEOs filled out a structured questionnaire and answered questions that arose from their responses.

- As in the earlier study, we assured our interviewees confidentiality, where needed or requested.[2]

- We did our first 18 interviews face to face. As we gained experience with the questions and process, we switched to phone interviews. Our early interviews extended to well over an hour—some ran to two; subsequent interviews took about an hour.

- Compared to the *Inc.* study, in which we approached a more or less random sample of founders and were rarely turned down, we faced significant obstacles in arranging interviews and therefore had to follow a more opportunistic approach. We approached CEOs through the VC firms that had invested in their companies. We got off to a smooth start because two partners of RRE Ventures were willing and able to persuade the CEOs of virtually all the companies in their firm's active portfolio to talk to us. It was similarly smooth sailing with ABS Ventures (seven randomly selected companies), Catamount Ventures (entire portfolio), and Atlas Ventures (four randomly drawn companies from their health-care portfolio). But several of the VCs I contacted refused to make introductions because they did not want to "distract" their CEOs (or "use up a chip"). Others did not respond to repeated communications (or they agreed to make introductions and then became incommunicado). Some of those who did make introductions first "screened" the CEOs for their interest in the project. The difficulty of reaching CEOs through their VCs made me supplement the sample by turning to former students who happened to be running VC-backed companies; they were helpful both in their willingness to be interviewed and in the introductions they provided to other CEOs.

Haphazard as this process may have been, I believe the sample of firms is—with respect to industry, stage of development of the company, and geographic location (of the companies and their VCs)—representative of the businesses that comprise the portfolios of typical mid- to top-tier VCs. The main problem of bias arises from the screening of companies by their VCs. I have good reason to believe (in some cases I was explicitly told) that we got a disproportionately large number of introductions to CEOs who had a strong interest in doing business overseas (or were already doing so) or were immigrants. We therefore likely observed a higher than average level of globalization (and of CEOs born outside of the United States). If I were using my evidence to assert that the world has become flat, such a bias would undermine my argument. As it happens, because I claim that the world is much less flat than many believe, a sample of companies biased toward globalization strengthens my argument.

The interviews suggest that, though the Internet has reduced the costs of selling and sourcing abroad, a lack of scale and maturity limits the geographic reach of most new and emerging businesses. In spite of the international bias of my sample of 106 venture capital–backed businesses, extensive cross-border activity was uncommon.

Certainly a few companies in my sample were—as described in the box—poster children for globalization: they intermediated or facilitated international trade, sold their products to overseas customers, used offshore manufacturing facilities or software development teams, and raised capital from international investors.

The Poster Children for Globalization

- Odyssey Logistics, based in Danbury, Connecticut, facilitated international trade. Odyssey was launched in 2003 to help companies in the chemical and process industries outsource the management and transportation of their raw materials and finished goods on a global basis. Odyssey operated in 74 countries, but (unlike UPS or Federal Express) did not own any transportation facilities; rather, it provided management services using a software platform developed and maintained by a team of programmers in Kiev, Ukraine. Odyssey's investors included Logispring, a venture capital firm based in Switzerland that invests in "businesses for global supply networks."[3]

- Vivre, based in New York City, also promoted international trade, but in luxury goods rather than bulk chemicals. The company was started in 1996 by Lebanese-born and Swiss-raised Eva Jeanbart-Lorenzotti, who was then a 27-year-old investment banker. Initially, Vivre helped a few brands, such as Bulgari and Ferragamo, sell their products to U.S. consumers through catalogues (including Vivre's own) and websites. By 2004, Vivre had signed up more than 100 European brands for its catalogue, which it mailed to more than 800,000 U.S. consumers. Like Odyssey, Vivre had sold some of its stock to a Swiss investor—a Geneva-based jewelry merchant.[4] It used an outsourcing company in India to maintain its website.*

- eSilicon, based in Sunnyvale, California, was, according to its founder and CEO, Jack Harding, built around "the fundamental trends of globalization and outsourcing." The company provided design and manufacturing services for customized, "application specific" silicon chips[5] used in products such as the iPod. To supplement design teams based in California, New Jersey, and Pennsylvania, the company acquired a design firm in Romania and formed a design partnership with the Japanese company Hitachi. It had sales offices in Israel and Japan and sales representatives in Europe. The company did not have any manufacturing facilities of its own;

---

* On the other side, Supplyscape helped discourage (illicit!) cross-border trade, protecting producers of pharmaceuticals in the United States (which may themselves be multinationals) from counterfeit drugs imported from labs in places like Brazil and China.

rather, it contracted with several companies, such as Taiwan Semiconductor Manufacturing Company, in the Far East. By 2005, it had raised $86 million in venture capital, including investments from Investor Growth Capital of Sweden and NIF Ventures and CrossBridge Venture Partners, both of Japan.

- Nexsan, a developer of data storage systems (its technology was used by the makers of the *Lord of the Rings* movies), was started in Derby, UK, in 1998. In its early years, it served customers in the UK (where it also had its manufacturing operations) and in continental Europe. In 2001, the company moved its headquarters to Los Angeles to improve its U.S. sales. It also opened a manufacturing facility in San Diego, but did not close its UK plant. In 2002, it opened an office in Seoul, Korea, as the central point for serving the Asian market. As of 2005, Nexan had acquired a Canadian software company and used contract manufacturing (for a portion of its production) in China and Mexico. Its main R&D remained in the UK.

- Cyota was incorporated as a Delaware company in 1999 by four Israelis, with its business headquarters in New York and its R&D in Israel. By 2005, the company had become a leading provider of software for credit card security to banks in the United States, Canada, the UK, and Japan, with data centers located on three continents and more employees outside the United States than inside. Financing was provided by venture capitalists in Israel, Europe, and the United States.

The poster children were however, exceptions—all told, only about a dozen or so of the companies we studied were global players. If the world were borderless and geography didn't matter, we should expect the typical business to derive two-thirds of its revenues from outside the United States (since the United States accounts for about a third of the world's GDP). But this proportion held true for fewer than 4 percent of the 83 companies for which we have revenue data.* More than 60 percent derived at least 90 percent of their revenues from the United States, and more than a third derived all their revenues from U.S. clients.

Only 34 of the 106 companies reported having facilities or offices outside the United States. Another five companies reported having overseas staff operating out of their homes. Moreover, the label *multinational* didn't

---

* Most of the companies for whom we do not have revenue breakdowns were "prerevenue."

quite fit the majority of the companies that did have overseas offices: 21 of the 34 had just one overseas office, and just four companies operated in five or more locations. Only 10 companies had more than 10 employees abroad.

A third of our interviewees had "outsourced" some part of their research or development function to offshore firms, but only six used offshore outsourcing to develop complete products. The most common use of offshore outsourcing was for the more routine activities of testing and quality assurance. Only 15 companies had outsourced any manufacturing to overseas suppliers, and only four had outsourced services (such as data entry, call centers, or transaction processing).

The somewhat indirect global engagement of the businesses we studied, namely the role immigrants play as founders and employees, was perhaps more significant than their overseas sales or offshoring activities. More than half the companies (57 out of 106) had at least one immigrant founder, and more than a third had an immigrant CEO. The overall proportion of immigrants to the total workforce in the median company we studied was slightly greater than 20 percent, compared to the 12 to 14 percent share of immigrants in the U.S. workforce as a whole.

More significant than the specific numbers on overseas sales, offices, offshoring, and immigrant participation was what we learned about the distinctive role of VC-backed businesses in the multiplayer innovation game, and how this distinctiveness affected their interactions with overseas players.[6]

This distinctiveness had several facets. First, in contrast to mature businesses, large or small, the mission of a VC-backed business—indeed, its very reason for being—is the creation of a new commercial enterprise. Second, because VC-backed businesses start from scratch, they have to develop many things—know-how and products, as well customer relationships and organizational structures. Third, a VC-backed business has only so much time and money for accomplishing its mission, and these constraints have a significant influence on how such businesses innovate. For example, they favor mid-level innovations, and they avoid cutting-edge research. Large companies, by contrast, also undertake new business initiatives to grow and renew themselves, but their time and resource constraints aren't as onerous.

In the chapters that follow, I argue that the distinctive manner in which VC-backed businesses participate in the innovation game often leads to an ambivalent posture toward global interactions: it stimulates long-term interest in overseas customers and offshoring, but only limited commitment.

How VC-backed businesses innovate also helps account for an apparently high participation of immigrants in them. I also discuss features of the overall innovation game that may be reasonably inferred from my observations and analyses of VC-backed players—particularly the difference in how this game is played at different levels.

In the next two chapters, I analyze how and why VC-backed businesses innovate in a distinctive way. Chapters 3 and 4 show how their behavior affects international marketing and offshoring initiatives. Chapter 5 analyzes the role of immigrants. Book 1 concludes with a brief discussion of research methods. The table "Highlights of Book 1" draws attention to what each chapter tells us about VC-backed businesses in particular, as well as the more general inferences and policy implications that will be described in book 2.

Table B.1
Highlights of Book 1

How the VC-Backed World Works	Broader Implications
1. VCs in new ventureland*	
• VC-backed businesses characterized by specialization in initiatives with "medium" uncertainty (especially about demand) and a strong technological base	• Innovation game requires many kinds of players → public policies should not tilt toward any subset (the theme of great variety runs through all the remaining chapters as well).
2. Advancing the frontier	
• How the "typical" VC-backed business develops mid-level know-how and products by extending and combining high-level know-how and products through a rapid, interactive and iterative process	• Mid-level innovators require (1) An ample supply of high-level know-how → expansion of cutting-edge research in China and India is a good thing for many U.S. innovators and consumers; (2) venturesome consumers who help innovators develop their products and then purchase them → policies should not be "biased" against consumption; (3) a wide range of "moderately" trained technical and nontechnical staff → training more PhDs in science and engineering may be counterproductive.
3. Marketing arenas	
• Why most VC-backed businesses rely on domestic "early adopters" to develop products, but then also continue to favor domestic customers for broader scale roll-outs	• Mid-level products are more "optimized" to local markets than are high-level products or know-how → the U.S. needs to worry more about the willingness of mid-level innovators to tailor products

(*continued*)

Table B.1 (*continued*)

How the VC-Backed World Works	Broader Implications
	for U.S. markets than about ensuring an "indigenous" supply of high-level know-how.
	• Sales and marketing play a crucial role in realizing the value of innovations → policy bias against sales and marketing is unwarranted.
4. Offshoring: the ins and outs	
• Why VC-backed businesses continue to develop their core products at home but are increasing their use of low-cost offshore locations for activities such as the testing of new products	• Many innovative activities, especially at the mid-level, will continue to be performed in the U.S.
	• Greater offshoring of testing (and other activities that are "well suited") will increase the development and use of products that improve U.S. productivity → offshoring is not a threat to U.S. prosperity.
5. Founders and staff: global at home	
• How the high participation of immigrants in VC-backed businesses reflects the supply and demand for scientists and engineers rather than the exceptional enterprise of immigrants	• "Run-of-the mill" immigrant engineers (who don't have advanced degrees) play a valuable "complementary" role—they broaden the variety of labor available for mid-level innovation rather than "displace" the native-born → immigration policies should reflect the value of "journeyman" technical labor and the comparative advantage of the native-born in nontechnical roles (such as management and sales).

* Chapters 1 and 2 will also provide the reader with context for understanding globalization choices made by VC-backed businesses and other mid-level innovators.

1

■ VCs in New Ventureland

VC-backed businesses differ from each other more than do barber shops or restaurants—for instance, in what they sell and whom they sell to. Yet they do share common characteristics. I will highlight some of them by comparing VC-financed firms with other kinds of new or emerging businesses. These distinguishing features will help explain the nature and extent of the cross-border interactions of VC-backed businesses. The comparison will also illuminate an important feature of the overall innovation game, namely the high degree of variety and specialization of the players. As we will see, even the relatively broad category of VC-backed business has many distinguishing features; and there is also considerable—and multidimensional—variety within the category.

For expositional convenience the analysis will be spread across two chapters: in this chapter we will see how and why VC-backed businesses have relatively large capital requirements, less novelty, more experienced founding teams, and a stronger technological foundation for their innovations than other kinds of start-ups. In the next chapter we will focus more closely on the distinguishing characteristics of their role in advancing the technological frontier.

In the best of times, and under expansive definitions, each year fewer than a thousand new ventures receive seed or early-stage financing from venture capitalists; in lean times only a few hundred receive such financing. In contrast, the total number of new businesses started in the United States every year ranges from half a million to two million.[1] The very low proportion of VC-financed start-ups—less than one-half of 1 percent of the total—reflects the low proportion of entrepreneurs who apply for venture capital as well as the extreme pickiness of VCs in selecting from the proposals they receive. Who makes it and who doesn't?

A useful way to highlight the distinctive features of successful applicants is to distinguish between three classes of start-ups:

- A large "C" class comprises many popular but low-potential businesses that start small and stay small.
- An elite "A" class comprises start-ups that receive venture capital funding. Not all elite start-ups survive, however; some enjoy extremely rapid growth and provide spectacular returns; others flounder or fail, sometimes spectacularly.
- Between the popular "C" and elite "A" ventures, we find "promising" "B" class start-ups that can evolve into so-called gazelles (from whose ranks *Inc.* draws its "500" lists), a few of which may then become multi-billion-dollar public companies. These promising class B ventures cannot, however, secure start-up capital from professional VCs, so their founders "bootstrap" their ventures with personal funds or those raised from relatives, friends, and individual investors.

In this chapter I argue that there are systematic differences in the three classes—growth and the availability of VC funding aren't simply the result of chance. I also suggest that the elite VC-backed start-ups tend to have a much stronger technological foundation than the other two kinds. This analysis will later show why VC-backed businesses are better positioned than other start-ups to do business abroad, but also why they tend to be cautious in undertaking cross-border initiatives.

■ Popular Cs, Promising Bs

Several attributes distinguish popular but low-potential start-ups from promising but less common start-ups. Traditionally popular ventures, such as beauty salons, auto-repair shops, and house-painting and housecleaning services, provide relatively low-unit-price goods or services to many consumers; by contrast, businesses that expand rapidly provide high-unit-price goods and services to a small number of customers.[2] Moreover, most popular C start-ups serve individual consumers, whereas high-growth B businesses tend to serve other businesses. Similarly, "popular" start-ups are mainly found in industries where the technology has matured and demand has stabilized. In contrast, many B businesses originate in high-tech fields such as the computer industry that are in a state of flux.*

Frank Knight's theory about the nature of profit helps provide a unifying explanation for many specific differences between class B and class C ventures.[3] According to Knight, real profits (as opposed to the returns to labor, capital, or other resources earned in a competitive market) aren't earned by taking known, or precisely quantifiable, risks, such as betting on a roulette wheel. Rather, profits represent a reward for assuming unmeasurable and unquantifiable risk, which Knight calls uncertainty. "Knightian" uncertainty arises when novel circumstances preclude mechanistic extrapolations based on historic patterns—when past isn't necessarily prologue.

In class C start-ups new businesses closely replicate existing businesses, so there is little novelty of circumstance. According to Knight's analysis, they face little of the uncertainty that is necessary for making a profit. This is obviously not the case for class B start-ups in high-tech markets such as the computer industry, where ongoing innovations constantly create new circumstances (whether or not the start-up itself stirs things up). But B start-ups that sell high-ticket goods and services such as fancy handbags also often face the uncertainty of novel circumstances, albeit in a more subtle way. For instance, to get buyers to pay $1,000 for a handbag, sellers often have to satisfy some amorphous want, such as the customer's desire to be cool or trendy. In the absence of any proven method for creating coolness, history provides a poor guide for assessing the prospects of such a start-up. Therefore, even if the genre of luxury handbags is well established, every start-up's idiosyncratic effort to achieve coolness involves novel circumstances.

Knight's analysis doesn't imply that simply starting a business under novel circumstances guarantees profits and growth. Making a profit in turbulent computer markets or the ineffable handbag industry may require

---

* More than a third of *Inc.* 500 companies were in the computer industry, which has long been in a state of technological flux.

talent, skill, hard work, and luck. Moreover, ventures started under novel circumstances do not survive at a higher rate than ventures that do not.* Rather, novel circumstances are a necessary—not a sufficient—condition for a true economic profit (that exceeds the normal return on capital and labor invested in the venture).

Novelty may nevertheless allow some class B start-ups to enjoy great long-run success in the following way: High uncertainty deters ambiguity-averse entrants—many individuals and firms don't like games in which they have to guess about the risks and returns. The attenuated competition gives entrepreneurs who are willing to plunge into uncharted waters a chance to earn high profits, at least until the uncertainty is resolved. At that point, exceptionally capable—and a little lucky—entrepreneurs can parlay their initial profits into a valuable franchise. For instance, even if most ventures to produce luxury handbags may fail, Kate and Andy Spade were able to sell their business (to Liz Claiborne) for over a $100 million. Similarly, while most of the people who were assembling PCs in their bedrooms in the 1980s are forgotten, Michael Dell has accumulated a net worth of $14.2 billion (according to *Forbes*'s 2006 estimates). Such rewards are not available to the most hardworking and capable owner of a barber shop.

If novelty is a necessary condition for the commercial success of any enterprise, then the elite VC-backed class A and class B start-ups should have it. What, then, is the difference between the As and the Bs? As we will see next, VCs tend to invest in a narrower subset of novel ventures—they favor the high-tech novelty of a computer, not the aesthetic novelty of a luxury handbag.

■ Qualifying the Chosen

Barbers and florists don't seek financing from VCs, but a fair proportion of the founders of promising class B companies do solicit such funding. About 30 percent of the *Inc.* 500 companies I studied in my previous research had approached VCs. Although a majority of promising start-ups don't search

---

* Indeed Knight himself speculated that in the aggregate, uncertain ventures produce negative returns.

for venture capital, enough of them apply to deluge VCs with potential deals. Of the many who apply, only a small proportion gets a serious response, and very few get funding.*

Start-ups that can raise venture capital have some of the attributes that distinguish promising class B ventures from low-potential C ventures: they usually sell high-ticket goods and services to business customers (rather than to individual consumers), and they are concentrated in high-technology industries.

But there are crucial and somewhat subtle differences between class A start-ups and the more common variety of promising class B start-ups. VCs have a strong preference for ventures where there is an *objective* basis for expecting a *large* payoff through a public offering or acquisition by another firm (aka an "exit" or "liquidity event") in a five- to seven-year time frame.† In contrast, self-financed entrepreneurs are more willing to act on pure hunches (i.e., they have higher tolerance for novel, data-scarce circumstances), and to pursue opportunities where the foreseeable payoffs are small and where the route to a five-year exit is not obvious.

Their desire for objective criteria for predicting large payoffs in five years leads VCs to consider three factors when they screen proposals. The first, and the most frequently emphasized by VCs, is a management team that is capable of rapidly building an enterprise that's sizable enough to produce a large payoff. VCs sometimes talk about hard-to-pin-down qualities—John Doerr, of Kleiner Perkins, says he looks for "outstanding management" with a "tremendous sense of urgency." Charles River Ventures assesses "the capabilities and charisma of the founding team. Can they attract the best employees? Do they have the capability to shift the direction of an industry?"[4] But before these subjective factors come into play, there is an objective hurdle: to use the words in a brochure produced by Primus Venture

---

* According to the managing partner of Highland Capital Partners, a top-tier VC, the firm receives about 10,000 "qualified" business plans, which lead to about 1,000 meetings, followed by 400 company visits. In the end, Highland makes about 10-20 investments a year. (Source: Robert F. Higgins, "Venture Capital and the Entrepreneur," presentation at Columbia Business School, November 4, 2004).

† I provided a detailed "Knightian" explanation for the nature and underpinnings of VC investment criteria in my 2000 book and in a follow-up article. "How Novelty Aversion Affects Financing Options" (Bhidé 2006). Mainstream finance theories ignore Knightian uncertainty and focus on information asymmetries—the so-called lemon problem that my fieldwork suggests is of less concern to real-world investors and entrepreneurs than the contracting problems that arise because of Knightian uncertainty.

Partners, "competent management with deep experience in the industry or markets they address."

The importance of two other criteria is sometimes obscured by such pronouncements as, "We'd rather invest in a great team with a good plan than a good team with a great plan." But even the most competent team cannot turn water into wine. So VCs also assess market potential: is the "space" (to use the now common term) large enough to accommodate a sizable enterprise? Potential investors also evaluate the venture's prospects for establishing durable competitive advantages or "barriers to entry": an undifferentiated enterprise may earn transitory profits in a rapidly growing market, but under normal circumstances, it cannot provide a satisfactory exit for its investors. Moreover, such an exit also requires that the advantage be owned by or embedded in the firm, such as a proprietary technology, brand name, or tacit and difficult-to-replicate knowledge.

Note an important distinction between the criteria for *teams* on the one hand, and for markets and durable advantages on the other: Tried and tested teams are desirable, and VCs would rather get superstars at premium prices than rookies for a bargain. VCs, however, avoid businesses that serve mature markets and have well-established competitive advantages. Rather, they look for markets they expect to become large, and firms they expect to develop proprietary advantages. They want to profit from—and to some extent facilitate—these changes.

In assessing market potential, VCs usually don't go out on a limb. Their preference for objective data and fast exits causes them to avoid ventures that try to *create* a market. They even shy away from emerging categories where there is a small market but little hard evidence about when demand will take off. VCs tend to wait for evidence of sizable sales in conjunction with a large number of potential users who have not yet become customers. To use an epidemiological analogy, a good time to invest is when the epidemic has plainly started but much of the population has yet to be infected.

For instance, the technological buzz about nanotechnology dates back at least to the early 1990s. I supervised a student research project at the time that anticipated a soon-to-be booming field. As it happened, it was the Internet that took off. The excitement about nanotechnology didn't go away, but in the absence of any large commercial applications, nanotechnology companies have accounted for a modest share of VC investment. In the VC-backed companies I studied, only two (one a developer of systems for conducting cell culture experiments, and the other of advanced batteries) made any mention of their use of nanotechnology.

The case of Verdiem (another company in our sample) also points to the reluctance of VCs to invest in markets that aren't yet "ripe." The company (which started life in 2001 as EZConserve) developed software to help organizations with large networks of PCs monitor and reduce their electricity costs. As Verdiem's CEO, Steven Sperry, told us (in 2006):

> When I first went out to raise money for the company, it was pretty obvious that we weren't going to attract capital from the large venture capital firms. One reason was we weren't in a category that other venture firms were investing in. It's kind of a catch-22: how does a new category start if nobody wants to invest in it? Somebody has to prove that there's a market opportunity before investors are going to move into that space. I think that's happening now in our space; every four weeks or so I receive a call from a large venture fund that's interested in the green-technology, energy-infrastructure space. But it wasn't until last year, 2005, that we really established traction to the point where I could say to an investor that we're no longer trying to prove that there's a market for this type of software. We now have 60-plus customers and a twenty-million-dollar pipeline, so there's clearly a market.

Identifying the potential to establish durable competitive advantages before they have been realized is more challenging and limits the kinds of start-ups eligible for VC funding. Considerations of exit require advantages that transcend the personal capacities of the individuals running the company. Selling a business or taking it public is problematic if the key assets are controlled by a few of its employees. Moreover, in many kinds of advantages that belong to or are embedded in a firm, objective evidence of potential is scarce. For instance, in businesses like handbags and shoes, brands names can be worth billions. Similarly, in fast foods and big-box retailing, developing the tacit and multifaceted knowledge required to sustain an effective and efficient business system can create large and valuable franchises. But it is very difficult to research whether a particular start-up has what it takes to build a successful brand or business system. In the absence of objective evidence, VCs tend to stay away.

Instead, VCs usually earn their keep by focusing on start-ups whose plans for building proprietary advantages have important technological foundations. Plausible candidates for funding seek to build their business on or around a patent for a new molecule, gizmo, or process (or an invention around someone else's patent), an ingenious design, a repurposed technology, an algorithm or a solution to an engineering problem. Such a technological foundation permits objective, fact-based assessments of the start-up's prospects. VCs can, for instance, research the strength of the venture's intellectual property (IP) and the price-performance of competing technologies; solicit the reaction of potential customers to the prototype; and consult industry experts about the technical problems that remain to be solved. In other words, VCs can kick real tires: they don't have to take all the critical premises of the founders on faith.

Most of the companies in my sample could provide VCs with some demonstrable evidence of an incipient technological advantage. For instance, 50 interviewees reported that they had filed for or secured a patent (or exclusive rights to the use of a patent) *before they received funding from VCs*; only 44 said they had not; and 12 did not tell us (in most such cases, the interviewee had joined the company after it had received VC funding and was unsure of the company's history). It is also worth noting, as indicated in the box on the sources of pre-VC patents, that in many cases, company founders secured licenses to patents from other players in the innovation game. This suggests that VCs don't care where a company's technological edge comes from—as long as there is a source. The role of patents also provides an example of the multiplayer nature of the innovation game.

Sources of Pre-VC Patents

Our interviewees had secured their patents (or patent rights) from a variety of sources.

Twenty resulted from classic individual inventive activity of the founders. Biorexis Pharmaceutical's CEO told us that his company's chief scientist developed its proprietary protein engineering technology "literally in his garage. I have seen the garage!" Similarly, 4INFO, started to develop mobile search applications for cell phones, filed five provisional applications for patents[5] before receiving venture capital funding. All the development was done in founder Zaw Thet's living room.

Nine companies secured their "pre-VC" technology from another company or commercial research lab. Inxight developed software that analyzes text (in more than 15 languages) and organizes unstructured data (such as emails) into preset folders or classifications. Its core technology emerged from the Xerox Corporation's Palo Alto Research Center; in fact, Inxight was started as a wholly owned subsidiary of Xerox in 1997 and did not raise VC funds until 2001. Similarly, Alinea Pharmaceuticals secured exclusive rights to all compounds discovered at the Institute for Diabetes Discovery (IDD) in Branford, Connecticut, a research organization focused on metabolic disorders. Enpirion developed ultraminiaturized power systems (used in personal computers, laser printers, and so on) in one integrated circuit. The technology was originally developed at Bell Labs by scientists who went on to found Enpirion, securing a license from their previous employer.

Twelve companies secured technology licenses from universities. Brontes Technologies licensed technology developed by Douglas Hart, a professor of mechanical engineering at MIT. The technology, called active wavefront sampling, allowed the development of high-speed, digitized three-dimensional images that are highly accurate. MicroCHIPS Inc. (Micro Chemically Integrated Products) secured a technology license from MIT for a tiny polymeric chip with many microreservoirs that could be used to deliver drugs over time while implanted or ingested. One company, Paratek Microwave, licensed "phased array antenna technology" from the Army Research Labs that it expected to use in devices ranging from satellite systems to Wi-Fi networks.

Some of our interviewees who had started with a concept said they had to (or chose to) wait until they had tangible evidence of the viability of the enabling technology before they could get VC funding. Alex Gorelik and a couple of engineers started Exeros in 2002 to develop software that would increase the efficiency and accuracy of data integration projects as well as of data governance, that is, the process of identifying sensitive data, how it flows through an organization's systems, and who has access to it. Gorelik said: "We spent two years developing our product before we could get funding. Nobody believed it could be done. We had very innovative technology, which is like nothing else out there."

The CEO of Supplyscape, Shabbir Dahod, also chose to wait. His company helped its clients fight the import of counterfeit drugs. Its systems used radio frequency ID tags (RFIDs) to track drugs from manufacturers through distributors to retailers and pharmacies. Dahod told us, "We went a year without venture financing. We wanted to build up the core technology and get some

> market validation before we raised money. There were seven technical founders. My deal with them was, 'If you forgo salary and contribute your time, I'll pick all the baseline expenses for the company, make you founders, and give you appropriate quantities of shares.'"

■ Variations on the Theme

Although VCs evaluate all three factors—the team, the market, and prospects for establishing durable advantages—they may overlook the deficiencies in one area if another factor is especially strong. This can introduce variations in the kind of technological base that different VC-backed businesses start with.

For instance, the common claim that "the team comes first" notwithstanding, an exceptional technological base can compensate for the inexperience of founders. Rookie founders can secure financing if the market and technology story is sufficiently compelling simply by agreeing to work under the adult supervision of an experienced CEO. Indeed, many VCs say that hiring good CEOs and other top managers is one of the significant ways they add value to the businesses they invest in (see box).*

Building the Google Team

Google provides a famous recent example of how VCs may invest in businesses with inexperienced founders who have developed a great technological foundation and then help build up the company's managerial capability.

In 1996 Larry Page and Sergey Brin, two PhD students, undertook a research project to develop a new approach to searching web pages (using "back-links" instead of ranking the number of times a search term appeared

---

* In describing "What We Look for" on its website, Charles River Ventures starts with the "capabilities and charisma of the founding team." But a few paragraphs later, we are told, "We don't require a complete management team, since we can often help in building one." In recent years some other VC firms, such as Bessemer and Atlas, have hired senior in-house recruiters to help find managers for their portfolio companies.

on a page). The research led to a patent application in January 1998. In September of that year, Page and Brin incorporated Google with about $1 million raised from wealthy, high-profile Silicon Valley individuals (including $100,000 from Andy Bechtolsheim, a founder of Sun Microsystems). By then, companies such as AltaVista had already created a large demand for web searches. Google's technology and clean interface made it highly popular—by February 1999 it was handling about 500,000 queries a day. In June 1999 two leading VCs, Sequoia Capital and Kleiner Perkins, invested $25 million. Sequoia's Michael Moritz and Kleiner's John Doerr joined the company's board. The VCs helped Google quickly recruit seasoned executives, such as Omid Kordestani from Netscape. In 2001, Eric Schmidt, a 20-year high-tech veteran who was then running Novell, was hired as CEO. Schmidt brought in financial oversight and established standard business processes (such as sales forecasting), freeing Page and Brin to focus on technology.[6]

Conversely, exceptionally credible founders may lead VCs to suspend their normal criteria for evaluating potential markets or competitive advantages (see box "Bending the Rules"). In some cases this may lead to investments in businesses that have, to start with, no technological foundation at all. But as the box indicates, if the founders often have earned their credibility through high-tech ventures, VCs can reasonably expect them to create a technological edge.

Bending the Rules

John Doerr of Kleiner Perkins says he usually looks for a "strategic focus on a large, rapidly growing market." Doerr's investment in Segway Inc. was an exception to Doerr's normal preference for rapidly growing rather than nascent markets. Segway was started to produce a scooter-like vehicle, officially the Segway HT (Human Transporter), that used gyroscopes to mimic human equilibrium and motion. Passengers didn't steer—they simply leaned in the direction they wanted to go. There was no existing market since the HT was a completely new type of transportation. But the company's high-profile founder, Dean Kamen,[7] had the charisma and credentials to sell his "If we build it, they will buy it" vision. Doerr predicted the HT would become "as big as the Internet." In fact, the HT, which was unveiled in 2001 and was projected to sell 50,000 to 100,000 units by January 2003, had sold only 6,000 units by September of that year.[8]

In my sample, three unusual companies also received funding almost entirely because of the credentials of their founders. One is ThinkFire, started by Nathan Myhrvold—previously the chief technology officer at Microsoft—to help clients realize the value of their patents and help users of intellectual property to secure patents (and defend themselves against patent infringement suits). ThinkFire did not have a proprietary technology for providing its services—at its core Thinkfire was a cross between a high-end consulting firm and a merchant bank. Nevertheless, the company had no difficulty raising venture capital, because, according to its CEO and cofounder Dan McCurdy, "Nathan was seeking the funding. Here was a famous guy showing up saying, 'I have this great idea, and what I need to make it work are the relationships you have—and I have many of those too. And if you don't give me a huge valuation, you won't get to play because I will use my own money.' That was the first and foremost reason we got funded. We also had a very successful management team, who had demonstrated enormous success at a big company in getting money from IP: We had been generating half a billion dollars a year at Lucent [where McCurdy previously worked]."

A second instance of founders' credibility trumping evidence of markets and competitive advantage is Benu. The company was cofounded by Jeff Closs and financed by New Enterprise Associates (NEA), a leading VC firm in Silicon Valley. Closs recalls:

> We raised almost two million dollars as seed money with no business plan. We literally had two million dollars in the bank, with four cofounders and a big stack of blank paper.... [But] I had been a CEO at one of NEA's other companies, so I had a long relationship with the firm. Another cofounder had been a longtime CEO of PacifiCare, which is now part of United Healthcare. And NEA had looked at a number of business plans in health-care services, but they hadn't seen a deal they wanted to do—either they didn't feel comfortable with the management team, or they weren't persuaded by the business model or they didn't want to co-invest with some of the other people who were in the deal.

After nearly two years of evaluating different opportunities, the founding team started Benu in September 2000 to help midsized employers offer their employees a broad choice of health plans (as is common in large companies) instead of a single health plan. (The plan did involve developing a proprietary risk management system.)

The third example of the importance of a company's founders is Mangrove Systems, cofounded by UK native Jonathan Reeves. In 1996, Reeves and Thomas Shea founded Sahara Networks, raising $11 million from Bessemer Venture Capital and Greylock Ventures, two leading Boston-based VC firms. Two years later, before Sahara made a product, it was acquired by Cascade Communications for $212 million. In 1999 Reeves and Shea launched Sirocco Systems, with about $30 million raised from Bessemer (and other VC firms). Eighteen months later Sycamore Networks acquired Sirocco for nearly $ 3 billion.*

In the spring of 2002, Reeves teamed up with two former colleagues to launch Mangrove Systems. Thanks to Reeves's track record, he was able to raise $2.5 million in seed financing from Bessemer and $600,000 from other sources. By July of that year, the company had hired 10 employees, leased a 26,000-square-foot office (that could accommodate 120 people), and installed a sophisticated computer system—without having identified a product.[9] Eventually, Mangrove's management decided to develop the telecommunications industry's first "GFP (generic framing procedure)-based Transport Aware Switching™ system," and in April 2003 raised even more VC capital—upwards of $20 million from Bessemer and several other VCs.[10]

* Perhaps not coincidentally, Sycamore's cofounders had previously started Cascade the acquirer of Reeves and Shea's previous enterprise, Sahara.

Between the "great technology plus rookie team" and "great team plus no market, technology, or product" extremes, VCs tend to make a range of trade-offs. Explosive market growth and a good team, for instance, may encourage VCs to invest in a start-up that has not yet developed even the specifications of a product to serve the market. But these variations within the A class should not lead us to overlook basic differences between class A and class B start-ups. The next section, which discusses why B businesses fail to attract VC funding, will help place in sharper relief the distinctive features of class A businesses that affect how they play in the innovation game and engage in cross-border interactions.

■ Promising (but not quite enough)

Class B (or "promising") ventures—including those that go on to achieve great commercial success—often fail at the outset to meet VCs' screening criteria.

One reason is that founders of "promising" start-ups often lack a deep résumé containing objective evidence of their ability to rapidly build a large-scale business.*

Another reason is that unlike the founders of Google, they also lack a compelling market or technology story to compensate for their thin résumés. Sometimes, as was the case when Bill Gates and Paul Allen started Microsoft in 1975, there is no evidence of a large and growing market— when VCs invested in Google, it may be recalled, the demand for web searches was already well established. Even after a market has reached the takeoff stage, as was the case with the PC industry in the early eighties (see the box "Nothing Personal"), entrepreneurs may lack a proprietary product, patented technology, or any other verifiable, durable advantage. That was the case with Michael Dell.

Nothing Personal

In the sixties and seventies, VCs financed many companies (such as DEC, Prime Computer, Cray Research, Stratus, and Apollo) in the minicomputer and mainframe computer industry and earned handsome returns. Yet in the early days of the personal computer industry there was virtually no VC investment in such start-ups. The pioneering companies started between 1975 and 1980— MITS, Microsoft, Apple, Digital Research (which produced CP/M, the operating

---

* The individuals who start companies that go on to make *Inc.* 500 lists are, however, better educated than the overall workforce or the founders of the run-of-the-mill start-ups. For instance, more than 80 percent of *Inc.* founders have at least a four-year college degree (Bhidé 2000). And some of those who famously dropped out (Bill Gates and Michael Dell) attended brand-name colleges (Harvard and the University of Texas at Austin). In contrast, only about a quarter of the U.S. workforce—and small business owners—have college degrees (Hurst and Lusardi 2004). Participation in student activities and side-businesses may also give founders self-confidence in their commercial acumen, salesmanship, resourcefulness, and other such qualities that are invaluable in getting a promising business off the ground. But this does not constitute "the deep experience in the industry or markets" that Primus Venture partners and other VCs want.

system used by Apple), and VisiCalc (responsible for the first spreadsheet)—were launched with the founders' own savings and borrowed funds from relatives, friends, or so-called angel investors.[11] A major reason VCs didn't invest in start-ups during the early days of the personal computer industry was that there was no evidence of large market potential. When Bill Gates and Paul Allen launched Microsoft in 1975, their first product, the 8080 BASIC computer language, ran only on the Altair, a rudimentary personal computer made by MITS, a tiny Albuquerque start-up. MITS sold the Altair in kit form to hobbyists at a rate of a few thousand units a year. An additional deterrent in many cases was the absence of proprietary technology: there was nothing particularly proprietary about Microsoft's BASIC—it had no patent protection and could easily have been replicated by many competent programmers.

VCs started investing in personal computer start-ups after the success of the spreadsheet (launched in 1979) and the launch of IBM's PC in 1980 significantly increased demand for personal computers. In 1982, for instance, Sevin-Rosen financed the start-up of Compaq Computer and Lotus Development Corporation. Both companies targeted large and growing markets: Compaq had IBM's PC in its sights, and Lotus had VisiCalc's spreadsheet.

But although VCs became willing to invest in personal computer start-ups, most of the entrepreneurs who flocked to the field could not secure VC financing. Although the market was large and booming, most start-ups could not offer VCs evidence of a path to durable competitive advantages. The contrast between Compaq and Dell is instructive. Compaq's first computer, launched in March 1983, incorporated the solution of two technical problems: a computer that was both portable (although it was in fact more luggable than portable) and a legal clone of the IBM PC. In order to make the clone legal, engineers had to duplicate the functions of the BIOS (basic input/output system) without actually copying the code, through what is called "clean room" reverse engineering. Overcoming these technical challenges made Compaq the only alternative to IBM and enabled the company to ship more than 50,000 units in its first year. In 1985, Compaq even took the technological lead—its Desktop Pro 286 ran at faster speeds than an IBM PC.

Michael Dell started his business two years after Compaq, from his dorm room. He didn't need a team of engineers to make IBM-compatible machines—by then a legal BIOS could be purchased from third parties—and there was no other technological basis for the venture. The business was based only on

> the premise that by selling directly to end users (without a middle-man), Dell
> would "better understand customers' needs and provide the most effective
> computing solutions to meet those needs."[12] Eventually, by developing an
> effective supply chain (a "business system" innovation) Dell surpassed both
> IBM and Compaq in the personal computer market. But at the outset there
> was no evidence to suggest this outcome.

My previous study of *Inc.* founders suggests that the absence of proprietary products or technologies is pervasive even among the successful class
B start-ups. Only 6 percent of the *Inc.* founders I interviewed claimed to
have started with unique products or services. Nearly 60 percent said that
identical or very close substitutes were available, and the rest indicated
slight to moderate differences between their offerings and those of their
competitors. Fewer than 5 percent of the companies reported filing for a
patent.[13] What makes the absence of any technological edge striking is that
more than a third of my interviewees were from the computer industry.
The dynamism of the computer industry and high-tech sectors of the economy apparently allows businesses that don't have any technological capability of their own to participate in their growth. For instance, the rapid
growth of the computer industry has spawned *Inc.* 500 businesses that help
clients recruit part- or full-time software engineers. But the recruiters themselves do not develop any software.*

The factors that sustain the profits and growth of promising *Inc.* 500 companies have noteworthy implications for the distinction between class A
and class B ventures. According to *Inc.*'s own surveys, only 12 percent of the
founders attributed the success of their companies to "an unusual or extraordinary idea." Eighty-eight percent reported that their success was mainly due
to the "exceptional execution of an ordinary idea."[14] My prior research also
suggests that because in the initial stages there is no organization to speak of,

---

* This is exactly opposite to the pattern in VC-backed businesses. There, even companies such as
  Amazon that don't develop commercial software do make large investments in systems that are
  central to their business. In my sample of VC-backed businesses, aside from a few companies
  that are not in a high-technology industry and some that might be called faux high-tech, the
  overwhelming majority had devoted significant resources to developing new technology.

the "exceptional execution" turns on the founders' personal efforts and abilities. Furthermore, the comparative advantage of an entrepreneur's personal capacities (for instance in reading and satisfying fuzzy customer wants) lies in activities where there are significant diseconomies of scale. This reliance on personal abilities obviously discourages VC investment— VCs cannot bet just on an untested personal capacity to execute; and even a successful bet in a business with significant diseconomies of scale cannot produce a large payoff.[15]

The comparative advantage of class B businesses in activities with significant diseconomies of scale also has subtle implications for their role in the innovation game. As I have mentioned, although many such companies are classified as computer or telecommunications or health-care businesses, they may not develop new products or technologies. They can, however, play a valuable role in the deployment of innovations developed by other players in the innovation game (such as VC-backed businesses). For instance, many *Inc.* 500 companies have served as distributors and "value-added resellers" of computer equipment produced by large computer companies. These distribution activities have significant diseconomies of scale, but have also played an essential role in the IT revolution.

Similarly, reliance on the personal capacity and efforts of their founders limits the geographic reach of many class B ventures. Businesses that rely on the personal touch of an owner to make each sale cannot easily serve remote customers. Nor can they readily develop or produce their offerings in low-cost offshore locations.

■ Concluding Comments

All other things being equal, we should expect class A VC-backed businesses with strong technological foundations to have greater cross-border activity than class B (or class C) businesses whose profits turn on the exceptional personal capacities of the proprietors. When the differentiating features of a business's offering derive from a proprietary technology, its production can be decoupled from the sale—and neither requires the presence of the proprietors. As an empirical matter, high-tech companies in the United States have exported a larger proportion of their output than companies overall, and more recently they have been at the forefront of offshoring.

The preference of VCs for large absolute payoffs (and not just a high rate of return) also points to a high level of cross-border engagement: We should expect VCs to favor companies that target large global markets and avoid companies that serve small local markets. The larger scale should also facilitate offshoring.

This was in fact the case with CiDRA—the company derived well over half its revenues from international markets and had a high-profile relationship with Infosys, one of the top Indian outsourcing companies. Its CEO told us,

> When I was raising capital for CiDRA, I knew that VCs want to take swings with the bat. And if you want to raise money from top-tier firms—who see thousands of business plans—you have to have a compelling proposition that can give an 8X or 10X return in multi-billion-dollar markets, not multi-million-dollar niches. So you get pushed to be global from the beginning.

The preference of VCs for technology-based businesses that can produce large payoffs (which I was aware of before I started my study and which led me to focus on VC-backed businesses to begin with) explains why the VC-backed businesses in my sample were generally more global than the typical small business. The interesting question is, why wasn't vigorous global engagement even more widespread? Why was CiDRA an exception: why did so few of the other companies derive large shares of their revenues from overseas markets? What led so many to hold back from offshoring? To help answer these questions, we will now examine more closely the nature of the technological innovations that the companies undertook and the dynamics of their pursuit of them.

2

■ Advancing the Frontier:

The Nature of Mid-level Innovation

The role of mid-level innovators—as exemplified by many VC-backed businesses—has not received the attention it deserves. Many researchers and policymakers make no distinction between levels of know-how and product development, or they focus only on the development of high-level knowledge. I emphasize the distinctive features of the middle level for two reasons: As we will see in later chapters, how mid-level players innovate has a significant influence on their overseas marketing initiatives, and their use of offshoring and immigrant labor.

Understanding what mid-level innovators do—and what they need in order to flourish—will also buttress the analysis in book 2 of how policymakers in the United States and other advanced countries should respond to the expansion of high-level research in China and India. It will support the proposition that the United States should welcome more research from China and India, because an increase in the supply of high-level know-how helps mid-level innovators based in the United States develop products that increase productivity and wages in the United States. The material in this chapter likewise foreshadows the harmful unintended consequences of efforts to promote high-level research in the United States by training more PhDs in science and engineering.

Where and how do VC-backed businesses contribute to the development of new technologies—what's their role in the multiplayer innovation game?

This chapter highlights three features (briefly mentioned in the introduction) of innovations by VC-backed businesses. First, they seem to thrive in the middle of the innovation game, in terms of the know-how and products they develop. Second, they add value by combining or extending high-level know-how or products. Third, their modus operandi is quite unlike that of high-level scientific research: VC-backed businesses employ an iterative process akin to what engineers call "rapid prototyping," involving close, ongoing interactions with users.

■ Attractions of the Middle

As mentioned in the introduction, successful new high-tech products or services usually incorporate knowledge developed at several levels, ranging from high-level principles or concepts to ground-level know-how. For instance, the MP3 music files for iPods (and other digital audio players) incorporate high-level mathematical algorithms used to compress audio and video files; mid-level programming techniques for producing MP3 encoders; and the ground-level know-how required to "implement" an encoder in the hardware system used to generate the MP3 file.*

New products can also be stratified into levels according to their distance from end consumers: ground-level "consumer" goods and services (e.g., the iPod); high-level raw materials, platforms, or components (e.g., the chips used in the iPod, or even the silicon used to make the chips); and, at the mid-level, "intermediate" products (e.g., chipsets rather than individual chips).[1]

The sweet spot for innovation in many VC-backed businesses is at the middle level for both know-how and products. With respect to know-how, for such businesses there are several kinds of deterrents to working at either the high or ground level.

VC-backed businesses do not try to discover scientific principles in pure physics, chemistry, or biology, for example, because research labs (or individual scientists) whose sources of funding do not expect a financial return have natural comparative advantages. More subtly, and contrary to popular perception, VCs also shy away from ventures that pursue basic engineering

---

* The same kind of pattern may be observed even in low-tech business-system innovations. For instance, in the case of Starbucks, there is the high-level idea of transplanting an Italian style espresso bar to the United States; lower-level principles pertain to store locations, décor, and menus, and the very detailed operational knowledge of how to train baristas and manage a store.

or technological advances even if they may have commercial value. There are two reasons for this. First, commercial success in developing high-level know-how is rarely achieved within the five- to seven-year time frame that represents a successful exit for VCs. Second, as discussed in the last chapter, their limited appetite for Knightian uncertainty discourages VCs from investing in highly novel projects—such as efforts to break new technological ground. Here, individuals whose tolerance for Knightian uncertainty isn't curtailed by their responsibility to investors (because, for instance, they are self-financed or have faculty appointments) have comparative advantages.

VC-backed businesses are also unlikely to focus on developing ground-level know-how, also for two reasons. First, VCs avoid investing in businesses whose profitability depends mainly on detailed, tacit knowledge of individual circumstances (such as providing custom engineering or design services) because it is difficult for VCs to objectively assess the prospects—in other words, there is a high level of Knightian uncertainty about whether the founder has what it takes.[2] Second, the absence of economies of scale in such businesses usually precludes large payoffs to VCs. Here, too, the self-funded or informally financed entrepreneur has a comparative advantage.

VC-backed businesses therefore tend to specialize in mid-level know-how: they develop new products by building on high-level know-how secured from other individuals or organizations (see the box "Securing High-Level Know-How"). They also try to "outsource" much of the development of the ground-level knowledge needed to make their products useful to other players (such as consultants or the value-added resellers mentioned in the last chapter) or to actual users of the products.[3]

Securing High-level Know-how

My interviews suggest that VC-backed businesses build on high-level know-ledge secured from a variety of sources. In some cases, the know-how is licensed—about 14 percent of the companies in my sample started with a technology licensed from a university or research organization. Others build on know-how that has previously been embodied in a commercial product or released to the public domain: for example, many of the software companies in the sample mentioned that they had secured licenses from companies such as Microsoft and Oracle or were using "open-source" software such as Linux. In yet other cases, the founders of the company were responsible for a significant technological advance, but *before* they raised funding from professional VCs: the founders had an idea, built a prototype that provided a crude technical validation, and *then* secured VC funding. This followed the model of Larry Page and Sergey Brin, who developed a search algorithm as students at Stanford and then refined it using capital raised first from angel investors and then from VCs.

Turning now to products: nearly two-thirds of the VCs we interviewed developed mid-level intermediates (see box).

Products Developed

The majority of the businesses in my study—69 companies, or 64 percent—were developing intermediate goods and services. Forty (58 percent) of these 69 companies were developing enterprise software and systems. The rest offered a range of goods and services including workflow automation for hospitals, tax optimization models for corporations, systems for extending trade credit to the construction industry, managed-care programs for seniors, and web-based marketing programs. About 12 percent were developing goods and services that would be used—although rarely actually paid for—by individuals. These businesses included developers of an exchange-traded fund; a website for weddings; a platform for online gaming; interactive media for TVs and computers; online reviews of local service providers (such as plumbers); and a variety of applications for wireless phones. Thirteen percent were developing drugs, devices or tests that would be marketed to physicians but "consumed" by, implanted in, or performed on individual patients. Eleven percent were developing high-level products including semiconductor chips, disk storage devices, lasers, and a nano-tech lithium ion battery.

The tendency of VCs to favor businesses producing mid-level "intermediates" may be obscured by striking outliers at both ends. Speaking of once-VC-backed companies that operate on the ground-level, consumer side, Amazon, eBay, Google, YouTube, and others have captured the public's imagination because their products and services are widely used, and their success has produced breathtaking financial returns for their investors and founders. Similarly, on the high-level side, we have companies such as Intel that make the basic building blocks and "platforms" for our high-tech society. Silicon chips have become almost as common as potato chips, and although most people may have never seen a microprocessor, thanks to a spirited branding campaign, they know there is one from Intel Inside® their computer.* But these vivid cases are not representative of the VC-backed business.

The VC firm Kleiner Perkins is second to none in the returns it has made from its investments in companies (including Amazon and Google) that provide consumer goods and services. But, as the box "The Kleiner Perkins Portfolio" shows, the majority of its portfolio comprises companies developing mid-level products.

The Kleiner Perkins Portfolio

Of the 81 active portfolio companies listed on Kleiner's website as of this writing,[4] the majority (49 companies, or 60 percent) developed mid-level goods and services—more-or-less complete equipment or application software or services, versus basic materials or components—for use by other businesses rather than end customers. These included 23 companies developing so-called enterprise software and systems; six companies developing instruments used in hospitals and medical research (but not implanted in patients); and 20 companies developing sundry IT-based equipment and software such as data-center switches, imaging systems, and network storage systems.

Nineteen were developing ground-level consumer goods and services. These included three network or community companies; two broadband service providers (over wireless and satellite); two "e-commerce" companies (a "reseller" of tickets for sold-out concerts, shows, and sporting events and a "marketplace" for customized products); two providers of information for people on the move (in their cars and over wireless phones); a distributor of movies and videos over the Internet; a provider of "photoneumatic therapy" for hair and skin beautification; a financial services company (UPromise); and a restaurant guide (Zagat, which had been in business long before Kleiner Perkins

---

* Ubiquity has its rewards: not coincidentally, the market value of Intel's common shares is almost as large as Google's.

made an investment). Four companies were developing treatments (e.g. for obesity and vision) that would be marketed to physicians but "consumed" by (or implanted in) patients.

On the side of high-level products and services, 13 companies appeared to be developing basic materials or building blocks at a level similar to or higher than Intel's microprocessors. These included six "alternative" energy companies (developing solar power, cellulosic ethanol, bio-diesel, and natural gas derived from coal); a developer of fuel cells for wireless phones and other portable electronic devices; a company developing codecs for camcorders and digital cameras; four companies in the semiconductor industry (one developing specialized chips and three supplying tools and materials used by chip makers); and a biotechnology company developing *inter alia* engineered gene libraries, engineered cells to produce novel pharmaceuticals, and bio-refineries for the production of industrial chemicals.

Contrary to perceptions, VC-backed businesses do not dominate the development of new "ground-level" consumer products—or high-level building blocks. Rather, because large, well-established, and generally public companies dominate the sphere of ground-level and high-level products, new and emerging companies (whether or not they are VC-backed) have trouble breaking in. Lists of "hot new products" or "best new products" of the year published by magazines such as *BusinessWeek, Forbes,* or *Fortune* are filled with ground-level consumer products that their readers are likely to be interested in—the latest wireless phones, iPod-like music players, flat-panel TVs, DVD players, game consoles, printers, laptops, intelligent home appliances, hybrid cars, and so on. Most of them are developed by large companies such as Apple (notwithstanding its renegade image, the company has been public for more than 25 years), Dell, Electrolux, Honda, GE, Hewlett Packard (HP), Kyocera, Microsoft, Motorola, Nintendo, Nokia, Philips, Toyota, Samsung, Sega, and Sony. Start-ups, such as Tivo, with its successful launch of the digital video recorder, are notable exceptions. The first successful personal digital assistant—the Palm Pilot—was introduced by Palm Computing *after* it had become a subsidiary of the public company U.S. Robotics.*

---

* In software and consumer services, the dominance of the large companies is apparently less pronounced, but even here, once a category (e.g., spreadsheets or word-processing software) becomes well established, small new firms seem to have a hard time breaking in.

VC-backed businesses also account for little of the innovative action in developing high-level components and raw materials. Although there have been scores of semiconductor start-ups (typically the so-called "fabless semis" that outsource fabrication to third-party foundries), these companies usually target niche markets and represent a small portion of the semiconductor pie. New microprocessors from large, well-established companies such as AMD, Intel, and Motorola have dominated in terms of sales volumes and overall impact, and are largely responsible for the amazing improvements in price performance. Likewise, Corning, founded in 1851, has developed and produced most of the glass that goes into the liquid crystal displays used in laptops, computers, and flat-panel TVs. In 1970, Corning researchers also developed optical fiber that could be used in long-distance communication. The fiber now provides the backbone of the Internet— and Corning remains its largest supplier.

For convenience, I will refer to the focus of many VC-backed businesses on mid-level know-how and on intermediate goods and services simply as *mid-level innovation*. But as mentioned in the introduction, levels of know-how and product development represent only some of the ways innovations vary and innovators specialize. I will now briefly touch on some other dimensions of the space that seems to characterize the favored domain of VC-backed firms. We will later see how these dimensions affect the global interactions of VC-backed businesses.

■ Other Dimensions of the VC-Backed "Space"

I argued in the last chapter that VC-backed businesses have a higher tolerance for novel circumstances (Knightian uncertainty) than large corporations, but a lower tolerance than the self-funded entrepreneur. I also suggested that, whereas novelty is unrelated to the level of knowledge (decoding the genomes of another species in 2007 is arguably less novel than was opening Starbucks's first espresso bar in Seattle in 1987), it does go hand in hand with the maturity of the industry. VCs avoid getting in too early (while a self-financed entrepreneur may not), but do so before maturity has moved the comparative advantage toward large, well-established companies. They aren't pioneering explorers like Christopher Columbus, but they are early settlers in New Worlds.

VCs also tend to favor businesses in which rapid expansion has significant payoffs, such as those in which locking in a large share of customers deters competition from entering afterward. Opportunities where speed matters (in terms of expansion and not necessarily entry) favor VC-backed businesses that have more access to capital and other resources than do self-funded entrepreneurs.*

Additionally, VC-backed businesses seem to favor products and services used by service industries or by the service functions of their customers, rather than manufacturing. For example, they are more likely to serve businesses in health care, banking, and retailing than businesses that produce tangible products such as steel, automobiles, or toothpaste. Similarly, more VC-backed businesses develop enterprise software (that, for instance, facilitates the logistics capabilities of its users) than semiconductor chips used to produce widgets (see box).

Opportunities to Serve

At every level, most of the companies in my sample were focused on services or service providers. Of the 11 companies developing ground-level innovations for consumers, only one was developing a consumer product (a remote control for appliances). Among the innovators developing mid-level intermediate goods, 20 were serving customers that provided services (such as retailing, transportation and finance), and the other 32 were facilitating a "service" function (such as marketing, IT, or tax-optimization) in their customer organizations. Only 11 were developing products or services that would be used in making a physical good (e.g. embedded software for cell phones, a supply chain for chip producers, or a testing platform for biotech companies). Among developers of high-level products, however, all eight companies were producing physical goods or services used in the production of physical goods.

Given VCs relatively undiluted pursuit of financial returns, the propensity of VC-backed businesses to develop innovations for the service industry suggests a more general point: the service sector provides an attractive

---

* In some fast-growing industries, however, rapid expansion does *not* lead to any sustainable advantages, and in such cases VC-financed businesses do not have this comparative advantage.

target market because it contains a large number of customers who are ready and able to purchase and use high-tech products. Presumably, therefore, many kinds of innovators—not just VC-backed businesses—are likely to focus on service providers and service activities. This pattern, as we will see in book 2, has significant implications for an assessment of the globalization of innovation.

To summarize: VC-backed businesses tend to specialize in mid-level innovation, pursue opportunities where there is a middling level of Knightian uncertainty and potential for rapid expansion, and develop products that facilitate services rather than manufacturing. Next, I examine how VC-backed businesses innovate, and what this tells us more generally about mid-level innovation.

■ Extending and Combining

As mid-level players, VC-backed businesses often add value by building on or extending high-level know-how or products. Such enhancements, as the box on Brontes Technologies illustrates, may be so comprehensive that the value of the high-level inputs represents a small portion of value of the cumulative outputs.

Brontes Technologies

Brontes Technologies, a company in my sample, developed a scanner that allowed dentists to generate 3-D images of teeth instead of making plaster molds. The antecedent technology—"active wavefront sampling"—originated in Professor Douglas Hart's lab at MIT. In 2003, MIT's Deshpandé Center gave Hart and his students a grant to develop commercial applications for wavefront sampling. Hart's group used the grant to build an integrated prototype device. This took a lot of "busywork" (e.g., writing motor control programs) rather than research that could be published in scientific journals. But building the prototype helped identify the strengths and weaknesses of the technology and helped secure funding from VCs for a start-up (Brontes) to develop the dental imaging application.[5]

It took considerable additional innovation to extend the antecedent know-how. Hart recalled that "going from the prototype to a commercially

---

viable device that had the speed, accuracy, and the robustness necessary for dental use was a big deal. The Brontes R&D team had to come up with numerous innovations both large and small." Janos Rohaly, who was a post-doc in Hart's lab and then became the chief scientist at Brontes, added:

> We had to find ways to deal with freehand camera motion, and eliminate its influence on 3D recovery, develop a novel imaging model to accurately correct optical aberrations through digital processing, seamlessly and accurately stitch together and visualize the recovered 3D patches at video rate, and figure out what accuracies, resolutions, tolerances, tools, et cetera dentists needed. All the ideas we generated are now an important part of our IP.

Developers of mid-level products combine as well as extend: a significant part of their technological contribution (as the case of enterprise software described in the boxed text illustrates) comprises developing the know-how required to integrate many higher-level technologies and components.[6]

Developing Enterprise Software

Enterprise software (e.g., for accounting or payroll applications) is a favorite product category for VC-backed businesses. It usually comprises multiple "tiers,"* each of which runs on a different hardware platform and can be independently upgraded or replaced as technologies or requirements evolve. In a standard three-tiered architecture, the data tier contains the actual records (e.g. on the salaries, deductions, etc. of individual employees) and resides on a mainframe computer (or equivalent thereof). On top of that is the so-called business logic tier (or the "applications tier"). This is the brains of the application and runs on a workstation (which we can think of as a very high-end PC or a stripped-down mainframe computer). The top tier is the "presentation tier"—what the user of the application sees and interacts with. This runs on a PC or a workstation.

Developers of enterprise software use a variety of third-party building blocks in each tier. For instance, the data tier may use a relational database

* The tiers that are commonly used to describe the architecture of enterprise software *do not* correspond to my levels of know-how and products.

package from Oracle, or IBM's DB2 software. The applications tier might be created using software such as BEA's Aqua Logic, Red Hat's JBoss, or IBM's WebSphere, and the presentation tier might use Mozilla's Firefox or Microsoft's Internet Explorer browser. The building blocks commonly used for each layer change over time. For instance, according to one of our interviewees—Jim Dougherty, the CEO of Metamatrix—"some 30 percent of building blocks used in enterprise software are now open source—and some companies only use open source components." But, significantly, all developers of enterprise software now combine a variety of building blocks; the era in which vertically integrated companies such as IBM developed applications from the ground up is long gone. A crucial engineering challenge faced by developers involves the effective integration of components produced by other individuals and organizations (including the open-source community).

Commercially successful combinations also incorporate knowledge (or at least conjectures) about what customers want and what they will be willing to pay. The integration of marketing knowledge with technical design and engineering is especially critical in innovations that bundle several functions into a single product or service. For example, in designing something like a Swiss Army knife (as opposed to a meat cleaver) innovators must know (or guess) how different potential buyers will value different blade combinations in conjunction with figuring out the costs and technical feasibility of the possible combinations.*

In my sample, only a handful of businesses developed high-level products whose attributes could be reduced to a few key variables;† and virtually

---

* As it happens, it is hard to think of any real-life examples (including meat cleavers) of products or services that customers value for just one attribute. Even in a pure commodity like gold, customers care about purity, form (ingots or coins), and the terms and location of delivery. But as a general rule, purchasers of mid- and ground-level products have an interest in a broader set of attributes than the purchasers of high-level raw materials. For instance, purchasers of gold jewelry value design, the brand name, trendiness, the ambience of the jewelry store, and the helpfulness of a salesperson—not just the number of carats and whether the item is a bracelet or an earring.

† For instance, a developer of advanced batteries (for industrial use) told us that there were "three things that have increased or improved: power, safety and life." Similarly, the CEO of Gammabright, a developer of components (mainly diodes) used in laser systems, said that the key metric in the industry was dollars per watt of power for a given level of "brightness."

none of the companies developing mid- or ground-level products faced customers whose purchasing decisions turned on only one or two objective criteria. As will become apparent later, understanding what customers valued, and incorporating this knowledge into a product or services accounted for important sources of the value of these companies' innovations.

■ Iterative, Interactive, and Rapid

Let us turn our attention now to *how* VC-backed businesses extend and combine. I focus on three features that characterized the innovations of the companies I studied: (1) the process was iterative and incremental, that is, it was more evolutionary than "creationist"; (2) the process often involved close interactions with users; and (3) the iterations were extremely rapid, so the accretion of small changes could lead to large transformations. In the passages that follow, much of this is illuminated in boxed texts featuring the specific experiences of my research subjects.

Iterations—adjustments through "trial and error"—took place at multiple levels and, as I have stated, were most often incremental. In several cases, the companies had changed basic elements of their business model—products, target customers, and technologies. In many such cases, the changes moved the businesses toward the middle level: businesses that began by targeting consumers turned to developing intermediate goods and services, and businesses that began by developing general-purpose, high-level technologies and components turned their attention to more comprehensive solutions for specific "vertical" markets (see box).[7]

Moving to the Middle

Zensys moved from selling ground-level consumer products to mid-level consumer products. The company started developing kits for controlling home appliances in 1999. Following the Ikea model, the kits were to be sold to consumers who would install them in their homes. In 2001, Palamon Capital, a VC firm, agreed to invest (Zensys had initially been financed by its founders and "angel investors") on the condition that the company "focus on technology and technology sales" instead of on the consumer market.[8] The company then developed a line of products and engineering services to sell to manufacturers producing hardware and software for the "intelligent home."[9]

SoundBite also moved up from a ground-level consumer service. The company was launched in 2000 with a product that would allow consumers to send free voice messages ("telemails") to one or more recipients (such as members of their book club). The service was free—users only had to listen to a 10-second ad.[10] The model apparently did not work, and the company shifted its focus to the business market. By 2003, SoundBite had signed up "more than 80 new customers within key vertical industries such as financial services [and] publishing" who used SoundBite's services for providing service alerts and reminders of unpaid bills and renewal of subscriptions.[11]

The more common migration was from higher to lower levels—companies that started with a general-purpose tool reinvented themselves by developing lower-level products—but with a more comprehensive set of attributes aimed at specific market segments.

- Silverlink, according to its cofounder and CEO Stan Nowak, started out developing a remote monitoring technology to allow grown children to manage the care of elderly parents. But target customers didn't have "urgency, scale, and a willingness to pay," and the company was on the brink of running out of cash. Nowak recalled:

  The way we were selling was, "We have a great hammer, show us where your nails are." We needed to shorten the distance between the capability we had built and an application that customers would pay for. One of our angel investors introduced us to companies in the pharmacy benefit market and the managed-care market. One of them said, "Have you ever done refill reminders [for prescriptions]?" We said we hadn't, but we're willing to try. We started doing reminders, and we started to have success. That became a much shorter sales cycle. The next guys we talked to, we said: "Refill reminders! You've got to be doing that."

  We've now done over one hundred different things like refill reminders. We go to customers and say, "Here's the menu of things that we do for companies like you. This is what it costs, this is the return on investment, and this is how you do it." We've become a real solution-focused company.

- Sapias was founded as SecuraTrak in 1999. Its early products were relatively simple, using GPS and cellular networks to help track stolen computers and then stolen vehicles. Neither effort got very far, so in October 2001, a newly installed CEO put SecuraTrak into "stealth mode" to "develop new technologies to address the needs of the exploding mobile enterprise asset [aka fleets of commercial trucks] management market." The company emerged in October 2002 as Sapias (from the Latin *sapienta*: foresight, wisdom, and judgment), using "advanced wireless, GPS, Internet, and database technologies" to collect and transform "real-time, location-based data" about fleets into "customized business intelligence."[12]

Once the basic model had been settled, trial and error was important in designing and implementing the right bundle of product features. As the case of GTESS (see box) illustrates, identifying the so-called core value proposition or unique selling point of a product was simply a starting point. Achieving a commercially viable and technically robust offering required numerous iterations to add features that made it attractive to customers, as well as concurrent re-engineering and stabilizing of prototypes for large-scale, real-world use.

The Many Iterations of GTESS

The first rounds of iteration for GTESS took the company from trying to sell a high-level optical character recognition (OCR) tool to developing a lower-level system aimed at the health-care industry. The company's founder was a native of Poland with a PhD from a technical institute in Warsaw who was strongly committed to the idea that "technology should be used to eliminate human labor in the processing of paper documents." With the help of students from Warsaw (doing PhDs in artificial intelligence and mathematics), he developed OCR-based software, without any specific vertical market applications in mind. In the early 1990s, he sold the software to a variety of customers—a bank, a railroad, and a company in the nuclear industry. He was quite frustrated, however, because customers didn't know how to deploy it. By 1995, when he was approached by a small health plan that wanted to use his software to process paper claims, he chose to maintain control. "You send us the claims," he said, "and we will send you back the clean data." That started GTESS down the path of becoming a provider of automated health-care claims processing.

As GTESS moved into claims processing, "it became apparent that the company had to develop deep domain expertise to enhance the technology to service a single vertical." The company hired someone with 15 years experience (including running IT operations) for a health insurance company. She put together a team of technologists who focused on the specific problems of health-care processing. The company also realized that simply converting paper claims submitted by physicians to an electronic record had limited value, because the paper claims themselves were almost always "incorrect, incomplete, or didn't match the payments systems of GTESS's customers." The realization triggered a noteworthy innovation—GTESS developed a technology that "goes way beyond OCR technology." Rather than create records that match the paper claim, it used "deep domain knowledge" and artificial intelligence techniques to correct errors, omissions, and mismatches automatically, without costly human intervention.

The commercial success of a new product requires innovators to complement their technical advances with "nontechnical" development in areas such as organizational capabilities, marketing knowledge, and customer relationships. Such developments also utilize an iterative process. For example, a CEO described the process of working with a large multinational customer as "a matter of trial and error. Large companies are layered like onions, but the layers—appearing randomly and unpredictably—influence the relationship you're building. Unfortunately, you don't get to see all the layers the day you walk in. . . . Creating an intimate relationship with a customer like [the large multinational] is a complex process. It took two and a half years to reach the point where the relationship was complete on all phases, including, for instance, their receiving people actually taking delivery of the product and the financial people promptly paying invoices."

Close, ongoing interaction with users was, for many mid-level innovators an important feature of the iterative process. The detailed examples in the box "Interactions with Users" show that customer engagements had many connections with the development of our interviewees' products and businesses and involved a much more intricate process than, say, commissioning a structured consumer survey. Later, we will see that the kind of interaction described in this box has subtle but important implications for the effect on the United States of the increasing globalization of high-level research. Although these examples describe interactions with users from the innovators' perspective, these interactions would have been impossible without the willingness of users to engage in them. As I will argue later, the willingness of users in the United States to interact with mid-level innovators allows the U.S. economy as a whole to benefit from high-level scientific research and technologies developed abroad.

Interactions with Users

Several CEOs of mid-level innovators stressed the importance of starting an ongoing dialogue with potential users early in the development process and, often, of continuing this dialogue even after a product is released.

According to Netuitive's CEO, Nick Sanna, the company started with

> very sophisticated algorithms. Programmers often think that with code and time, they can solve any problem. But some performance barriers cannot be broken, unless you have a completely new approach. This company was born out of the encounter of mathematicians and statisticians with people who saw a problem in a space that could not be solved with existing approaches. That was the spark. But, turning breakthrough algorithms into a commercial product required a true partnership with customers. They were looking for a solution, but they couldn't find anything. They tried to build it themselves, but they found us and became our beta customers. They tested the product; they suggested extensions and validated the concepts. Step by step and incremental improvement after incremental improvement, we got to a solution that most of the market would want.

Aaref Hilaly of Clearwell Systems described a product development process that straddled engineering, customer feedback—and fund-raising. This process did not end with the first release of the product:

> This company has had a fairly classic path. There were six to nine months of prototyping and iteration by a small team before we raised any venture

funding. The venture funding paid for about eight guys working for a year writing the first version of the product. Its quality was low, it was missing key features. Nonetheless, we shipped it. This is common. If you look at successful software products, they tend to ship their first versions half-baked. You cannot logically deduce what needs to go into the product, and customers cannot give you feedback, until they use it—they cannot imagine using it. You just have to get [customers] using it as quickly as you can.

After we shipped the first version, we immediately got feedback on what was missing. We scrambled to put out a second version that included two key missing features. That was a very difficult release. But you only get your comments after someone has used a product, and by that time you are almost to the point where you need to be doing the release. It's a moving target for the engineering team. Now, we've hit everything that we need to in terms of basic features. The next step is to add a bunch of little things—the niggly things—and increase scalability and performance. You also need to increase supportability, which is the ability to diagnose problems efficiently when something goes wrong. These are the things you deliberately defer to later releases.

In other words, product development involves a juggling act in which innovators play close attention to what customers say and want but exercise their judgment about when and what to implement in their products.

Kevin Riegelsberger of Capital Stream said that, besides providing feedback, customers sometimes helped *fund* product improvements:

It's important to get your first product out the door so you have something to sell, so you can test your theories and learn from your customers. . . . Customers will tell you what more they want in your product. Your first product can be a Volkswagen—it doesn't need to be a Ferrari. If your Volkswagen is very good at what it's supposed to be—a small efficient automobile—then customers buy it for that purpose, but they'll pay you to customize it. Then its feature content builds up over the years, so it may become a Ferrari.

The evolution of a product through the addition of features suggested and financed by customers also involves judgment. According to Riegelsberger: "You have to be careful to do only those things, that can be rolled back into the core of the product,"

PatientKeeper, unlike many other companies we studied, developed a process to incorporate customer feedback *before* developing new products. The company provides mobile computing solutions to improve patient care and control health-care costs, for example by allowing doctor's hand-held devices to connect to and obtain data from hospital databases. CEO Paul Brient told us that the company's development process—among the best structured in my sample—started with product managers "getting on airplanes and talking to people in the field. I personally spend three days a week in hospitals."

Brient described how the company had recently started developing a nursing product:

> I spent two and a half days in one of our client's hospitals, in all the different nursing stations, shadowing nurses, understanding how our potential product would fit into their workflow. There is no third-party source from which you can get this information. You have to be out there with the people whose problem you're trying to solve.
>
> This knowledge feeds into a "requirements document"—a 30- to a 150-page document with screen layouts, workflow, data flow, a description of the end-user experience, what are we going to automate, what are the "gotchas," what the environment is like. For the nursing application we are building, patient care techs have no formal training. They are high school educated, so the user interfaces have to be very different than what we have for a physician-focused product.
>
> We then take the requirements document back into the field to potential customers—"co-development" partners. It becomes the basis for interaction and for feedback before we write code. After some revisions to the requirements document, a co-development partner signs a contract to receive the product. They pay us some money, but it's highly discounted. The quid pro quo is that they work with us while we build it and give us feedback. So they get a product that really works well for them. They are like a beta site except our interactions start earlier than in a typical beta, and customers get something that works really well for them. One important caveat to this is that we always work with at least two co-development partners to avoid writing a custom piece of software. Using two partners helps us sort out the customer-specific requirements from the industry requirements.

Once co-developers have formally signed off on the requirements document, we commission a development team. The product manager now, instead of focusing externally, focuses internally for the one-month or six-month development phase. Nevertheless, there is still a lot of interaction back and forth with the co-development partners. Requirements are not supposed to change in this development phase. The reality is that they do. This is partly because as you develop, you realize there is more detail required: you had written a paragraph or sentence in the requirements document, but you really should have written a page. So even when you get into the coding phase there are still a bunch of questions you have to answer. Or you have to make some changes because you encounter hard engineering problems. Or, through the interactions with the co-development partner, you come up with a better idea for the workflow, as they start seeing the actual software rather than the static pictures.

Then, when the development phase is complete, we go into what is a more traditional beta cycle. That can lead to even more suggestions from customers for changes.

Developers of high-level and ground-level products in my sample did not, however, make similar mention of the importance of customer dialogue. In fact, the CEO of a company developing a high-level software platform observed:

We didn't really develop for customers. We developed a very general product that we thought many customers would use. We've reached a stage now where we do take feedback from customers, but we're not like other people who almost develop their products as a consulting engagement. They custom build something for customers, and then they generalize it. We still build general products.

As the last example in the box indicates, an ongoing dialogue with customers does not seem to be equally important for every kind of innovation or innovator. In particular, developers of many pathbreaking, high-level components and technologies have worked in splendid isolation, for example, the Shockley team at Bell Lab that developed the transistor, John Backus's team at IBM that created FORTRAN, the first widely used programming language, and Timothy Berners-Lee and his associates at CERN, who invented the protocols of the World Wide Web. The marketing problem of determining the optimal bundle of features in these high-level innovations may not have been as onerous as solving the technical problems. With ground-level consumer products, especially for mass markets, customer feedback is valued, but a close iterative dialogue is usually infeasible. Consumer goods companies like Proctor & Gamble test customer reactions through focus groups and surveys. In radical innovations of any level, such as Xerox's first copier, consumer reactions to the concept or prototype cannot always be taken seriously. In other words, the kinds of innovators that derive the most value from close ongoing interactions with users happen to be the ones in the majority in my sample—developers of mid-level products with many, but not radical, features and functions.

Speed is another important characteristic of the innovation process of VC-backed businesses. We can think of the typical *Inc.* 500 start-up as a puddle jumper—a small commuter plane with limited range for any one flight, but with periodic refueling capable of traversing a great distance. A large company is like a battleship that can cross an ocean in one go, but at a measured pace. A VC-backed business in this analogy is like a spaceship: it can go much farther than a puddle jumper and faster than a battleship, but it flames out if it doesn't reach escape velocity (hit its "milestones") before its fuel runs out.

The requirement to make very rapid progress arises from both external and internal sources—from competitors in the marketplace and from venture capitalists who provide financing. As I have mentioned, VCs tend to invest in businesses that serve markets in which there is clear evidence (at least to knowledgeable observers) of large potential demand and in which securing a large share of the market early provides (somewhat) durable competitive advantages. This sets off a high-stakes race both to develop an attractive product and to secure a large number of customer orders. As one CEO put it:

> If you have a good technology and a product, you are going to have competition soon. When you introduce something, you have a narrow window to get on the right side of the chasm.* And it has very lit-

---

* The interviewee was referring to (as did many others we talked to) Geoffrey Moore's *Crossing the Chasm*, 1991, which has become enormously influential in the high-tech industry. Moore argues that there is a sharp discontinuity (or "chasm") between what it takes to win over early adopters as opposed to more mainstream buyers.

tle to do with having the best technology. Look at all the wonderful technologies that have been introduced by companies that go bankrupt. And look at all the companies that have succeeded with mediocre technology. Once you have a product that's competitive and have your first adopters, you have to go from being technology-centric to "go to market"-centric. Then it's all about how fast can you distribute, how well can you service, and how fast can you get the crack team with enough people to generate enough cash and have your product take off before a big player comes in and crushes you.

On the funding side, VC-backed businesses usually have substantially more capital than informally financed businesses, but they cannot as easily dial up or dial down their rates of growth. Nor, in contrast to publicly traded businesses, can they raise debt or equity from the public markets whenever they wish. Rather, they rely on milestone-to-milestone financing:[13] if they fall short of a pre-negotiated target, they risk being cut off entirely (and not just getting money under somewhat worse terms). Therefore, the venture has to race not just against competitors but also against the financing clock. As the CEO already quoted told us: "I have seen any number of start-ups in our industry go out of business because they weren't properly funded. They had wonderful technology and wonderful products, but they couldn't get traction with customers before the money ran out and their landlord kicked them out."

Moreover, unlike rocket ships that follow precisely calculated trajectories, VC-backed businesses don't have well-defined paths that are sure to get them to their targets before the money runs out; instead, as we have seen, they proceed through trial and error. Therefore, a venture's ability to beat the clock depends on how rapidly and well it conducts trials and utilizes the results, not on how fast it can race down a well-specified track. In fact, a comparative advantage of VC-backed companies (which face tight resource constraints) vis-à-vis the battleship corporations (which have ample resources) lies in undertaking initiatives for which it is hard to formulate a long-term plan. In such domains, small, flexible teams can have the upper hand.

■ Contrasts with Scientific Research

The three features of mid-level innovation I have just discussed—iteration, interaction with users, and speed—vary in their importance in different

VC-backed businesses. Similarly, other kinds of innovators who develop mid-level products may not exhibit these features to the same degree. For example, large companies that have easier access to capital markets may face less pressure to innovate rapidly. Such variations aside, the "logic" of mid-level innovation uncovered in my interviews suggests that the three features—especially iteration and interaction—will be found in the processes used by a wide range of players who undertake such innovation, and not just by VC-backed businesses. In other words, there is something distinctive about how innovation proceeds at the middle level.

To further clarify this distinctiveness, it will be helpful to contrast the general nature of mid-level processes with the standard procedures used to develop high-level knowledge in the physical sciences. Although in both cases we usually have hypotheses and experiments, there are profound differences in methods. Physical scientists seek to discover causal relationships that already exist in nature. Innovators utilize the profoundly human capacity of imagination to create goods and services that did not previously exist. Whereas scientists believe that there is just one causal pattern in nature waiting to be discovered, innovators can imagine a vast array of possibilities.

The innovator's experiments have, in some senses, a narrower purpose. Scientific experiments test whether a causal principle is generally true by trying to falsify it under a broad variety of circumstances. Innovators don't test general principles; rather, they conduct trials to find whether a particular product or service does what it's supposed to do under the specific kinds of circumstances where it's intended to be used. If something works, innovators don't particularly care why it works, except to the degree they might be concerned about the conditions under which it might fail. Moreover, the failure of an innovation under conditions that lie outside a product's intended use is inconsequential.

From a different perspective, however, the innovator has a broader purpose. Scientific experiments are intended to produce a binary outcome: it either falsifies the hypothesis being tested or it does not. Innovators utilize their trials more broadly. They do want to find out whether something works—whether a new process is more efficient or whether customers will buy a new product. The innovator's experiments are usually intended to generate ideas about remedies and improvements. The developer of a new product wants to know what might be added or changed to increase its value. This dual purpose is succinctly captured in the common exhortation: "Try it, fix it."

The design and conduct of experiments in the two domains reflect differences in their purpose. A well-designed scientific experiment, for example, has controls intended to maximize the generalizability of the result and minimize the chances that the outcome is an artifact of a particular investigative procedure. A good experiment can be replicated; this helps reduce the likelihood of spurious results that may arise because of conditions prevailing in a particular lab; and replication generates a large number of observations that can be subjected to statistical analysis. Experiments are also expected to generate objective unambiguous results: a scientist's creativity and skill is expected to contribute to the design of the experiment, rather than to interpretation of the data it generates.

An innovator's trials, in contrast, generally don't have the kinds of controls that scientists consider essential. This is partly because of a more "pragmatic" orientation—the innovator is often much less concerned about generalizable results and must make do with whatever is available. An innovator wanting to try out a new product on a large number of representative customers may in fact have to rely on the feedback of a few "alpha" or "beta" customers; such "early adopters" are, almost by definition, not in the mainstream. Similarly, the "try it, fix it" approach (e.g., through the ongoing tweaking of product features) precludes replicability. By design, each new observation reflects conditions that are different from conditions under which the previous observation was made.

Finally, the results of each trial are fraught with ambiguity ("Knightian uncertainty") that requires the innovator to make risky, subjective judgments. Suppose a beta customer suggests a change in the design or the addition of a feature. The innovator has to guess whether mainstream customers will have the same preference; moreover, if the innovator does incorporate the suggested change, returning to a design stage prior to that change may be costly or infeasible. (The innovator does, however, have the advantage of being able to engage in a dialogue with early customers who have a common interest in the successful development of the new product. In the physical sciences, experimenters work with mute subjects who do not have a stake in the results.)

The difference between the processes of mid-level innovation and scientific procedures has implications for the human capital required by these two kinds of activities. As we will see later, mid-level innovation does not require a large cadre of staff with PhDs in engineering or science—for most positions in an organization developing mid-level know-how, a basic level of technical knowledge is sufficient. Policies to increase public funding for PhD programs may increase the availability of staff required to undertake high-level research, but they do not do much for increasing the labor supply used by mid-level innovators.

■ Intellectual Property

Differences between high-level research and mid-level know-how extend beyond the processes and human capital inputs used in their production. As briefly mentioned in the introduction, there are basic differences in the nature of the outputs as well: high-level know-how comprises general principles, whereas mid- and ground-level know-how is tied to specific products, processes, or local conditions. In Newtonian physics, for example, force always equals mass times acceleration, whereas the designs for microprocessors will vary with the desired "clock speeds," and optimal conditions for producing microprocessors can be different for individual fabrication plants. We also find related differences in the degree to which know-how at different levels can be codified and transmitted. Newtonian physics can be reduced to compact formulas that anyone can read. Microprocessor designs may be described in blueprints that are usually much more complicated than Newton's laws, but aren't always complete and may need to be "explained" by the designers. And the ground-level knowledge of operating a particular microprocessor fabrication plant often has a high tacit component that cannot be reduced to text, formulas, or diagrams.

As a practical matter, the differences in the degree to which know-how can be generalized and codified affected how the producers of the know-how in my study realized its benefits. Researchers who produce scientific knowledge that is general and codified publish their results—and such publications lead to career advancement, prizes, and research grants. Developers of high-level technologies can secure its commercial value through patents. Lower-level know-how that is less general and codifiable is harder to patent. As we will see next, my interviews suggest that the difficulties of patenting mid-level know-how—in conjunction with several other factors such as tight resource constraints—discourage many VC-backed businesses from making heavy investments in patents. They rely instead on other ways of realizing the commercial value of their intellectual property.

All 22 of the companies in my sample that developed drugs or devices regulated by the FDA invested heavily in patenting their intellectual property. As we will see in the next section, however, FDA regulations give ventures that fall under their jurisdiction a special character; I will therefore limit the discussion of patenting in this section to the companies that weren't regulated by the FDA. In these 84 companies, there was an almost even distribution among those making a heavy investment to acquire a broad portfolio of patents (27 percent), those seeking to acquire a limited number of patents for defensive reasons (26 percent), those making small and often inconclusive efforts (21 percent), and those making no effort at all (26 percent).

Twenty-seven percent of the companies made a significant investment in securing patents. Interestingly, the CEOs of these companies had little to say about the benefits they expected from the basic right that patents confer, namely the right to "exclude" competitors from using their technology. Rather, as indicated in the box "Reasons for Prolific Patenting," they cited more subtle benefits.

Reasons for Prolific Patenting

CiDRA, a company that developed process-monitoring technologies, filed for more than 800 patents and also acquired a Norwegian company for its (patented) technology. Its CEO said: "I believe in overinvesting in IP. It helps you get top-tier business partners and VCs. From the VC point of view, IP is extremely important since it helps determine the exit value."

Another CEO said his company was serious about investing in patents from the start because one of its early investors was an inventor who "made a fortune around a voicemail patent." The company's first acquisition was "strictly about patents," and since then the company had built up its portfolio through a combination of acquisitions and internal development. The company now had two in-house and two outside patent counsels and a "patent committee that meets quarterly with board supervision."

The CEO of an enterprise software company regarded the long-term value of patents to be more important than the immediate right to exclude:

> We have a hint that other companies might be violating our patents. But we're not putting our patents to work, because it would be a major distraction. We should win on our own merits. At the same time, we know that one day, if the business grows very large, we may have the time, and maybe the need, to protect ourselves from that point of view. So it's an insurance policy for the future.

Another CEO observed:

> We have a patent portfolio that is really the basis for the value we will realize for our business. There are many disputes in the industry, and it is not uncommon to see a lot of litigation. But it's usually the bigger companies that are involved, not start-ups. Even if our patents were being infringed, we would be very reluctant to sue. If the infringer is another start-up company, it makes no sense to do anything until it actually becomes a competitor. But the fact that we could sue is of value to a potential acquirer.

Twenty-six percent of the companies in my sample (excluding the drug and device companies) devoted resources to securing patents primarily as a defensive measure (see box).

Playing Defense

"Our attitude is, let's have a few patents so that if somebody sues us, we can sue them back," said one CEO. "If we were doing something that I thought was truly breakthrough in terms of technology, I would feel differently, but for us, it's really about execution."

Another CEO noted:

> Patents take three to five years to be granted. You can't use them in an offensive way until they are granted, and as a start-up, you don't know if you're going to be around in five to 10 years. So, it's silly to invest too much. But you want to be defensive, and when you do become a big company and people start chasing you, then it becomes

> really useful to have those patents, to go after people who try to go
> after your market.

Similarly, the CEO of an enterprise software company that had filed for six patents said:

> This is not the pharmaceutical industry—you cannot sit on a patent and
> print money. Patents are not our core IP; they are like a security blanket
> that you keep under your pillow. You take them out if an acquirer comes
> calling. Or, if you're sued for patent infringement, they give you a bargain-
> ing chip. Plus, it motivates the engineers. They love it.

A third category, accounting for about 21 percent of the (nondrug and non-device) companies in my sample, made only a token effort (see the "Token Efforts" box) to secure patents. And strikingly, not a single such case involved developers of high-level products; in every instance, the company was developing mid- or ground-level products.

Token Efforts

We asked one CEO whose company had just filed for its first patent why it had done so: "That's a good question. I don't really know. Perhaps it will protect us against competitors. I personally had mixed feelings about this."

Another CEO said:

> Our VCs asked us to go file some patents. . . . They are very big on that. I'm
> not a big believer in the value of patents in this business, but I didn't
> want to pick a fight, so I put our patent attorney on a contingency plan: I
> said, "I'll pay you only if you get them." To his credit, he got two out of the
> four we filed for, and we wrote him a big check.

A third said:

> We have one patent granted and three that are in process. The decision
> to apply for them was made prior to my time in 2000–2001. Since that
> time, we have come to the conclusion that it's not worth the money. So
> we haven't applied for any more patents, even though we have written a
> lot of software since then and we could file for something.

Finally, 26 percent had never filed for any patents. And here too, every non-filer was a developer of mid- or ground-level products.[14]

Two interviewees said that the failure to file had been a mistake, but in all other cases we were told that not filing was a sensible choice and the decision deliberate (see box).

Mistakes and Choices

"The company has no patents whatsoever, which is very sad," one CEO said, "because when I look at the IP, there is a fair amount of it which I believe is patentable. But the founders who bootstrapped the start-up decided it would cost too much money. Now it's too late, because we've been selling the product for five years."

It was also too late for a company that acquired its technology from a company that was started by "a typical professor who blew it by publishing everything before getting into the patent process."

All other CEOs whose companies hadn't filed for patents had no regrets. The CEO of a company that abandoned a patent application explained:

> When I joined the company, it had applied for a patent on 70 different aspects of the product. I reviewed the patent application and decided the cost of pursuing a patent was not worth the return.
>
> The only reason to have a patent in the software industry is because investors will ask, "Do you have a patent?" That's misguided. If you have some unique or deep technology, a patent clearly is an advantage. But for the vast majority of start-up companies, patents are really just window dressing for investors. If you can explain to the investors why a patent is not necessary, why it's not valuable, why it's not a barrier to entry, they'll get past that issue.

The CEO of a health-care services company had a similar view about the utility of patents in his industry. "I come from the medical devices industry where patents are all and everything. But [with] health-care services, there is usually no incremental value in patents. We thought long and hard about this and had discussions with our VCs. They said, 'Uh-uh. Don't spend the money.'"

Was it coincidence that all the nonfilers (and "casual" filers) were developers of mid- or ground-level products?

Some of the reasons that CEOs gave us did not seem related to the level of the innovations their companies had undertaken. Some cited the need to conserve capital (see box).

Conserving Capital

According to one interviewee:

> You have to decide whether to make IP a major part of your business. You can't dabble. There's no such thing as "just filing a patent." You have to file a whole patent strategy, say, eight or 10 patents, around your seminal concept. That's time consuming and expensive. Unless you do a lot of work yourself—which requires distracting your engineers—you run about $20,000 per patent.[15] That's fine if you are Texas Instruments, but for a venture-backed company, that's a fair amount of money. And then the real cost is in enforcing your patents. One of my friends received the seminal patent for a "system on a chip" design, which is sort of the holy grail of our business. He notified several very large companies that were using his architecture. They said, "Fine. Sue us." But that's multiple millions of dollars, and he just didn't have the resources to do it. You would have thought he might have been able to monetize that somehow and give it to someone else. But other people also felt like it wasn't worth the risk or the hassle.

Similarly, the CEO who had stopped patenting activity after his company had secured a patent (and filed for three others) told us,

> We saw something that a very large company had done that sure as hell looked to us like a violation of our patent. They came back with a very interesting defense, and it was clear it was going to cost us a ton of money to win anything, ever. It wouldn't have been large amounts of money to them but it would have been for us to win.
>
> We looked at our chances of winning—it looked only a little bit better than fifty-fifty. We just dropped it.

Similarly, a few of the interviewees said that that rapid obsolescence of technology made the issue of patenting moot (see box).

Moving Targets

The CEO of a company that developed antispam products said, "We are not worried about patent protection. Spam is a team-on-team sport; the software is always changing and a new threat is always coming."

Another CEO said, "[The] churn in our market is now so fast that the half-life of useful ideas is six to 12 months versus the five or 10 years that it used to be. So your patent might be irrelevant before you recoup the money you spend on it."

Other reasons for not patenting, however, *were* related to the kinds of innovations the companies undertook: The basic nature of innovation in mid- and ground-level products made patenting difficult. Innovations, as the box "A Mélange" indicates, were like Isaiah Berlin's fox ("who knew many things") rather than the hedgehog ("who knew one big thing").

A Mélange

"Our [enterprise software] application has years and years of domain knowledge built in, but not any deep technology."

"Our IP [for supplying customized semiconductors] is a whole bunch of little things based on customer and domain knowledge that has been built into the product, rather than one concrete idea. I see a similar phenomenon with many other companies that are selling [semiconductor] chips merely as platforms to where they really add value through software. It's hard to identify their "great idea"; their uniqueness comes from the combination of their hardware and software, rather than a particular hardware circuit."

"Much of the value of our [surveillance] systems is in the interfaces that we have written for video integration. There are many different lighting systems, cameras, digital video recorders that are out there, and we have interfaced our software to each of those devices."

> "What really distinguishes us is the integrated system, developed for tracking retail traffic in stores. It has optical scanning devices to collect the data. It then pushes the data back to corporate headquarters [of clients] every night after midnight. And then we manage the data for the clients and serve it up to them, either in an extract if they have a data warehouse or we provide a web-based reporting tool."

As a legal matter, establishing the novelty and nonobviousness of such innovative mid- and ground-level combinations—to the degree required to secure a patent—is difficult. As an extreme case, think of a recipe for a new cocktail, dress, handbag, or even laptop computer. Because the individual elements have been previously integrated, the nonobviousness and novelty of even a genuinely new configuration is hard to demonstrate. Even if one of the elements is, in fact, new, and consumers find it better than prior combinations, its novelty and nonobviousness may not be sufficient to sustain a defensible patent. Furthermore, patent applications must contain a specification that meets what is known as an "enablement" standard—it must provide sufficient information to enable a knowledgeable person to make or use the invention. But some of the critical features of mid- or ground-level combinations are hard to pin down. To cite a trivial example: along with countless others, I switched from AltaVista to Google in 1999 for searching the Internet. I did not observe any great improvement in the search results, but I found Google's interface cleaner—a feature that cannot be specified in a patent filing.

Some interviewees didn't want to file for "weak" patents because if they didn't get the patent—or couldn't defend it if they did—they would merely end up tipping off competitors (see box).

Keeping It Quiet

"Our solution isn't technology based," one CEO told us. "It's kind of knowledge and know-how based, so even if we spent a lot of time and money to get a patent, it wouldn't be very strong. Our competitors would be able to come up with a way around it. We decided there was no point in telling the market how we do what we do by filing a patent application and [decided] to keep our knowledge as a trade secret."

> Another CEO said his software business had developed "fantastic technology. We did very well with it. But we elected to not file a patent because we felt that it was riskier to expose the ideas and then have to defend it than to never discuss it."

A large number of CEOs said that the process of trial and error created not just products valued by customers, but also barriers to entry vis-à-vis competitors. They didn't see the point of investing in patents of questionable value when the difficulty of replicating know-how (and relationships) developed through an iterative process provided strong protection against competitors (see box).

Not Really Necessary

The iterative, trial-and-error process common among mid-level innovators often makes patenting unnecessary. The CEO of a company that develops software to manage large networks of servers said:

> You could have the sharpest software engineers on the planet sit in a room and try to build a solution that competes with ours. But there's no way that they could think through every potential problem or feature until they had actually been in the field and tried to sell their products to customers. We've accumulated about 150 customers—customers whose size and pedigree are second to none—whose feedback is already in our product. That's the key to our competitive advantage.

Similarly, the CEO of a company that developed software to manage geographically dispersed assets (like the cell towers of wireless companies) said:

> Even if a big, strong player tried to do what we do, it would take a minimum of two years to get there. The software is so detailed and complex that by the time you developed it and you got the extra pieces and you integrated those pieces and you made a few mistakes along the way, you would have chewed up at least two years. And it's more than just writing code. For example, we are very good at doing this software for the wireless industry. That is because we have people in the company whose early

careers were in wireless. They have subject matter expertise that goes into our product and makes it useful to wireless carriers. If somebody wanted to compete with us, they would have to figure out how to get that expertise.

Another CEO emphasized the robustness of his company's software:

It's impossible to have a software product that actually works until you battle test it in 50 accounts and have had people beat on it hard. You just cannot test these things in a lab. Inevitably, you're integrating your software with the customer's existing systems—which are all configured differently—and your software can crash if it encounters something that's running slightly differently. So having a product that actually works in a variety of environments is a sustainable competitive advantage. Putting 300 people on it doesn't work: they still have to battle test on 50 accounts.

The CEO of a company that developed energy management software talked about the knowledge the company had developed of how to sell their product as a barrier to entry:

Although we have a software system, we don't sell to IT managers. We sell primarily to energy managers and facilities managers. We had to go through a significant learning curve to understand how to sell to these people. For instance, we found that you had to have a relationship with utilities and energy companies who can give rebates to customers who buy energy efficiency products the utility has approved. If you try to sell to energy managers, one of the first questions they're going to ask is, "Can I get a rebate on it?" So we had to learn how to develop relationships with utilities, how to apply for rebate programs, and how to get our product qualified for them. You're not going to find that knowledge in a software company, and that's a barrier that protects us.

Other CEOs talked about the advantage of having secured the confidence of customers—the value of the knowledge accumulated on the other side of the sales process, as it were. For instance, the CEO of a software company that served banks said:

We're not worried about start-up companies trying to create a product to compete against us. It's a very difficult thing to sell to a bank, because they like to buy from mature software companies, not risky start-ups. We

> were lucky enough to persevere for long enough to the point where we're now considered a safe player to buy from.

Similarly, another CEO observed:

> It's extremely hard to reproduce our track record. We now have 11 years of experience doing this. We have 13,000 installations of our software. My main competitor right now has exactly zero instances that I know of. So when I go into a company, and I've got 13,000 and he's got zero, who do you think they have more confidence in? Patents have nothing to do with it. It has to do with confidence and trust.

The reasons we have just reviewed suggest that other innovators, such as large companies, that have access to more capital may be more willing to invest in patents than VC-backed businesses; but, in general, all innovators who develop mid-level know-how tend to rely more on laws protecting trade secrets and copyrights and less on patents to secure the value of their intellectual property than do developers of high-level know-how. Mid-level players, however, tend to file some defensive patents, especially under laws that grant patents easily and favor patent owners. As we will see later, this has implications for the kinds of activities innovators are willing to offshore as well as for how changes in patent laws are likely to affect the innovation game.

■ Drugs and Devices: A Special Case

About 20 to 30 percent of total venture capital investment goes to ventures in health care. Health-care ventures can be divided into businesses whose activities are regulated by the Food and Drug Administration and those that are not.[16] The former category comprises mainly companies developing drugs (through conventional means or biotechnology), medical diagnostics, and medical devices. Such FDA-regulated ventures are much closer to the techno-nationalist stereotype of high-tech innovation than the other companies in my sample. Their attributes therefore help put into relief the characteristics of the more representative mid-level innovators.

An analysis of FDA-regulated businesses also illustrates a crucial feature of the multiplayer innovation game that is usually omitted from the techno-nationalist argument—the great variety and specialization among players. The FDA-regulated companies were more closely connected to scientific research than most other companies in my sample; but in most cases they specialized in activities that did not involve cutting-edge scientific research. We will also see that FDA regulations profoundly affect both drug and device developers, but not in the same way. As a result, the innovative roles of drug developers and device developers are different from those of mid-level innovators and cutting-edge research labs—and from each other.

I begin this discussion with drug developers—the category where differences with mid-level innovators that aren't regulated by the FDA are particularly striking. The agency's regulations have helped make (for better or worse) the process through which new drugs are now brought to market long and expensive—it takes about 12 years and $400 million from start to finish (see box).

Drug Discovery and Development

In the past, new drugs were discovered by serendipity or by isolating the active ingredient from traditional remedies. Over the last couple of decades, the industry has adopted a more systematic or "rational" process that we can say (at the risk of oversimplification) comprises the following steps. First, researchers identify a "target" that, if suitably altered, will cure a particular disease. For instance, the development of Mevacor and Zocor, Merck's cholesterol-lowering drugs, started with an effort to block the enzyme that can stimulate the overproduction of cholesterol.[17] Then large libraries of chemical compounds are tested (typically using "high-throughput screening") to find ones that hit the chosen target (e.g., block the enzyme that stimulates the overproduction of cholesterol) but don't affect other related targets. When good candidates are found, medicinal chemists may then try to modify their structures to increase their activity against the chosen target and reduce effects on unrelated targets.

Even if a compound hits a target, there is no assurance that this will actually effectuate a cure. So the next step involves more direct tests against a "model" of the disease itself in test tubes ("in vitro") and in animals such as rats and mice ("in vivo"). After further tests—for instance, to assess potential toxicity and safety in humans, among other things—and finding a suitable

---

dosage and form (tablet, capsule, liquid, etc.), an investigational new drug (IND) application is filed with the FDA, which includes everything that is known about the compound. If the FDA doesn't object in 30 days, the IND is approved and human clinical trials begin.

Phase 1 of the trials tests whether the drug is safe and can be tolerated by humans, and phase 2 whether the drug actually works and in what dosage. Both phase 1 and phase 2 are small-scale trials, usually with less than a couple of hundred patients. Drugs that pass phases 1 and 2 trials then enter much larger-scale and more comprehensive phase 3 trials. These can involve several thousand patients and are intended to generate data about the drug's effectiveness for specific indications, to test for a broad number of potential side-effects, and to identify good ways for administering and using the drug.

In addition to the phases 1 through 3 studies, the FDA also requires "bio-availability" studies in healthy volunteers to document how the body absorbs and excretes the compound's active ingredients and evidence that the drug can be manufactured on a large scale, while both avoiding the introduction of impurities and maintaining uniformity from batch to batch.

The process involves considerable risk. According to a report of the Congressional Office of Technology Assessment, only five out of 5,000 compounds that go into preclinical testing make it to a phase 1 human trial, and only about one of those five is ultimately approved by the FDA.

The costs and nature of the process in turn encourage VC-backed businesses to specialize, possibly to a greater degree than in other industries. Large pharmaceutical companies that have the time and money can see the process through from beginning to end, but VC-backed businesses cannot.[18] Rather, they focus on a relatively narrow part of the process. For instance, virtually all the relevant companies in my sample started with compounds that had already passed through several early-stage hoops, and were licensed from a university lab or company that did not want to take it forward.[19] To use the somewhat misleading terminology of the industry, the companies I studied were in the business of drug "development" (which, as described in the box "Drug Discovery and Development," actually involves a lot of testing) rather than the preceding process of drug "discovery."* Contrary to popular perceptions, therefore—but like the mid-level innovators in the rest of my sample—the biotech companies drew on, but did not themselves undertake, razzle-dazzle research.

There was a significant difference, however, between how the drug developers and mid-level players in my sample innovated: the FDA's "scientific" orientation and rules make it very difficult for drug developers to use a process that is either iterative or particularly rapid. For one thing, although ground-level consumer products (like the iPod) tend to be more complex and multifunctional than higher-level products, prescription drugs are neither complex nor multifunctional[20]—although they are at least in some sense ground-level. This is principally because a "scientifically minded" FDA has traditionally had a very strong preference for simple "single molecule" drugs that can be proven to cure a specific indication.[21] The scientific orientation of the FDA is also reflected in rules requiring well-specified, controlled experiments to test the efficacy and safety of new drugs.

This regulatory posture does not leave much scope for innovators to develop drugs using the "try it, fix it" approach. Good judgment and good practice can reduce risks (see box), but once a compound has been picked and the FDA has approved a testing protocol, the developer is in the same position as someone conducting a science experiment: it is what it is. A skilled chef can make up for a missing ingredient by modifying the recipe, but if a compound is discovered to have an unexpected toxicity, the "single molecule" approach of the FDA makes it impossible to effect compensatory adjustments by adding something to offset the toxicity. In fact, because FDA-approved protocols (like good science experiments) are more or less cast in stone, once a trial is under way, the developer cannot adjust the dosage or other aspects of how the drug is administered to patients.

Similarly, beyond a point, the rules of nature and the FDA make it impossible to speed up development. In vivo and in vitro tests and clinical trials have natural minimum time requirements, and, especially in large-scale phase 3 trials, developers cannot act unilaterally and have to rely on many

---

* For instance, Achillion was developing antiviral drugs for HIV and hepatitis that originated in the lab of one of its founders, Dr. Yung Chi Cheng at Yale, or were licensed from companies such as Wyeth. Another company in my study, Ascenta Therapeutics, was developing cancer treatments from compounds licensed from the University of Michigan and the National Institutes of Health. Ocera Therapeutics sought licenses for compounds to treat gastrointestinal and liver diseases. Finally, Novalar was repurposing an "old" drug for a new application—to reverse the effects of local anesthesia used in dental procedures quickly.

organizations and individuals who may not have the same incentive or ability to act quickly.

Good Judgment and Good Practice

Because little can be done to rectify a "bad" choice of a compound for trials, drug developers often put a lot of effort in avoiding such "mistakes." One CEO in our study described how his company mitigated the risk that "preclinical studies do not reliably predict human outcomes." It formed "a scientific advisory board with half clinical and half basic-science people, . . . forced them to talk to each other, [and] only worked on those targets that the clinicians and the basic scientists agreed were the right intervention points."

To a degree, companies can also try to minimize the time and expense required to undertake trials. For instance, one CEO told us:

> We are an exclusive oncology development company—we focus only on cancer. I am a medical oncologist. My chief medical officer is an oncologist. Our VP of research is an oncologist. And we've also hired people who are clinical project managers who know oncology very well. Unlike other companies our size, we don't outsource our trials to a CRO [contract research organization]: in fact, I think the expertise that CROs often bring to oncology trials is somewhat limited. We have developed all our procedures and standard operating procedures with which we have been able to complete a phase 1 trial in 10 months when many companies would take 18 months. We also completed one phase 2 trial in four and a half months—at less than half the cost that we would have incurred with a CRO.

The CEO did acknowledge, however, that there were limits to how fast trials could proceed: for the phase 3 trial, his company would have to use a (presumably slower moving) CRO to enroll the large number of patients needed for the trial.

The high costs of the regulatory process—and the low probability of success—make it imperative for FDA-regulated businesses to secure patents so that products that do make it all the way through provide a commensurately large return. Therefore, all the FDA-regulated companies in our sample had made a significant investment in securing their IP through patents.

The only significant patenting question mentioned by their CEOs (as we will see in the next chapter) was about which foreign countries in which to file for patents.

Medical devices, like drugs, are regulated by the FDA in a manner that makes their development lengthy and expensive. But, there are wrinkles that make the process of developing devices more iterative and interactive than the development of prescription drugs: unlike single-molecule drugs, devices are complex combinations of many components. And the complexity of the human body makes it impossible to develop effective and safe combinations without considerable trial and error (see box "Developing Devices").[22] This does not however, mean that medical device companies have as free a hand as, say, the mid-level developers of enterprise software: their iterations do have to conform to FDA rules. And as we will see in chapter 4, the perceived rigidity of the FDA in this regard encouraged some of the companies in our sample to undertake the development of their devices in countries with friendlier rules.

Developing Devices

Developing a device often involves a great deal of iteration, not just binary, "yes or no" type of testing used for safety, efficacy, and so on. As one of our interviewees pointed out:

> Medical device development is an iterative process. It's not like a drug, where you have a molecule and you take that through clinical trials. If most people looked behind the curtain, they'd be mortified by how imprecise and unscientific the process really is. That's one of the dark secrets of medicine.
>
> The human body is very complex, for one thing, so there are a lot of ideas that simply don't work. You imagine them and you try them, and they don't work. Moreover, devices have to be finely engineered and manufactured according to precise specifications. But you can't tell the engineers exactly how to build something that's never been built before.
>
> You do your initial development in animals, and you try to find an animal model that's as close to the clinical condition as possible. But animals

are imperfect proxies for humans. So something that functions in animal models invariably doesn't work at all when you get into your first group of patients. And you shouldn't be surprised. You don't know how it won't work or why it won't work, but almost inevitably, that's what is going to happen. Devices have to be iterated dozens and dozens of times.

The development of medical products is like the development of medical skills. Physicians have to practice on somebody. If you go into a hospital and you are treated by a fellow, you are going to get inferior care and there is a higher risk of something happening. You'll say, "Gosh, that's horrible—I never want to be treated by a fellow." But if everybody said that, fellows would never become doctors—they have to practice on somebody. It's the same thing with devices. When you first start using them, they are imperfect. They are like fellows—they need to grow up, and if you said you don't want to try something on humans until it was perfect, you would stop innovation.

The CEO of another device development company observed:

It's very exciting in the conceptualization phase, but when you touch a human body, it gets extremely complex. We hate biology. The world of pharmaceutical sciences hates biology because everything looks great until you actually come near a human. The human body is such a complex mechanism that it's largely nonpredictive. It is trial and error. Trial in animal models, error in some humans.

Earlier in the chapter, we distinguished between VC-backed businesses that developed mid-level products and VC-backed businesses that develop high- and ground-level products. We also saw that mid-level innovators, who happen to represent the majority of companies in my sample, combine high-level know-how and inputs using an iterative, interactive, and rapid process. Now we have seen how the introduction of FDA regulation complicates the picture: it tends to slow down the development process and discourage trial and error, but not to the same degree for device companies as for drug development companies. These differences, in the relatively small world of VC-backed businesses, suggest that the broader universe of innovators is highly specialized and diverse. Although much of my argument simplifies innovation down to three levels, the greater complexity of the real world strengthens my critique of the techno-nationalist focus on high-level research.

■ Concluding Comments

The next three chapters examine the relationship between how VC-backed businesses innovate and the nature of their cross-border interactions. We will pay particular attention to how developing mid-level innovations through rapid, interactive iterations with users affects how VC-backed businesses pursue overseas customers, use offshoring, and involve immigrants as founders and employees.

The analysis and evidence in this chapter also informs some of the more general propositions that I sketched in the introduction and will develop in book 2.

Although the spotlight has been on VC-backed businesses, they are obviously not the only players in the innovation game even at the middle level. Other players, such as the *Inc.* 500 companies and large corporations, also undertake mid-level innovations that combine and extend higher-level know-how and products. These other mid-level players may innovate in ways that are somewhat different and possibly complementary. For instance, we would expect large public corporations to have a comparative advantage in undertaking mid-level innovations that require substantial amounts of capital but where speed is not of the absolute essence.*

My larger point is that there is an important role for many mid-level players who develop valuable innovations through a process of iterative engagement with users. Although this may seem trivially obvious to anyone who has any familiarity with the real world of business, in the much-vaunted Schumpeterian model, there is no place for this kind of innovation. For Schumpeter, there is but a single über-innovator who does everything of consequence and is then followed by a swarm of "mere imitators." Furthermore, in that model, innovation occurs in one fell swoop and without iterative engagement with users. As Phelps puts it, "The Schumpeterian chef

---

* Indeed, we often find the following kind of complementarity: VC-backed businesses exploit their comparative advantage in undertaking "quick and dirty" trials to establish the commercial viability of an innovation and then sell out to large corporations that add the capital and further refinement necessary to realize its full potential.

works away in his kitchen to zero in on the exact recipe that fills the bill." By contrast, in Friedrich Hayek's theories—which in my view more accurately capture the essence of modern innovation—the chef who has "little idea of what diners would like [and] experiments on his customers." My research suggests that mid-level innovators are like the Hayekian chef; moreover, their customers are active rather than unwitting or passive participants in the experiments—they make suggestions, possibly even in the kitchen as the dish is being cooked.

As we will see in book 2, however, the misrepresentation of innovation isn't confined to Schumpeter's rhetoric: alarmists such as Richard Freeman also invoke Schumpetrian assumptions. Taking into account how most innovations unfold in a modern economy causes the alarmist thesis to unravel.

3

■ Marketing:

Edging into International Arenas

Advocates for free trade and globalization argue that rapid economic growth in China and India is good for the United States because it expands opportunities for U.S. exporters, particularly of advanced technology products. As evidence, they cite the fact that international sales of high-tech companies such as Intel and Microsoft have boomed. But export opportunities are not equally attractive for all U.S.-based players in the innovation game; high-tech products don't comprise a homogeneous category like soybeans or corn. As we will see in this chapter, only a small number of the VC-backed businesses in my study pursued customers abroad in a big way.

What kept the majority from mounting all-out efforts to serve customers abroad? Some reasons discussed in this chapter apply mainly to VC-backed businesses, whereas some reveal aspects of the innovation game as a whole. For instance, we will see why developers of mid-level products are more likely to focus on U.S. rather than overseas customers than are the developers of high-level products.

The reluctance of mid-level innovators to pursue overseas customers will disappoint those who use the exports of high-tech products as their touchstone of U.S. economic strength. In fact, as I will argue in book 2, the United States benefits from the eagerness of mid-level innovators to optimize their products for U.S. customers and focus their sales and marketing efforts on U.S. markets. I will then further argue that the United States should be more concerned about the willingness and ability of innovators to serve U.S. customers than about maintaining its primacy in high-level research. The material in this chapter will also highlight the importance of sales and marketing activities in the innovation game; I will use this observation in book 2 to question the wisdom of a public policy tilt in favor of training more scientists and engineers—and to argue for protecting the interests of "venturesome consumers" of innovations who aren't too hard a sell.

As the box "Gung-Ho, Slow, or No-Go" indicates, our interviewees varied widely in their enthusiasm for overseas customers.

Gung-Ho, Slow, or No-Go

ThinkFire (an IP company mentioned in chapter 1) targeted international customers from the very beginning, according to its CEO: "The company was founded in July 2001. Within two months, we were in Tokyo meeting with companies like Fujitsu, Hitachi, NEC, Yamaha, and Matsushita."

The CEO of Gammabright[1] (a developer of high-power laser diodes) also had a global view: "We've always worried more about what vertical market to crack rather than which geography we want to penetrate. Whether target customers find value in our product differentiation comes first. Then [comes] the potential revenues we can get. Geography comes third."

Others, such as the CEO of Active Networks, an online registration company, took a middle ground: "We are at an inflection point—for six years, we stayed focused on the U.S. to prove our model. We'd sublicensed our technology to a company in Europe, but they didn't do too much with it. Now we're planning to re-enter Europe on our own."

Another CEO observed that "we have only recently turned cash-flow-positive. Our number one goal has been to stop using investors' money, and we did everything we could in North America to achieve that. Now we can start looking outside."

Yet others, such as the CEO of a Massachusetts-based health services company, had no interest in overseas markets: "We are about to expand into two regions: upstate New York and central Connecticut. We are completely. domestically focused and have no plans in the near term or long term of doing anything abroad."

Similarly, the CEO of a company providing consumer services said: "Every year, we analyze whether we should [either] add a product or expand into a new geography, and every year, we decide to go with new products. Some years ago, we bought a European company whose sales were principally in Europe, but then we came to the conclusion that the U.S. would be a bigger and better market for its product, so we shut it down and moved its entire staff to the U.S."

As it happens, most businesses fell into the "when-the-time-is-ripe" rather than the "as-soon-as-possible" or "never" camps. As box "Revenues Derived or Expected from International Customers" shows, only 4 percent derived more than half their revenues from outside the United States. But when we asked CEOs what share of their total revenues they anticipated overseas customers to account for after five years, provided things went well for their companies, 25 percent expected overseas customers to account for over half their total revenues.

The box also shows noteworthy differences between types of businesses. Developers of high-level products derived a much larger proportion of their revenues from customers abroad than did developers of mid-level and consumer ("ground-level") products;[2] and businesses that targeted customers in service industries (or provided a service function) were less international.[3]

Revenues Derived or Expected from International Customers*

Distribution of companies in my sample by their current and anticipated percentage of international sales to total sales

- More than 50 percent from international customers: now 4 percent of companies, anticipated after five years by 25 percent of companies
- 26–50 percent from international: 22 percent of companies; anticipated by 48 percent
- 11–25 percent from international: 14 percent of companies; anticipated by 10 percent
- 10 percent or less international: 61 percent of companies; anticipated by 18 percent

Median percentage of international sales to total sales

By type of product developed

- High-level: 30 percent
- Mid-level: 10 percent
- Ground-level: 0 percent

By type of customers served

- Manufacturing: 65 percent
- Service industries or functions: 0 percent

* See tables 3.1 and 3.2 for details (see appendix for all numbered tables). Numbers exclude FDA-regulated companies.

What factors account for such differences? What might deter developers of mid- and ground-level products or products for the service industry from serving overseas customers? Could these be spurious correlations? To address these questions, this chapter first examines the strong attraction of overseas markets for some VC- backed businesses. The main body of the chapter then discusses what caused many to hold back—why as a rule, VC-backed businesses, especially those playing at the middle level of the innovations game, tend to develop their products, sales, and marketing processes and organization close to home—and in the absence of compelling overseas opportunities, pursue growth in domestic markets. The rest of the chapter elaborates on the main ideas: why many VC-backed businesses favor European customers over Asian customers; what is special about FDA-regulated developers of drugs and devices; and why large firms often derive a larger proportion of their revenues from international markets than do VC-backed businesses. These topics will further illuminate the relationship between innovation and international sales and marketing.

■ No-Choice Internationalism

Most of the companies that derived more than half their revenues from overseas customers (or expected to do so quickly) were developing telecommunications hardware, software or systems (e.g., for the wireless industry) or high-level components (such as batteries and semiconductor chips) for manufacturing companies. The CEOs of these companies said that overseas markets were more advanced or growing more rapidly, and that their companies could not reach the critical mass needed for long-term viability if they focused on only U.S. customers (see box).

Irresistible International Calls

"We had no choice," said the CEO of a company developing products for the telecommunications industry."The number one equipment provider in our market, by far, is Ericsson out of Sweden. They have about 28 percent of the market. The next largest is Nokia, from Finland, with 13 percent of the market. That's 40 percent of the market right there. The next largest is Siemens, which is German, then Nortel, headquartered in Canada. The U.S. companies, Lucent and Motorola, are numbers six or seven."

Said another: "The market we are in is delivering high-bandwidth-to-wireless handsets, and 3G [third generation] wireless is ahead in Europe. It makes sense to focus on Europe, and then bring back our products to the U.S."

"Our main customers, the Tier 1 mobile operators, are scattered all over the world, and the center of innovation in mobile telephony is Europe and Asia," said a third."Also, the technology in Europe and Asia is more homogeneous, so we can sell the same products to many different operators in the market. The proliferation of technologies in the U.S. makes this hard."*

"Our software takes content, applications, and broadcasts to mobile devices, so, for instance, you can watch interactive TV on your cell phone," said another."This is, for now, not as appealing in the U.S. because the primary interface to the Internet for Americans is through a PC. Abroad, many people don't have PCs with broadband access. Their access to the Internet tends to be mainly through a mobile device. If you go to Finland or Sweden, the phone is part of people's life—you buy a Coke with a phone."That makes the adoption of mobile services of the sort we want to provide faster overseas."

* In the United States, some wireless carriers, notably Sprint PCS and Verizon, use CDMA technology, while Cingular and T-Mobile use GSM.

Companies that developed hardware components used in PCs also had to sell abroad—to the so-called original design manufacturers (ODMs), principally located in Taiwan.[4] But, as described in the boxed text, they also had to concurrently market to the customers of the ODMs, many of which were located in the United States.

Dual-Mode Marketing

ODMs are successors to traditional contract manufacturers and have some role in designing the computers they manufacture for companies such as Dell and HP. This gives ODMs a say in what goes into a computer, but not complete authority; their customers (Dell, HP, etc.) also exercise influence, as do the producers of the microprocessors such as Intel. Therefore, companies that develop computer components often have to "sell" to both ODMs and U.S.-based computer manufacturers and chipmakers—in the United States and in Taiwan.

A CEO whose company develops chips to manage power and clock speeds explained how this plays out:

> Intel publishes what they call a "reference design" for different kinds of computers and a list of approved vendors for all the components in that design. Your chip has to be on Intel's list, but it's not for Intel to buy anything. Who specifies your chip depends on whether the product is of strategic value to a Dell or HP. If the computer is a high-visibility kind of model, then Dell or HP is likely to pick the bill of materials.[5] But that's usually not the case, particularly if the component is 20 dollars or below. Then they let the ODM pick the chip. So if we can't get Dell or HP to specify our chip, we have to work on the ODM, who then has to get Dell or HP to approve. This is what happened with our first design win. We explained the value of our chip to the ODM in Taiwan, which was longer battery life. The ODM then convinced *their* customer [in the United States].

Two CEOs said the small number of potential buyers for their products in the United States required them to look for customers abroad (see box).

A Numbers Game

One CEO said: "The market in the U.S. for our equipment is in the billions of dollars, but this doesn't have to do with the size of the market—it has to do with the number of customers. Our customers are companies that develop protein therapeutics. They are very sophisticated, and there are not a lot of them—roughly 200 worldwide, and 100 in the United States. If you believe any of the Geoffrey Moore theories on "crossing the chasm," critical mass is 50 customers. Fifty customers would [be] half the market in the United States. That's really, really hard. To get 50 accounts, you're going to have to go abroad whether you like it or not."

The CEO of Gammabright noted: "About 80 percent of our commercial revenues* are from fewer than seven or eight customers. The universe of potential customers is in the range of about a hundred. . . . We have to be geography agnostic. . . . We build the devices that go into the systems. For us to be a successful player, we need to make sure that wherever the devices are used, we have a presence there."

* Gammabright also served the military market just in the United States.

■ International by Choice

Businesses may, of course, try to secure customers abroad even if the domestic market can sustain a viable enterprise. For some businesses such as Blackswan[6]—a company that helps clients check proprietary software for open source code that might infringe on open source licenses*—the profit opportunity abroad was too good to pass up. Its CEO told us: "Our thinking was, international companies have the same issue with open source as U.S. companies. In fact, in some countries, the open source movement is stronger than in the U.S. It's one of the reasons we're interested in Germany. We're also looking at companies that embed software in devices; these embedded

---

* Under the terms of the General Public License (GPL), any software utilizing code covered by the GPL has to be made "freely available." Blackswan helped companies identify and manage the licensing obligations of this and other open-source licenses.

software companies may be more active outside the U.S. than within the U.S. We think we could easily get more than half our revenues from international, if we do a good job developing the international marketplace."

Other companies played the international card to secure long-term competitive advantages by preempting rivals abroad or locking up under-served customers abroad. Or they served U.S. multinationals abroad to so-lidify relationships with such companies and prevent rivals from poaching them (see box).

Jockeying for Competitive Advantage

The CEO of a company developing antispam and security products for email that derived 40 percent of its revenue in international markets said: "We saw that our competitors in the U.S. market hadn't gone international, so that was a kind of greenfield opportunity. It's important to penetrate a country's mar-ket quickly. Vendors of software security products are like Coke and Pepsi. Once you get in, it's tough to unseat you. We wanted to get high market share in as many markets as we could."

Preemption was cited by two other CEOs as well. "We can't wait for com-petitors to develop products abroad. So, defensively, we filed for patents in all the places we thought competitors might emerge," said one. "We are also try-ing to suck the oxygen from [competitors] by selling to companies in se-lected countries."

Said another: "We've reached the point where some markets have hit the maturity needed to sustain a business, and we'd be exposed if we delayed much longer. We aggregate buyers and sellers [for online advertising], and once someone has built the first marketplace, the cost of entry for someone else [is] very high. That's sort of what happened to eBay in Japan—someone else built an auction site first."

The CEO of Bladelogic was attracted by the lower intensity of competi-tion: "We sell software to companies with very large data centers: that's the world's largest 1,000 to 2,000 companies. We obviously target the *Fortune* 500 companies in the U.S., but there are also quite a few large accounts in France, Germany, and the UK. Our bet was that those companies were terribly under-served compared to U.S. companies because everyone focuses on North America."

One CEO said that even nominal sales in overseas markets helped create a valuable image of being a "global" company that provided advantages in the U.S. market. "My last company was relatively small in the U.S.; but, outside the U.S., we were larger than most of our major domestic competitors. This gave us some cachet with our clients, who were large advertising agencies. We could also use their subsidiaries that we had served abroad as references for getting their domestic business."

Two CEOs said they had expanded abroad to maintain their standing with multinational companies that they served mainly in the United States. One of those CEOs, whose company sold devices and systems that counted shoppers in a store, said, "We have counting device[s] in 43 countries. Many of our clients are global, and they have dragged us along whether we wanted to go or not. We serve a discount shoe retailer whose stores are all over Central and South America, and a couple in Japan. Another customer is a luxury retailer with outlets in 39 countries."

The other CEO's company (which provided email-related services) developed an international capability without actually creating a physical presence outside the United States: "We need to be able to serve customers globally, because customers deploy email globally. Even if the decision-maker is based in the U.S., and our product will be used mainly in the U.S., our capacity to provide service abroad becomes another box to be checked. And even if customers' staff abroad don't make the purchasing decision, they can veto a vendor. So we need to be able to tell an international story. But because of advances in technology, we don't need to have any people or equipment abroad—we can do everything from the U.S."

The phenomenon of U.S. customers who demanded international service did not seem to be widespread—only a handful of CEOs talked about it. Apparently, U.S. multinationals do not always require vendors to provide their products and services globally—the requirement depends on the organizational structure of the multinational, or more precisely, the structure of the function buying the product or service. For instance, a vendor selling to a globally centralized IT function may have to provide global support for the product; this may not be the case if the sale is made to units that operate independently in each country.[7]

Other factors that encouraged some companies to serve customers abroad (when there was no compelling short-term need) were the urgings of investors and the goals or predispositions of founders (see box).

Other Stimuli: Investors and Founders

Two CEOs cited the role of their investors in their overseas initiatives: "Our first institutional [i.e. nonindividual] investor was a publicly traded Japanese computer-services company that opened an investment arm to invest in U.S.-based technologies. They also got us to open a fifty-fifty joint venture with them in Japan. It didn't make sense, because we hadn't yet established a successful business model in the U.S., and we didn't have the resources or the focus to put into the joint venture. But they were willing to fund it."

The other recalled that in 2000, his company "opened offices in Tokyo, Paris, Stockholm, and Munich and started a joint venture in the UK. The Internet bubble hadn't yet burst, and our VCs were saying to us, 'Expand, expand, expand!' Then, we had to shut them all down." After such experiences, said this and several other interviewees, VCs became wary of "premature" expansions into overseas markets.

In two other companies, the ambitions and mind-sets of the founders and top executives provided the impetus. When we asked the CEO of an "Israeli-origin" software company why it had made an all-out effort to get clients in many parts of the world, he said: "I can't recall the answer. Perhaps it was just 'more! more! more!' We had this Wild West, gold rush outlook. We knew all the banks in the world would have to implement a product like ours, and there were three viable vendors. One was a company started by an Indian immigrant in Boston, another was an Irish company, and the third was us. We were called the three I's: Indian, Irish, and Israeli. Wherever we submitted a proposal, we would find that the other two had as well."

The CEO of a software company told us: "Our goal is to become a billion-dollar company. If all we wanted to do was get acquired, we wouldn't be going after the international market so aggressively."

As a general rule, however, long-term ambitions and beliefs provided a brake, rather than an impetus, for international expansion. For instance, one CEO, explaining her company's reluctance to expand overseas, said: "We have a mission to be a world-class provider of tax-management software. So we first want to make sure we take really good care of our customers in the U.S. market. As a young company, you don't want to take on too much: It's just as important to know what to say no to as it is what to say yes to. Many companies have asked us about teaming together or partnering abroad, but to really be world-class, we have to know what's required before we go into those markets."

Next I turn to why the more representative cases in my sample hadn't made a serious investment in securing customers abroad. First we will see how, regardless of long-term mission or vision, most CEOs believed that it was crucial to "get it right in the U.S. first." Then I will discuss four reasons that encouraged the companies in my sample, especially the mid-level innovators, to continue to focus on the U.S. market even after their product and business model was refined.

In a Nutshell: Why VC-Backed Businesses Focused on Domestic Customers

- Initially, engaging with nearby customers facilitated the iterative development of products and sales processes.

Even after development was substantially completed, many companies continued to focus on domestic customers because of

- uncertainty about whether product combinations (and sales processes) developed for the United States would click abroad.

And they faced higher costs (compared to expanding domestic sales) of

- localization of products, marketing and support;
- managing international sales activities;
- establishing an effective sales channel.

■ Iterating at Home

Some products, like Beaujolais Nouveau, Microsoft's X-box 360, and *Spiderman 3* (the movie), are launched nearly simultaneously in many parts of the world. This was certainly not the approach of the companies I studied.

Virtually all of them focused on customers in the U.S. market—or even a narrower geographic area—until they refined, through the iterative process described in chapter 2, their product and sales process (see box).

Developing Products and Sales Pitches: The Power of Proximity

Even in an era of cheap telecommunications and travel, most CEOs relied on engaging with proximate customers to develop and refine their products and sales processes.

As the CEO of a Silicon Valley software company said:

There are companies that understand who their customer is, why they buy the product, and where to find more of them. Most early-stage venture-backed companies, like us, don't. We have 15 or 20 customers, but we don't have a repeatable sales process yet, so we need to be close to every data point. We need to touch and feel every customer and get a detailed understanding of exactly how they are using the product and its other potential applications. We need to hear off-the-cuff remarks—they can reveal a great deal. Pretty much every executive goes to customers—not just the sales guys—to take a close look at what they are doing.

Ideally, I want people who are a bicycle ride away. We haven't been able to do that, because a bunch of our customers have their corporate headquarters on the East Coast. But it's much easier for a California company to go to the East Coast than to go to Japan. If you can't meet your revenue targets in California—never mind the United States—when the revenue targets are relatively low, you don't have a business. California itself is the sixth biggest economy in the world. You are not going to solve your problem by getting on a plane and going farther away—there is something else that you should be focusing on.

The way you have to sell enterprise software in Europe and Japan is also not conducive to a start-up company. You have to go through resellers and third-party channels. So you touch your customer much less. The customers themselves are often more risk averse and leery of adopting early stage technology from a small U.S. company."

A Boston-based CEO expressed similar views:

> When you are getting your initial product out, you want to be right there on the customer site, helping the deployment and learning about missing features so you can feed that back into your product and sales pitch. Unless you can establish a repeatable sales process in your backyard, it's very challenging and risky to go anywhere else. In fact, even though the U.S. as a whole tends to be fairly accessible, our initial customers were all in the Northeast. As it happens, our most successful vertical [markets] are financial services, insurance, and retail that tend to be headquartered in the Northeast. More than 70 percent are located in a small area, going north from Atlanta and east from Chicago. But [even in companies where customers are more broadly distributed], it's common for West Coast start-ups to have their first dozen or so customers cluster west of the Mississippi, and for East Coast companies to have them east of the Mississippi.

The CEO of another Boston-based company said: "We knew we wanted to serve a global market, but initially we went much narrower because we believed in the Geoffrey Moore model: 'Pick a market where you feel you can win, and be successful there first.' We picked Florida. We said that would be where we would get all our sales for the first year. We grew at a very rapid rate in Florida and have now become the market leader in the U.S."

The less usual "have-to-sell-overseas" companies also faced pressure, of a different kind, to focus on U.S. customers first. "We're a software company in the telecommunications space, specifically in wireless, and the adoption of wireless drives the demand for our software. Korea, China—those are the two big ones for us. Korea is a small country, but it has one of the most sophisticated high-speed wireless networks and mobile penetration of any country. But typically, Chinese and Korean customers prefer that you test your product with somebody here before taking it there. So our business in general is 'U.S. first.' "

The only company that didn't initially focus on U.S. customers was Broadwing[8]—also a supplier to the telecommunications industry. This was, according to its CEO, because of unusual circumstances:

> There is an obvious advantage to having your first customers close, not far away. But we happened to hit our full product stride [in 2001] just as the telecom market in the U.S. imploded. Our target customers were in

disarray and not in a position to try any new products. So we put a sales team into Asia to see what we could do. It was survival behavior. We needed to build our order book, and we wanted customer feedback—as they say in our industry, "If you don't deploy the product, then you won't have any bugs." And we had a talented bunch of techies; with no one buying the product, they were getting demoralized. . . . We always planned to go global, but if it hadn't been for the market problems, we would have built a bigger base of business in the U.S. first.

Other factors induced caution in venturing abroad early as well. As we saw in chapter 2, VC-backed companies use an iterative process not only to develop their products and sales processes but also to refine their organizational structures and routines. The latter can be a more protracted process, and CEOs spoke of the value of deferring international expansion until that process was more advanced. One said: "From one to one hundred employees, you are setting up systems and infrastructure, something that must be done before going global. My philosophy is, don't touch the global market till you figure out the local market and create a sense of who the company is. So many things can go wrong. You have to keep your group together and learn to operate together."

Another CEO indicated that VCs reinforce a "U.S.-first view": "I'm on the board of several venture-backed companies," she told us. "In every case, the VCs say, 'Lets conquer the U.S. first; don't even think about international before that. If you can do it here, then you can always get the product to market internationally later.' " Apparently, the "Grow or go home" motto of some VCs at the turn of the millennium has ceased to hold sway.

The dictum *Get it right at home first* helps explain why the older businesses (and businesses with more overall revenues) derived a larger portion of their revenues from abroad. As the box below shows, the median ratios of international to total revenues for businesses that were at least 10 years old was greater than for businesses that were between five and 10 years old; for businesses that were less than five years old, the averages and medians were even lower. The medians and averages were also much lower for companies with less than $5 million in revenues than for companies with more than $20 million in revenues.

Median Proportions of Total Revenues Derived from International Customers*

The median percentage of international sales to total sales was greater for older companies.

- Five years old (or less): 0 percent
- Older than five but less than 10 years old: 10 percent
- 10 years or older: 25 percent

Median percentages were also higher for companies with larger total revenues.

- Revenues of $5 million or less: 0 percent
- Revenues $5–$19 million: 5 percent
- Revenues $20–$49 million: 21 percent
- Revenues $50 million and greater: 25 percent

* See table 3.2 for details. Numbers exclude FDA-regulated companies.

The data in the box also, however, shows that even many "mature" firms in my sample did not derive a significant proportion of their revenues from international markets. For instance, the median international share for businesses that were from five to 10 years old was just 10 percent, meaning, of course, that half of this age cohort derived 90 percent or more of their revenues from U.S. customers. In fact (although this is not shown in the box), 37 percent of the 5-to-10-year-olds and 34 percent of companies that were 10 years old or more had *no* overseas sales. In the sections that follow, we will look at factors that might have deterred these more mature businesses from securing international customers.

■ Uncertain Prospects

Uncertainty about the demand for a company's products was a common deterrent to pursuing international sales. The cases discussed earlier of companies that "had to sell abroad" because overseas markets were larger or more advanced were the exceptional ones, accounting for less than a fifth of my sample. Most businesses developed products and services for which the domestic market was more advanced and vibrant than any foreign one, or at least contained enough potential customers to satisfy aspirations for rapid growth. In fact, the size and growth of the U.S. market had encouraged six firms to relocate their headquarters to the United States. Moreover, the six had immigrated from "advanced" rather than "backward" economies (where demand for high-tech products often is low): two started in Israel, two in the UK, one in Denmark, and one in Australia.

The attractiveness of the U.S. market was also evident from the competitors faced by the companies I studied. Even businesses with no sales outside the United States faced competition from non-U.S. firms: of the 34 businesses whose current revenues were derived just from domestic customers, more than 40 percent faced foreign competitors. For the CEO of a company developing exchange traded funds, for instance, the main competitor was Barclays, the UK-based bank. But the international competitors (of the domestically focused companies) weren't just multinationals such as Barclays and Siemens (from Germany) that have a long-standing presence in the United States. In more than half the cases, they were small- or medium-sized companies for whom serving the U.S. market was presumably a considerable stretch.

This is not surprising: as discussed in chapter 1, VCs tend to invest in businesses that operate in what is, according to the evidence VCs can obtain, a large and growing market; and, at least in the normal course, a U.S. VC will want to see evidence of such a market in the United States.

But because of the huge size of the U.S. economy, from the point of view of a U.S. VC, evidence of a large and growing market abroad isn't a must. Therefore, for some companies in my sample, there was no evidence that they could ever sell products abroad. As one CEO whose business developed automatic voice-messaging products told us, "The market for our technology is really ill-defined outside the U.S.—automatic voice messaging is unknown. It's not sure whether it will work or not, even in Europe, let alone Asia."

Other companies were deterred by the problem of predicting when overseas markets might take off. Some products, like DVD players, can catch on at the same rate in many places. In other cases, there can be considerable differences in how quickly markets "develop" or "mature." Wi-Fi networks for home computers took off much more rapidly in the United States than in Europe; conversely, text messaging on wireless telephones caught on much more slowly in the United States. After the fact, experts may give reasons, but reliable predictions of growth rates are not on offer. For VC-backed businesses, good timing—not too early or too late—is crucial.

Businesses that face saturated or stagnant markets at home can feel impelled to take chances on uncertain opportunities in international markets. But VC-backed businesses that faced palpably large opportunities in the United States had little incentive to gamble on nebulous prospects abroad (see box).

Why Take the Chance?

One CEO (who was resisting pressure from U.S.-based multinational customers to expand overseas) said: "I *know* I have a pretty fertile hunting ground right here in my backyard. And then somebody tells me that if I climb Mount Kilimanjaro and get past the lions and tigers and the cold and the snow, I might find another good hunting ground. Well, why don't I hunt in my backyard for a while and see how I can do?"

The CEO of a company selling anticounterfeiting solutions to the pharmaceutical industry said his company had not yet made a serious effort to sell outside the United States even though he anticipated great potential in the long term: "From a technology perspective, we are ready to take advantage of opportunities in Europe. But the question is, are the markets ready to invest in an anticounterfeiting solution? Generally, companies only do what they *must* do, not what they should do. We've been successful in the U.S. because our customers know they must use our technology because of financial, competitive, and legal pressures. It's only now that these drivers are emerging in Europe. Companies may be realizing that counterfeiting is a significant issue that they must do something about. But I'd have to be confident that European companies are at the point where they feel they *must* do something before we'd make an investment in developing those markets."

In addition to not knowing whether or when demand for their product category will materialize abroad, U.S.-based innovators also face uncertainty about how well their specific product will sell abroad. Will customers abroad value features developed and "battle-tested" for U.S. customers to the same degree—or even at all?

These uncertainties about features and attributes are usually greater with lower-level products such as cars and computers than higher-level products such as silicon and sheet metal. This is partly because whether a lower-level product attracts buyers often depends on amorphous attributes, such as styling and user interfaces, and it is difficult to predict whether a look or design that draws domestic customers will resonate with the tastes of overseas customers. Also, as discussed in chapter 2, even if the attributes are concrete (rather than amorphous), the attractiveness of many mid- and ground-level products often depends on assembling the right combination. A combination that has proven its appeal in the domestic market may flop abroad because of subtle differences in local conditions. More frugal customers abroad, for instance, might prefer cheaper (or more durable) combinations with fewer bells and whistles.

Similarly, the commercial success of an innovation also requires discovering, usually through a process of trial and error, an effective sales and marketing approach. Approaches that work at home may not work abroad. Advertising campaigns developed for the home market have famously offended consumers abroad. Although problems with using the domestic formula for business-to-business sales abroad are not as well known, they can be equally vexing.

Of course, there are several examples of mid- and ground-level products developed for the U.S. market that have been successful in improbable locales—Starbucks has clicked in countries where the traditional beverage of choice is tea. But the record of the successes and failures of previous products provides little guidance to an innovator assessing the chances of the next—the innovator faces high Knightian uncertainty. The prospect of having to start the iterative process from scratch encourages companies such as Judy's Book (see box) to maximize the return on the effort they have already made by sticking to their home market.

Sticking to Seattle

The CEO of Seattle-based Judy's Book (an advertising-supported website with reviews of local businesses) said, "International is not on my agenda. Our business hypothesis is that advertising is primarily national. It's a $100 billion industry in the U.S. that's going to be moving online. The hypothesis also is that the U.S. is the leading Internet market, and local businesses are likely to move here first." Getting the Judy's Book model to work abroad was also a powerful deterrent: "We have a hard enough time getting this to work in Seattle. I've had to learn a lot about what does and doesn't work right here. For instance, initially we defined our business in a very horizontal way: any advertiser in the Yellow Pages. But that created a critical mass problem in terms of data, so we had to figure out which categories to target. We've also had to solve a consumer-attention problem—people have the need for plumbers and pest control, but they are not necessarily passionate about writing reviews on the web about them. And to make our kind of business work overseas, you would have to be on the spot to solve these kinds of problems."*

* Being shut out of overseas markets did not, however, concern the CEO of Judy's Book: "It's inevitable. I've been in communication with a guy in Germany who's doing a very similar thing. Someone's doing it in Toronto. The recognition is that they are not coming here and we are not going there. In fact, we try to help each other out."

In contrast to Knightian uncertainty about whether a product will click abroad, there is almost never any doubt that starting to sell overseas will require—as we will see in the next three sections—a larger investment of funds and management time than is necessary to increase the domestic sales effort. And the payoffs from investing resources in international marketing are in most cases also predictably realized more slowly (even if the product does click). The combination of greater resource requirements on the one side and highly uncertain, slowly realized returns on the other would naturally give pause to any innovator who contemplates mounting an international sales effort. For a VC-backed business, the larger requirements of money and managerial time and the slower payoffs are especially daunting.

As I have mentioned, round-to-round financings limit businesses, between rounds, to what one CEO called "my fixed bag of money." Moreover, VCs are loath to "replenish the bag" if the venture fails to make rapid—and verifiable—progress. Managerial capacity—or "bandwidth"—is also limited.[9] Constraints of money, time, and managerial capacity understandably cause VC-backed businesses to stick to initiatives that have fast, verifiable payoffs. Therefore, even if international initiatives have a "positive expected net present value," VC-backed businesses have an incentive to defer them until an IPO (or acquisition by a large company) provides more ready access to capital and managerial capacity.

As one CEO said: "We very much want to develop a market overseas. But it's a question of when—do we have enough dry powder to make the investment, because it *is* an investment. And it's probably an investment that would take two years [to turn] into revenue, whereas domestically, I can turn an opportunity into revenue in six months."

■ Localization Costs

Adapting products and associated services to local conditions creates obvious additional costs when businesses start selling abroad. The adaptations range from the relatively straightforward translation of interfaces and manuals to conforming to local business practices and regulations (see box).

"Going Native"

Selling a product abroad that was originally developed for the U.S. market requires expenditures to adapt or change the product for local conditions. Often, the user interface needs to be translated—and the translation updated as the base-language interface changes. An obvious example is Google's and Yahoo's search and email websites. If the product requires manuals or documentation, these too need to be translated. For users who need individualized support, a U.S. vendor may need to establish a help desk or help line with staff who speak the local language and operate in the local time zone. According to one CEO:

> We created a Spanish version—that cost about $120,000. But even if you give customers in Spanish-speaking countries a Spanish translation, they don't want to call your support line and speak to someone in English; they expect a Spanish speaker. At a minimum, you need to have some kind of reverse-translation software at the customer support desk so the customer can point to where they are having a problem and you can see in English what they are seeing in Spanish. That too, as you can imagine, costs money.

For some products, translation issues go beyond words. One company used artificial intelligence to archive text documents, and needed software that could handle characters not used in English (for instance the cedilla and circumflex in French). Another, whose product incorporated voice recognition, had to develop versions for different dialects of the same language.

International customers often derive more value from products if they are optimized for local conditions and taste. A web search optimized for German users might provide different results—and advertisements—than it would for U.S. users, even if the underlying search engine used the same technology. One interviewee, whose company operated a music website, told us that even though users from all over the world listened to the same songs (there was more than an 80 percent overlap between his Japanese and U.S. customers' choice of music), there was "almost no end" to the localization of the website his company would undertake abroad—if it had the resources.*

Some products incorporate context-specific knowledge that has to be localized. The CEO of a company that developed a spam-blocking product needed different rules in different countries for detecting spam. Moreover, the rules had to be constantly updated—in each country—to keep up with ever-changing forms of spam.

Mid-level products and services in particular have to be adapted to differences in the needs and business practices of business users. A simple example is accounting software developed for small- to medium-sized businesses in the United States that typically do not do business outside the country. Selling the software overseas, where many small- to medium-sized businesses engage in international trade, can require a "multicurrency" capability. More extensive localization can involve adapting to the idiosyncrasies of prevailing business processes.

Some products also have to be altered—or at least "recertified"—to satisfy local rules. For instance, a CEO (whose company developed fleet management systems that used wireless networks) said that doing business in a new country would require getting the company's systems certified to run across a local carrier's network. Besides out-of-pocket costs, managing the process might take from six to nine months of an employee's time.

---

* The interviewee also said that when he asked a leading search company (through high-level contacts) to share its localization tools and techniques, he was told these were considered highly confidential and of great strategic value.

The CEO of Cognio (a company that helped identify and correct problems with local area networks) also spoke of the expense and opportunity costs of regulatory compliance: "One of our first customers, Microsoft," he recalled, "asked us to solve a problem that they were having with interference with their wireless networks in Portugal. But then our servers were held up in customs while the product was certified by the Portuguese equivalent of the FCC."

According to some of our interviewees, anticipating the need for localization when a product is initially developed can reduce the ultimate costs (see box).

Preparing for Localization

Some companies in our sample, particularly those selling enterprise software, apparently developed products keeping future international sales in mind. One CEO said: "Our product was developed from the beginning with the issue of localization in mind. We have Japanese and Chinese versions of our product, and our product can be very easily localized. For example, we have external tables with text files. So you just translate those files, you push a button, and it's in another language."

Another CEO said:

We spent a significant amount of time visiting all our target customers, understanding the diversity of their operational processes and their technology infrastructure. We tried to come up with an architecture that could fit within those diverse elements. Many software companies start with one customer who has one way of doing things. Then their next customer has a different way of doing things and a different infrastructure that hasn't been factored into the product design. What you should do at the start is survey the marketplace and find canonical solutions that can fit into the diversity of environments your software needs to operate in. And we didn't restrict ourselves to U.S. customers. My cofounder, who is from Singapore, urged me to visit Italy, where companies were having the same problem, and they had a different approach to it. We

> believe our solution has factored in that approach—and when we start selling there, we will find out.

The CEO of a company developing software for banks added:

> From my past history in enterprise software, I learned to not develop a product for just one market. So if you are a bank and you say, "I have these five steps in my credit process," I don't create a product that has just these five steps. I create a workflow that has an unlimited number of steps, even though to you, it's defined as only five steps.

Building in flexibility for future international sales is not, however, a "free option"—it does require up-front investment. Doing research on "canonical solutions" takes up time. Developing more flexible software also entails writing more code; this is not only more costly in and of itself but adds to the cost of testing the software. Businesses that start with limited resources may therefore have to forgo the flexibility that would later help reduce localization costs.

Costs of Flexibility

Businesses have to incur up-front costs to reduce the subsequent costs of localizing their products. As the CEO of the bank-software company (quoted above) observed, "Some people say developing more flexible programs has gotten cheaper because the tools for developing software have evolved. I'm not convinced. I believe that testing code is as costly as writing code, and testing a larger set of variables makes testing exponentially more difficult."

Another CEO—whose company had not invested at the outset in a flexible architecture—bemoaned: "Most companies who are boot-strapping don't think about architecting for other languages, because it's expensive. You've got very little cash on hand, and you start making decisions on how to get the product out in the fastest possible way, without any bells and whistles, so a client can use it. You start down this path, and it becomes easy to keep going down this path and not add those bells and whistles. You end up with an architecture that, from the point of view of a new CEO, and for the purposes of serving an international market, is inadequate.

Market conditions and the nature of the product usually had the most influence on the degree of localization (see box) that the companies in my sample undertook. All told, approximately 30 percent of the CEOs said they sold their product abroad with little to no localization. At the other end—about 14 percent of our sample—were businesses for whom the issue of localization was moot because CEOs believed there was no demand (without radical reconstruction) for their innovations outside the United States. In between were businesses—about 45 percent of the total—where modest localization (e.g., of the user interfaces) was required to serve customers overseas, as well as those—about 11 percent of the total—where the localization requirements were extensive (see box).

Degrees of Localization

The degree of localization undertaken by the companies I studied varied considerably, with market conditions and the nature of the product playing a significant role. At one extreme in my sample was a CEO who told us: "Our software is easily transportable across boundaries—in most countries, the people who use our product understand English. There is very little localization needed, and we, at this point in our maturity, don't do any at all. Our sales are a little slow in Japan because we don't have a localized version; it might help us there."

Said another: "At some point, there may be a need to localize the marketing materials, and maybe the user interfaces, but currently, that has not been a problem for us. The folks that use our product are generally developers who speak English. Besides, our software is the only thing like it on the market. We have one small competitor, but their product is nowhere nearly as advanced as ours. People abroad have been willing to engage with us simply because there is nobody else to engage with."

At the other extreme was the CEO of a health-care services company:

Fundamentally, we are solving a U.S. problem of physicians who are not well automated. The manifestations of the problem vary a lot, even at the local and regional level; California is different from the Southeast, which is different from the Northeast. We have sold our system to one hospital in Canada. That was about half-an-order-of-magnitude more difficult than a typical installation in the United States. You might think, "Canada is like the 51st state. Overall, it's not that different." But health care is practiced differently, and people have different expectations. So we can't just sell the same systems everywhere.

As might be expected, we found that the extent of localization necessary was correlated with the proportion of revenues that businesses derived from their overseas sales (see box).

**Median Proportions of Total Revenues
Derived from International Customers***

The median percentage of international sales to total sales varied with the extent of localization necessary to serve customers abroad as follows.

- Extensive localization (9 companies): 0 percent median international sales
- Modest localization (38 companies): 10 percent median international sales
- No localization (25 companies): 25 percent median international sales
- 12 companies reported no overseas demand for their product or service

The median percentage of international sales to total sales was greater for companies reporting "early" overseas revenues.

- Early overseas revenues (23 companies): 30 percent median international sales
- No early overseas revenues (47 companies): 0 percent median international sales
- Of the 47 companies that did not have early overseas revenues, only 15 went on to serve customers abroad.

* See table 3.2 for details. Numbers exclude FDA-regulated companies.

Also noteworthy was a relationship between companies that secured customers abroad "early" (i.e., within six months from the time they first started generating revenues) and their "eventual" proportion of revenues derived from overseas. Almost every company that had "early" overseas revenues had done so without any proactive international marketing effort; in one case, a computer-disaster recovery service, the company was approached by a Scottish bank and a French company through the good offices of a Google search. Naturally, little localization went into the product. As shown above, the median proportion of international sales for companies that had early customers abroad was 30 percent. In contrast, the median proportion for companies that did not have early overseas customers was zero. In fact, only about a third of these businesses eventually started selling abroad. In other words, if a company's product or service did not naturally "fit" overseas markets early on, more likely than not, it wouldn't fit later.

■ Organizational and Managerial Problems

Another deterrent to pursuing customers abroad was that starting international sales and marketing organizations and getting them to function smoothly consumed scarce top management time.

The problems of managing the conflicts that arise in large multinational organizations have been extensively studied. As illustrated by the boxed text below, small and emerging businesses aren't immune to these problems, even if their only activity abroad is selling their goods and services in a few countries.

Overcoming Intramural Conflicts

According to the CEO of a software company that derived more than a quarter of its sales in Europe:

All companies, large or small, wherever they might be located, tend to be ethnocentric, and as a result, sales productivity tends to be highest in the home country. It's not conscious, but as a result of having the same culture and proximity, the default tends to be the support of the local sales effort.

For instance, in the U.S., we have a marketing staff that manages our participation in trade shows. In Europe, the sales people do this on their own. But they don't know how to set up exhibits or even where to get T-shirts to give away.

The default mentality is almost tribal: why do we have to give our salespeople abroad company cars? Why do they have different rules for travel and entertainment?

The neglect and suspicion become a self-fulfilling prophecy. Sales efforts abroad that aren't properly supported confirm people's beliefs that opportunities abroad aren't worth pursuing. This kind of ethnocentrism isn't just a problem with U.S. companies. I used to be the head of the U.S. sub of a UK company, and even though the U.S. was a larger market for the company, it got proportionately less sales and marketing support.

The tendency to have self-contained operations in each country makes things worse. When I first arrived here, we had a subsidiary in each country in Europe, headed by a sales person who thought of himself as a country manager. Each country did its own collections, invoicing, and accounting. Each country managed its own renewals of maintenance contracts. Now we do all invoicing out of the UK and the contract renewals out of Germany. The salespeople are salespeople and not administrators.

Another cited "the classic international business problem of splitting the commission when the sale crosses territory." "It's a very contentious issue," he said. "When a French multinational bank installs our product in its New York office, who gets the credit—the Paris office or the New York office? The international and domestic sales teams are constantly at war about this."

Addressing these problems consumes management time that is a scarce resource in VC-backed businesses. And rapid expansion of domestic customers and employees itself (one CEO observed that the majority of his staff had been hired in the last six months) can use up managerial capacity as quickly as the company can add it. The management capacity problem is exacerbated when that executive team has limited experience coordinating geographically dispersed subunits; two-thirds of the companies in my sample had just one facility in the United States. Therefore, matters that in a large company would be disposed of through the application of informal routines or policy manuals required the intervention of top management.

The high opportunity cost of scarce managerial capacity naturally reinforced businesses' reluctance to serve international markets. "When you go international," a CEO said, "you're taking focus away and attention away from your core in the United States." Another explained why his company had closed its London office: "With $6 million in revenue, it was impossible to service the European and American markets. It was a matter of focus."

The international backgrounds and experiences of some CEOs (and their staff) seemed to bolster their confidence about managing overseas sales organizations and dealing with other problems in serving customers abroad.

Familiarity Breeds . . . Confidence

CEOs said that their prior relationships and knowledge of markets abroad enhanced their willingness and ability to serve overseas customers. For example, Nick Sanna, the CEO of Netuitive and a native of Italy, told us: "Our chairman is of Iranian descent. Our CTO is Canadian. Our product manager is from France. So although we are based in the States, we did everything from the beginning with a global mind-set."

Another CEO said: "Because I am a UK native, I have always had a European bent. In previous companies, we were also oriented globally, especially towards Europe. In the first company I founded, Deutsche Telecom was one of our first three customers. In the second company, the first customer was French."

A (U.S.-born) CEO recalled that the previous company where she had worked "was international from the start. One reason that this worked so well was that it had a highly international workforce. That took away the fear and the strangeness; it wasn't just a bunch of Americans doing business in Europe. The staff also had contacts in their home countries that helped the company."

But ultimately, how much difference did the international backgrounds of the CEOs and their staff actually make?

It is difficult to question the oft-heard proposition that ignorance and unfamiliarity make it difficult for companies to serve overseas customers.* Many U.S. businesspeople do have limited exposure to conditions abroad. I was once told by a former executive of the credit card company Capital One, who had been charged with formulating a strategy for international expansion, that most of his colleagues at corporate headquarters (in Richmond, Virginia) had never applied for a passport (even though a UK native cofounded Capital One). And indeed, by many estimates only between a fifth and a quarter of the U.S. population had passports in 2005.[10]

That said, humans are gregarious creatures with the capacity to learn. They can—and do—turn chance meetings into lifelong friendships and acquire new knowledge. The world of commerce, in contrast to many other walks of social life, seems especially open to the formation of new relationships. There certainly are cases (e.g., in the diamond trade) where outsiders may be excluded from closed trading networks, but this does not seem to be the rule. In the normal course, determined outsiders with the right skills and personality can form business relationships, no matter how hidebound society as a whole might be. Trollope's Augustus Melmotte, in *The Way We Live Now*, is a fictional character but accurately portrays how astute strangers can work around severe class prejudice and xenophobia. What you know can make up for whom you (don't) know, especially if the "what" includes knowledge of human nature.

The data in my sample certainly do show a correlation between the national origin of the CEOs and the ratios of their international revenues to total revenues (see box). But the correlation is far from perfect. The low proportion of immigrant CEOs in companies that have no international sales may simply reflect the comparative disadvantage of immigrants vis-à-vis the U.S.-born in running highly domestically oriented businesses. The absence of immigrant CEOs in health-care service companies in my sample, for example, may be result of the deeper domestic knowledge of native-born CEOs in these fields.

---

* The value of prior relationships in lubricating commercial transactions also seems indisputable and has been repeatedly demonstrated by studies of "networks" (which take issue with economic models that assume trade between anonymous agents).

Correlations of Overseas Sales and CEO Backgrounds

Companies with immigrant CEOs had higher median proportions of international sales to total revenues, but the correlation wasn't perfect.

- Immigrant CEO = 20 percent median international sales
- Native-born CEO = 0 percent median international sales
- A third of the companies with immigrant CEOs *did not* serve customers outside the United States.

The proportion of immigrant CEOs was also higher in "have to sell overseas" telecommunications and semiconductor companies than in the "no market abroad" health-care services companies

- Immigrant CEOs (in all companies) = 36 percent
- Immigrant CEOs in telecom and semiconductor companies = approximately 50 percent
- Immigrant CEOs in health-care service companies = 0 percent

---

The modest correlation of CEO backgrounds and international sales is consistent with what the CEOs told us: having backgrounds and connections helped them sell abroad, but other factors mattered even more.

Helpful but Not Essential

"Personal relationships were useful," the CEO of Cognio told us, "but not imperative in selling outside the U.S." The CEO of a telecommunications company (a UK native) told us that he had used his personal connections with a large buyer in France and those of a top engineer to reach out to a large Chinese customer. Did this mean, we asked, that they had actually chosen targets on the basis of prior relationships? Not so, he replied: "We exploited the people and the connections we had, but regardless, we would have found some way in.... The company has become very visible because of its R&D. We did a demonstration at a Swedish research institute. That got Deutsche Telecom and a number of other European operators looking at us."

Another (U.S.-born) CEO whose company derived nearly half its revenues from international sales told us: "Even though we didn't have international experience, we compensated by doing our homework. Our VP international who set everything up was very methodical. For each region, we talked to five companies about who they had used and who we needed to talk to."

Our interviews also suggest that a factor that requires businesses to look for customers abroad, namely a small number of customers overall, can also make up for the lack of prior relationships.

As the CEO of Gammabright said: "The [laser systems] industry is fairly small—it's not like the semiconductor world, which is where my roots are. If you spend some time in this field, you will get to know a lot of the players. You'll see the same faces at the trade shows. Trade shows usually give us a lot of information, especially the ones that are well attended internationally. You also learn that certain customers will buy from certain suppliers, and at the fully integrated systems level, this might be binding, but at the component level, it doesn't matter. There are clear metrics for price performance, and if you are at the cutting edge, you get customers. If you fall behind, your position will erode."

Like personal connections, overseas investors played an ambiguous, and in my interpretation even less important, role in influencing how vigorously or successfully a company pursued customers abroad. Just over 40 percent of the businesses in my study received financing from wealthy individuals, VCs, and strategic investors who were based abroad. As with immigrant CEOs, the presence of international investors did correlate with proportions of overseas revenues: the median proportion for companies with international investors was 21 percent compared to zero for those that did not have international investors. But I doubt this was because overseas investors helped companies find customers abroad (see box). Rather, overseas investors likely picked companies that did business internationally.

Do International Investors Facilitate International Sales?

Only one CEO mentioned a customer relationship that was initiated by an overseas investor. Others were positively skeptical. Speaking of international VCs, one CEO said: "You get all your early-stage investors from the U.S. The international VCs who invest in U.S. companies are mostly later-stage investors. As the business is about to take off, they put money in, especially if you have customers in their home country. They *say* we have all these contacts, but it's all BS."

Some of the companies had received funding from the in-house or affiliated investment arms of multinational companies based overseas, but these also apparently did little to facilitate sales, even though in most such cases, the "parent" multinational was a potential customer for the products the companies were developing.

One interviewee told us that the investment staff based in the United States had "a big-company mentality. They couldn't sneeze unless headquarters told them to get a Kleenex. All they did was to put us through a drill to make sure that they didn't embarrass themselves, and they closed the investment only after we had sold our product to their bosses."

Another who received a strategic investment from a multinational called his experience a "nightmare. They said they wanted to partner with us, but they ended up competing while they were on the board."[11]

■ Sales Channels—a Hobson's choice

The last obstacle to serving international customers that I will discuss—the difficulty of establishing effective sales channels abroad—deserves special emphasis because it illuminates an important policy question: Should public policies discourage sales and marketing activities? In the view of many policy pundits—and not just techno-nationalists—sales and marketing activities constitute a waste of resources that should be devoted to more productive activities such as research. In the introduction, I laid out the opposite case, that sales and marketing activities are essential to realizing the value of innovations. Unless new products are effectively sold, their developers, users, and society at large derive no benefit. Next, we will see that selling is as challenging as it is necessary—innovators often have to set up their own "direct" sales forces because using "indirect" channels is infeasible or ineffective. Selling abroad magnifies the problem: whereas setting up a direct sales channel at home is expensive, doing so abroad is prohibitive. Therefore, many innovators make do with whatever sales that ineffective indirect channels can deliver abroad—or they don't bother with international customers.

Few new products, especially those developed by an up-and-coming innovator, sell themselves, at home or abroad: the innovator has to communicate information about the features and modes of use, sometimes to buyers with tepid interest in learning about them. Moreover, selling requires more than just communicating information. The buyer has to be convinced to make a leap of faith that the innovation will provide benefits in excess of the costs, and that the vendor will be around to provide ongoing support and upgrades.* These concerns are acute for innovations such as enterprise software systems, where the costs and benefits are realized over the long term and a break in vendor support can cause significant disruptions. Assuaging such concerns usually requires face-to-face persuasion—supply-chain management software, for instance, cannot be sold just by providing technical specifications or a catchy ad campaign.

Selling also requires an up-front investment: salespeople have to be trained and marketing materials developed before the innovator realizes any revenues. The sales process itself can take time: the sales staff has to secure appointments, make multiple calls, and possibly fill out requests for proposals. Months if not years can pass before any orders are signed. The costs can be material, particularly for mid-level innovations where uncertainty about a customer's long-term costs and benefits makes selling the product challenging.

Therefore, the return on sales and marketing investments (or what some CEOs called the "productivity" of their sales efforts) can have a substantial impact on overall profitability—and on the availability of the next round of financing, especially after a product has come out of the "beta" testing phase. Because time is of essence, the speed with which a new salesperson starts generating revenues also is crucial.

In principle, a VC-backed business could ameliorate the difficulties of selling its products by using third-party (or indirect) distribution channels instead of investing in its own direct sales effort. Channels do exist in the markets of interest to VC-backed businesses. For example, there are numerous distributors of enterprise software (formerly known as "value-added

---

* In book 2 (chapter 11) I argue that, like the developers, buyers of new products face Knightian uncertainty.

resellers" or "systems integrators" but who now call themselves "channel partners"). Since channel partners don't have to hire more salespeople and have relationships with customers, "outsourcing" the sales function to channel partners should—in principle—generate revenues for small companies with little additional cost.

In practice, however, as many interviewees told us, VC-backed businesses usually have a hard time realizing significant revenues through third-party sales forces, especially for complex, mid-level products (see the box "Limitations of Indirect Channels"). Overall, only about a third of the revenue-generating companies in my sample used indirect channels to any significant degree to sell to customers in the United States; two-thirds relied mainly on their own sales force. We didn't ask each interviewee *when* they started using indirect channels, but by comparing the median "revenue-generating ages" of the users and nonusers, we inferred that this was likely to have been later rather than earlier.

Limitations of Indirect Channels

As one CEO said:

> Resellers are exquisite if it's the same box to be sold over and over and over in the same way. But our product is very customized by the time it lands on a client's desk. The sales process for our kind of product is also very complex and personal. You have to attract a senior-level person and make them understand the value proposition. You also have to attract a user at a lower level who is in pain on a daily basis and get both of them, preferably with one of them leading, as the champions of your product. In every single case it becomes complex—we don't have a single sale that's taken as is. The typical reseller would have a very hard time with this.

In recent years, large companies such as IBM have joined the ranks of channel partners, selling the products and services of other companies alongside their own. These relatively new channel partners do have sales forces capable of dealing with complex products and purchasing processes. But the number of such channel partners is small—according to one interviewee—less than five. Moreover, the good channels (and their individual sales personnel) are usually unwilling to risk investing their time and effort in trying to sell an unproven product. One CEO said:

> In our space, you have to be fairly large before you go indirect. I learned that the hard way. We spent a lot of time with Accenture and Deloitte and IBM early on. They would happily take the meeting, but then nothing would come of it. Eventually it worked great, but we could have saved a lot of time and money if we had waited until we had a larger business.

Similarly, Nick Sanna of Netuitive recalled:

> We started trying to sell right after 9/11, and nobody wanted to buy IT from small companies. [So] we thought going with channel partners would be easy and the right thing to do. However, when we knocked at the door of the large companies we wanted to partner with, they told us, "You have a very nice product—come back after you have a dozen customers." We realized we would have to convince the first customer ourselves. Only then would we have the right to talk to the big guys who we wanted as our partners. It was hand-to-hand combat for our first dozen customers in the U.S., but we did it.

Although most companies we studied preferred to invest in more expensive—and more effective—direct sales force in the United States rather than use indirect channels, many companies abroad preferred the less effective but lower-cost indirect route. An important reason for this was that the economics of building a sales force abroad invariably looked unattractive when compared to expanding the U.S. sales force—the investment required was greater and the sales generated lower and slower (see box).

The High Costs of Building a Sales Force Abroad

When faced with a choice between adding salespeople to a preexisting domestic sales force or creating an international sales force from scratch, the companies in our sample usually chose the former. Several reasons made it more costly to create and establish a direct sales channel abroad:

- Even if the actual wages (or commissions) of sales staff were the same or lower abroad, other costs were onerous: social security contributions and the cost of perquisites (such as a company car) were usually higher in Western Europe and many parts of Asia.
- Legal, tax, accounting, and other kinds of overhead support for a sales organization in a different country was higher than in a different state.
- Overseas sales staff could not as easily use corporate resources, located at headquarters (wherever that might be)—for example, to prepare a marketing presentation.
- Sales staff abroad usually needed "real" offices. To paraphrase slightly the observation of a Boston-based CEO, customers in Portland wouldn't care if their local salesperson worked out of a home office, as long as the company had "real" headquarters they could visit in Massachusetts. Customers in Paris, however, would be concerned about the soundness of a U.S. company that didn't have a proper office and address in France.

The time and money it took for an overseas sales force to generate revenues was also greater because of the absence of local relationships and references. One CEO told us that, even though his previous company dominated a niche for accounting software in North America, "that didn't make any difference to customers in China. The accountants we were trying to sell to would ask their accountant friends, 'Have you heard of this company?' This made breaking into the Chinese market really hard. Having a large number of North American customers meant nothing."*

But especially for companies selling complex, mid-level products, securing confidence and forming close relationships with clients is as crucial abroad as it is in the United States. The CEO of the company that aggregated buyers and sellers of online advertising said:

* Many other CEOs shared the same view. One of our interviewees, however, had a different perspective on the portability of references: "It depends who the references are; if it's Mike's Photo Shop, no. If it's Visa, American Express, you know, certainly. And your references don't have to be huge; they just have to be known in their segment. If you're selling to retail, it has to be Kmart or Wal-Mart or Target.

> Google has been able to internationalize with very little sales or infra-
> structure investment because they didn't have to deal with things like
> business processes in other countries. As long as Google's search engine
> can index pages in the local language and consumers use it, then the
> small advertisers—who are even more underserved outside the U.S.—
> will advertise on Google. That's not the case for most businesses like this.
> You *have* to establish relationships with traditional media companies
> and ad agencies in each country.

While companies allocated all their funds for building a sales force to their U.S. operations, many companies used indirect channels abroad, even though they did not use such channels at home (see box).

Indirect Sales in the United States and Abroad

Of the companies in my sample that had sales both in the United States and abroad,

- half used indirect channels (to a significant degree) abroad but not in the United States;
- one used indirect channels in the United States but not abroad;
- half used indirect channels both outside and inside the United States.

Indirect channels were especially commonly used in Asia:

- More than four-fifths used indirect channels in Asia.
- Two-thirds used indirect channels in Europe.
- One-third used indirect channels in the United States.*

* Includes all companies selling in the United States whether or not they had international sales

---

Using indirect channels allowed companies to sell abroad without having to incur the up-front cost and overhead of developing their own sales forces. Particularly in Asia, indirect channels could provide crucial local connections and references. But the basic problem of the ineffectiveness of indirect channels didn't go away: it was no easier to get the attention of good indirect channels abroad than it was at home. Using indirect channels also limited the kinds of customers that could be served abroad. One CEO said, for instance, that the company's use of resellers outside the United States didn't bother its multinational clients, "like Siemens, who are willing to be supported by our U.S. staff." But without setting up its own offices, the company could not satisfy a broader clientele of customers who "demand a local number where they can talk to someone locally."

Distributors in Asia who might provide an entrée to the local market didn't, as it turned out, give away the value of their connections. "In my last company, we had a joint venture in Korea with a very large, family-controlled conglomerate," one CEO told us. "The company became the number one online advertising technology provider in Korea, and it still is. But we had to give 80 percent of the revenues to our Korean partner. So markets like Korea or Japan are very appealing and may draw you in. But what does it really do for your business? The money all stays over there, and you don't make much more than if you had just licensed your technology."

Most companies (apart from the exceptions described in the box, "The High Costs of Building a Sales Force Abroad") picked indirect rather than direct sales channels simply because they were the lesser of two evils. Indirect channels helped provide evidence of global potential (which could be valuable at the time of "exit") without consuming significant resources. But they did not generate significant international revenues. Faced with an unappealing choice of channels, many companies decided not to sell abroad at all.

Exceptions That Didn't Find It Harder to Sell Abroad

A handful of CEOs reported they did *not* face significant challenges (or high additional costs) in selling to customers abroad.

Nick Sanna of Netuitive said that, once the company demonstrated its mettle through direct sales to U.S. customers and signed up a top-tier channel partner, the channel partner had no problem in signing up customers in Japan. "We never even met these customers," said Sanna. International customers— almost all secured through the channel partner—subsequently grew to account for about half Netuitive's total revenues. And Netuitive didn't have to worry about geography: "We just have to train their sales force—we only have to deal with their headquarters. They market worldwide. It's been easy."

Gammabright was also able to sign up good distributors—including Japan's best—in all the places it wanted to sell. In fact, to the CEO's surprise, the distributors' competence largely compensated for Gammabright's lack of local engineering support, which the CEO "originally thought would be a big handicap."

Cybrel Security Systems signed up its first UK customer without a local sales force or indirect channel. Instead, its CEO said, "We went to London all the time. We were there so often, it didn't even occur to them that we weren't a local company. At some point, we did set up an office in a tiny room with a shared secretary, just to have a presence in the UK."

These cases, however, involved exceptional circumstances. Netuitive developed a one-of-a-kind product that required very little localization, for instance. After the value of the product was demonstrated with U.S. customers, its channel partner (a household name in the computer industry for half a century) could easily sell the product to its customers in Japan.

Gammabright (as mentioned in the previous chapter) produced high-level devices whose value turned on a small number of measurable attributes. According to the CEO, the company's devices were "differentiated at particular wavelengths and power levels." That helped distributors "round out their portfolios. Otherwise we would not have merited much attention."

Cybrel's three competitors were, as mentioned, all relatively small, young companies, and none was based in the UK. The Irish competitor that might otherwise have had an advantage selling to a British bank apparently lost out because (according to Cybrel's CEO) it "took the order for granted."

To summarize what we have covered in this chapter so far: International markets have a much stronger draw for companies developing high-level physical components than they do for companies developing mid- and ground-level products or products used in service industries or functions. International markets also become more attractive after a company has finished refining its products, but this attraction is tempered by the uncertainty of overseas demand, the costs of localizing the product, the managerial capacity consumed, and the difficulties of establishing effective—but not prohibitively expensive—sales channels.

The theme of variety, central to my overall thesis, has been evident: Different types of businesses are attracted to international markets to different degrees, and even within a "type," the specific combination of problems a particular business encounters affect its enthusiasm for serving overseas customers. The next three sections further illuminate the variety of the international sales efforts undertaken by different innovators. I start with the question of which specific markets abroad become the focus of different VC-backed businesses. As one CEO said: "You never go 'international'— you go to selected markets that are appropriate for your business." In the section that follows, we will see how the factors that affect whether a business markets abroad also influence its decision of where to go.

■ Which Markets?

The choices of which particular international markets to target closely paralleled the trade-offs faced by the companies regarding whether they should try to serve customers abroad: The "no choice" internationalists had no choice but to follow the geographic distribution of potential customers. So companies developing high-level components for products such as personal computers focused on the Far East, where many of the manufacturers are now located. Similarly, producers of components whose customers were widely dispersed were "agnostic to geographies."

As I have mentioned, businesses that were making a modest effort in international markets typically did so to demonstrate their long-term potential for serving customers abroad rather than to generate significant sales. These companies didn't pick markets where they might eventually realize the largest revenues and profits; rather, they seemed to favor places where they could serve and secure customers quickly and without spending much money or management time on localization and marketing.

The UK was apparently a top choice for these companies. It was the country most often mentioned when we asked CEOs where they got their "early" customers abroad; and it was, by far, the number one country for locating sales and marketing offices and signing up distributors. English-speaking countries with advanced economies (Australia, New Zealand, and Canada) and European countries where English is widely spoken (Scandinavia and the Netherlands) were also popular.* The lower incremental

---

* As shown in table 3.3, of the 29 companies that had sales offices abroad, 15 had one in the UK. Of the 28 companies that had distributor relationships overseas, nine had a distributor in the UK. English-speaking countries with advanced economies and the smaller West European

investment required to secure customers in English-speaking countries apparently was one attraction. For instance, when we asked a CEO why he had established a sales presence in Australia (which has a small market and is very far away) but not Europe, he said: "It's just easier. In Australia, all we had to do was hire one person and could easily do one million in sales. Europe has issues with multiple languages."

The VC-backed businesses I studied seemed to have two other preferences about where to market abroad. One was for technologically advanced economies. Apart from China (where five companies had sales offices), there were no other emerging economies where the companies had established a sales presence. Every other sales office was in an industrialized country. Apparently, the kinds of innovations developed by the companies I studied just did not have a significant market in fast-growing but still substantially backward economies. As one CEO said: "India and China are still struggling with trying to cover their basic needs. They are a long way from getting to the problems that our products solve, and I don't think they will get there for another 50 years." (An important implication of this difference in economic development—as I will discuss in book 2—is that advanced economies are more likely to benefit from innovations, regardless of where such innovations originate.)

The companies in my sample also sold more (and presumably devoted more of their marketing efforts) in Europe rather than in Asia. For example, 22 companies got 10 percent or more of their revenues from Europe, while only 13 got this proportion from Asia. "Everybody talks about the huge growth in Asia," one CEO said, "but when you look at the numbers, the more attractive market for companies like ours abroad tends to be in Europe."

On the surface, this seems surprising, given that Asian economies are regarded as more dynamic than European economies. But as the example in the box illustrates, this dynamism was often offset by their distance from home—physical, economic. and social—which increased the investment required to serve them.

---

countries, where English is widely spoken, came next: four companies reported sales and marketing offices in Australia, New Zealand, or Canada, four in a Scandinavian country, and one in the Netherlands.

Worlds Apart

The following explanation from a CEO—an immigrant as it happens—about why his company thus far made a much smaller effort to secure customers in Japan than in Europe encapsulates the sentiments of several other interviewees:

In Japan, we have to have a distribution center, and a local representative who speaks Japanese and understands Japanese business practices. With Germany, France, and Denmark, it's not necessary. We support Germany, France, and Denmark from the States.

In Europe, you are only eight hours away. If you need to have an engineer in Europe tomorrow morning, it's doable. You have four hours where people are working in their offices on both sides, so you can work through issues on the phone in real time. In Asia, your work hours do not overlap. If one of my Japanese customers has an issue, I may not have any qualified personnel in the U.S. available right away to respond to any of their questions, and you are 16 hours away on a plane. Our customers are all engaged in fairly critical research and development. So if something goes wrong, they cannot wait 36 hours for you to go and fix their problem.

Germany, France, and Denmark are also very much Western countries. They work with the same practices and philosophies as the United States. Japan is a completely different business culture. Let me give you one very dumb example. I cannot go fix up a robot in Japan without my senior contact knowing about it, even though it may not concern him, and his technical personnel may be perfectly capable of handling it. In the U.S. or in Europe, if a service guy gets a call that says a machine is broken, he goes directly to the factory, takes out his tool kit, and fixes the thing.

In Japan, you call Hiro San, you apologize profusely for the machine not working. You assure him time and time again that this is not a sign of flawed design, that you have looked into the problem, and you found that this is the first time it has happened, and that you have all the personnel and the knowledge needed to fix it. You promise that you will keep him posted and secure his blessing. Then you go and fix the machine. Then you call him back and explain to him what happened and why it won't happen again. You give him your cell phone number, you give him your home number, and you tell him that if he has any questions, he can call you at any time. Of course he would never do that. But you have to tell him that.

Imagine what would happen if I sent my service engineer from here, who is not well versed in Japanese business practices: he could offend my customers by not going about it the right way, and I could lose my business. That's why we are proceeding so slowly: Japan's a great market in the long term, but if we aren't careful we could easily blow it.

■ Special Cases: FDA-Regulated Drugs and Devices

FDA-regulated businesses provide a different angle on the variety of ways in which VC-backed businesses pursue opportunities in international markets.

One might think that markets for the developers of pharmaceutical drugs and medical devices would be especially global. As one CEO said, "The U.S. doesn't own hypertension or heart disease." Others, however, pointed out that there are in fact important differences across countries. For instance, the CEO of a company developing a new technique for performing breast cancer biopsies said that Europe would be a difficult market because "screening mammography is less aggressive and takes smaller samples in Europe. If doctors find a palpable mass, then they tend to go directly into surgery. We'd have to create the market there." Several mentioned differences in price regulations and reimbursement policies. "The U.S. is the Wild West," the CEO of a drug development company said. "I can basically charge what I can get away with. In Europe, I'm going to have to really prove that our drug has a real economic benefit to the health system at the price we want to charge." The CEO of a company developing a diagnostic technology added that "reimbursement from the government is complicated and kind of screwball in the United States, and just god-awful, terrible internationally."

Differences in infrastructure also created obstacles: "It's no problem having refrigerated drugs in the U.S.-supply chain management system," said a CEO. "In China or India, a refrigerated supply chain is a problem.

Also, in the U.S., consumers can put our drugs, which they take once a week, in their refrigerator. In China and India many consumers don't have refrigerators."

But to what degree did these differences affect concrete choices made by companies about where to market their products? As mentioned in chapter 2, FDA-regulated drug and device companies face long development cycles, and none of the companies we studied had reached the stage where they could generate significant sales either in the United States or abroad. In fact, most were "prerevenue." So the questions facing most of these CEOs pertained to what steps, if any, they should take to exploit opportunities in international markets far in the future. As we will see, developers of drugs and the developers of medical devices faced different kinds of choices from each other.

Many drug developers didn't expect—for the period in which they remained VC-financed—to directly sell the therapies they developed to doctors or patients. Rather, they hoped to advance compounds through clinical trials to the point that a large pharmaceutical company ("big pharma") would want to license the compound or acquire the development company itself. Therefore, said one CEO, "My real customer is big pharma."[12]

It so happens that because of the global consolidation of big pharma over the last 10 years, many such companies now have their headquarters in Europe. But that didn't seem to make much of a difference to the practical choices made by my interviewees. The geographic distribution of the markets big pharma was interested in did, however, seem to have a material, albeit indirect, impact in the following manner.

According to our interviewees, large pharmaceutical companies (regardless of their domicile) regarded the United States as their prime market because of its size as well as the freedom to charge what the market will bear. Nevertheless, the United States wasn't the only market of interest; even if they can't charge full price outside the United States, the low marginal costs of production (once the development costs had been incurred) encourages companies to sell their products wherever they can cover their variable costs.

This concerned our companies because, in order to interest their "customers" (to license the drugs they had developed or to make an acquisition offer) they needed to secure patents outside the United States. But because of the expense, many were hesitant to "patent everywhere"; therefore, figuring out where to file patents was a key variable in their "international marketing strategy."

Where to Patent? Cost versus Coverage

Patenting, as several drug company CEOs pointed out, was an expensive proposition. One CEO (who had previously been a lawyer) told us:

> It is relatively cheap and easy to file in the U.S. International filings often have very significant costs associated with them in translations and local counsel. I don't add up what we spend on it because I don't want to get myself sick, but I lay 10 to 1 we spent a million and a half dollars last year. If we'd filed just in the U.S., my expenses would have been a quarter what they were. It's not huge, absolute money, but for a small R&D company, it's stunning—huge, huge time and expenses. You don't want 10 percent of your R&D budget going to patents.*

Costs apparently forced many companies to consider carefully what to patent, and where. One CEO said:

> There are generally multiple phases in filing for patents. There is a relatively cheap initial phase where you get broad patent exclusion. Then, after about three and a half to five years, you go into the more expensive national phase, when you need to file in every single country. While it's cheap, you file everywhere. In the national phase, you need to make decisions about whether that is the most effective use of your money. In smaller companies, you don't file every patent in every country on the planet. You'll certainly file in key markets—the U.S., Europe, and Japan. And then you'll think about whether you file these patents in other large markets—China, Brazil, India, Australia, and Canada. Then, for places that don't care about patent law or those that don't represent significant

---

* Another CEO offered a lower estimate of the incremental cost of his company's international filings. His company spent about $45,000 to $50,000 a year, per patent and about a third of that was for European patents. But he too considered it a "significant" cost and commented that the company was "constantly looking at which patents to support."

pharmaceutical markets, you may not file at all in the national phase. It also depends on what you are doing. We're developing drugs that we expect to license to large pharmaceutical companies, so we'll file wherever we think it's going to be important for them to retain patent rights. But if a company is developing technology that will be used in drug discovery, then it might be okay to just file in places where there are drug discovery labs.

Device development companies also expected to eventually be acquired by large companies and also took seriously the question of where to file for patents. There were, however, noteworthy differences in two other respects.

First, we were told that, when it came to acquiring device manufacturers, potential acquirers usually preferred to wait until a device had proven its commercial viability and not just secured regulatory approval. This was because, among other things, the market acceptance of a device is harder to predict than that of a drug. Therefore, unlike drug companies, device developers had to choose where to market their innovations. Focusing on the United States was in many ways compelling; the market is large, and regulations and reimbursement policies do not limit prices to the same degree as in many markets abroad.[13]

But there was apparently one disadvantage to picking the United States. As we will see in the next chapter, the stringency of FDA regulations encourages many device developers to test, refine, and secure regulatory approval in Europe before entering the regulatory process in the United States. And this posed the question (discussed in the box) whether to use the regulatory approval secured in Europe to actually start marketing the device there.

Regulatory Hopscotch

A CEO, whose company had secured regulatory approval for its device in Europe first, told us:

Many companies make the mistake—and I have been guilty of this myself in previous companies—of seeing a quick path to commercialization in Europe after they have secured regulatory approval there.

They think the cash they generate in Europe will fuel their development. In fact, what happens is that marketing in Europe doesn't generate cash; it uses up cash because there are a lot of fixed start-up costs. We decided instead, after we got European approval, to use all our resources for our U.S. trial. Apart from the cash issue, when you have 40 employees, you can either use them to conduct a randomized trial or to commercialize; you can't do both things well. Now that we're finished with the U.S. trial and are in FDA limbo for a year and a half while we wait for approval, we're trying to commercialize on a very small scale internationally. It will never get us to profitability or even to break-even, but it could contribute some cash, and it gives us something to do while we wait for FDA approval."

■ Contrasts with Large and *Inc.* 500 Companies

Looking at the international initiatives of large public companies and the much smaller *Inc.* 500 companies provides a third, and much higher-level, perspective on the different approaches to serving customers abroad.

The typical, large public company derives a considerably larger share of its revenues from overseas markets than did the VC-backed companies I studied. In 2005, the median international share for the top 100 companies on the *Fortune* 500 list was slightly over 33 percent (compared to 10 percent for the VC-backed companies), and the average was 32 percent (compared to 18 percent for VC-backed businesses).[14] The share of international revenues for the subset of *Fortune* 100 companies in the sorts of "high tech" industries that VCs favor is particularly large. In 2005, the median international share for *Fortune* 100 companies in information technology industries (semiconductors, computers, software, networking equipment, and so on) such as Motorola, IBM, Dell, and Cisco was 54 percent, and for the pharmaceutical and medical device companies (such as Merck and Johnson & Johnson [J&J]) the median share was 42 percent.

Many interviewees pointed out that large companies have an obvious advantage in selling products and services overseas because they have the financial wherewithal.[15] One CEO recalled what happened to his previous company after it was acquired by J&J. He described J&J's policy of growing through acquisitions, whereby the acquired companies are left more or less intact but are provided with ample resources (and encouragement) to expand internationally. As a result, his company, which was once a purely domestic enterprise, quickly became global.

Large companies face many of the same problems in international markets as VC-backed businesses, but also with some noteworthy differences. Large companies may have already exhausted the easy growth possibilities in their domestic market (at least for a significant proportion of their revenue mix), so they have a strong incentive to enter overseas markets. Selling a new product abroad does not involve starting from scratch; the large company may not, for example, have to set up an overseas subsidiary. A broad portfolio of products and activities provides a critical mass for overseas operations attuned to local conditions; a European subsidiary can offer European-style benefits to employees without having to seek clearance from headquarters. And large companies have the funds to pay for the upfront costs of localizing a product, creating marketing materials, and so on.

The advantage of abundant resources was invoked by many interviewees: "If only we had what the large companies have" was a frequent refrain. One CEO cited the acquisition of his prior company by J&J as a "controlled, albeit 'one dog' " experiment. J&J, as is its wont, didn't break up or try to integrate the company with its other businesses, but it did make money and resources available. In quick order, the business became global.[16]

On the other side, most new or emerging businesses, including high-fliers on *Inc.* 500, derived a lower share of their revenues from overseas customers. As I wrote in the preface, in my previous study I found that only a negligible proportion of companies on *Inc.*'s 1989 list served customers outside the United States. Now, research associate Shira Cohen and I found that the proportion of companies doing business abroad on *Inc.*'s 2006 list was considerably larger than it was in 1989; even so, the *Inc.* 500 companies secured a much lower proportion of their revenues from customers outside the United States than did the VC-backed companies I studied.

What accounts for the generally lower share of international revenues of the *Inc.* companies? As it happens, they weren't significantly smaller or less mature than even the "postrevenue" VC-backed businesses. When we asked *Inc.* CEOs what discouraged them from doing business abroad, they said more or less the same kinds of things as the CEOs of VC-backed businesses. My hypothesis, based on my previous research and examination of the publicly available information (but no in-depth interviews), is that *Inc.* 500 companies develop more context-specific (or 'ground-level') know-how and products. Given the size of the U.S. market, such innovations can support quite an attractive business, but they cannot as easily sustain cross-border commerce to the same degree as the somewhat higher-level and more "generalizable" innovations undertaken by many VC-backed businesses.

■ Concluding Comments

The kinds of businesses VCs tend to invest in—such as computer hardware and software, telecommunications equipment, pharmaceuticals and biotechnology, and medical devices—have long been at the vanguard of U.S. exports. For instance, as far back as 1988, according to International Trade Administration data, 21 percent of computer equipment and 20 percent of the pharmaceuticals produced in the United States were exported. Since then, export ratios have further increased. As we have seen, *Fortune* 100 companies derive even higher shares of their revenues from overseas markets. Although the VC-backed businesses I studied served more customers overseas than the typical small business or start-up, they were laggards in comparison to other companies in their industries, and especially *Fortune* 100 companies.

In this chapter, we saw that the basic attributes of their innovative activity discourage many VC-backed businesses from an early and vigorous pursuit of overseas markets. Their objective is to refine and demonstrate the long-term potential of their technology and business model to the satisfaction of public markets or acquirers. A high proportion of VC-backed businesses develop mid-level combinations whose complex features require extensive tweaking for local conditions and a labor-intensive, time-consuming process of building relationships with customers. All this is more quickly and cheaply accomplished by focusing on the U.S. market. In contrast, high-level products often require less localization, and the sales process is not as burdensome because, to some degree, their features speak for themselves. Therefore, companies developing high-level products are more likely to pursue customers in overseas markets.

How the firms innovate also affects their interest in overseas customers. Good mid-level combinations often evolve through a dialogue with users. Engaging users in the domestic market for this purpose has natural advantages, but combinations developed for local users may not be optimal for customers abroad. Therefore, the more iterative the process, the less likely the business is to sell overseas. Moreover, unlike organizations such as IDEO, SRI International, or Battelle that only develop know-how, leaving it up to their clients to commercialize their designs and inventions, VC-backed enterprises have to secure customers and build an organization. This juggling act—the iterative, interconnected development of products, sales-and-marketing processes, staff and organizational routines—has to be performed under tight financing deadlines and constraints and often in the face of vigorous competition. Small wonder, then, that the default choice for many businesses is to focus on domestic markets (that are typically expanding rapidly and have high long-term potential) and to defer the exploitation of overseas opportunities.

Some of the factors that discourage many VC-backed businesses from an all-out pursuit of overseas customers affect, to a greater or lesser degree, many other players in the innovation game. For instance, limitations of capital and management bandwidth will more significantly affect the market choices of small, self-financed businesses, but may not be of great concern to large, publicly traded companies. We should expect, however, certain other factors to affect all businesses, regardless of their size or sources of financing. Importantly, we may surmise that most mid-level innovators prefer to rely on local customers to provide ongoing feedback in the development process. In the postdevelopment stage, we would expect all innovators to face higher localization costs for lower-level products than for higher-level products or for products used by service industries rather than manufacturing industries.

In other words, the specific case of VC-backed businesses suggests the general proposition that the world isn't flat to the same degree for all kinds of innovations. High-level innovations travel relatively easily, whereas mid- and ground-level innovations are considerably more sticky, as are innovations developed for customers in the service industry. These differences in the cross-border mobility of different kinds of innovations will play an important role in book 2 when I argue that the expansion of high-level research abroad is good for the United States.

A second general inference from the research in this chapter and critical in book 2 concerns the range of activities that are important in the innovation game: the commercial success of innovations turns not just on the attributes of the product or know-how, but on the effectiveness and efficiency of the innovator's sales and marketing process. This point is utterly obvious to those in the business world but, as we will see, is often ignored in discussions of public policies toward innovation, which tend to focus on R&D and other "technical" activities.

A final and closely related point: innovators tend to favor markets where users are willing and able to take a chance on new products. For example, markets in China and India may be large and their economies growing at more than twice the rate of Western economies, but many innovators focus on the United States and Europe, where they expect their sales and marketing efforts to yield higher returns. This receptivity of markets to innovations, I will argue, has a more profound effect on prosperity than does the place of origin of the scientific or technological breakthroughs that led to the innovation.

■ Offshoring:

The Ins and Outs

Colonial powers once went to war to secure overseas markets, but today export opportunities do not have a significant place in the popular consciousness. Rather, offshoring—which leads to the importing of goods and services—dominates the discourse on trade. Populist critics, such as Lou Dobbs, oppose offshoring of any and all jobs, while techno-nationalists don't mind "mundane" offshoring, as long as the United States can offset that exodus by creating high-paid employment in activities such as R&D. But according to some techno-nationalists,[1] that's no longer happening: witness the rush, they say, by VC-backed businesses to relocate their development activities to low-wage countries.

In fact, given their small share of overall innovative activity, offshoring by VC-backed businesses cannot significantly affect U.S. employment. But could it be the canary in the mine providing a warning of an explosive change? My findings in this chapter suggest otherwise: VC-backed businesses aren't relocating their development activities abroad on a wholesale basis, because offshoring is attractive for only some of the many activities that they—and other players in the innovation game—undertake. Offshoring does not seem well suited—either now or in the foreseeable future—for the "complete" development of many mid-level products, although it is becoming an increasingly attractive option for testing such products or for developing certain of their subcomponents.

This assessment is based not just on what the companies in my sample were currently doing, but, more importantly, on their reasons for what, where, and how they chose to offshore. The complex pluses and minuses of offshoring the CEOs described contrast sharply with the highly abstracted models of trade theorists and the contourless conceptions of flat world gurus. The assertion that modern technology makes it possible to do anything anywhere and that it is therefore only a matter of time before all innovative activity migrates to low-cost locations abroad does not even modestly approximate the reality that I observed. In fact, as we will see in this chapter, in figuring out what, where, and how to offshore, businesses weigh a wide range of idiosyncratic factors, such as the nature of the activity in question, the firm's capacity to attract and manage high-quality employees or outsourcing companies, and the legal and regulatory regimes in different countries.

These observations suggest that across-the-board offshoring of innovation is unlikely to occur anytime soon; because several factors make it difficult to offshore activities that are now best performed in the United States, no single change is likely to stimulate their exodus. These observations also provide the groundwork for an optimistic assessment that I will offer in book 2, namely that greater offshoring of well-suited activities tends to increase rather than decrease the volume and value of innovative activities performed in the United States.

In this chapter, after summarizing overall patterns in my sample, I discuss the unusual cases—companies that rely heavily on offshoring, including work on core product development—and the special reasons for their orientation overseas. The main body of this chapter discusses why the more typical companies in my sample, especially the mid-level innovators, developed their core products domestically but were using or experimenting with offshore resources for other activities, such as testing. The remaining sections—on the factors affecting choices about "how and where" to offshore, the special case of FDA-regulated businesses, and contrasts with large and *Inc.* 500 companies—bring out the diverse and complex interactions between innovation and offshoring.

■ Overall Patterns

As with the pursuit of international customers, we found a wide range in the use of offshoring among the companies we studied. For some companies, offshoring was of great consequence because their entire development staff was located abroad. In these cases only their headquarters, sales, and marketing staff were in the United States. Others had become satisfied customers (see box) of outsourcing companies (instead of having their own offshore development staff).

A Satisfied Customer

CiDRA's founder and CEO said that he previously worked with Tata Consultancy Services, the largest of the Indian outsourcing companies, and "this went extremely well." CiDRA itself signed up with Infosys, another top Indian outsourcing services provider:

> CiDRA was one of the first companies to use the offshore model for product development. The talent [Infosys] sent us was incredible. They had five to six people working with us in the U.S. and 30 in India. The arrangement gave us lower costs and faster delivery. Infosys is an amazing company. They have a software-factory approach. They give you a date and then meet it—for us, the cost of software [development] pales against the cost of being late.

The companies that relied on offshore development were outnumbered, however, by those that were considering it but had not yet tried, had tried and failed, or had decided not to try.

No Thanks

> "We will outsource someday, but not now. Right now, we need to focus, and we don't need a lot of people. All I have now are a couple of Stanford PhDs, master's from MIT, and a few industry-experienced people."

> "We gave it a try. It did not matter how good they were in India; we could not make it profitably work for us."

> "We have analyzed outsourcing every year, and every year we've concluded it doesn't make sense. Our company is very high-end and specialized. We have historically put everyone not just in the U.S., but in the same building."

> "We're *just* getting to the scale where it might make sense. We have enough of a backlog of initiatives and enough modularity to the product so that we could take pieces of a development and push it to an outsource provider."

Overall, offshoring the development of new products was apparently no more significant or widespread than initiatives to serve international customers; in fact, by some measures (see box), offshore development was less significant than overseas sales and marketing.

Overseas Sales and Marketing versus Offshore Product Development

Own overseas offices

29 companies in my sample undertook sales and marketing out of their own overseas offices.* In contrast,

Only 24 companies undertook some form of offshoring activity from their own offices. Of the 24,

- 19 used their offshore facility only for the *development* of new products rather than the manufacturing of parts or the provision of technical support to customers;
- Only 11 of those 19 companies used their offshore facility for developing a core product or a critical component, as opposed to ancillary subcomponents or software testing.

Relationships with other companies abroad

28 companies used overseas relationships for sales and marketing.*

40 companies used the relationships for offshoring. However,

- Only 29 companies used these relationships for any kind of product development activity;
- Only eight of those 29 companies used offshore relationships to develop core products or components of core products.

* As discussed in chapter 3. Note that "offshoring" does not include sales and marketing activities undertaken abroad

---

■ Unusual Cases: Heavy-Duty No-Choice Offshoring

Most of the companies in my study that reported heavy reliance on off-shoring fell into three categories. One group comprised companies whose innovations were embodied in physical goods, typically high-level components, that were produced in high volumes. For these companies, using subcontractors in Asia was, although sometimes challenging, virtually inevitable (see box).

An Unavoidable Asian Connection

"In our business, which is making novel miniaturized components," said the CEO of a semiconductor company, "we could not function without a supply chain outside the U.S. Fabrication, packaging, and testing of semiconductors all have to be in Asia."

Another consideration, according to the CEO of a battery company, was time and capital:

> You could build a fully automated, 24/7, 365-days-a-year, high-quality manufacturing facility. Because labor costs wouldn't matter, the facility could be located anywhere. But this would cost at least $100 million and take several years to bring on line. That would be very challenging to a VC-backed start-up. Instead, we decided to use the manufacturing base in China. China provides a manual or semiautomatic manufacturing alternative whose quality isn't quite as good as with the fully automated alternative. But it has been proven over the last 10 years to be adequate, the variable and startup cost is lower, and the people availability is great. So we were able to enter the market with reasonable volumes and supply batteries to tier 1 customers on a price-competitive basis.

Dealing with suppliers in China—or any remote location—this CEO noted, was problematic, but given his company's strategy, unavoidable:

> Twenty-five years ago, I was in a technology start-up company in Boston, and we were struggling with trying to coordinate our marketing and manufacturing when the president moved the manufacturing facility to Vermont. Every time we had a meeting, we had to drive two and a half

hours each way. I used to curse that guy. Now I've started this business where the manufacturing is a 24-hour flight away in China. But what is the alternative?

Our strategy was to focus on high-volume applications. If we were a niche player making specialty products in low volumes for specialized military, aerospace, or medical applications, we could have done all our manufacturing in North America. But we decided to become a tier 1 supplier globally. That meant that we had to have high-volume, high-quality, and low-cost manufacturing, otherwise even with our technology differentiation, we would not long survive.

North American companies abandoned the advanced battery market 10 or 15 years ago, and all the advanced technology work has been done in Asia. Ninety percent of the equipment manufacturers that serve this market are in Asia, 90 percent of the materials that are utilized in the industry are procured from Asian sources, and a very large part of the intellectual knowledge base resides in Asia. So if we were going to play on a global basis, we'd have to have a presence in Asia.

A second category, comprising four firms, "had to have" offshore relationships because the firms served as "value-added resellers" of offshore resources. I have already mentioned three members of this group: Vivre, a reseller of European luxury goods; Odyssey, the logistics management outsourcing company; and eSilicon, which helps small- to medium-sized developers of customized chips (including one in my sample) use fabrication, packing, and testing services offered by providers in Asia. A fourth company, Virtusa—which had programmers in 10 locations abroad—was, according to its CEO, "an IT services company, pure and simple."

Notice that for both these categories, the "unavoidable" offshoring did not involve the development of new products or technologies, although in many cases, it did utilize the specialized skills and assets of the offshore provider.

This was not the case for the third category of the "no real choice" companies—six businesses (mentioned in the last chapter) that had started overseas. Unsurprisingly, their development teams were located overseas as well.[2] Although in principle the developers could have been relocated to the United States when the headquarters and sales and marketing staff had migrated to the United States, this would have been disruptive and expensive for a small company. Similarly, the CEO of a company that had started in the UK told us that when he tried to move some engineers to the United States, they refused. So, practically speaking, these companies didn't have much of a choice.*

We could also reasonably include in (or place at the periphery of) the third "no real choice" category five companies whose offshore development facilities came through the acquisition of other companies.[3] Here too, in principle, the inherited offshore facilities could have been shut down and the staff or projects repatriated to the United States. And indeed, in one case, the CEO had tried—unsuccessfully—to do precisely that, with a facility based in Israel. But, according to that CEO, the supply of engineers at home had become very tight, and visas to relocate the Israeli staff to the United States unobtainable. So he reluctantly kept the facility open. In the other cases however, CEOs saw no reason to shut down the acquired facility. In one instance, a company in the telecommunications industry, the CEO in fact expected to *expand* the acquired facility, based in Belfast (Northern Ireland). This CEO cited the "need to augment our development quickly. British Telecom has a large operation in Belfast, and the area has a highly skilled and stable workforce. There is not the turnover that we've seen in California. And they are in the same time zone as our European customers."

■ Offshoring, by Choice

The boxed text "Reasons for Choosing Offshoring" contains the comments of CEOs whose companies were not impelled to pursue offshoring by a lack of a domestic manufacturing base or the happenstance of their origins or acquisitions. These CEOs had a range of views about the role of costs. Two said the only reason to offshore was to reduce costs, while one insisted costs played no role. A more common response was that costs did matter but less than other considerations—particularly tightness in the local labor market and the need for speedier development.

---

* It's also worth noting that it probably wasn't low wages that encouraged these companies to keep their development centers in their countries of origin, since the companies had originated in advanced economies where wages weren't much lower than in the United States.

Reasons for Choosing Offshoring

"There is a wealth of highly educated resources abroad available at a fraction of the cost here. That was a key motivator for us; and, honestly, if anyone says it's anything other than cost, they're lying."

"Our majority shareholder has investments in a number of outsourcing companies in India. They have whispered in my ear—they are marvelous, they never shout—for a long time, to look at offshoring for our back office operations and our customer support function. We found some things that might otherwise have been put on the back burner, and we are doing a science experiment on it now."

"Two years ago, we hired someone who was born in Pakistan who had extensive experience outsourcing major projects to India. At about the same time, we had a project that some of our customers wanted us to do, but we didn't want to spend too much money or resources because it wasn't critical to our business in the long term. Also, all my competitors were outsourcing—every entrepreneur I knew was doing some form of outsourcing—and my VCs told me that around 80 percent of their companies were."

"Our concern was, if our competitors outsource, would they have a competitive advantage? In today's business environment, you have to take [this] seriously. If you expect to be a world-class organization, and you are not doing some things offshore, you are probably not a world-class organization."

"We tried outsourcing and it failed. So then for about two years we didn't bother. Then I started feeling pressure. It was clear we had to dramatically increase our development capacity, and we just could not hire people at that rate here. Our motivation wasn't cost, it was capacity. We just needed more output. Customers were demanding more functionality, the rate of innovation was increasing, and we could not service that demand."

"We were 18 months into the company when it became hard to hire in the DC area. We said, 'Let's go to other places where there is an abundance of competencies in software for call processing.' We went to Dallas, where my cofounder had managed a site for Nortel, and Montreal, where I had managed a large R&D team. The folks in Montreal were more interested, and we felt we could hire people there who wanted to work for us."

"Last year, the unemployment rate here was less than 5 percent, and we had an average of 15 open positions in our operations department. I hooked up with a portfolio sister company, and they were able to fill those positions in India."

"We started using an outsourcing company in India close to a year and half ago. There are three principle value-adds that we get. The first is a skilled labor force. We're having a tough time finding the kind of software developers we need here. It's amazing to me. We have job requisitions open with high pay, and we're having a tough time filling them. Secondly, it's a flexible workforce. We can flex up, we can flex down. It's not like turning a light switch on and off, but it's less pain than doing it here. Third, and I ranked it in priority, is cost. It's not an 80 percent reduction, but it is 50 percent."

"We started doing offshore development in India from day one. We raised money at the end of 2002, which was a difficult year to raise financing, and we wanted to figure out cost-effective ways to make that money last. One of the VCs was recommending that start-ups establish offshore development. They had invested in an outsourcing company and were great believers in the capital efficiencies even a start-up can get from offshore. My cofounder had 10 years' experience in offshore development and knew how to organize teams here and offshore so that you could get 18-hour productivity days from the engineering team."

Cynics might suggest that even if cost savings were paramount, very few CEOs would admit as much. It is also common knowledge that many VCs have prodded their portfolio companies (see box) to use offshoring to "improve capital efficiency"—aka to reduce development costs.

Pushing Offshoring

VCs apparently have a different view of offshoring then they do of serving overseas customers. As we saw, except in the bubble period, VCs usually counseled a cautious approach to pursuing overseas markets, whereas they facilitated or strongly encouraged offshoring initiatives. Three CEOs, for instance, said that their VCs had connected them to "sister" portfolio companies that provided outsourcing services (from offshore locations). One CEO said he learned about the dos and don'ts of offshoring at a conference organized by the VC firm Kleiner Perkins. Others noted that VCs used offshoring as an investment criterion. "I was told by a VC," one interviewee said, "that unless you are doing offshore development, the decision to invest will be much more difficult." Another said: "Three-quarters of the VCs that I talk to will raise the issue of offshoring: 'Are you going to? Have you?' "*

* The CEO did add that "there are some VCs whose experience with offshoring has made them skeptical."

But whether or not the CEOs revealed the true reasons for offshoring, one thing seems fairly clear: few companies were developing their core products offshore. Development facilities that originated abroad with the company itself (or that were later inherited through an acquisition) accounted for all but four of the 11 offshore facilities developing core products or components of core products. Most of the offshoring that companies started after they were up and running was for activities such as data entry, customer support and testing (also known as "quality assurance," or simply QA). In the next six sections I discuss the reasons (summarized in the box below) that discouraged all but a handful of companies in my sample from offshoring their core development.

Reasons VC-Backed Businesses Did Not Offshore Core Development

- Communication problems (with customers and with other internal staff).
- Partitioning problems—development projects could not be broken up into well specified pieces.

- Managerial capacity constraints—offshore development consumes scarce top-management time.
- Not any faster—using large teams of lower-cost developers does not actually speed up product development.
- A less-than-suitable supply of the kind of experience and skills required for product development in many overseas locations.
- Discouraging testimonies (of other companies that tried to offshore their development).

Note that these reasons pertain to product development. Later in the chapter, I argue that the problems of offshoring activities such as product testing are less severe than the problems of offshoring product development.

■ Communication Problems

In the last chapter, we saw how the value of an ongoing dialogue with customers ("co-development partners") for mid-level innovators—who comprise the majority of the VC-backed businesses in my study—led those businesses to focus on the domestic market as they developed and "battle tested" their products. As the boxed text below indicates, the perceived value of having developers meet face-to-face with customers—and with the "internal" marketing and sales staff—also discouraged these companies from locating R&D personnel offshore.

Critical Conversations

One CEO said this about why he had refrained from offshoring development to India:

> I have an Indian friend who lives in Portland but has an outsourcing company in India that sells programming services to large U.S. companies. He tried to sell me on the idea they could develop our core development as well, but I ultimately decided not to do it. We are developing a product for an emerging category where interaction with customers drives innovation. All our customers are now based in the U.S., and it's

very important that the people who are developing our software are in regular communication with our customers, and not just by talking with them on the telephone. They need to be visiting the customers' physical locations, see how the software is being used by talking to end users, and use that knowledge to design new features and capabilities.

Another CEO said his company gave up on efforts to develop products offshore because "you have to tell the people offshore exactly what you want. Programmers in the U.S. can figure things out for themselves, because they're involved in developing the prototype; they go to customer meetings, and they understand the underlying business process. Offshore programmers are one step removed. So when time is critical, when you have a rapid development cycle, you don't go offshore."

Keeping the R&D staff at home also facilitated communication with sales and marketing staff who might have even closer contact with customers. One CEO said this about the value of putting the engineering staff in the same location as sales, marketing, and product managers:

If you're outsourcing a function where all the processes are very well defined work, then it could be interesting. But where you need responsiveness and constant innovation, it is better to deal with local people. It's not just the time difference and language barrier of dealing with a country like India. You also struggle with communication in the same country, even in the same location, because engineers speak a different language from salespeople and product-marketing people. Even with everybody being American, if you have a development center somewhere in the middle of the U.S. and the rest of the team in California, you really run into problems. It's not a question of cost. You want people right next to you, not in India or Alabama.

One of the very few companies that apparently did not have a problem with a remote development facility was Cybrel, which, from the start, located its R&D in Israel. But as its CEO explained, this may have owed to its staffing policies and the nature of its product:

Coordinating the R&D staff—which is still all based in Israel—with sales, business development, marketing, and professional services—which are based both in Israel and the U.S.—has never been an issue. We don't have a head of Israel and head of America. We have functional departments, and except for R&D, the departments have people in both countries. It's never been a major problem probably because we have moved a lot of people from Israel to the U.S. They bring along all the knowledge and contacts, and then you have just a two-minute call or IM [AOL's Instant Messenger] and you get things done. It also helps that many of the Americans we have hired are fluent Hebrew speakers; we have just three flat-out Americans. And the nature of our projects doesn't require you to be on-site with customers much. You need a kick-off, a couple of follow-up meetings, and three or four face-to-face meetings in a six-month period.

The other company, which started and continued with Israel-based R&D, faced, its CEO (a "flat-out American" by all appearances) said, more significant coordination problems:

The R&D organization had a product focus, not a customer focus. They developed what they thought was needed and wouldn't accept feedback the U.S. team got from customers. There was a large emotional and political gap and a lot of conflict between the two teams. When I arrived, Israel was not even on the same email system as the U.S. Then after we merged the email systems, I once sent an email to all employees announcing a successful sale we had made. I got an email back from the manager in Israel saying: "Don't tell my people anything—they will just ask for raises."

■ Partitioning Problems

Communication of development staff with customers and other members of the organization does not, however, require that all the developers be in the same location. Why not have some developers in the United States close to customers, and sales and marketing staff and other developers in low-cost, offshore locations? One of our interviewees said that his company couldn't do so because they were developing hardware—physical objects that could only be worked on in one place. Software development, he volunteered, might be different. And indeed, the development of open source software, such as Linux and Firefox, suggests that software can be developed by a widely dispersed team—a model that had in fact been used by two companies in my sample (see box).

Virtually Offshore

One company, using dispersed programmers offshore, was developing an interactive web access tool—a "social browser" whose features included tools for blogging and sharing photographs and bookmarks. Its founder previously headed marketing and business affairs for the Mozilla Foundation and coordinated marketing activities for Firefox, its open-source browser. The social browser incorporated some of Mozilla's technology as well as its open-source approach—including working with widely dispersed programmers. Virtually all "telecommuted" from their homes over the Internet—18 from locations within the United States and seven from abroad.

The other company was developing software for law enforcement. Its founder and CEO, who was a proponent both of what is known as "extreme programming" and of remote development, explained:

> In extreme programming, new features do not go through the old school marketing requirements and external-specifications and internal-specifications routines. We create "use cases" that come directly from end users. We then code a module or unit to "solve" that case. We then implement that module as part of the whole project. Developers are closely involved with users in that process to make sure that what they code is what the case represents, or to figure out if the user interface is easy to use.
>
> In the past, the user and the programmer would have to sit next to each other. But now, with IM and "live person" technologies, that's no longer necessary. We take an extreme view of extreme programming and of remote development. I don't care if I have a developer in the Midwest or in New York or in Florida. They just basically get onto our virtual development site and are constantly in contact through IM or other communication mechanisms. We use Skype regularly for conferencing. These electronic mechanisms bring you close to the customer without your needing to be there.
>
> It happens that all six of our programmers are in Vancouver, Canada. We have a small office outside Simon Fraser University, where our base technology was originally developed. Four out of the six people typically

work out of their homes. The office is primarily used when our VP of engineering and products and our CTO, who live in California, travel up there. They go over when we need large changes in the architecture and technology and discuss next versions. We have toyed with using people overseas in Japan and Indonesia, but that hasn't happened yet.

The CEOs of other companies were aware of the open-source model, but they believed that their particular software (including an application with a Linux "base"!) could not readily be developed by dispersed teams. In part, the difficulty they faced derived from the complexity of the mid-level combinations that the majority of them were developing. To recall an earlier analogy, they were developing Swiss Army knives, not meat cleavers. The blade, the bottle opener, screw driver, and wire stripper had to fit together; they could not be developed independently. In principle, a master designer could specify rules and interfaces so the designer of the bottle opener did not have to interact with the designer of the wire stripper—and indeed the modern style does favor the development of software modules. But in practice, most of the CEOs we interviewed said this was extremely hard to do.

This was the case because, for one thing, the complexity of most mid-level combinations—and sometimes their interconnections with lower-level products*—is considerably greater than that of a Swiss Army knife. Making sure numerous components of a product integrate properly is easier when the developers of the individual pieces work side by side. But open-source applications also have many components that have to work together. Linux and Firefox, for instance, have been developed—and continue to evolve—through the efforts of individuals whose interactions were usually limited to periodic exchanges over the Internet. Why shouldn't this also be a good model for the innovations of VC-backed businesses?

The answer lies in the more rapid, iterative, interactive process used to develop mid-level combinations. Developers of open-source software such as Linux and Firefox work off a stable "kernel" or "code base," and many of

---

* For instance, one CEO said that "our software has to communicate with highly complex applications that our customers have installed, and there are no open APIs [application programming interfaces] to write codes to."

the features they add are not new in that these features have already been implemented in earlier operating systems or browsers. And, because Linux and Firefox are not commercial products, the problem of determining the optimal bundle comprising the most attractive trade-off of cost and features doesn't arise. Nor does speed particularly matter—the developers can set their own pace, usually while holding down other day jobs. For mid-level innovations, in contrast, companies add or remove features as they sequentially discover what "combinations" their customers value. Sometimes they also have to stabilize and extend the base technology. Moreover, competitive races and financial pressures demand rapid progress.

The dynamics of this process made it difficult for our subjects to partition development into tasks or subprojects that could be undertaken by remote individuals or teams. As the boxed text below indicates, most interviewees believed sending detailed market or product-requirement documents to an offshore organization was neither feasible nor desirable. Rather, it was important for the entire team to be located in one place so that members could jointly make changes to the individual products as quickly as possible.

Coordination in Real Time

The fluidity and pace of his company's development process, according to one CEO, made it difficult to make plans for who would do what and when:

> We often don't know what we want until the day before we do it. There are many spontaneous "Ahas!" in our technical development. We are building and piecing together things that have never been put together before. There are a lot of moving parts, and there isn't a clear roadmap.
>
> We've found that no matter how much you try to define something up front, it's going to be somewhat wrong. Moreover, in the very early stages, when you are building a team, you don't have a product manager, let alone a product management process.
>
> A formal development process is fine if you are a mature company with long development cycles. It's much tougher when you have only one product that you need to get out quickly. Our iteration cycle has to be very, very fast. If we get a request from a customer, we have to respond very quickly.

Another CEO recalled his experience in a prior company:

> Our head of engineering was an Indian national who wanted to move back. He was thrilled when I told him he could be our Indian development officer. The setup seemed perfect. The guy knew the code inside out, he wanted to be there, and he hired a dozen people. But guess what—within six months it made no difference if we knew him or not. It all comes down to how well you can prepare the work. If your specifications are absolute by the time they leave your desk in North America, maybe it will work when it's being developed in India, but I don't know anybody who's that perfect, so it ends up requiring midnight conversations with the team in India. And the number of change-order requests makes the price of whatever you are trying to develop about the same as having it done here.

The need to make frequent, coordinated changes also required, according to one CEO (who as it happened, *had* instituted a sophisticated product-management process), co-location of the entire development team:

> We have communication challenges, just with one product manager and 15 developers. There are times when you have to grab everyone, put them in the room and sit at a whiteboard. I have personally pulled developers for three or four sessions in the last four weeks, where we made major breakthroughs in terms of what we were trying to do. You couldn't do this on email. You couldn't do this even one-on-one. . . . If a customer has an issue or we have an idea for a new feature, because we have all our developers in one place, we can turn around our software in a big hurry. I know it's conceptually possible in offshoring mode, but in practice, I think you lose the speed and that spark of innovation you have with a lot of really top-quality developers in one room.

> One CEO did take the opposite view: "If you have a seasoned engineering chief who has defined your procedures, selected good development tools, and instituted a well-documented quality assurance process, and you have excellent market-requirement documents and product-requirement documents, there is no reason, even if you are a small company, you can't hand over pieces of your development to an outsourcing organization. An awful lot of start-ups lack that discipline."

This was the only interviewee who made such a claim, however. The view of all the others may be encapsulated in the words of a CEO who told us, "We need tremendous interaction between the teams working on the different components of our product; what we do is not something that can be reduced to a tight requirement and thrown over the ocean for a development team to work off."

■ Managerial Capacity Constraints

The experience of the companies in my study that developed their products abroad suggests that the coordination problems of offshore development go beyond those of simply exchanging information—they include basic organizational and cultural conflicts. And while these problems may not be intractable, the CEOs of companies that did have offshore development centers told us that solving them consumed precious management time and effort. This consumption of "managerial bandwidth" creates yet another deterrent to the offshoring of development (see box).

A Time Sink

"During the bubble years, we had money and wanted to expand our development team," said one CEO. "My cofounder's brother had an outsourcing company in India, and he dedicated about 50 people to us. It took three years to get it to work—it was a constant battle. One big problem was the reporting structure. We had one guy responsible for the overall management in India and one for the U.S. We also had directors who were responsible for different functions. The developers were confused about who they were supposed to report to. To make things worse, there were conflicts between the functional directors, and the organizational structure was constantly evolving. Managing people itself is different in different places. India is very process focused. The U.S. is more fluid. We needed systems in place to make sure that the definition of the work was very clear."

> The previously mentioned (non-Israeli) CEO described a considerable effort required to coordinate the company's developers in Israel with its U.S.-based marketing staff:
>
> > We had to change the manager of the development unit. The new guy is an Israeli who has worked in the U.S. We changed the development process; the team had been very bootstrapped in their approach. They had taught themselves how to develop the system by reading a book. We installed a video-conferencing system and hired a U.S.-Israeli consultant for cultural training. We made lots of trips back and forth. We got a few customers in Israel so the development team would have direct contact with some real users and not just a marketing team in the U.S. A lot of the tension has gone, and the relationships are more positive. But it took a lot of effort.

■ Not Any Faster

The manufacturing companies discussed at the start of this chapter also had to use up their scarce managerial capacity to work with their suppliers in Asia, but low manufacturing costs—and access to resources that weren't available in the United States—provided adequate recompense. In software, however, one of the main benefits that offshoring is supposed to offer—faster development through larger, cheaper teams—was, according to my interviewees, hard to realize.

Some fans of offshore development claim that it can help businesses accelerate innovation, because the same amount of capital can pay for larger development teams. Skeptics, however, question whether team size actually increases development speed. Nine people may dig a ditch in a third the time it takes three people, but as Frederick Brooks wrote in his celebrated book *The Mythical Man-Month: Essays on Software Engineering*: "When a task cannot be partitioned because of sequential constraints, the application of more effort has no effect on the schedule. The bearing of a child takes nine months, no matter how many women are assigned." In fact, "Brooks's Law" suggests that increasing the size of software teams may delay development, a significant reason being that large teams entail high communication overheads.* Many believers in "small is beautiful" go one step further to argue that it is better to pay a premium for a few star programmers than to employ many average programmers.

A strategy of using small teams of highly talented programmers does not go well with offshoring, however. Star programmers may not be abundant in low-wage locations—among other things, someone's willingness to write programs for a low wage (instead of emigrating to the United States or securing a high-paid job in management) invites questions about that individual's "star-worthiness." And even if low-cost stars can be found abroad, small team sizes can make the economics unattractive: the total savings on the wage bill of a small team may not offset the irreducible out-of-pocket costs and management capacity used to set up and operate an offshore facility. The skeptical view was dominant among the CEOs we interviewed. Most believed that the optimal size of their teams was too small to justify offshore development (see box).

A Few Good Developers

Most CEOs believed that product development in their companies was best undertaken by small teams of great programmers.

> "We are an ASP [applications service provider]. Our process is highly integrated and dependent on doing everything quickly—we are making changes to the software all the time. It's not like enterprise software with big but infrequent releases. We need tight-knit, small teams."

> "The concept of software factories with the people as cost is wrong. I'm willing to pay four times the money for somebody who is really good, because they are going to generate one hundred times the value. Running around to get programmers for twenty thousand dollars a year makes no sense when what's between their ears is incredibly important."

> "The right engineers who are really top-notch will vastly outperform large numbers of novice engineers."

---

* The number of "communication channels" increases as the square of the number of people: with twice as many people you have four times the number of possible interactions.

"What we needed when we were starting was very deep but not very broad. We didn't need a lot of people to do standard stuff. We needed a few people to do very specialized stuff."

With small teams, the benefits of lower wages couldn't justify the over-head of offshoring.

"We have 16 developers. Even if we offshore the whole thing, the economics don't work out."

"If you have development teams of a thousand or fifteen hundred people, and you have specific applications that can be compartmentalized, then offshoring is fine. We have a development team of fewer than 30. I cannot be convinced that the economics outweigh the value of having all of them in the same building."

"We did some calculations and found we would need at least 15 overseas developers to support the additional management overhead, and we're not there."

"Multisite management is hard and expensive. I used to work at Nortel [a large telecommunications company]. We had 100 people in Bangalore, with three senior level people in North America managing them, traveling back and forth, training them and making sure they were on track."

"I used to work for a multinational. The company was so big that we could put our own bricks and mortar in India, hire our own people, and not just bring people from North America. We had 300 there and, guess what? When you do it that way, it does work out very nicely. The results were the exact opposite in one venture-backed company I worked with."

Once companies had established a small development team in the United States, they found it more economical to expand capacity than to open a new center abroad. One reason was fixed set-up costs: Just as it is cheaper to add sales staff at home than in a new sales office abroad (because no additional set-up or fixed costs have to be incurred), it is also cheaper to add another developer to an existing development team. The fixed costs of coordinating the work of developers abroad and at home tends to be larger than the fixed costs of managing a sales office abroad. Therefore, where businesses might think of opening a one- or two-person sales outpost abroad, they have to decide whether to add many developers or none. At home, developers can be added one at a time. The quirks and nuances of complex projects and technologies and the norms and interactions of social groups also favor adding staff in existing locations (see box).

Expanding at Home

"We have a product that has evolved over five years," one CEO told us. "The team that built it here knows its inner workings, and it's not productive to train *anyone* on it, let alone an offshore team."

Another CEO of a software company explained why it had decided against starting a development center in China (in spite of the fact that one of its cofounders was an immigrant from China).

> Our software has these enormously complex econometric models. When we hire scientists here, it takes them months to understand what's going on inside the models. How do you hand that knowledge to a team in Shanghai? It's not a language issue—it's the fact that they're at the end of a telephone line and not sitting next to you for months.
>
> The easiest time to [offshore] is when the company is being formed or is changing to a different technology path. Neither is true for us. Our technology was created here in the U.S. We have programmers who have been here from the start, are very loyal to the company, and are a close-knit group. Their knowledge base is pretty deep, and a lot of it is almost tribal knowledge that they carry around in their heads. I wouldn't say that all our design documents and structural documents and coding reports are always detailed or up to date. At this time, it would be hard to do any offshore development. If we got to an inflection point where we were starting something totally new, we'd think about it.

■ A Less Than Suitable Supply

Besides the problem of finding "star-quality" talent, many CEOs said they were discouraged from undertaking development in low-cost locations abroad because of the scarcity of individuals with the specific skills and experience needed for the projects.

In a few cases, the CEOs indicated that developers were unavailable because of a lack of consumers for—and therefore knowledge about—their product (see box).

Unfamiliar Terrains

The developer of an advertising network for online games wanted programmers who were avid "gamers" and would have knowledge of the "context" for the code. But low-cost locations such as India had few online gamers, because few young people could afford the necessary high-speed Internet connections.

Another CEO said that his company developed the core part of its application in the United States because the necessary actuarial expertise in health insurance was unavailable abroad. "You might find actuaries in the property and casualty field—for instance, Lloyds of London has many. But you don't have many medical insurers outside the U.S.—it's all government-run, so you just don't have people with the skill sets to underwrite and predict medical costs."

The distinctive features of the U.S. health-care system upset the efforts of a health-care services provider to develop products in India: "We were approached by an outsourcing company from India, said the CEO. "They were part of a group that runs a chain of hospitals. They came over to us and said, 'We know hospital stuff. We'd like to be in the U.S., and you might want do something in India. We'd be a great partner for you.' They have very aggressive people, and so we tried it. It was a dismal failure. At some point, people have got to understand how the U.S. system works and develop a bunch of company-specific and context-specific knowledge. Even though this group knew something about health care, because they didn't have the specific knowledge we needed, their productivity was unbelievably low."

We did encounter an example of a company that had opened an offshore development center—as it happens in a relatively high-cost location—because of the local availability of specialized expertise. A document-processing company had set up a software development center in Antwerp, Belgium, in large part because a department in the university was a leading center for research in computational linguistics and graduated many well-trained students in the field. But this was an exceptional case. As I will discuss in the next chapter (and in book 2), many countries may train the kind of talent that U.S.-based innovators want, but a good bit of that talent emigrates to the United States. The U.S. labor market therefore provides a "one-stop shop" for a wide range of expertise, making it convenient for innovators who need a wide variety to locate their development in the United States.

Some CEOs cited problems with the "style" of overseas developers. One said that the software developed by his company's center in Switzerland "was less clever, more process oriented. Its look and feel wasn't particularly innovative—it just seemed like old things being reused." Another said his company had stopped using programmers in Russia because of "language issues and a different focus on quality—the code wasn't as buttoned up as we expect it to be here." A third said his previous business used an outsourcing company in India, but found that "the style of coding was different, and it was difficult for us to look at the comments in the code and understand."

A more common issue with offshoring development, especially in India, was simply that the demand for capable programmers was greater than the supply. "Software engineers cost a third as much, but their quality isn't great so they are only half as productive. It's not worth the hassle," said one CEO, who happened to be of British-Pakistani heritage (his company had hired a small engineering team in India because "one of our key guys wanted to move back to India"). Moreover, as the example in the boxed text illustrates, competition from large multinational companies makes it difficult for VC-backed businesses to attract and retain the more capable programmers (at wage rates that make it worthwhile to incur the additional costs and hassles of managing offshore development teams).

A Difficult Homecoming

"We launched our company after the Internet bubble had burst, and VCs were very tight with their money," one CEO told us.

My cofounder and I are from India, so we tried to figure out how to leverage our dollars there. We couldn't, for a number of reasons.
  One was domain expertise. We are a systems management company, and we wanted very sophisticated, OS [operating system]-level developers;

those people are tough to find, although there was a plethora of people with backgrounds at the applications level. We also wanted people with 10 to 15 years' of hard-core development experience, but most of the people had fewer than four years. In India, people always seem to aspire to get into management. If they haven't become managers after four years, I think their parents would start wondering, "Is this person an idiot or what?" But once people get into management, they lose technical skills. In the U.S., there are people who thrive on working on complex development architectures—it's what they want to do as a career.

We also found that professionals wanted to work for large U.S. brands. It was important for them to tell their parents or their spouse: "I'm work-ing for GE or Microsoft or HP or IBM." If they worked for a start-up with no name recognition, it would be viewed as "OK—you weren't good enough for IBM so you had to settle for the second or third choice." Also, good people want to see some long-term commitment by the U.S. company—they don't want to work for a fly-by-night operation. They want to see a team of 20-plus in place. That's easy for Microsoft, HP, Sun, and IBM, but hard for us. And we're not going to have the big glass tower building and our name on the outside of the building in lights.

So we had a tough time really attracting the best of the best in India. And if we could find someone good, they'd leave—the turnover was tremendous.

We retrenched, but not fully at first. We still had a core group of people here in the U.S., so we tried co-development; we naively thought we could do round-the-clock work on the same projects between the U.S. and India. But time and distance made interactivity between the U.S. and India very problematic. Then we gave them a project that they could manage on their own. That didn't work either: as a start-up, you don't spend much time dotting every *i* and crossing every *t* when you're doing technical specifications. You use gut instinct, you build something, you test it in the market, come back and iterate. But you can't say to a team in India: "Here's kind of what I want . . . can you go take a crack at it?" You end up with huge disconnect in terms of what they thought they were sup-posed to do versus what your expectations were, because they don't have a really good appreciation of your core business. Ultimately, we just gave up.

Why should the experiences of my interviewees be so contrary to the popular notion of an India containing a limitless supply of hard-working, highly talented software engineers? Could this be the result of a fluke or bias in my sample? Or is the popular notion mistaken?

Certainly there is no shortage of individuals in India willing to offer their services as software programmers. The outsourcing company Infosys famously receives more than a million applicants for entry-level jobs each year. But the number of capable programmers is much smaller: if the supply really were abundant, companies such as Infosys, which in 2006 hired fewer than three out every 100 applicants, would not have to raise wages by 10 to 20 percent a year, nor would it face high (10 to 20 percent per year) employee turnover. Moreover, research that Professor Kumar of the Indian Institute of Management in Bangalore and I undertook in 2004 suggests that VC-backed businesses have an especially hard time competing for good or even acceptable talent against large multinational companies or companies such as Infosys, whose principal clientele comprises large companies in the United States and Europe.

■ Discouraging Testimonies

The last in my list of reasons very few companies developed their core products offshore pertained to what their CEOs were told by their peers and employees.

As mentioned in the earlier sections of this chapter, some companies retrenched from offshore development after having failed to make it work. Their comments also indicate that some CEOs learned from their previous experiences that, although offshoring might work for a large company's well-defined projects, it was not well suited for the more fluid development projects undertaken by VC-backed businesses. Therefore, they never tried offshore development. Other CEOs did not have direct experience with offshore development, but were discouraged from giving it a try by the cautionary tales of others.

What Others Said

CEOs who had no direct personal experience were dissuaded from offshoring by hearsay.

"I know a lot of people who have chosen to outsource and who have not gotten the price benefits they thought they would get because they end up spending a lot more time. The price per hour of work is a lot less. But if it takes three times as many hours to get the job done, you haven't saved any money."

"What I'm finding from other colleagues is that it takes a tremendous amount of effort to get it up and running properly and to really get any time-to-market advantage and to really get any reasonable cost saving. Yes, there are cost savings, but they're not to the magnitude that people have been talking about. The only reason to move overseas is if you really need lots and lots of people to do something who can be quickly trained up on what you need them to do, and then they're going to be very productive and deliver to you in time-to-market advantage for lower cost. I mean significantly lower cost, because other than that, it's not worth it."

"Once or twice per year, a subcommittee of my board comes together to look at our technical direction. One of our board members is the former CTO of Texas Instruments, the other is CTO of United Healthcare. These are executives with vast experience in development around the globe. One of the questions we asked them last week was: 'We have an application that we want to enhance and probably rewrite; is it time now to think about possibly doing this offshore?' They said, 'Absolutely not. You're just too small to manage it remotely.'"

Two CEOs said they encountered resistance to offshoring from their U.S. development staff. "To some degree, they were concerned about their own jobs," said one CEO. "They also seemed to be genuinely concerned about the quality of the work being done in India."

The other CEO recalled, "Early in 2003, we decided to move a component of R&D to a low-cost region to be competitive over the long term. Nevertheless, employees in the U.S., especially in the Indian community, got very upset. They thought we were going to shut down the U.S. operation and didn't believe us when we said we wouldn't. We stopped and waited until 2004. The business grew substantially in the meantime, and when one of us restarted the process, young star employees came forward and asked to head up the Indian organization. Now we have a sizable staff in both countries."

Similarly, the CEO of a company whose development was based in Israel said the Israeli programmers weren't "culturally and technically" comfortable moving software development out of Israel and vetoed starting a development center in India. Ultimately, by way of a "compromise," the company decided to move QA to India because the function could be "easily expanded and contracted."

There are natural variations from company to company in the degree to which the six reasons discussed above discourage them from offshoring their product development. Problems of communication will not trouble developers of high-level products (who do not need much ongoing interaction with customers) to the same degree as they will developers of lower-level products. Similarly, large companies will not be as deterred from offshoring development by the additional managerial capacity this requires. My broader point is that there are *many* reasons that encourage innovators to keep their core development activities—especially of mid-level products—at home, close to their target customers. The fact that some companies are undertaking high-level research abroad does not contradict my point: Microsoft may undertake advanced research in artificial intelligence and speech recognition in China, but the bulk of the development of its bread-and-butter mid- and ground-level products (such as its operating systems and Office suite) is done in Seattle.

The kind of problems that discourage the offshoring of mid-level product development can be further highlighted by examining the kinds of activities that the companies in my sample *did* choose to offshore.

■ Candidates for Offshoring

The challenges VC-backed businesses encounter or anticipate with the offshore development of new products are apparently less severe in the case of what one CEO called "operational things like data entry and call centers." These tasks are more easily routinized and partitioned. The activity doesn't change very much over time; therefore, there is plenty of time to amortize the set-up costs. The skills required typically aren't deep or specialized—data entry, for instance, doesn't require much more than the ability to read and type. And the basic technology and managerial know-how necessary for remote data entry and telephonic sales and support were refined well before the current offshoring boom got under way. For instance, banks long ago figured out how to operate remote call centers and data-processing operations in places such as Iowa and Utah rather than at their branches and headquarters. It was therefore not a huge leap—at least technically and managerially—to replicate these activities in places such as India, once the necessary communications infrastructure was established. In contrast, the remote development of software is of fairly recent vintage. Through about the 1990s, most Indian outsourcing companies sent programmers from India to work on their customers' premises in the United States. Indeed, as of this writing, the premier Indian outsourcing companies such as Infosys still get nearly half their revenues from so-called on-site projects.

But VC-backed businesses, which are usually still developing their products and building a customer base, do not generate a high volume of transactions or phone traffic. Therefore, even if the obstacles to offshoring data entry and call centers are modest and the economics attractive, only a small number of companies in my sample used offshoring for these activities—most simply had no need.

Offshoring manufacturing is also relatively easy—the partitioning and decoupling of the stages of production is commonplace, and the path to contract manufacturers in the Far East is even better trodden than the path to Indian outsourcing companies. In fact, as mentioned, for the producers of many physical goods, having Asian suppliers is considered unavoidable—"fabless" semiconductor companies have to deal with remote silicon foundries. Therefore, in my sample, all but two companies that *could* use offshore manufacturing did so. But as with data entry and call centers, the total numbers were relatively small—because of the preponderance in my sample of companies that developed software and other services, few had their own manufacturing facilities offshore or used third-party suppliers (see box).

Uses of Offshoring (excludes core product development)*

Ongoing services (including software maintenance, technical support, and transaction processing)
- Four outsourced.
- Six companies had established their own centers, but these all provided high-end services to local customers, such as design support, and were located in the UK, continental Europe, and Japan.

Manufacturing
- 10 used contract manufacturers.
- Two had their own manufacturing facilities.

Testing or quality assurance (QA)
- 14 outsourced.
- One had its own facility.

Development of ancillary products
- 10 outsourced.
- Six had their own facilities.

* See tables 4.1 and 4.2 for details. Numbers exclude FDA-regulated companies.

Offshore testing or QA was a little more prevalent than offshore manufacturing, and considerably more common than the offshoring of services such as data entry and call centers. Although offshore testing was not a "must" like offshore manufacturing, more companies needed to test than manufacture. Like data entry, testing did not pose as many obstacles as complete product development, in part because there was not a lot of ambiguity about the tasks and expected outcomes, and it was easier to direct offshore staff. Problems of labor availability and turnover were also less acute—unlike programmers, testing staff didn't have to be "outstanding," replacing someone who left in the middle of a project was less disruptive, and, the benefits of speeding up development were easier to realize.

Testing Advantages

As one CEO pointed out, testers in the United States and offshore could more easily collaborate on the same project than programmers writing code, and this could in fact speed up product development:

> Our QA runs around the clock with a combination of U.S. and Indian resources. People here in the U.S. do testing during the day and then hand it off to people in India who do further testing overnight. The next morning, when we come in here, we see the results of those tests. It is hard to imagine John in the U.S. writing code for 10 hours and handing it over to Ashok in India to write additional code. Ashok would have to spend a lot of time trying to figure out what John wrote, and vice versa.*

> Another CEO said locating his company's QA team abroad was "very important because it allowed 24-hour development. Our programmers here sent off the code they wrote during the day to China, and when they arrived the next morning, they had a long list of bugs they needed to fix."

* A few CEOs did say they used offshore and U.S. programmers to work on the same project. In all such cases the actual number of offshore programmers was small (four or fewer), and most CEOs thought it was a bad idea.

Some companies who kept their "main" development activity at home were developing components of their core or "ancillary" products offshore. These efforts were invariably cautious; and this caution (as the text box below indicates) was self-reinforcing, making it difficult for the companies to make the transition to riskier development projects.

Playing It Safe

As the comments below indicate, some CEOs said their primary reason for offshoring the development of ancillary products was to reduce costs. But they chose projects to minimize the risks of offshoring, thus limiting the magnitude of the cost savings:

> "We build and test components of the product in India that are relatively easily partitionable or [do] jobs that no one really wants to do in the U.S.

For instance, [our offshore programmers] are developing a couple of adapters that allow our products to integrate with other products. We created a general template, and they just need to populate the template with the specifics of the product that we are integrating into. They also do the "build engineering"—the not-exactly-sexy, 'Does it work?' stuff."

"We are pushing a project out that really isn't core to our application. It's adding some things to a dashboard and reporting and some other stuff that is more commoditized than the IP that we rely on. I just don't see us ever outsourcing that."

"We started with data entry and that turned out to be a homerun. We now do 70 percent of data entry overseas and 30 percent in the U.S. Offshoring software development, however, has been slow. You put your maintenance projects or stable stuff overseas. Our approach is to get it started in the U.S., and when it's scaled up, we send it offshore."

"We send off stuff we don't like to do—for instance, getting rid of the duplicate data items—noncore stuff that's on the periphery but needs to get done and can be clearly identified."

"Very early on, we created a company in India. We hired engineers who supplemented our own technical staff for the more mundane technical activities, such as the lower-level identification of certain pieces of information that needed to be gleaned. We found an abundance of people who could perform tasks that did not require deep technical expertise, and they were much less expensive."

In one telling instance, a company brought a development project back to the United States after it unexpectedly turned out to be of strategic importance: "A few customers asked us to implement a new standard. Our developers didn't think the standard was going anywhere, so we decided to do the implementation in India. But the standard became a big deal, and important customers started asking for it. Fortunately, our chief architect had been attending all the meetings of the body that was setting the standards, and he had the expertise from a design and conceptual point of view, and we were able to rebuild the hands-on development expertise in our U.S. staff as well."

An unusual perspective on what to offshore was provided by a CEO who said:

Companies produce proprietary software by assembling components. The highly proprietary, highly competitive pieces are developed at home. When teams of people from engineering, product management and marketing develop something with a lot of messing and tweaking of prototypes—that's difficult to offshore. The rest, if it can be properly documented, you can send offshore. But onshore and offshore aren't the only two options: there is also now open source. We are evolving to a three-tiered process of developing software: utilizing open source where we can and offshoring the things that have less competitive advantages, and then developing the pieces that are of high competitive advantage at home.*

This cautious approach to offshoring may be self-reinforcing. Companies often selected mundane, low-risk projects for offshoring in part because they expected a high turnover of staff; this was arguably a self-fulfilling prophecy.

As one CEO said: "There is a high turnover rate in India. That's because so much of the work done there is considered lower level. If you want to attract and retain people, you have to give them something they can sink their teeth into—something they will be proud to own."

At another point during the interview, however, the same CEO said his company's developers in India were working on "projects that do not require a deep knowledge of the core technology, are generally add-ons—like more ways for customers to slice and dice data—and don't require senior architects and aren't threatening to the team in the U.S." Similarly, to the degree that U.S. companies use their Indian employees (or outsourcing companies) mainly to execute routine projects, the offshoring capability in India for such projects improves, thus attracting even more routine work.

* Although no other CEO raised this as a third option, many did mention, in different contexts, that they were using open-source components in their products. And to the degree that open-source components are developed by individuals dispersed all over the world, we can regard their use as a disguised form of the offshoring of noncore development.

An appreciation of the great variety that I have illustrated in the preceding sections—in the roles of innovators, the cross-border activities that fall under the rubric of globalization, and the interactions of innovative roles and cross-border activities—is, in my view, essential to a proper understanding of how the modern economy is evolving. In this chapter we have already seen how differences in the "level" of innovations and the kinds of innovative activities (e.g., core development vs. testing) lead to differences in the potential for offshoring. In the remaining sections of this chapter I examine other dimensions of variety in offshoring. I start with the practical question faced by any innovator who wants to offshore an activity—whether to "outsource" the activity or use an in-house facility abroad.

■ Outsourced versus In-house Offshoring

In some cases, differences in whether companies outsource or develop in-house facilities arise because of classic "make or buy" considerations that have little to do with offshoring issues. For instance, low internal demand compared to the minimum efficient scale explains why (as we saw in the box "Uses of Offshoring") most of the companies in my sample outsourced their offshore manufacturing. All the semiconductor companies were "fabless" simply because their requirements were too small to support an in-house facility; whether to use a domestic or overseas foundry was a separate issue. Conversely, software companies were more likely to use in-house facilities for product development than for testing; this was because the problems of writing and monitoring contracts with outside vendors—another standard "make or buy" issue unrelated to offshoring—were more severe for product development (see box).

Contracting Problems

CEOs of software companies were reluctant to outsource product development for reasons that happened to concern foreign outsourcing companies but would also apply to a U.S.-based outsourcing company: "A lot of outsourcing shops in India are set up for big companies," said one CEO. "They want all the data before they bid on contracts. Now when a Citibank says, 'I want to move my trading system from Cobol to C++ on a Sun server,' it's easy for the outsourcing company to reply, 'That will cost three million dollars;

we'll have it in seven months.' But that's the wrong model for a start-up. You don't know much—you can come up with a specific plan that isn't real world, but then if your product requirement changes, engineers in India will say,'Oh my god, you can't do this. It's going to cost you another 500 K.' Or, you can do time and materials [contracts], but then you can't control your costs."

Another CEO described his reservations about using an Israeli outsourcing team:"The challenge for a small company is that you get 10 engineers in Israel who build something great for you in six months. But then suppose a year later, we have to modify. Now what? Am I going to generate a long-term contract for these guys? Probably not. I need people on staff even if this means we're paying substantially higher prices." The same concerns would presumably arise if the outsourcing company were located in California rather than Israel.

Whether to offshore did, however, interact with the question of whether to outsource in some other ways: outsourcing mitigated some of the problems of offshoring and amplified others. How much it mitigated or amplified those problems varied across companies and activities. For many VC-backed businesses, in-house or outsourced was such a Hobson's choice that they did not offshore at all.

An important plus for outsourcing, according to our interviewees, was the lower fixed cost and time required to set up and manage an offshore operation. A minus was that most creative talent abroad often preferred to work for in-house development centers rather than for outsourcing companies.

Outsourced Offshoring: A Basic Trade-off

As mentioned earlier, many VC-backed businesses used offshoring for "non-critical" activities often performed by a small number of employees. Several CEOs said they were encouraged to outsource such activities rather than start and manage an in-house offshore operation because they could not justify the considerable time, money, and effort required for the latter. "Even though it's more expensive per person," one CEO said, "we just didn't have the infrastructure to rent buildings, hire people, pay taxes, and do whatever the hell else we'd have to do to have a facility in India. We couldn't build the infrastructure, because we didn't have the economy of scale—we started with five people. And we didn't have anyone on staff that had experience in managing a remote facility."

On the other side, some CEOs said outsourcing increased the problems of getting and retaining good staff abroad: "Outsourcing companies can't attract the top talent in engineering, because they can't offer the stock options and challenge [that product development companies can offer]. Many of these outsourcing companies therefore hire a lot of junior-level people who are not as productive. I once ran development for a large company. We used an outsourcing company in Romania. They were using right-out-of-school grads. I shut it down and moved everything to our own center in Israel."

Although outsourcing could reduce the time and expense of starting an offshore operation (because some of the organizational and physical infrastructure was already in place), it does not eliminate the set-up costs. As one CEO, said: "The process was quite grueling and very expensive. I hired a consultant who had set up relationships there before. We set up strict criteria for evaluations. We set up pilot projects. Getting it to work has been more difficult than we would have expected."

Similarly, the costs and problem of coordinating activities across time zones, languages, and national cultures did not go away, and may well have increased because communications also had to cross organizational boundaries. Several CEOs said, for example, that it was important to have a liaison from the outsourcing company in the United States to "translate" their exchanges with the remote staff. "There is a Srinivas in India and a Srinivas here in the U.S.," said one CEO. "They've worked together over many years. Our core technical team tells the Srinivas here what they want built in India—generally stuff like management consoles and reports that the core team doesn't want to do. The Srinivas here then deals with the Srinivas there who manages the six developers who do the coding."

The problem of getting good staff "through" outsourcing companies was particularly acute for VC-backed businesses. As described in the box below, the projects of VC-backed businesses don't interest the large outsourcing companies, so VC-backed businesses are drawn to the smaller outsourcing companies with whom their interests are better aligned.

Attention Deficits

The offshoring projects of VC-backed businesses often don't interest the large offshoring companies. This is because offshoring companies share in, if not fully pay for, start-up and ongoing management costs (such as the salaries of the Srinivases mentioned in the previous box). Outsourcing companies therefore prefer clients with large, long-term projects in which they can more easily recover their set-up and management costs. But the kinds of projects that VC-backed businesses usually try to offshore are often small and peripheral. And VC-backed businesses have short time horizons. "My goal is to accelerate development," one CEO said. "When outsourcing companies talk to me about two-year development time frames, I start to sweat. I can't think that far ahead. I'm thinking about six-month development—that's the longest possible lead time."

Unsurprisingly, many CEOs we interviewed found that the premier outsourcing companies did not devote much attention to small customers or did not allocate their most talented staff to their projects. "I worked with [a large Indian outsourcing company] in my last start-up," said one CEO. "They tried to give us the attention we needed, but I don't think we got as much attention as we would've gotten from a smaller company. We then tried working with three different outsourcing firms. But because we couldn't commit to the number of heads and the duration of contracts that a larger firm could commit to, we couldn't get the best talent in the talent pool of the outsourcing company. We always got the B or C teams—the A team would work on large projects for some *Fortune* 500 company."

There were exceptions. One CEO said

We are a customer of Wipro—probably the smallest customer they have. We've never had more than six or seven people assigned to us when they typically have six hundred. They aggressively sought our business because they said they wanted to break into the advertising industry. My friends who had worked with them said we'd be crazy to try to work with them because they're such a slow, bureaucratic, careful organization. But we thought, if we put in the right processes, we could use them for things like very routine data infrastructure management projects. It's been going on for about a year. They have one employee here, and their engineers there are queuing up trying to work on our projects because normally they only get to work for large banking clients.*

In the normal course, however, the smaller companies that couldn't easily compete for *Fortune* 500 clients were more interested in serving VC-backed start-ups—and vice versa. As one CEO said: "We're looking for outsourcing companies that have between five hundred to a thousand developers. That is still relatively large, but a contract to engage between 20 or 30 of their developers is more meaningful to them than it is to somebody that has 6,000 developers." Another said, "We gravitated to a small company where we could have reasonable mindshare."

* The CEO later emailed: "Thought you might like to know. . . . the Wipro experiment ultimately failed . . . they tried hard, but just were not equipped to deal with nimble projects. Nice folks, but we terminated the relationship after a year or so." So the "exception" also migrated into the "rule."

The mutuality of interest doesn't solve the basic problem described in the boxed text—the mismatch between high set-up and overhead costs of offshoring on the one hand and small, short projects on the other. One way or the other, market forces tend to drive scarce resources—good engineers—into their highest-valued use, namely large, long-term projects. In India, the brightest and the best (who don't find their way to Silicon Valley!) have their wages bid up by the large outsourcing companies. The smaller outsourcing companies that undertake the less economically attractive projects can't afford to pay for high-quality talent and have to make do with the candidates who have been rejected by the larger companies. So as the interviews that Professor Kumar and I did in Bangalore suggest, smaller outsourcing companies keep losing their good employees.* Or as the example below illustrates, if small firms do become successful, they too lose interest in the kinds of projects VC-backed businesses have to offer.

* One owner of a small outsourcing company told us that his firm had become "a training and recruiting ground for the large companies." His engineers were "all looking for their 'Infosys card.' And when they get the call, how can I tell them not to go?"

Growing Apart

A CEO of a software company, and native of India, recalled the history of a troubled outsourcing relationship:

> Our outsourcing partner was originally started—by someone I had known for a long time—to develop a new product company, but then ran out of funds. We provided a financial lifeline. Our understanding was that if this project worked out, we would acquire them. We carved out something that one customer wanted but wasn't strategic for us. We provided most of the architecture and design.
>
> But apparently our interests weren't aligned. When they found a more attractive opportunity, they lost interest in our project. Also, there didn't seem to be the notion of consequences for them—they were far away and they didn't have a name to lose in the U.S. We disengaged as fast as possible, and decided not to think of doing any more development abroad until we had enough heft so that vendors in India would pay attention to us.

To get around the lack of interest of large outsourcing companies, one CEO said his company joined up with three other companies of similar size to set up a dedicated outsourcing operation. The circumstances were unusual: all four companies were "telecom-centric," but they weren't competitors. All of them were outsourcing data-entry tasks that made it easy (compared to developing software) to redeploy staff across projects. It also helped that, together, the four companies could support about a thousand "seats."

The hybrid, "build-operate-transfer" model (as illustrated by the Stoneriver[4] India example in the box below) was a somewhat more common approach to solving the attention problem of outsourcing while also reducing the cost and hassle of setting up an in-house facility abroad.

Stoneriver India: The Build-Operate-Transfer Model

In the build-operate-transfer model, a local entrepreneur takes responsibility for setting up an offshore center and hires its staff ("builds"), manages the operation for some transitional period, and ultimately transfers ownership of the operation (or sometimes just its staff) to a U.S. company. Throughout the period, as the CEO of Stoneriver, a company that was trying out this model, explained, the offshore staff is treated "as if they were employees of the U.S. company":

> They call themselves Stoneriver India. They spend 100 percent of their time working for us. They have company email addresses. As soon as they're hired, they come here for a five-week stint. They work in our offices, they go back, and then they come back here seven or eight months later. We even paid them a bonus this year, when my VP of engineering went over there last week. That's very unique. We weren't obligated by contract, but we're trying to engender some goodwill and some loyalty, and boy, that, that went over really well.

It was not clear to me, however, that the hybrid model could fully square the circle, as it were, in attracting and keeping top talent. The CEO quoted above, for instance, also revealed that the number of employees would expand and contract according to the timing of a big product release. A flexible workforce has many benefits, but presumably employee retention is not high on that list.

However, although the build-operate-transfer model has been well tested with large companies, its durability with VC-backed businesses is thus far unproven: in most of the companies we interviewed, the experiment had been in operation for about a year; only one company actually reached the "transfer" state. If it can be made to work, it would further broaden the menu of offshoring options available to VC-backed businesses and other small innovators.

■ Where to Offshore?

The choice of overseas location represents yet another source of offshoring variety. This choice, my interviews suggest, is neither random nor driven just by differences in wage rates. Rather, the companies in my sample seemed to pick different locations for different kinds of offshoring. Offshore manufacturing (which was predominantly outsourced) was concentrated in the

Far East, although NAFTA countries (Canada and Mexico) and Western Europe were also represented, as table 4.1 indicates.

The development of "complete core products" offshore took place exclusively in advanced economies. This was predominantly undertaken in in-house facilities; in turn, most such in-house facilities either started offshore along with the companies themselves or were secured through acquisitions. Some other kinds of in-house offshoring operations were also primarily located in advanced economies: all the in-house service operations abroad were in Europe or Japan, mainly because they were intended to provide local support to customers; as we saw in the last chapter, most companies targeted customers in advanced rather than emerging economies.

The case of India deserves special mention. India, it will come as no surprise, was a favored location for outsourced development activities such as testing and outsourced services, such as data entry. But the same popularity appeared to stimulate a search for alternative locations—often in countries with somewhat higher per capita incomes than India.

Offshoring in India: A Self-Limiting Snowball?

India was the offshoring location of choice for many activities: 16 of the 28 companies in my sample that had outsourced development (to any degree) did so only in India, nine did not outsource in India, and three had outsourcing relationships in India and some other country. Of the 14 companies that outsourced testing, nine did so in India.

The popularity of offshoring to India reflects historical factors. India was, early on, a low-cost source of programming labor, initially on-site and then increasingly offshore. Over time, the number of Indian vendors and their total capacity for providing outsourcing services grew substantially, as did the number of individuals in the United States who used their services. Therefore, when we asked CEOs why they chose an Indian outsourcing company, a typical answer was: "Our VP of engineering and I had both worked with people in India, and we knew how outsourcers in India work." Some CEOs also mentioned receiving emails and phone calls from Indian outsourcing companies "practically every day."

Although to some degree, the success of Indian outsourcing fed on itself—awareness and knowledge begat more awareness and knowledge—

there was also a self-limiting element. Shortages of qualified labor in India, and the emergence of competitors in other countries attracted to the business by the success of Indian outsourcing companies, encouraged some CEOs to look elsewhere:

> We are looking at the Ukraine and the ex-Soviet republics. One of our partners has an operation in Ukraine, and perhaps we will get some people through them. India strikes us as overplayed. The price advantage is not as great as it once was, and there is an employee loyalty issue. We hear it's a very cash-driven market now. A software developer is paid about $30,000 to $36,000 a year. Guys will go across the street for another thousand a year.

> Two CEOs said they set up outsourcing relationships in China because of personal relationships there. One went to Canada because of "the difficulty of managing outsourcing in India—the savings of going to India weren't worth it, and we wanted something safe and predictable."

■ Legal Issues

Concerns about the loss of intellectual property—sometimes based as much on idiosyncratic beliefs as on objectively verifiable facts—affected choices made by different companies in my sample about what to offshore. As mentioned in chapter 2, much of the value of mid-level combinations cannot be secured by patents. Often the only legal protection is through copyright laws, trade secrets, or confidentiality agreements with employees. Several CEOs lacked confidence about such legal protections outside the United States and were hesitant to let the crucial features of their IP "out of the building," let alone out of the country (see box).

Keeping IP Secure

The difficulty of protecting mid-level IP made many CEOs in my study extremely cautious about what they would offshore.

"I don't feel comfortable with our IP traveling all over the world to [places with] different cultures and morals and laws. What is actual law in one place and what is actual law in another place is different. And then there is standard practice—doing business in Italy is an entirely different scenario, whether it's against the law or not."

"It's a very long, drawn-out process abroad for defending your IP and prosecuting those who took it. Things that we just take for granted in the U.S. are vulnerabilities abroad."

"We are very careful about not handing enough of the product over to be an IP risk. We have different levels of trust with our outsourcing partners, and we don't trust *anyone* to handle the complete IP."

"We do QA and documentation outside the U.S., but we are not ready to move our engineering. We might save 60 percent on our development costs, but it's not worth the risk—one weird guy could destroy the business."

"The core team here in the U.S. has all of the IP. The things that are given to the offshore team are things that, even if they stole it, we would be happy."

The decision of *where* to offshore was also influenced by CEOs' beliefs about the safety of their intellectual property.

How Beliefs about IP Theft Affected Location Choices

A CEO whose company was about to start outsourcing from India said, "I believe that the Indian outsourcers have a process and a method for maintaining confidentiality. I don't have any clue about whether folks in other countries have that process or not." Another said he ruled out Korea because in his previous venture, he had found that, although the quality of programmers was high, "there is no way you can protect your code there."

Concerns about China were widespread. One CEO said his company was tempted to switch to a competitor of his existing Taiwanese supplier who offered much lower costs, but because the competitor was based in China, "we decided not to risk it—if our IP gets out, that's the end of the company." Another CEO told us "My CTO is from China and is paranoid about outsourcing from there." A third opined: "In China, they steal. I don't know how else to say it. They steal. They'll take a picture of Snoopy and sell it as Shoopy. What I'm told by people from China is that when somebody sees a CD, their immediate thought is, 'How many copies can I make from this and how many can I sell?' Maybe it's not really rampant, but I didn't have the time to get the data to find that out. We went with India with people who we could trust."

Concerns about IP also influenced how companies "organized" their offshoring, sometimes taking elaborate measures to minimize the chances of its theft (see box).

Divide and Defend

A CEO whose company's manufacturing operations and suppliers were located in the Far East described protecting intellectual property by distributing production among five facilities in three countries:

There are four steps to making our product. The first is making the ingredients. We developed one of the ingredients—a unique powder. We make that ourselves, because it is the most unique differentiator for our technology, in China. We've split the process across two factories that are an hour apart by car so that employees don't have access to the entire process: a lot of the trade secret theft in China occurs by the employees at the engineering level who start their own business.

Sometimes the management team sets up a satellite operation to produce the same material for the China market without the parent company being aware of it. So the Chinese nationals we hired to run the plant are Western-educated, with families and legal-resident status in the U.S. If they got caught stealing, they'd be subject to North American courts. They are also highly compensated with stock and have a significant upside in the success of the company. In step 2 of the process, the powder is blended with other ingredients to make a liquid coat that is applied to a metal foil. A subcontractor does this for us in Korea, which is a little bit more secure than doing it in China. The coated materials get

> shipped back into China, where a subcontractor assembles the "guts" of the product in a remote location. There is some IP in the mechanical aspects of assembly, and we do run some risk that people could knock off some of the things we've done. The output is then sent to a subcontractor in Taiwan for the final step.

The influence of IP concerns on offshoring choices stands out when contrasted with the negligible role of worries about enforcing contracts: Many CEOs said they had little confidence in their ability to enforce their contractual rights abroad, but this seemed to have little effect in their companies' offshoring arrangements.* This doesn't mean that the companies in my sample did not negotiate contracts with their overseas suppliers—for reasons discussed in the box "A Ritual, but with Some Substance," many

---

A Ritual, but with Some Substance

Why did CEOs bother to negotiate contracts in places where there was little hope of enforcing them? One CEO simply said, "Because it makes you feel good." Another said his VCs insisted he negotiate the right to hire [the employees of the Indian outsourcing company who worked on his company's projects], even though such contracts would be unenforceable—anywhere in the world.* A third said that even though his Chinese suppliers had a "relaxed attitude" toward contractual obligations, they believed that "Western companies are contract-oriented, and they would think us not very serious if we didn't negotiate a 30-page contract and just shook hands instead."

* "Imagine what would happen in the U.S." the CEO said, "if we fire an employee with whom we have a noncompete agreement and then he goes and works for a competitor. There is no way we could enforce the noncompete. The only way to keep your employees is to have them want to work for you."

---

* One reason for this might be that, even in the United States, flagrant breaches of contract or take-it-or-leave-it demands for renegotiation are a normal fact of entrepreneurial life. Aggrieved parties may, in principle, be able to secure relief through a lawsuit, but this is not availed of in practice. As Howard Stevenson and I once found, the strong do in fact routinely get away with a lot: the usual response is to accommodate or terminate the relationship when firms or individuals who have more market power or financial clout breach their contracts or promises. Retaliation or suing to recover damages is an unusual last resort (Bhidé and Stevenson 1990).

But there were more substantive reasons for negotiating contracts as well. Some CEOs regarded contracts with suppliers as useful "mutual planning devices." For instance, a fabless semiconductor company entered into a contract with a foundry to reserve line capacity for $10 million worth of goods a year. The supplier couldn't really "hold the customer's feet to the fire" on this, but it was useful in establishing production schedules. Contracts similarly helped clarify mutual expectations (for instance, about service levels) and provided a modicum of protection against personnel changes. If, for instance, individuals moved on, their successors would have some knowledge of what their predecessors had agreed to.

Negotiations could also help build relationships, because, as a CEO said, "when you spend day after day going over a contract, you get to know each other better."[5] And given the significant potential for miscommunication and misunderstandings in cross-country commerce, it is reasonable to have serious negotiations over contracts, regardless of the legal problems of enforcement.

did make a serious effort. My point is simply that concerns about the lack of enforceability had very little practical effect on offshoring choices, especially in comparison to concerns about IP protection.

■ Special Cases: Drugs and Devices

In chapter 2, I showed how FDA regulations give a special character to how VC-backed businesses developing drugs and medical devices innovate. We saw, for instance, that FDA regulations encourage drug developers to focus on "single molecules" (instead of "combinations") and allow for little to no trial and error in the development process. With medical devices, combinations are unavoidable as is some trial and error; but FDA rules do limit their extent. In the section below I examine the distinctive choices that FDA-regulated companies make about offshoring.

To start with drugs, recall that many companies that we studied "in-licensed" promising compounds that they expected to "develop" (or what in other industries would be called "test") through a few phases of clinical trials. The companies were also highly virtual, and expected to retain a contract research organization (CRO) to manage the clinical trials. What were the benefits and problems of offshoring these activities, and how do these considerations compare to the offshore testing of software?

The principal benefits of testing abroad were easier enrollment of patients and easier approval by local regulatory authorities (see box).

Why Test Abroad?

CEOs who were doing testing abroad cited easier access to the patients and samples they needed. "We were driven to doing trials [for a treatment of Crohn's disease] in 10 countries in Europe because there is less competition for patients and more availability," said one CEO.

"There are places in Eastern Europe with a high incidence of Crohn's disease. And we were looking for patients who had not been previously treated by a certain compound that is used broadly and aggressively in the U.S., but not in Europe."

Two other CEOs noted:

"We want to enroll as many patients as quickly as we can, because the clock is ticking, and doctors in Eastern Europe are incented to enroll much more quickly. In Prague, for instance, cardiologists make the equivalent of 500 U.S. dollars in a month, but if they participate in our clinical trial they can make a year's salary. So they enroll patients quickly."

"We're developing a noninvasive test [for endometriosis]. All we need is a little vial of blood [taken before the patient gets the traditional laparoscopic test]. We found clinical researchers in Europe who were collecting samples for other trials, and they were able to share those samples with us. When we approached physicians in the U.S. who were doing studies on endometriosis, more often than not, the physician said:'I'm sorry, I cannot share my samples because your use is different from what's allowed in my IRB [institutional review board] approval.'"

CEOs also cited the value of overseas tests for getting regulatory approval to market their drug abroad. Said one CEO:"We're very active, even today, in engaging overseas opinion leaders in what we're doing and getting their thoughts on our next set of trials. If we want approval to sell in Japan, we will have to run Japanese trials."

In contrast to companies that were testing software, drug company CEOs did not expect to realize costs savings. One said that in principle the cost of human trials in India was much lower than in the United States, but the low-quality of CROs was a serious deterrent (see box).

Not Quite a Bargain

One CEO (an immigrant from India) told us:

> You can do clinical trials in India for a third or a fourth of what it would cost in Europe or the United States. There are a significant number of patients available and their compliance rate is very high, because they don't get the drug for free.
>
> The problem is, you don't want to use a bad CRO, even if they're willing to work for you pro bono. CROs can screw up by giving the wrong drug, giving the wrong dose, or forgetting. These kinds of screw-ups are critical. The regulations describe pretty much to a T what needs to be done, and any deviation from that is not acceptable. And you have to report everything to the FDA. If an accident takes place in India, you have to report that to the FDA.
>
> All this requires a great deal of technical skill: these people have PhDs, and like MDs, they have to go through board certification and take continuing education credits to keep their board certifications active. But you still don't have CROs in India and other developing countries who have this kind of ability yet.

Only one CEO said his company tried to take advantage of lower labor costs abroad:

> We started off as a virtual company, but then because we advanced our pipeline faster than we had expected, we needed a lab to do a lot more preclinical work. We selected Shanghai because of cost savings. I wouldn't say that we do cutting-edge work in China. The people all happen to have PhDs, but the work could be done by well-trained technicians. We do a lot of high-throughput work. We run an awful lot of in vitro and in vivo studies—for about 10 percent of the cost in the U.S.

> The CEO also added that coordination with the China lab had not been a problem:
>
> > It's not like IT. Say you develop a new concept for an IT product. By the time you have the development set up in China, the concept can already be outdated. In biotech, you have a longer cycle and there are components of preclinical development that are pretty standard and straightforward. We can define the work very specifically with very clear outputs. Also, we only have 14 people, which we could grow to 30—it's not like we have a hundred people.

The companies in my sample also had a problem with using CROs that could do international trials in advanced countries: CEOs thought that top-tier CROs that had the capacity to manage trials in many different countries were insufficiently attentive or too expensive for a small business (see box).

Misaligned Interests, Redux

"Paraxel and all the big global CROs will tell you that they care just as much about small companies as they care about Merck," said one CEO, "but in my experience, that's not true. The small, domestic CROs care about your business a lot more than do big, huge companies for whom you're a fraction of their business."

Another CEO said his company worked with "the smaller unglobal CROs that are well less than half the cost of the Paraxels. We are basically shopping the Kmarts and the difference in cost is incredible."

But why not use one or several small overseas CROs? Because, as our interviewers said, this option would require more management capacity than could be justified by a small, early-stage trial. As the CEO of a company developing a drug to treat diabetes said: "We evaluated a site in Lima, Peru, of all places. South America has a very high incidence of diabetes and is an excellent place to do diabetes research. But we concluded that given the small size of our initial studies and given that we are dinky players with limited management ability, we had to stay in the U.S."

In contrast to developers of drugs, developers of medical devices more routinely undertook (or seriously considered undertaking) human trials abroad before doing so in the United States. CEOs said this was because the more flexible regulatory regimes outside the United States facilitated the trial and error necessary to develop the devices (see box).

Arbitraging the Rules

"There is a lot of iterative invention in devices, and we need clinical input," said a CEO.

> But doing that in the U.S. is very time consuming. We first did animal studies and bench work here, and the first patient we treated was in Melbourne, Australia. We then aggressively recruited sites outside the U.S., based on their regulatory hurdles or lack thereof. So, after Australia, we ended up in Hong Kong, Brazil, and then throughout Europe. Fortunately for us, whatever you figure out through iteration abroad will also work at home, but it still would have been much more convenient for us if we could have done the trials here first. This is our primary market—there are 3 million people in America who could use our device. In fact, there are a lot of reasons we would have focused on the U.S., were it not for that regulatory component."

"We're not in humans yet; we do expect that when we go into humans, our first human implants will be outside of the U.S.," said another CEO. "That's largely because the regulatory bodies of other countries are less risk averse. Obviously, no matter what the regulatory body is, you would never put anything in a person that you thought would harm them. But going overseas allows you to quickly determine safety and efficacy. Then you and your investors have the confidence to proceed. It also allows you to refine your product before you take on the system in the U.S. It's very difficult and very expensive to make changes once you start the U.S. process, so you really want to make sure the bugs are worked out somewhere else first."

"Do not attribute this to me, but I think the FDA prefers testing to be done outside the United States first," were the candid words of a third CEO.

"That's not a politically correct statement, but that's my impression. It's easier to do testing in other parts of the world because the regulatory hurdles are lower."

Interestingly, even those companies that performed human trials abroad kept all their employees in the United States. Their reasons for doing so were similar to those of many non-FDA-regulated VC-backed businesses discussed earlier in this chapter: the greater availability of applicable skills in the United States; the desire to have all functions in one facility to enable fast and clear communication; the precedence of "getting it right" over cost savings; and the desire to move through iterations quickly.

■ Contrasts with Large and *Inc.* 500 Companies

In our analysis of international market opportunities, we saw that *Fortune* 100 companies, especially in the IT and pharmaceutical sectors, derived a significantly higher share of their revenues from overseas customers than did the VC-backed businesses in our sample. We do not have a similar measure to compare offshoring; by all accounts, however, large companies have been ahead in taking advantage of this as well. For instance, nearly every IT company in the *Fortune* 100 has a large and visible presence in Bangalore, whereas only a handful of the VC- backed businesses had operations in Bangalore. And Bangalore is, of course, just one offshore location where large companies secure goods and services and undertake R&D.

Many of the advantages that large companies enjoy in serving international markets also give them a boost in their offshoring activity. These include ample financial resources, managerial capacity, and extensive experience doing business abroad. Multinationals such as General Electric, Citibank, and American Express, whose in-house and outsourced activities catalyzed Indian offshoring, had been operating subsidiaries and joint ventures in India for many decades before.

The activities of large companies are also more suited for offshoring. As I have mentioned, a large proportion comprises stable, high-throughput operations (such as sending and collecting on bills) that can be codified and consolidated in one low-cost offshore location. Moreover, even though the proportion of routine activities in *Fortune* 100 type companies may far exceed the proportion of innovative activities, the overall size of the companies is enormous; therefore, their portfolio of innovative projects is also substantial. At least some projects from this portfolio are attractive candidates for offshoring because the requirements can be specified up-front, and they do not require ongoing interactions with customers. Examples include the development of utilities for existing products (such as printer drivers), the porting of software from one hardware platform to another, and upgrades of in-house mainframe systems. Large corporations also undertake some basic—or what I have called "high level"—research (that VC-backed businesses typically use but do not produce). Such research, too, can be done without interactions with customers—and at a more measured pace than commercial development.

Their size and scope also provide large companies with advantages in recruiting local staff and in building relationships with high-quality outsourcing companies. Locals are attracted by the job security and career opportunities available in the international networks of large employers. High-quality outsourcing companies find the economics of working on the kinds of projects that large companies outsource more attractive: routine activities such as billing are more "contractible" (because, for instance, the requirements can be more easily satisfied), and the fixed costs of marketing and maintenance of the relationship can be amortized over multimillion-dollar, multiyear deals.* As I have mentioned, these advantages of large companies allow them to pay wages that make them the employer of first resort for the best local talent, leaving VC-backed companies with slimmer pickings.

This does not mean that large companies can, or do, or will in the future, offshore all their development activities. Their large innovation portfolios also contain even more activities that, for reasons discussed in this chapter, are best performed in the United States. Microsoft's and Google's China research centers get a lot of attention, but it's not without reason that these companies have been trying to recruit as many engineers as they can for their development activities in Washington and California.

---

* The effort required to start and manage software development projects is certainly more substantial, but the magnitude of the projects justifies the considerable time put into the planning and oversight. Moreover, in large complex projects, the additional effort required for remote development represents a small proportion of the total effort that would normally be put into an equivalent on-site project.

■ Concluding Comments

The tight capital constraints that may encourage VC-backed companies to focus on the domestic market create pressures in the opposite direction when it comes to offshoring. Many VCs apparently strongly encourage their businesses to take advantage of low development costs overseas. Nevertheless, the use of offshoring by the companies we studied was limited. Very few businesses chose to develop their core products in low-cost locations, because of the value of proximity and the difficulties of partitioning. Companies that focused on relationships with domestic customers from whom they could get rapid feedback also wanted their developers close to these customers and to the other members of their staff. Several other factors also reinforced their reluctance to offshore. These included the scarcity of managerial capacity, the relatively small savings that could be realized from offshoring small teams, the limited supply of capable staff available in offshore locations, the competition from large companies for this staff, the difficulty of communicating across time zones and cultures, and the fear of losing their intellectual property.

These difficulties, however, appear to have been less of an impediment in the offshoring of activities such as testing and the development of ancillary products. Here, proximity to customers was not critical, and the tasks could more easily be partitioned and sent to a remote location. These activities also did not require as much managerial attention or the brightest and the best talent, and did not put the company's intellectual property at risk.

If we look beyond the problems facing VC-backed businesses alone, the analysis in this chapter suggests that there are many impediments to offshoring, especially of activities undertaken by mid-level players, whether or not they are financed by VCs. Therefore, there is no single floodgate that, if opened, would unleash a torrential outflow of mid-level innovative activities. Moreover, all the impediments to offshoring mid-level innovation are unlikely to decline quickly or even at the same rate. For instance, as people and firms in additional low-cost locations abroad learn how to provide offshore services—and knowledge of their capabilities disseminates—the scarcity of labor there may decline. It is not at all clear, however, when—if at all—technology will allow full and deep communication (not just the exchange of words and numbers) across time zones, cultures, and working styles, and will provide a good substitute for real meetings around a whiteboard or a visit to a customer's site.

The offshoring of manufacturing and of routine services, it is also worth noting, wasn't restrained by many of the problems that hold back the offshoring of mid-level innovation today. In the former case, specifications of what is to be manufactured can be precisely communicated. There is little need for ongoing dialogue—the buyer can simply examine the goods produced and see if they meet the agreed-on specifications. This is rarely the case with mid-level development projects because the outputs are difficult to specify in advance. Therefore, ongoing engagement with remote staff is important.

Second, in many manufacturing activities (and in some routine services), the notion of an unbounded supply of unused labor (that can do the job) is closer to reality than is the case with innovative activities, where the supply is limited. Moreover, when a source arises (as might happen when garment exporters set up shop in Bangladesh), it is not difficult for customers to test whether that source is up to the mark. Therefore, additional supply can enter the market with relative ease.

Third, in manufacturing (although usually not in services), an intermittent supply can be satisfactory. For instance, the requirements of a small semiconductor company can be satisfied by a day's output from a production line in a foundry once every quarter. With software development, however, a continuous supply, preferably of the same programmers, is necessary. Labor requirements cannot be satisfied by securing the services of the entire staff of an outsourcing company for a day or two.

That said, innovators are increasingly undertaking some activities, such as testing offshore, the significance of which should not be underplayed. Testing may not be glamorous, but it does account for about half the time and expense of developing software, according to many experts.

There are two ways to interpret the significance of such offshoring. One is that it takes jobs from U.S. workers who would otherwise have been employed in such activities (or, at the least, it reduces their wages). The other interpretation is that the total output of innovations increases because the costs of undertaking projects decline. In this view, offshoring frees some of the labor that might have been absorbed in routine activity; as a result, employment in higher-paid and more interesting development work also increases. Even more importantly, from the point of view of the overall good, the innovations enhance the productivity of their users. In book 2, I will make the case for this second, more optimistic interpretation.

5

■ Founders and Staff:

Global at Home

The participation of immigrant scientists and engineers in the U.S. high-tech industry is in some ways a forerunner of and a substitute for the offshoring of innovative activities. Programmers from abroad working "on-site" (on client premises) in the United States paved the way for offshoring; and now that offshoring is well established, overseas programmers can work for U.S.-based companies as immigrants or as offshore workers. Like offshoring, immigration evokes anxiety and debate. Critics argue that immigration depresses the wages of scientists and engineers in the United States. This discourages the native-born from pursuing careers in these fields and makes the United States dangerously dependent on the labor of foreigners, presumably because they might decamp if they find better opportunities in their native lands. Advocates, however, claim that highly qualified and enterprising immigrants help create many new jobs in the United States by starting new businesses or helping established high-tech firms that can compete in international markets.

My detailed examination of the role of immigrants in VC-backed businesses suggests a complex reality. On the one side my analysis raises questions about the extent to which the exceptional enterprise or brilliance of immigrant scientists and engineers actually matters to many players in the innovation game. On the other side, I highlight the valuable role that immigrants who may not be wizards play in providing the run-of-the-mill technical labor required for mid-level innovation.

Many venture capital–backed businesses I studied were more globalized through the role that immigrants played in starting and staffing them than through their sales to overseas customers or through offshoring. The median proportion of international to overall revenues was 10 percent, whereas for the economy as a whole, exports account for 11.5 percent of GDP. In contrast, the median percentage of immigrants to total (U.S.-based) employees in my sample was 20 percent, while the foreign-born percentage of the U.S. civilian labor force in 2005 was only 15 percent.[1]

The proportions did vary considerably in my sample, however. In about 15 percent of the businesses, immigrants accounted for only 5 percent or fewer of all employees—versus the above-mentioned 15 percent of the civilian labor force. I also found considerable variation by level and by function: for instance, the proportion of immigrants was higher among the CEOs and other top executives than in the rank and file. In addition, the technical staff had more immigrants than the sales and marketing staff.

In this chapter, I analyze why the participation of immigrants in the businesses that I studied was higher than in the workforce as a whole, as well as why it varied by firm, by level, and by function. I connect the role that VC-backed businesses play in the innovation game to their demand for labor and to their natural sources of supply. My explanations cast doubt on a romantic view, not limited to a few successful immigrants, that immigrants have an exceptional taste and talent for entrepreneurial activity and that high-tech ventures offer them an escape from the glass ceilings of large established firms.

I also examine whether immigrants, especially in the top ranks, increase the propensity of VC-backed businesses to pursue overseas and offshoring opportunities. And as in previous chapters, I discuss how things are different in large corporations and in *Inc.* 500 companies.

Some demographic profiling is in order: In the box below, I review some data about the distribution of immigrants in my sample.

The Distribution of Immigrants (in my sample)

CEOs provided us with information about national origins and functional roles at three levels of their companies—the founders, the top executives (the CEOs themselves, and their direct reports), and their overall (U.S.-based) workforce.

The data on top executives is the most accurate because, in many cases, we were able to use profiles posted on company websites as a starting point. With the founding teams and the overall workforce, we have the CEOs'"best guesses."

Founding teams

According to CEOs' estimates (see table 5.1), 60 percent of the founding teams included immigrants. The table also shows that (as we might expect) larger teams were more likely to have an immigrant founder. Of the 290 founders overall, 104 (36 percent) were immigrants.

CEOs provided more complete (and presumably more accurate) information on founders who remained actively involved in the companies at the time we did our interviews. About 44 percent of the companies had an active founder who was an immigrant,[2] and 39 percent of active founders were immigrants. Also noteworthy is the distribution by role (table 5.2): nearly three-quarters of the founders—immigrants or U.S. natives—who were still active in their companies served as CEOs (37 percent) or in a development function, for example, as chief technology officer (CTO) or chief scientist (36 percent).[3] Immigrants were especially well represented in the latter roles—48 percent of founders active in a development function were immigrants. Similarly, the proportion of founders in development roles was higher among immigrants (44 percent) than in the U.S.-born (31 percent). Conversely, 40 percent of U.S.-born founders served as CEOs (compared to 33 percent of immigrant founders), and about 29 percent performed some other role (compared to 23 percent of immigrants).

Top executives

Our data covers 581 CEOs and their direct reports. Less than a quarter were also founders; more than three-quarters had been hired to replace founders or to fill new positions. About 27 percent of the 581 executives were immigrants, which is lower than their 36 percent share of founders. In other words, immigrants were more likely to found companies than to be hired as executives in already formed companies.

As before, we see (table 5.3) a strong "match" of immigrants with development roles: 39 percent of development executives were immigrants (and 36 percent of immigrant executives were in development roles.) The percentage of immigrants was a bit lower among CEOs (36 percent) and a lot lower in the other "nontechnical" functions. For instance, only 18 percent of sales executives and 11 percent of finance executives were immigrants. Similarly, among 63 finance executives (who included just one founder), only 11 percent were immigrants.

We also see a "founder effect" in development roles: the proportion of immigrants among development executives who were hired later (34 percent) is lower than among those who were founders (48 percent). We do not, however, see a founder effect among CEOs. Although nearly half the CEOs were hired later—and almost certainly had replaced individuals who were founders—the share of immigrants among the CEOs who were hired later was about the same as in those who were founders. To talk of a "founder effect" in the ranks of the nontechnical executives is not very meaningful because only a few of such executives were founders.

All U.S.-based employees

According to the CEOs' "best guesses," immigrants comprised about 21 percent of the total U.S.-based employment of the companies in our sample.[4] The average of their percentage of immigrants to total employees was 23 percent, and the median of this percentage was 20 percent. In other words, the proportion of immigrants was highest among founders, lower among top executives, and lowest in the rank-and-file.

CEOs also provided distributions of their immigrant and total employees (table 5.4) by four functions: technical (including staff engaged in any kind of engineering or technical role, and not just development); marketing and sales; core management (not including those managing a technical activity or marketing or sales); and all other employees (such as operations or administrative staff). The total U.S. technical staff numbered 2,579—about half the total domestic employees of these companies. The marketing staff was 1,112 (22 percent of the total). Core management numbered 335 (7 percent), and other staff—mainly operational employees of companies that were well past the development stage—numbered 1,082 (21 percent of the total).

Following the pattern of the founders and top executives, we found a close match between immigrants and the technical function. Of the 2,579 technical staff, 800 (31 percent of the total) were immigrants, and of the 1,078 immigrants, (74 percent) were technical staff. The average of the percentage of immigrants to total technical employees was 29 percent, and the median of this percentage was 26 percent. By contrast, just 6 percent of the 1,112 marketing staff were immigrants.

In the next section, I offer an explanation, more prosaic than the one cited earlier, for the patterns reviewed in the box above: immigrants represent a large proportion of the supply of the engineers and scientists that VC-backed businesses require (to a greater degree than required by the "average employer" in the economy).

■ Demand and Supply

Starting with the demand side: Let us look at why VC-backed businesses need workers who have scientific and engineering skills, and how these requirements change as VC-backed businesses evolve.

We have seen that venture capitalists tend to invest in businesses that have a strong technological foundation. Even so, these businesses themselves do not undertake much cutting-edge research; they often extend and combine research that is cutting edge. Founding teams, therefore, often comprise individuals with advanced degrees in engineering or science who are familiar with (and may have personally helped develop) high-level knowledge and components and have the skills to design good combinations. These include not just the technical founders—the CTOs and the chief scientists—but in many cases, the CEOs themselves. Specifically in my sample, 20 percent of founders had master's, and 24 percent PhDs, in engineering or science (table 5.5).[5] The proportions were especially high among founders in development functions—26 percent had master's degrees and 45 percent PhDs. Even among CEOs, a quarter had a master's or PhD—although the degree of choice was an MBA (which 40 percent of CEOs had).*

As firms grow and add rank-and-file staff, their demand for individuals with advanced degrees in engineering and science declines, not in absolute numbers but as a proportion of their total employment (see box).

---

* The proportion of immigrant founders with master's and PhDs was somewhat higher than for U.S.-born founders, but this seems largely the result of the high proportion of immigrants in development functions. Looking just at the founders playing a development role, we find virtually no difference between the qualifications of immigrant and U.S.-born founders. The proportion of "founding" CEOs with master's and PhDs seems noticeably higher for immigrants; however, the actual numbers are rather small.

The Declining Demand for Advanced Degrees

In my sample, 24 percent of founders, 14 percent of top managers (table 5.6), and just 6 percent of overall staff (table 5.7) had PhDs. Similarly, 20 percent of founders, 16 percent of top managers, and 11 percent of all staff had master's degrees.

I do not have similar data just for the technical staff—I have estimates for the proportion of employees who worked in a technical function and had master's degrees and PhDs, but not how many with master's and PhDs worked in a technical function. Making the admittedly extreme assumption that all master's and PhDs (below the level of top management) worked in a technical function, I calculate that 15 percent of the technical staff had PhDs and 25 percent had master's, compared to the 39 percent of top mangers in development with PhDs and the 28 percent with master's. The true difference is probably much greater. In other words, the demand for advanced degrees also declines with level "within" the technical function.

An obvious reason the relative demand for advanced technical degrees tends to decline as firms grow is that the proportion of their technical staff declines. VC-backed businesses start with high proportions of founders in a development function; but the addition of executives in functions such as marketing, sales, and finance reduces the proportion of technical staff in top management teams. In my sample, two-thirds of top executives who were hired after the business was formed were in nontechnical functions. For instance, only five of the 73 sales executives and just one of the finance executives were founders. As might be expected, the proportion of executives with master's and PhDs in these "new" functions was low. (2 percent of CFOs and 4 percent of sales executives had master's in engineering or science, and none had a PhD.) Similarly, the rank-and-file employees also had more nontechnical employees than founding teams. As we have seen, more than 40 percent of the rank-and-file staff in my sample comprised sales and marketing and operations personnel. I don't have data on their educational qualifications, but it is likely that there weren't many master's or PhDs among them.

But, as indicated in the box, even if we look just at the technical staff, we see that the proportion of PhDs and master's is also lower in rank-and-file *technical* positions than among the founders and top executives. One reason is that as firms mature, more of the technical staff is responsible for operational activities and the implementation of projects rather than the development of know-how or products. A more significant reason, from the point of view of the broader argument of this book, pertains to the nature of the development tasks in the many VC-backed businesses that undertake mid-level innovations. As discussed in chapter 2, the kind of trial and error used to develop mid-level products from high-level know-how and products is in important ways different from high-level scientific research. Therefore, apart from a few individuals who serve as "bridges" to the high-level know-how, VC-backed businesses that undertake mid-level innovations do not need a lot of individuals with advanced degrees on their technical staff (see box).

Superfluous Qualifications?

Many interviewees were skeptical about the need for technical staff with advanced degrees in engineering or science. Even in cases where employees did have advanced degrees, CEOs said they weren't necessary:

"We have a couple of PhDs. They made career mistakes getting a doctorate. Who knows, some years from now, we may have a real need for them."

"About 30 percent of our employees have a master's in engineering or science. Not that we need them. . . . I'd say, it just so happens that they had advanced degrees. Some of these people were born in India, finished their master's there, came to the U.S., and then got hired by us."

"We hire people who have a lot of practical experience. Many of them just happen to have master's degrees."

In some cases, PhDs were valued, but their numbers were small. "We have three PhDs," one CEO said. "It really helps. One of the guys has a PhD in vision engineering. He is working on algorithms to improve the ability of our devices to count [the number of shoppers in a store] and designing new devices that count better."

The very different composition of the technical staff in research labs of large corporations supports the conjecture that advanced degrees are more useful in cutting-edge research than in the development of mid-level know-how and products. Although I do not have access to the personnel data of many companies, my ad hoc inquiries about the labs of large corporations—which undertake more cutting-edge, high-level research—suggest that they have a significantly greater demand for individuals with master's and PhDs. At IBM's "research" labs, 55 percent of the staff had PhDs and 27 percent a master's in engineering or science. "Development" labs at IBM, which typically employed more technicians and other support personnel, nonetheless had only slightly lower proportions: 42 percent had PhDs and 27 percent master's degrees. Similarly, at General Motors, 49 percent of the R&D staff had PhDs and 22 percent master's.

Turning to the supply side, immigrants comprise a significantly higher proportion of the U.S. workforce with technical qualifications—and particularly, those with advanced degrees—than they do of the overall workforce. According to a National Science Foundation report, 25 percent of college-educated workers in science and engineering (S&E) occupations in 2003 were foreign born. The proportions were even higher in S&E workers with PhDs: "Among all doctorate holders resident in the United States in 2003, a majority in computer science (57%), electrical engineering (57%), civil engineering (54%), and mechanical engineering (52%) were foreign born."[6]

It is striking, therefore, that the proportion of immigrants among the PhDs working in the companies I studied—38 percent—is considerably *lower* than the proportion of all PhDs working in the United States who are immigrants. This may be because, contrary to the romantic view, the typical immigrant who gets a PhD in engineering or the sciences is *less* likely to be an enterprising renegade, and more likely to want a secure job in a university, government, or large company lab, than a U.S.-born PhD. The immigrant PhDs who start or join new businesses provide striking exemplars of immigrant entrepreneurship, but they may not be representative.* Another possibility is that comparisons with highly aggregated census data may be misleading because immigrants may be concentrated in subspecialties, which are less likely to spawn new businesses.

---

* As we will see, India accounts for a high proportion of immigrant engineers in the United States. The typical Indian who gets an engineering degree and then emigrates to the United States isn't likely to be an out-of-the-ordinary risk-seeker. I can report from firsthand experience that getting an engineering education in India is considered a much safer and mainstream choice than enrolling in a liberal arts program.

In any event, resolving this conundrum is outside my scope. For my purposes, it is enough to observe that the demand and supply factors seem to explain pretty well the variations in the proportion of immigrants at different levels and functions.

The low proportions of immigrants in the sales and marketing staffs in my study also support the supply-and-demand story discussed previously—and, as we will see later, the broader propositions of this book. Only 6.1 percent of the total number of U.S.-based employees in sales and marketing (across all the firms in my sample) were immigrants. As it happens, the foreign-born percentage of people in sales and related professions in 2005 overall was somewhat lower than the foreign-born share of the civilian labor force, according to Bureau of Labor Statistics data. But, at 11.25 percent, it was nearly twice the percentage of immigrant sales and marketing staff in my sample. What is the explanation for this significant gap in immigrant proportions in sales jobs in the economy as a whole and in the companies I studied? Greater xenophobia seems improbable—businesses with immigrant CEOs should be no less likely to employ immigrant sales staff than businesses with U.S.-born CEOs. Rather, our interviews suggest a widespread belief that, given what the businesses were trying to sell (complex, high-ticket, mid-level products rather than insurance, automobiles, or real-estate), and whom they were trying to sell to (other businesses rather than individuals), the fit between the available supply of immigrant labor and the nature of the sales task was poor (see box).

Misfits?

"The sales and marketing side is very localized and we don't find many suitable immigrants for those jobs," one CEO told us. "The makeup of our sales staff [in terms of their national origin] reflects the makeup of their customers," said a second. A third commented, "In engineering, it's easier for me to think of how many native-born Americans there are. I can think of only three, out of a team of 23. In sales, if you count two Canadians as Americans, I'd say pretty much the entire sales team is American."

The view that immigrants aren't well suited to selling high-tech products isn't confined to native-born CEOs: This last observation was made by an immigrant of South Asian heritage, born in the UK. Over the years, fellow alums from the Indian Institute of Technology who have started high-tech businesses in Silicon Valley say they also favor hiring U.S.-born sales staff. However, a few have predicted a change in this pattern as the proportion of immigrants making the purchasing decision, on the customer side, increases.

The countries of origin of the immigrants (see tables 5.2, 5.3, and 5.8) also reflect the distinctive nature of VC-backed businesses' demand for labor and those businesses' natural sources of supply. Although the immigrants in my sample hailed from many countries, the distribution of countries did not match overall immigration patterns. Mexico—according to the U.S. Census Bureau, the largest supplier of immigrants in 2000 (27.6 percent of the foreign-born population)—was represented by just one CEO in my sample (and he happened to be half-Lebanese). Other countries with a top 10 "overall rank" in their share of the foreign-born in the United States—such as the Philippines (number 3), Cuba (5), Vietnam (6), El Salvador (7), Korea (8), the Dominican Republic (9), and Germany (11)—were represented by no CEOs in my sample, very few members of the founding teams, and negligible shares of the overall workforces.

Conversely, immigrants from China, Israel, and English-speaking countries (the UK, Canada, Australia, New Zealand, and especially India) accounted for a much higher percentage of founders, top executives. and rank-and-file staff than their share of the overall population. For instance, Indian immigrants accounted for a third of the active immigrant founders in my study, a third of the immigrant CEOs, 24 percent of the immigrant executives, and 30 percent of the overall immigrant staff[7]—but only 3.5 percent of the foreign-born population in the 2000 census. Similarly, immigrants from the UK accounted for 15 percent of the active immigrant founders, a quarter of the immigrant CEOs, 20 percent of the executive teams and 5 percent of the overall staff—but just over 2 percent of the overall foreign-born population in the United States. All told, immigrants from just seven English-speaking British Commonwealth countries[8] accounted for nearly two-thirds (62 percent) of active immigrant founders, 69 percent of immigrant CEOs, 57 percent of immigrant executives, and 41 percent of the overall immigrant staff.

The demand for scientific and engineering skills by the VC-backed businesses I studied helps explain the patterns favoring English-speaking immigrants over non-English-speaking immigrants in my sample. Indian immigrants, who accounted for 30 percent of overall immigrant staff in the companies I studied, also accounted for about 14 percent of the foreign-born scientific and engineering degree-holders in the United States in 2003 and more than 40 percent of the recipients of H1-B visas.[9] Moreover, as I have mentioned, many of the technical staff in VC-backed businesses need to communicate externally with customers and internally with colleagues in marketing, sales, and product management. Here, immigrants from English-speaking countries, even if they are considered too "alien" for a job in sales, have an obvious comparative advantage. (Language issues are, however, less likely to matter in high-level research and development, where communication usually takes place within small teams of scientists and engineers.)

Some other patterns, particularly the very low number of women and U.S.-born minorities, are harder to explain. Only 6 percent of the 106 CEOs in my study were women. None were African-American, and only one U.S.-born CEO had a Spanish surname. Although we did not keep count, when we looked at websites to collect the preliminary data on top executives we observed the same pattern: relatively few women or (as far as we could tell) Hispanics, and no African-Americans. To some degree, this reflects the low representation of women and minorities in science and engineering jobs and student enrollments. According to a National Science Foundation report, in 2000, women represented 25 percent of those in S&E occupations, African-Americans 6.9 percent, and Hispanics 3.2 percent.*[10] But the shares of women, African-Americans, and Hispanics were even lower in my sample. As for positions such as finance, among 63 top executives in the companies we studied who had titles such as chief financial officer (CFO), only one was a woman, while 8 percent of the *Fortune* 500 companies had female finance chiefs in 2005.[11] Nearly half of the CFOs in my study had MBAs, and women earned 34.8 percent of MBA degrees in 2004.[12]

---

* The low proportions of African-Americans and Hispanics are consistent with their relatively low share of the college-educated workforce. But this is not the case with women: the NSF report notes that women made up 48.6 percent of the college-degreed workforce, African-Americans 7.4 percent, and Hispanics 4.3 percent.

In my judgment, the strong focus on maximizing financial returns makes it unlikely that old-fashioned discrimination or prejudice plays much of a role in the hiring decisions of VC-backed businesses. As one CEO told us:

I'm Mexican, of Lebanese origin, living in the United States; I have the two ethnicities that people in the U.S. are the least happy about. I get stopped at every airport. So any kind of prejudice that I could have had has been completely eradicated from me. The worth of someone depends on what he or she does, not where he or she comes from, or the color of his or her skin. We have tried to inculcate this culture in the company. We have looked systematically for the best people for each one of the positions.

While cynics might attribute such sentiments to posturing, it should be noted that the great competitive and financial pressures that VC-backed businesses face create a strong incentive to exclude any "noneconomic" considerations from their hiring decisions. Rather, the low proportion of women and minorities likely reflects conditions in the specific "micro–labor markets" that VC-backed firms recruit from (which I will discuss in a later section) and the absence of the pressures faced by large corporations, the public sector, and nonprofit organizations to undertake proactive efforts to recruit women and minorities. Whatever the causes, the underrepresentation casts serious doubt on the romantic notion that VC-backed businesses have a high proportion of immigrants because they are a natural home for historically disadvantaged segments of society.

The preceding analysis suggests that as VC-backed businesses mature, the proportion of immigrants on their staff tends to decline—a progression explicitly predicted by one (U.S.-born) CEO: "Generally, sales and marketing people are U.S.-born. Most of the others here are not. Right now, with the new money we're raising, we're going to grow sales. If sales become more than half the company, more than half [the employees] will be U.S.-born."

But what explains the considerable variations in the proportion of immigrant technical staff from company to company? The number of companies far removed from the mean and median proportions (of 26 and 29 percent respectively) of immigrants in the technical staff was quite large. In about a tenth of the companies, the immigrant share was more than 50 percent—but in nearly a fifth of the companies the immigrant share was less than 10 percent. By contrast, in the sales and marketing staff, the proportion of immigrants was uniformly low.

As we will see next, a variety of factors—notably, *not* including differences in efforts to drive down wage costs—led to variations in the proportion of immigrants in technical staffs. Examining these factors will help us better understand the interplay of supply and demand in markets for the kind of labor used by VC-backed businesses, and thus to assess the claim that immigrants drive down wages in these markets.

■ Tolerating Headaches

First off, note a contrast between the recruiting of immigrant technical staff and offshoring. At some high level of abstraction, we can think of an immigrant engineer as a substitute for an offshore engineer. And quite concretely, this is a question on the minds of individuals abroad: whether to work "at home" for a U.S. company or try to emigrate to the United States and seek employment there. But that's not how most of the CEOs we interviewed looked at it. Whereas they made a conscious decision—usually involving cost—about whether to offshore, this was not the case with hiring immigrants (see box).

Accidental Outcomes

Several CEOs told us that hiring immigrants was not a deliberate choice:

"I've never really thought about it that way. Our constant drive is to find the best people."

"We've hired a lot of immigrants. This wasn't a strategy on the company's part. It just so happens that many of the people in photonics are Chinese-born, and photonics expertise is very relevant to us."

"The workforce is as it is. We have not made a deliberate attempt to get five people in from India, three people from Europe, and so on."

"We have a diverse workforce by chance. We conduct rigorous interviews before bringing people in, but we don't look at their nationality."

In particular, CEOs told us that, in contrast to offshoring, reducing costs didn't come into the picture at all when hiring immigrants. Rather, they said hiring immigrants on H1-B visas entailed *higher* costs, and brought on the "headaches" of securing visas. All other things being equal, they would rather hire a U.S. citizen or permanent resident (see box).

Higher-cost Hires

One CEO, whose technical staff included a sizable number of engineers with H1-B visas, said:

> I really don't care whether they're local or foreign, whether they're green card, red card, or whatever. All I care is that I need to get the work done, and I would never hire someone of less capability because they didn't have [the right immigration] status. But it costs me. I have to pay the standard wage, and then I have to spend about ten to eleven thousand dollars managing their immigration process. I guarantee you that if I were interviewing two people of equal caliber, I would hire the American. It would not be because of prejudice, it would be because the American would cost $120,000 a year and the other $135,000 a year; I have a duty to choose the most cost effective.

On top of the legal fees and administrative costs of processing H1-B visas, employers faced a variety of "headaches" and disruptions:

> It's a legal nightmare. I want to hire somebody right now, but he's working at a company that is sponsoring his visa. If he were to leave, he would have to go back to India for a year. We'd have to figure out a way for him to work for us there, and then restart the visa process after that—and somehow reassure him that the company will be around for the two to three years it takes to get completed.
>
> One of our guys got a notice that he had 11 days to fix his visa status or he'd be deported. He thought he'd done everything correctly, but the INS[13] said, "Nope, you didn't fill out the forms right, and we didn't notify you because it's your responsibility to do it." We ended up having to send this guy and his wife to the other side of Niagara for two and a half weeks while his paperwork was fixed.

As the box "To Sponsor or Not to Sponsor" indicates, visa-related problems discouraged some CEOs, but not others, from employing anyone who needed an H1-B visa. Attitudes toward visa sponsorship, therefore, may explain some of the variation in the proportions of immigrants (in technical functions across firms) at the companies I studied.

To Sponsor or Not to Sponsor

As the comments below show, the CEOs we interviewed held a wide range of views about whether sponsoring an immigrant for a visa was worth the hassle. The quotations are ordered from those who were most willing to sponsor to those who were not:

"My cofounder and I are not only American, we are New Jersey Americans. But our business is competitive on a global basis. If we said, 'Let's hire the best software programmers in New Jersey,' we would get killed. We have to employ the absolute best we can find, wherever they live, whatever their race, color, religion. You pay dearly for it. You have to support their H-1 visas."

"I just want the best people. I don't care where they come from. Not only will I do an H-1, but for anyone who wants it, I will sponsor for a green card. And in fact, you can't really recruit an H-1 guy without agreeing to do that, because that's going to be his main criteria. [Sponsoring for] a green card is a pro and a con. The con is you have to spend five to ten grand on lawyers to get it through the process. The pros are, they can't leave; you've got them for the duration it takes the INS to do the paperwork."

"It's difficult to deal with immigration issues. But there is always a way around the system. If I want to hire someone, there's always an answer. Usually it comes in the form of money."

"We're not against getting visas for immigrants, it's just hard. You have to do it in a certain timeframe, and we need people when we need people."

"Every immigrant who works in this company already has permission to work in the United States. We're a small company. We try to avoid going through all the visa hassles."

"Having been through this at least twice in my previous lives, I find it gets to be very complicated. . . . We have 13 engineers. If one or two have [visa] problems, then it gets to be a major issue for us, so we stay away from it."

Difference in attitudes toward sponsoring immigrants for visas cannot, however, account for all the variation we observed from company to company in the proportion of immigrants in technical staffs. NSF data indicates that the great majority of immigrant scientists and engineers working in the United States already have permanent resident status (aka green cards) or U.S. citizenship. Such individuals could have been hired without visa headaches. More significantly, as we will see later, quite apart from visa issues, there simply isn't a good fit between VC-backed businesses and foreign-born scientists and engineers who don't have green cards or U.S. citizenship, particularly freshly graduated students. What other factors, then, besides attitudes to visa sponsorship, might contribute to the hiring (or not) of immigrants?

In the sections that follow, we will look more deeply into whom, where, and how VC-backed businesses tend to recruit. I will argue that different businesses recruit not from a general ocean of scientists and engineers, but from subpools differentiated by qualifications and experience, connections with the networks of top executives, and geographic location. Because of history or chance, different subpools have different proportions of immigrants. Therefore, even if businesses don't specifically look for or avoid immigrants, they can end up, rather randomly, with many or few.

■ The Role of Résumés

The qualifications and experiences that companies in my sample sought in their recruits had an important albeit indirect influence on their hiring of immigrants.

As a rule, all VC-backed businesses tend to rely on experienced personnel rather than individuals just entering the workforce—at all levels in the organization. It is more common to encounter inexperienced founders (such as

Bill Gates and Michael Dell), as mentioned in chapter 1, at self-financed class B start-ups. In these cases the founders can remain at the helm, learning how to manage large complex organizations in real time as their businesses grow. We also find inexperienced individuals rising to the top after starting at the bottom of large organizations—in the mailroom of movie studios, as linemen in a telephone company, or as gold-bar and coin salesmen in an investment bank. But this is not how senior positions in VC-backed start-ups are filled. VCs have a strong preference for seasoned management teams; and when VCs finance inexperienced founders, they often require the company to hire industry veterans. Or if VCs enter the picture at a later stage, they are not shy about replacing unseasoned managers.*

Experienced executives in turn hire experienced staff rather than fresh graduates, as indicated in the box "No Learner's Permits." Overall, nearly half the businesses in my sample did not hire employees from a college, master's, PhD, or postdoc program. Another 41 percent hired 10 percent or fewer of their staff directly from a university, and only four companies hired between a tenth and a fifth from universities. The preference for people who, though more expensive have "been there and done that" reflects the time pressure faced by VC-backed businesses—and as also indicated in the box, the mid-level innovations many undertake.

No Learner's Permits

"Even though we are located in Austin, we haven't hired a lot of UT [University of Texas] graduates," one CEO said. "In fact, we rarely hire people directly out of any college. We have a saying around here: 'There are only so many people we can have on our staff with learner's permits.' Even in the cases where PhDs were hired into the rank-and-file technical staff, the recruitment was not directly from university labs. "We need PhDs because we are doing very high-end automation—we're not assembling Lego robotics kits," one CEO said. "There are really fundamental principles of physics and chemistry that get involved. But most of the PhDs who work for us first worked for a company before coming here—almost exclusively large companies like GE or Perkin Elmer."

---

* Recall that nearly half the CEOs in my sample were "replacements."

The preference for experienced staff seemed to reflect the nature of the innovations that these businesses undertook: "You don't have time to train people; there is no learning on the job. You want people who have done this job three times before and could do it in their sleep," said one CEO. Another commented,

> We are a drug development company—there is not much in the way of investigative discovery coming from here. If we were a discovery company and looking at, say, how to manipulate cell processes and we needed to invent, then we would have bright-eyed and bushy-tailed recent PhDs or one-year postdocs. We want people who have experience. When you develop a pharmaceutical product as opposed to *discover* a pharmaceutical product, you can't make it up as you go along. You have to know what the next step is. You can't build a manufacturing facility for the first time. You can't conduct a clinical trial unless you have people who have conducted clinical trials before.

The relatively few people who had been recruited from college often started as interns, doing operational or low-end technical jobs such as quality assurance (QA). For instance, one CEO said that because Georgia Tech was located nearby, his company hired interns who could provide a "pair of hands." As my previous research suggests, businesses started without VC financing that can't afford experienced employees sometimes make do with inexperienced ones. If the business subsequently gets VC funding, though, only those employees who have grown into their jobs stay on. More often, they can't make the transition to professional management, and they move on. (As the box "Moving On" indicates, this was also apparently the case with one company in my sample—with the added twist that many of the employees who left were immigrants.)

Moving On

"We had seven people here originally, before we received VC funding, who are no longer with us because they could not transition to a more mature company," an immigrant CEO said.

> Four of them were immigrants who came straight from the university. They were very enthusiastic, creative people. They saw us as the proto-typical American dream company: "Let's work hard, everybody roll up your sleeves." They were very excited about being part of this. That's why they came to the U.S. in the first place. When we start getting managers and heads of sales and people like that, [these employees] were completely out of the water, because they didn't have any experience of working for a real company in the United States. All they knew was a whole bunch of people doing cool stuff. When we actually started doing serious work, they said, "This is not why we came to America."

VC-backed companies look for both general experience (e.g., building and managing a sales force) and specific experience. A case study about a VC-backed business I once wrote involved recruiting a chief marketing officer for a company developing systems to manage local area wireless networks (Wi-Fi). Apart from "good marketing skills," candidates were also required to have experience in network-management software, preferably in data rather than voice networks. The job specification specifically ruled out individuals who had worked only in companies producing hardware (rather than software) for networks. In the current study, we were told that companies had similarly specific requirements for technical knowledge. The CEO of a New Jersey-based company that was developing miniaturized "power systems on a chip" said they were looking for designers of integrated circuits (ICs) with experience in power management. This expertise was hard to find in New Jersey—there were many IC designers, thanks to Lucent, but these were specialized in communications rather than power-management applications. As one CEO said, "Hiring an engineer is not like buying a hard disk. Engineers may be all over the place, but we need people who know something about file sharing through wide area networks."*

For whatever reason, immigrants (and native-born) scientists and engineers are not evenly distributed across all fields and subfields. National Science Foundation data show that in 2003, the foreign-born share of chemical engineers whose highest degree was a bachelor's, was 17.5 percent; for elec-

---

* The company developed software that gave remote users easy access to centrally maintained files.

trical engineers it was 28.1 percent. In the physical sciences, the foreign-born share (at the bachelor's level) in the geosciences was 8.3 percent, compared to 26.6 percent in physics/astronomy. The shares of the foreign-born vary at the doctoral level as well: 37 percent of PhDs in chemistry are foreign-born, compared to 57.4 percent in computer sciences.[14]

Similar variations also apparently exist at the level of skills. When we asked a CEO and cofounder of a software company, who was a native of India, why his business employed very few Indian immigrants, he replied, "The average person we hire has about 13 or 14 years experience in implementing network and systems management products like BMC's Remedy. Although you can find a lot of Indians who are software engineers, they tend to be in applications rather than on the operations side of IT infrastructure, doing things like network management. We were able to find Remedy experts, however, in Brazil and South Africa."

As this CEO's comments and other data in this section reveal, VC-backed businesses—and presumably many other players in the innovation game—look for technical employees with very specific qualifications and experience. For reasons that are beyond the scope of this book, the representation of immigrants in different subgroups of qualifications and experience isn't uniform. Therefore, employers who need employees from a subgroup that contains a high proportion of immigrants will, without making a conscious choice, end up with a large number of immigrant employees.

■ Network Effects

Differences in the personal networks of the top executives in my sample represented a second reason for inadvertent variations in the proportion of immigrants on technical staffs.

The companies in my sample did not recruit on college campuses. Nor did they extensively use arm's length techniques such as professional recruiters and online job-postings. Rather, as the comments in the box "Whom They Knew" illustrate, they relied primarily on personal networks. The use of personal networks apparently led to less representative selections than would have recruiters or postings. As the box also indicates, the backgrounds and connections of the founders, top executives, and early employees, especially in technical functions, sometimes had a significant influence on whether the business hired many or few immigrants. According to our interviewees, immigrant CEOs and CTOs tends to have more fellow immigrants in their networks than native-born CEOs and CTOs; therefore, their rank-and-file staff, particularly in technical functions, had more immigrants.

Whom They Knew

The CEOs we interviewed said their companies relied heavily on personal connections to hire employees. "Eighty percent of the team is people I've worked with and have been successful with in the past," said one CEO. "Out of the 10 engineers, seven of them are people I have worked with before. Across the company, most people come from one degree of separation. We use recruiters very little because we're not at the point where we're out of the pool of our own referral net."

Another said his company had a process whereby they paid $3,000 if an employee brought in a friend: "I'm not sure that there is a single one of our stars in our organization who we hired through a recruiter.... [This] doesn't get us entry-level support people, but most of the senior folk, most of the development team, they came in through current or former coworkers or they are one step removed from my network."

The demographics of personal networks, then, affected the demographics of a company workforce. One Silicon Valley CEO, an immigrant from the UK of Pakistani heritage, told us: "In my experience, technical teams tend to be a reflection of the technical founder. You really need to seed a team with outstanding people, and it's really hard to recruit those guys. So the technical founders always end up going to guys they know, and they know people kind of like themselves. In the last company I started, I had a smart, young white guy out of Stanford. He recruited a bunch of really smart, young white guys out of Stanford. This time I have an old, experienced Indian guy, and he's recruited a bunch of older experienced Indian guys."

A U.S.-born, Boston-based CEO whose technical staff of 32 had just four immigrants explained

Our hiring process is immigration blind. We have the legal staff that could deal with H1-B visas, and I'm happy to do it. And we're very MIT-centric—20 percent of our staff is from MIT, which you would think would generate a lot of international applicants. But it actually hasn't. Most of our MIT people are white and grew up here. That's certainly not the MIT demographic. So we are kind of selecting oddly out of MIT, or there's some kind of self-selection going on. Perhaps it's because we're not hiring people directly at MIT. The company was started by someone from MIT in 1998. He brought in a bunch of people, from his class, many from his fraternity. Maybe we're getting most of our people from the classmates of the early employees or from the fraternity. Even if you are five years removed from somebody, you feel that you're a fraternity brother or sister.

Similarly, the CEO of a Chicago company (a Texas native) attributed the high proportion of immigrants on the company's operations staff to "our hiring practices. We pay recruitment bonuses, so we end up with friends and relatives. For a while, we had three members of one family. One was in accounting, one in data services, and one in installation. But they tend to be more in operations than anywhere else."

For my sample as whole, the proportions of immigrants in the workforces of companies with immigrant CEOs and CTOs was indeed higher in companies with native-born CEOs and CTOs (see box "The Correlates of Immigrant Employment"). The data in the box are also consistent with the suggestion of some of our interviewees that, because the networks of immigrant executives are skewed toward their compatriots, so is the makeup of the employees of their companies—companies with founders and CTOs of Indian origin, for instance, tend to have relatively high proportion of immigrants—many most likely of Indian origin[15]—on their technical staffs.

The Correlates of Immigrant Employment

Differences in the median proportions of immigrants employed by the companies in my sample varied with the backgrounds of the founders and executives in the following manner.

- Median percentage of immigrants in workforce in businesses
  Without immigrant founders   10
  With at least one immigrant founder   26

- Median percentage of technical staff in workforce in businesses
    Without immigrant founders   42
    With at least one immigrant founder   58
- Median percentage of immigrants in businesses
    Without immigrant founders   24
    With at least one immigrant founder   33
    With native-born CTO   28
    With immigrant CTO   33

At least some of these differences likely reflect the higher proportion of technical staff: in companies with immigrant founders, the proportion of immigrants in a technical staff tends to be higher than in a nontechnical staff. But as the data below show, the proportion of immigrants is higher in businesses with immigrant founders, even if we look just at technical staff.

If we look just at the subset of companies with at least one immigrant on the founding team, and categorize this subset in terms of those with and without an Indian founder, we see the following "India effect":

- Median percentage of immigrants in technical staff in businesses*
    Without an Indian immigrant founder   33
    With at least one Indian immigrant founder   60
- Median percentage of immigrants of Indian origin in businesses
    Without any Indian immigrant founders   23
    With at least one Indian immigrant founder   41

Businesses with a CTO from India also had a higher proportion of immigrants who were natives of India, compared to businesses where the CTO was an immigrant from another country (73 percent vs. 25 percent).

The correlation between backgrounds and proportion of immigrants is, however, far from perfect. Although the medians *across* the various categories are different, there is much more variation *within* the categories.[16] Therefore, a sizable number of businesses in categories with a low proportion of immigrants actually had a greater proportion of immigrants than some businesses in categories that had a high proportion of immigrants. For instance, over a third of businesses that had no immigrant founders (the "low" category) had a higher proportion of immigrants on their technical staffs than

---

* Immigrant-founded businesses with or without an Indian founder had approximately the same median proportion of technical staff to overall staff (59 percent).

the bottom half of businesses that did have immigrant founders (the "high" category). Similarly, nearly a fifth of the businesses with immigrant founders who weren't from India (the "low" category) had a higher proportion of Indian immigrants than the bottom half of businesses that had an Indian founder (the "high" category).

The box also shows, however, that the correlation between the national origins of executives and the proportion of immigrants on their staff is far from perfect. Three factors seemed to dilute the tendency of immigrant founders and executives to rely on their personal connections with their compatriots to staff their businesses. First, the business might need specific skills that are not widely available in the compatriot pool: we saw an example of this earlier in the business that needed Remedy expertise, which Indian immigrants tended not to have.

Second, although the personal networks of immigrant founders and executives might be biased toward compatriot immigrants, they also included connections that had nothing to do with national origins. A CEO (and cofounder), for instance, told us that although he and his cofounder were both from India, the proportion of Indian immigrants in their workforce was low. But there was a very high representation of Hewlett Packard (HP) alums, because both founders were veterans of that company: "One of our first hires was my former manager from HP. Now we have about 350 years of HP experience in the company."

Third, differences in the backgrounds of the founders added diversity to the networks they recruited from. As mentioned, most VC-businesses in my sample (86 percent) were started by teams rather than individuals; and, a surprising 25 percent[17] of the founding teams comprised founders who hadn't known each other before starting their business.[18] The other 75 percent included many cases where some members of the founding team had a previous connection but others did not. For instance, two colleagues might decide to start a business, then recruit a stranger to round out the team. This kind of team composition presumably helped broaden the recruitment net, as it were, and helped reduce concentrations that might result if the search were limited to one individual's network or the networks of teams with similar backgrounds.

■ Microclimates

The composition of the labor supply in the specific "catchment area" where the companies were located was a third factor that influenced the proportion of immigrants on their staff.

Virtually all employers tend to do most of their hiring in the place where they are located. The unwillingness of VC-backed business to hire freshly minted graduates reinforces this tendency, because experienced staff who have put down roots in their communities are less willing to relocate. Recruiting through personal networks rather than using head-hunters and ads also nudges VC-backed businesses toward employing local residents, because founders and top executives have more and better contacts in their local communities. Therefore, the companies in my sample that were located in places like Silicon Valley that have a high proportions of immigrants (with high-tech skills and experience) usually had higher proportions of immigrants on staff than companies in Seattle—which has a lot of high-tech workers but a lower proportion of immigrants (see box).

Silicon Valley versus Seattle

California's Silicon Valley famously has a high proportion of immigrants working in scientific and engineering occupations. In 2005, 53 percent of engineers and scientists in Silicon Valley were foreign-born, compared to immigrants' 38 percent share of the population of the area overall.[19] In contrast, according to the 2000 census, Seattle's foreign-born accounted for under 17 percent of that population (i.e. less than half of Silicon Valley's 2005 share).

VC-backed businesses in Seattle therefore apparently did not find many immigrant candidates for their jobs. As a CEO who lived in northern California before moving to Seattle told us:

Some areas of northern California are fairly homogeneous, but overall it's amazing how much of the world is represented there. At my previous company, we hired a senior technical person from India, so we had

---

a significant Indian population in the technical staff. Up here, we don't have that. This is a very homogeneous area, to the point where my wife and I have discussed whether this is a good place to be raising our children.

The larger share of immigrants in the California workforce naturally made it more likely that businesses located in that state would hire more of them. Overall in our sample, the median proportion of immigrants in companies headquartered in California was 24 percent, compared to 18 percent for all other states. The largest share in the five companies in the greater Seattle area was 13 percent—in the other four Seattle companies, immigrants represented less than 10 percent of overall employment.

Companies headquartered in California (or even in the Bay area) did not, however, have uniformly high proportions of immigrants—a third of the California companies had shares below the median for all other states. The other factors that affect the hiring of immigrants discussed earlier apparently outweighed the ample local supply.

Places like Silicon Valley known for their ethnic diversity were not, however, the only places where immigrants were well represented in VC-backed businesses. Twenty-seven percent of the 71 employees of a biotech company in the state of Georgia were immigrants. When I expressed some surprise—according to the 2000 census, Georgia's foreign-born share of the population was 7.1 percent, compared to the national figure of 11.1 percent—the company's UK-born CEO responded: "On the contrary, it's a center for scholarship, and there are 16,000 employees here working for 250 companies in the life sciences industry. People come to where the opportunity and the wealth lie. Georgia is a remarkably easy place to be successful."

In other words, the specific, "micro" factors pertaining to a particular business and its managers often trumped the overall shares of immigrants in the local population.

One Los Angeles–based company had developed a system to hire internationally—but it was the only one in my sample that had done so (see box).

An Exceptional Recruiter

The U.S.-born CEO of a Los Angeles–based company described a process to use the connections of immigrants on his staff to recruit internationally:

> What we want is the best talent that we can find to work for us in L.A. Our product is a very high-margin product; for us, one great engineer is better than 10 so-so engineers. So, we screen résumés from all over the world, and then we test people via emails. It's a three-hour test. If they ace the test, we fly them to L.A. and interview them in person and have them take another test. If they ace that, and if we think they can integrate culturally, and if they have basic English skills, we will get them into the U.S. one way or another. We have more people working with H1-Bs and in the green card processes than virtually any company of our size I know.
>
> It started when we hired a Russian who was working in Canada. He knew three other people in Moscow. Now we have a team of engineers from Russia, a team from southern India, a team from northern India, and people from Canada. Once you get the first person from an area, they know who the other smart people are.

This was the only such case, however. As a rule, the VC-backed businesses did not stray far from home in their recruiting efforts. The CEO of a San Francisco company, a French native, said: "Recruiting is a very complex activity, just in the U.S. or even in the Bay Area. It's supercompetitive. If we could have systems to hire from abroad, we would. But we don't really know where we could find people in places like Russia. . . . I used to have a huge network in France, but I've lost my European connections. My network is now all here, mainly in the Bay Area. It's a shame. We have some engineers from Europe, but they too have been here for many years."

Another immigrant CEO, who previously worked at Microsoft, similarly noted: "Microsoft has become a UN, [partly] because Bill Gates went around the world and plucked talent from everywhere.[20] If I could do that I definitely would, but I don't have the time. If I had some intelligent recruiter who could find the world's best talent, I would definitely leverage that."

■ Do Immigrants Increase Cross-Border Engagements?

What bearing, if any, did the proportion of immigrants among founders, top executives, and rank and file have on their companies' propensity to do business abroad? I have already noted a modest positive correlation between the proportions of immigrant founders and CTOs and the hiring of immigrant technical staff. I found a similarly positive modest correlation (see box) in the proportion of immigrants in a business and the extent of its international marketing and offshoring activities. We have no way, however, of knowing the direction of the causality—do immigrant founders face a comparative disadvantage in starting businesses where the market is principally in the United States, or does having an immigrant founder stimulate and facilitate the search for international customers? I suspect it is a little bit of both, and we will just have to leave it at that.

A Modest Correlation

Having an immigrant founder or CEO was modestly correlated with a company's propensity to serve customers abroad or have an office or facility abroad, in the following manner:

- Percentage of companies serving customers abroad, in companies:*

Without any immigrant founders	44
With at least one immigrant founder	62
With U.S. born CEOs	47
With immigrant CEOs	63

- Percentage of companies with office or facility abroad, in companies

Without any immigrant founders	39
With at least one immigrant founder	38
With U.S.-born CEOs	47
With immigrant CEOs	33

    Similarly, having an Indian founder or CTO was somewhat correlated with having a development center or outsourcing relationship in India.

- Percentage of companies with development centers in India, in companies

Without any immigrant founders	0
With an immigrant founder, but not from India	6
With an Indian-born founder	26

* Excludes companies without revenues.

- Percentage of companies outsourcing development in India, in companies

  Without any immigrant founders   22

  With an immigrant founder, but not from India   11

  With at least one Indian-born founder   33

- Companies with India centers or outsourcing (percent of companies)

  With U.S.-born CTO   20

  With an immigrant CTO but not from India   33

  With Indian-born CTO   50

The reader should not attach too much significance to such correlations, however. As in many of the other distributions I have described, even if the averages and medians *between* categories were different, there was even more variation *within* categories. For instance, the proportion of international revenues for businesses with immigrant founders ranged from 0 percent to 65 percent and for businesses with exclusively U.S.-born founders from 0 percent to 70 percent. Forty-four percent of businesses with exclusively U.S.-born founders had higher proportions of international revenues than the median for the businesses with immigrant founders. Therefore, the probability that a randomly drawn business from the immigrant category would have significantly higher proportions of international sales than one drawn from the U.S.-born category is quite small. In addition, the measures do not control for factors such as total revenues and localization costs, which, as I have argued, have a significant effect on the proportion of international to total sales. And, as I will argue in chapter 6, there is no sensible way to control for such factors.

■ Contrasts with Large Corporations and *Inc.* 500 Businesses

Even if large corporations are more global in their pursuit of international customers or offshoring opportunities, my analysis suggests that the proportion of immigrants among their top executives is probably much lower than the proportion among the top executives of VC-backed businesses. We were able to identify from public records the countries of birth for 771 (52 percent) of the 1,480 top executives of *Fortune* 100 companies in 2005. We found that 88 percent of these executives were U.S.-born, and 12 percent foreign-born, compared to 73 percent and 27 percent in my sample of VC-backed businesses. For the 709 executives for whom we could find no record of their place of birth, there was a very high probability that most were also U.S.-born, judging by factors such as where they attended high school.[21] Therefore, the percentage of U.S.-born executives was probably between 88 percent and 94 percent.[22] The proportion of immigrants at the CEO level of the *Fortune* 100 was particularly low: we counted six immigrants, 81 U.S.-born, and 13 who were likely U.S.-born, whereas in our VC-backed businesses, 35 percent of CEOs were immigrants.

The lower representation of immigrants in the top echelon is surprising given those companies' much larger involvement in cross-border activities. IBM, for instance, reported in 2005 that its international revenues represented more than 60 percent of its total revenues, and that slightly under 60 percent of its workforce was employed abroad. But nearly all members of its executive committee were U.S.-born. This may be less meaningful than meets the eye, however. The relatively low proportion of immigrants in top leadership positions probably reflected the fact that large corporations have lower demand for individuals with advanced degrees in engineering or science than do VC-backed businesses—a segment of the labor pool in which the proportion of immigrants is high (as mentioned). For instance, only four of the CEOs had PhDs (two of whom were immigrants), compared to 18 percent of the CEOs of VC-backed businesses; five had master's degrees in engineering or science compared to 18 percent for VC-backed businesses. Of all the 929 executives for whom we could determine their highest degree earned, 4 percent had PhDs and 6 percent had master's degrees in engineering or science, compared to 19 percent with PhDs and 22 percent with master's degree in the VC-backed businesses.*

In terms of functional responsibilities, fewer of the *Fortune* 100 CEOs served in some "developmental" capacity, which could also account for the lower proportion of immigrants in the top echelon, since, as we have seen, in the VC-backed businesses immigrants tend to be concentrated in technical functions. Of the 1,348 executives whose titles indicated their function, 3 percent were CTOs, heads of R&D, chief innovation officers, or chief development officers, compared to 25 percent in VC-backed businesses. In keeping with the preceding inference, 16 percent in this category (compared to

---

* The share of immigrant executives with PhDs (23 percent) and master's (11 percent) was greater than for the *Fortune* 100 executives as a whole.

6-12 percent overall) were immigrants, and virtually all (immigrant or U.S.-born) had a PhD or master's in engineering or science or an MD.

The distribution of the countries of origin of immigrant executives was also somewhat different, although, as with VC-backed businesses, high proportions were from English-speaking countries. Of the 90 identifiable immigrants, the largest contingent was from the UK (22 percent), followed by Canada (14 percent) and India (12 percent). Other English-speaking countries—Australia, New Zealand, and Ireland—accounted for another 9 percent.

The proportion of immigrants in the rank-and-file employees of the *Fortune* 100 was unavailable. But there is no reason to suppose it is any lower than in the workforce as a whole. Our earlier discussion suggests that, for certain job categories and educational levels, this figure could actually be higher than in VC-backed businesses. As I have mentioned, the labs of large companies not only have a higher percentage of staff with advanced degrees (who are more likely to be immigrants), they are also more prepared to hire freshly minted graduates, and these graduates, if they are immigrants, are in turn reluctant to leave their employers before they get green cards. Large companies that have extensive staff employed in their operations can also move them to U.S. operations without much difficulty, under the L-1 visa program for intracompany transfers. So at least in some respects, large companies may be more hospitable to immigrants than are VC-backed businesses.

According to our telephone survey of a randomly selected subset of the companies on the *Inc.* 500 list for 2006, the median proportion of immigrants in the rank and file was 9 percent—well below the 20 percent median of the VC-backed businesses.[23] The lower proportions probably reflect, per the arguments I have previously made, the fact that although many *Inc.* 500 companies participate in high-tech industries, they often don't themselves develop high-tech products based on cutting-edge technologies. Rather, they typically focus on creating the ground-level know-how necessary to sell and deploy such products. Accordingly, the proportions of founders and rank-and-file employees with advanced degrees in engineering or science are relatively small. Surveys indicate that the proportion of founders of *Inc.* 500 companies with any sort of graduate degree besides an MBA tends to be around 15 percent,[24] compared to 50 percent of the founders of the VC-backed businesses in my sample. Similarly, according to my telephone survey of companies on *Inc.*'s 2006 list, the median proportion of rank-and-file employees with a PhD or master's in engineering or science was 5 percent, compared to 22 percent for VC-backed businesses.

■ Concluding Comments

In chapters 3 and 4, we discussed the nexus between the innovative activities of VC-backed businesses and their international marketing and offshoring activities. Here we extended the analysis to a third kind of international interaction: the use of immigrant labor. In this chapter, I suggested that the relatively high use of immigrant labor by VC-backed businesses, especially in their early days, reflects the essence of their innovative role. Even if they don't need platoons of PhDs to undertake mid- and ground-level innovations, they do need a few to lead the process of combining and extending high-level know-how. A high proportion of such individuals happen to be immigrants. These businesses also employ more individuals in their rank-and-file development staff whose knowledge of specific tools and technologies is more important than the sort of training provided by master's and PhD programs. Here, too, immigrants account for a higher share of the qualified individuals than they do of the workforce as a whole. As these businesses grow, however, they require more staff in sales and marketing positions, which they tend to fill with U.S.-born candidates.

The analysis has some general implications for innovative activity in the United States. Most obviously, it suggests that immigrants do play a significant role, not just in the cutting-edge or high-level innovation that takes place in R&D centers, but also in mid- and ground-level activity. Taking into account what we discussed in chapter 4, we can further infer that these activities are of a different nature than the immigrants could perform in an offshore location (i.e., writing rather than testing code).

The kind of labor supplied by these immigrants also is noteworthy. Much is made of the contribution of immigrants with advanced degrees; however, technical personnel who don't have advanced degrees play at least as important a role in mid-level innovations.* Moreover, immigrants not only expand the quantity of technical labor available for innovation but, just as importantly, the variety. As we have repeatedly seen, in contrast to, say, the

---

* In my, sample there were three and a half times as many immigrants who did not have advanced degrees in engineering and science as those who had such degrees.

cultivation of corn, innovation is a many-splendored thing. This is quite obvious on the output side; clearly, the range of new products and technologies developed by innovators is greater than the varieties of corn grown by farmers. But different innovators use different inputs, including, importantly, in their technical staff. Leaving aside those with PhDs and master's with highly specialized educations, even engineers with just bachelor's degrees are not as fungible as, say, the fertilizer used by a corn farmer.

Moreover, multiple factors, such as skills, location, and the timing of their availability, may make a particular engineer highly valuable to one innovator but not to another. A COBOL programmer isn't a substitute for a C++ programmer. A programmer who won't move from Boston is of little value to an employer in California. Similarly, a programmer available three months from now is not particularly useful to a company that needs one today. VC-backed businesses may demand specific skills more urgently, but it is hard to imagine many innovators who can afford much delay.

The contribution of immigrants in providing the right kinds of skills in the right place and at the right time is ignored by those who argue that immigration should be restricted in order to force employers to retrain U.S. engineers. The role of sales and marketing staff in realizing the value of high-tech innovations also escapes the notice of those advocates who wish to curb the immigration of engineers. Curbing immigration might raise the wages of engineers and scientists and thus encourage more U.S.-born individuals to pursue careers in these fields, but to what end? How does diverting the U.S.-born from occupations where they have natural advantages—and that help produce and disseminate valuable innovations—increase the public good? It certainly won't help innovators (such as the VC-backed businesses in my sample) who would face higher costs and tighter supplies for their technical *and* nontechnical staff.

This brings me to the end of what I call, borrowing from the legal lexicon, the "discovery" or "witness testimony" phase of my inquiry. In book 2 I focus on the big picture—the implications of this research for U.S. prosperity and public policy. But before book 1 concludes, chapter 6 draws a contrast between the methods of this inquiry and the normal scholarly approach. Doing so will clarify why, in the just-completed discovery phase, with all the data that I collected, I have adopted a literary, or what some scholars call "hand-waving," style of exposition and analysis. It will also help lay the groundwork for the big-picture analyses in book 2.

6

■ On Methods and Models

Some scholars will ask why I have not tested my conjectures (about, for instance, what factors affect the number of immigrants employed by a firm) through a regression analysis. A traditional econometric procedure would start with a linear "model" of the form

$$Y = a + b_1 x_1 + b_2 x_2 + b_3 x_3 + \ldots + b_n x_n + \varepsilon$$

In this equation, Y, the dependent variable, could be the number of immigrant employees; each x would represent an independent or explanatory variable—the revenues of the firm, the number of immigrant founders, whether or not it is located in California or has an immigrant CTO, the number of patents filed (or better yet, cited in other patent filings), and so on; the bs are regression coefficients; and, ε is a random error term.

I would then use a standard statistical package to identify factors that are unlikely (say with 95 percent confidence) to affect the number of immigrants employed, and to provide a quantitative estimate of the impact of the factors that did matter. For instance, I might find that, controlling for all other independent variables, whether or not a firm has immigrant founders actually has no statistically significant impact, whereas a California location increased the number of immigrants by 8 percent.

Researchers use this approach (or versions thereof) to distill scientific facts from mere opinions and to provide authoritative, quantitative estimates about a variety of social and economic phenomena. For instance, according to a well-known labor economist recently cited in the *Wall Street Journal*, adjusting for work experience and gender, employers now pay college graduates 75 percent more than they pay high school graduates, while 25 years ago they paid 40 percent more.[1]

The numerical estimates of the study seem far more informative and authoritative than simply saying that the employers now pay a lot more for college graduates. They also help us isolate the effects of attending college from other changes in the composition of the workforce and thus allow us to assess how the premium for a college education has fared against the rise in college tuitions—has going to college become a better or worse deal?

As it happens, I am a great fan of numerical analyses, but I am also wary of how they are often done in the social sciences.[2] What gives me the most pause isn't what social scientists usually fret about: the direction of causality (might the dependent variables, in fact, be driving the independent variables?), accidental correlations, and omitted or unobserved independent variables. Rather, I am troubled by two crucial assumptions that are routinely made in regression analyses but rarely exposed, as Oliver Wendell Holmes might have said, to the disinfectant of sunlight.

One problematic assumption is not only that the models include all the independent variables that matter (i.e., the dreaded excluded variables have all been invited to the ball), but also that the variables have been "put together" in precisely the right manner. In the example above, it would be arbitrarily assumed—without an empirical or theoretical basis—that the right equation has the simple linear form $Y = a + b_1 x_1 + b_2 x_2 + \varepsilon$.

Arbitrary specifications can be valuable. For instance, standardizing the dimensions of a foot (or meter) gives every one a uniform way of comparing lengths. Similarly a linear specification for regression models may serve as a useful social convention for researchers. It provides a natural focal point—in the economist Thomas Schelling's language—that all researchers agree to use, so that everyone analyzing a certain data set arrives at the same result. Otherwise, different researchers using different models might reach completely different conclusions about what was or wasn't statistically significant.

At the same time, arbitrary specifications can mislead. Using a straightedge foot ruler to compare the lengths of twisted rods is not a sensible procedure: It can lead every one to mistakenly agree that one rod is longer.

And, a foot ruler will provide especially misleading results if used to measure rods that are twisted into quite different shapes. Similarly, in my view, linear models are often used in situations where there is no reason to suppose that the data are like straight rods.

We know that in nature, many multivariate relationships *aren't* linear. The surface area of a closed cylinder of radius r and height h equals $2(\pi r^2 + \pi rh)$, and that of a right circular cone equals $\pi r(r + \sqrt{r^2 + h^2})$. When the ends of a wire of length l, radius r made of a metal of conductivity σ is connected across a battery of voltage V, the current that flows through the wire equals $V/(\sigma \pi r^2 l)$. Even single variable functions often aren't linear—the sine of an angle of 20 degrees *isn't* half the sine of an angle of 40 degrees. So why would the complex phenomena that social scientists research be governed by simple linear equations? How can we *know* that the *right* equation is really the linear $Y = a + b_1 x_1 + b_2 x_2 + \varepsilon$ and not, for instance, $Y = a + b_1 x_1^2 + b_2 x_1 x_2 + \varepsilon$ (as in the surface area of a cylinder) or $Y = a + b_1 x_1 (x_1 + \sqrt{x_1^2 + x_2^2})$ (as in the surface area of the cone)?

If there were just one or two alternatives to the standard linear equation, we could simply use the one that "fits" the data best. But the number of possible equations is literally infinite. It is one thing for me to suggest that having immigrant founders increases the number of immigrant employees (or for a labor economist to claim that education and work experience increase wages). It is quite another to divine the right form in which the number of immigrant founders should be used in a regression equation. And as the thought experiment in the box at the end of this chapter suggests, unless by some chance the equation is right,* the seemingly precise, scientific estimates can be quite wrong.

One reader has pointed out that "if you regress surface area on radius and height for randomly selected cylinders and cones, under most conditions you should find a significant linear relationship." To me, that's precisely the problem: even if the result is "statistically significant," because it was based on an incorrect equation, it can't provide dependable predictions of surface

---

* Nonparametric models can ameliorate but do not eliminate the problem that we can never know the true equation. As it happens, these are not extensively used in empirical research. Instead, research papers will sometimes claim that their result is "robust" for a "wide range of specifications." What this really means is that the researchers found "statistical significance" using three or four specifications—out of the infinitely large set of possible model assumptions. The width of a "wide range" apparently lies in the eye of the beholder.

areas. And regardless of the *t*-statistics, a claim (for instance) that "controlling for height, every 1 percent increase in radius will lead to a 5 percent increase in surface area" is spurious. But that is precisely what one finds in a lot of research published in top-tier journals—and in estimates that the premium for going to college has increased from 40 percent to 75 percent after "controlling for gender and work experience." In this specific case, all that can really be said is that controlling for gender and experience in a particular—and quite arbitrary—way, the premium increased from 40 percent to 75 percent. Using a different kind of equation would lead to different estimates of the premium, but it is impossible for anyone to know which equations and estimates are the "right" ones.

A second (and related) problem with using linear regressions lies in the assumption that the same equation or process generates all the observations in a set of data. This is obviously untrue in the cylinder and cone example—in both cases, surface areas increase with radius and height, but the equations are certainly different.* Therefore if a "sample" contains both cylinders and cones, a single equation regression cannot produce meaningful estimates of how surface areas increase with radius and height. If, by chance, the equation happens to be "right" for one, it will certainly be "wrong" for the other.[3]

In a great many situations where regression analyses are used, the assumption may not be as demonstrably false, as with cylinders and cones, because we cannot know what the right equations are. But in many situations, the assumption is highly implausible, and the use of a single model becomes akin to using a foot rule to measure the lengths of rods twisted in quite different shapes. In my study, for instance, I would expect that for some businesses, having immigrant founders might lead to "exponential" increases in the number of immigrant staff, and in other cases, immigrant founders might have more muted, "linear" effects. Similarly, in analyzing the relationship of incomes and years of work experience, we would expect a consistently positive relationship between incomes and experience in some professions (e.g., lawyers and surgeons); in some cases (e.g., assembly line workers) we would expect incomes to flatten after a few years; and in yet others (e.g., fashion models and professional athletes) we would expect an inverted U-shaped relationship between incomes and experience. In other words, it's not merely that the slopes (or other such parameters) are

---

* *Not* just the parameters of the equations.

different, but that the basic equations most likely are not the same for different occupations.[4]

It would be fine if models with arbitrary or even bad assumptions were used as starting points and were then tweaked with experiments and experience to match them to the real world; a similar process helped the ancients construct trigonometric tables. We could also imagine an engineer who doesn't know the formula for the surface area of a closed cone starting off by examining regressions of area against height and radius and then using experiments to construct a series of graphs or tables relating area, height, and radius. Indeed, engineering handbooks are full of such graphs and tables; they may appear ad hoc, but they are an essential tool of the engineering trade.

Unfortunately, good experiments on social and economic phenomena are hard to come by. And unlike the developers of trigonometric tables of old—and modern engineers who cheerfully change equations to fit the data—social scientists consider it bad form to deviate from standard linear (or log-linear) equations.* A pragmatist also might not care much that a model was based on arbitrary or dubious assumptions if it did a good job of explaining variations in historical data and yielded reliable predictions. For instance, the "right" formula for the surface area of a sphere ($4\pi r^2$) happens to be such that the arbitrary choice of a log-linear model will produce excellent estimates.

But how often do models with statistically significant results actually explain 90 percent or more of the variation? I cannot, for instance, think of many individual organizations (let alone large and diverse economies) for which a model using as independent variables college education, years of work experience, and gender would explain 90 percent of the variation in the wages of employees. Far more often than not, graphical representations resemble Rorschach-like clouds that a computer has drawn a line through. Or to revert to an earlier analogy, researchers routinely use straight-edged foot rulers to measure the lengths of visibly twisted rods.

---

* Imagine the following scenario: I use a standard linear (or log-linear) equation to test the statistical significance of the effect of immigrant founders, but I find none. Then, because I happen to believe immigrant founders really do matter, I keep trying other forms of equations until I find one where the effect is statistically significant. This would be considered a serious breach of good practice, *even if the equation discovered through this "fishing expedition" actually fit the data better than the standard linear equation.*

The forecasts drawn from regression models are even less assuring. Economic models notoriously fail to predict booms, recessions, inflations, and accelerations and decelerations in productivity—not to mention significant changes in interest rates, exchange rates, and stock prices. Alan Greenspan, former chairman of the U.S. Federal Reserve, recently told an interviewer that he had used a "big mathematical model of forecasting the economy" and had "been in the forecasting business for 50 years," yet said, "I'm no better than I ever was, and nobody else is. Forecasting 50 years ago was as good or as bad as it is today."[5] In fact, I have a rather hard time thinking of many sophisticated economic models that do much better than the naive forecast that "tomorrow will be like today" (or that today's trend will remain in place). Forecasts also call into question the degree to which quantitative models are more objective than qualitative inquiries and analyses: If the models are truly objective, why do individual forecasters, who all have access to the same data and statistical methods, make different predictions? Surely, there is as much art as science.

I am not advocating that we abandon regressions, much less that we ignore numbers. Regressions do have value in suggesting hypotheses and as first cuts for looking at patterns in the data. Rather, I am suggesting that they be used judiciously, bearing in mind the fundamental unknowability (or Knightian uncertainty) of the underlying models and equations. The following rules of thumb can help.

One is to emphasize simple statistics rather than subtle relationships teased out with high-powered econometric techniques. Where the medians and means (and basic cross-tabulations) don't persuade, the argument probably isn't worth making. There is a reason business executives, medical researchers, and engineers—who do rely heavily on "hard" data—use advanced econometric techniques in exceptional circumstances rather than as a matter of routine. And I don't think it's because they are less sophisticated or capable than social scientists. Executive ranks are replete with driven, intelligent MBAs who were trained by faculty who are deeply committed to the statistical methods of the modern social sciences. And these are not innumerate individuals to start with—the proportion of MBAs at top schools with undergraduates in engineering or the natural sciences is many times this proportion in the college-educated population as a whole. If regressions and other advanced statistical methods are nonetheless rarely used by individuals who will look for any edge to get ahead, that tells us something.* Even social scientists themselves, I should note, almost never use statistical models to manage their departments and schools.

Second, we should stick to regressions where we are confident that the values of the dependent variable have all been generated—at least roughly—by the same process. For instance, in using a regression analysis to verify the equation for the surface area of a cone, we may tolerate small variations in the shapes of the cones used in a sample. We should not, however, include cylinders, whose surface area is related to height and radius in a completely different way. Unfortunately, researchers routinely mix cones and cylinders. For instance, observing new businesses from the ground up for about two decades has left me with no doubt that there are significant structural differences between different types of start-ups. Yet study upon study assumes uniformity, using a single equation to "explain" the number of *all* new start-ups, from biotech firms to hot-dog stands.[†]

Third, we should rely on regression results only to the degree to which they are corroborated by other data. A hypothesis should not be accepted or rejected on the basis of regression results without consideration of a wide range of relevant "case facts." For instance, we can expect changes in the wage premiums for attending college to roughly track the costs of attending college. If they do, we need not worry much about the arbitrariness of the assumptions used in the estimation procedure. But imagine instead an analysis claming that costs have grown much faster than wages. This is not an impossible result: a college education could initially have been a steal and then gradually become fairly priced; or the escalating social cachet of a college degree may have allowed tuitions to rise faster than wages. But the credibility of the result would turn on the strength of the evidence that can be marshaled to support the underlying explanation. In the absence of such corroborative evidence, we should treat the anomalous result (of sharply

---

* So does, I believe the blowups of "quant funds," such as the collapse of Long Term Capital Management (whose partners included two Nobel laureates in economics). A popular explanation for the blowups is that the funds use models that underestimate the likelihood of out-of-the-ordinary events. A complementary view suggested by my analysis is that all such models incorporate totally arbitrary assumptions in their basic structure; when many such models are in play, with the passage of time, some proportion of them will inevitably blow up.

[†] Harvard Law School's Mark Roe points to a similar problem with "legal origin" research that assumes "common law" or "juries" work in the same way in Britain and the United States as they do in British colonies like India (Roe 2007).

divergent costs and wages) as an artifact of arbitrary assumptions. We should be particularly suspicious of results contradicted by other circumstantial evidence: If something seems too "freaky" to be true, it probably is.

Two contrasting examples of the use of data analysis illustrate these rules of thumb. One is that of epidemiological studies of smoking, which reported, inter alia, that men born between 1900 and 1930 who smoked cigarettes "died on average 10 years younger than life-long non-smokers."[6] These seminal papers did not use sophisticated statistical methods, and it is unlikely that they properly controlled for all other risk factors. Nonetheless the studies are persuasive because they are of a piece with other studies, as well as with data on the carcinogens contained in tobacco, on the presence of carbon monoxide in cigarette smoke and from X-rays of smokers' lungs. The congruence of the statistics and detailed, multilevel explication of the causal mechanisms is compelling.

On the other side are studies claiming that immigration has reduced the wages of the native-born in periods when the rates of immigration and wage growth have been robust and unemployment low. It is certainly *possible* that the research is right in that wage growth may have been even higher (or unemployment lower) if immigration rates had been lower. But is it *probable* given that the "model" ultimately represents an arbitrary choice for a vast number of possibilities?

Take for instance Harvard economist George Borjas's study that concludes, "The analysis shows that increases in the number of foreign-born doctorates, primarily through the foreign student program, have a significant adverse effect on the earnings of competing workers, regardless of whether the competing workers are native-born or foreign born. An immigration-induced 10 percent increase in the supply of doctorates in a particular field at a particular time reduces the earnings of that cohort of doctorates by 3 percent."[7]

The conclusion seems questionable for several reasons. First, whereas the effect attributed to smoking—death through lung cancer—is directly observable, the reduction of wages attributed to immigrants can only be inferred vis-à-vis a model of what wages would have been in the absence of immigration. And because regression models are inevitably based on arbitrary assumptions, Borjas's assertion that his results "show" (rather than "suggest") a result seems unwarranted.

Second, the assumptions in Borjas's model are not only arbitrary, but also, in my view, highly implausible. His procedure exploits differences across disciplines in how the proportions of foreign-born PhD students have changed (because different disciplines have been "hot" or "cold" at different times).[8] At the same time, Borjas's regressions assume that foreign-born PhDs depress wage rates in all fields at all times in the same way. In fact, as I suggested in the last chapter, immigration can have significant "complementary" effects: in other words immigrants may "fill up spots on the team" that could not otherwise easily be filled with native-born students or employees. The impetus to do so is much stronger when a field is hot. As with the effects of radii and heights on the surface areas of cylinders and cones, the effect of immigration on wages is therefore likely to be quite different across hot and cold fields, and not the same.

Third, Borjas's results seem utterly at odds with palpable trends. National Science Foundation data show that wages of PhDs have increased many times faster than overall wage rates.[*9] Wage growth has been particularly robust in hot fields that have trained and employed a high number of immigrant PhDs. This (and other circumstantial evidence that I will review in a later chapter) suggests that, at least in some fields, immigrants have helped raise wages and have not reduced them.

In previous chapters, my concerns about the unknowability of the true equations limited me to reporting simple medians and means—and only in cases where the numerical result was supported by qualitative evidence from my interviews. In book 2, where I focus on the broader questions of globalization, I *will* use the results of the existing body of traditional empirical research. But as mentioned in the preface, I have taken—and will continue to follow—the comprehensive approach of a common-law trial. I will therefore use the results of traditional empirical research as pieces of evidence rather than the last word.

---

* Epstein (2006, 165) offers a similar criticism of Donahue and Levitt's (2001, 379) celebrated claim that "legalized abortion appears to account for as much as 50 percent of the recent drop in crime" principally because it "has a disproportionate effect on the births of those who are most at risk of engaging in criminal behavior." In fact, according to Epstein, while crime rates dropped, births of "those . . . most at risk of engaging in criminal behavior" actually increased; abortion's only effect was to slow the rate of increase. Therefore, abortion couldn't have reduced crime rates by 50 percent, although it is possible that the rate was lower than it might otherwise have been.

A Thought Experiment

Suppose an inventor speculates that mixing a little silver into copper will produce an alloy whose conductivity is much higher than that of copper. To test whether—and by how much—the conductivity of the alloy is in fact higher, the inventor produces several wires, some from the alloy and some from copper. Each wire is then connected across the ends of a 12-volt battery, and the current passing through the wire is measured with an ammeter.

If all the wires are of the same length and diameter, figuring out the difference in conductivity is simple: for each observation, the inventor calculates the reciprocal of the current (read from the ammeter), then computes the means and standard deviations of the reciprocals for the copper wires and the silver-copper alloy wires, and finally compares the means (applying standard "difference of means" tests) for the two kinds of wires.

Now suppose instead that the wires are of the same length but not of the same diameter. The inventor could try to "correct" for the differences in diameter either by multiplying each observation by the diameter of the wire before calculating the reciprocal, or by including the diameter as an independent variable in a standard regression. In fact, however, diameter matters, but not in a simple linear fashion—the inventor actually needs to correct for the cross-sectional *area* of each wire by dividing each observation by the *square* of its diameter before calculating the reciprocal. If the inventor doesn't know this (and therefore uses the wrong regression equation), estimates of the conductivities will also be flat-out wrong.

But why does the inventor need to know the right relationship in advance? Simply plotting the measured current against the diameter would make it obvious that resistance increases with the square of the diameter. And indeed, if the readings weren't "noisy," the inventor would easily see the right relationship.

But what if the voltage of the battery and the length of the wire also vary from observation to observation? A standard linear regression with length, voltage, and diameter as independent variables would again lead to erroneous results. The "right" correction (per the equation in the main text) requires dividing each observation by $voltage / (length \times diameter^2)$ before calculating the reciprocals. Plotting observations isn't likely to make the correction factor obvious: the inventor would have to either conduct a large number of additional controlled experiments or consult a textbook.

What does this imply for the reliability of research in the social sciences? As discussed in the main text, controlled experiments are usually infeasible, and there is no textbook to tell you what the right equation actually is. Moreover, even if the researcher sees that an equation of the sort that governs the flow of electricity through a wire fits the data better than the standard linear (or log-linear) equations, it would be *verboten* to use the "unorthodox" equation simply because it fit the data better. Therefore, remember this, the next time you read "significant at the 95 percent confidence level": the significance *assumes* that an arbitrary model is the right one.

Book 2

Embrace or Resist? ∎

There were six or seven emails in my in-box this morning, and let's see: there is one from a European pharmaceutical company who we are in business discussions with; there is one from an Australian investigator who is on our scientific advisory board about introducing our company's materials to another overseas pharmaceutical company, and then there's one from a business-licensing executive at a third major European pharmaceutical company. My next appointment is with my chief scientific officer to go over in-licensing opportunities. I would expect that between 50 and 70 percent of the opportunities that we are going to spend the most time on are overseas opportunities. I don't think that globalization is at all fake or unreal.

I've been around start-up companies for 23 years. I think you will never see an "A"-round company doing any offshore development. Most "A"-round investors like to stop by; they like to know who the engineers are, they like to touch and feel the company. What is changing is with series "B" and series "C" companies, where you have a product, have customers endorsing it, and are now trying to add to the product. Now many venture groups are asking you to look offshore.

In the 1980s we used to make products like the T-1 multiplexer for the U.S. market first and then add a module for overseas. Now companies design with the world front and center. This is partly because many standards are now set globally. For example, now many regulatory bodies have opened the frequency bands for 2.4 GHz in an unlicensed way, so now one technology can play anywhere in the world.

In book 1, I suggested that globalization is not proceeding at breakneck speed on all fronts. But to deny that economic engagements across great distances have increased—including those involving innovative activities—is like questioning the spheroidal shape of the earth. Our interviews with VC-backed business represent a snapshot—albeit one with a nearly two-year exposure—not a movie. Although my findings suggest that the global engagement of VC-backed businesses is less than many make it out to be, it is almost certainly greater than it was just a couple of decades ago. For instance, many interviewees told us that although localization costs, capital and managerial capacity constraints, and other factors discussed in chapter 3 encouraged them to focus on establishing a base of U.S. customers first, they tried to anticipate what their overseas customers would require and build in the flexibility and features that would minimize localization costs when they did venture abroad later.

Some interviewees further suggested that the development of products that can be relatively easily adapted for international markets has increased over the years. The increasing number of top executives at VC-backed businesses who have previously worked at large multinational companies accounts for this in part. Whether U.S.-born or immigrants, they are conscious of the opportunities offered by international customers and try to anticipate the challenges of serving them. On the technical side, products are more often designed to conform to industry standards, and increasingly, these standards are global rather than national. In addition, in products such as enterprise software, modern programming practices reduce localization costs, even though this was not why the practices were initially adopted. For instance, software is now developed in modules, or Lego-like blocks of code, in a manner that happens to make it easy to localize by altering just a few of the blocks.

Similarly, although we saw that most companies undertook the development of their core products in the United States, many (although far from a majority) were using outsourcing firms or their own facilities abroad to test their products or add features to products that had matured. The emergence of this kind of offshoring is almost certainly a feature of the new millennium. Ten years ago, the swarm of outsourcing firms in Bangalore offering testing (or build-operate-transfer) services to small U.S. firms did not exist. As mentioned in chapter 4, until 2000, outsourcing firms did little offshoring; rather they sent their staff to undertake projects on the premises of their U.S. clients. As the capacity to deliver services abroad has increased, so has the number of stateside individuals who know how best to take advantage of this capacity.

The role of immigrants has expanded. Immigrants have long played a prominent role in the development and use of new technologies—for example, Andrew Carnegie from Scotland helped revolutionize the steel industry. This continued into the modern IT era. To cite just one instance, Andy Bechtolsheim from Germany and Vinod Khosla from India teamed up with U.S. natives Scott McNealy and Bill Joy to start Sun Microsystems in 1982. The proportion of immigrants employed as scientists and engineers in the United States has increased significantly—from 11.2 percent in 1980 to 19.3 percent in 2000.[1] And as we have seen, the proportion of immigrants among technical founders and rank-and-file technical staff of VC-backed businesses reflects their share of the overall scientific and engineering workforce in the United States; we may reasonably infer that it is significantly greater now than it was in 1980.

The use of high-level know-how developed abroad by U.S.-based VC-backed businesses has very likely increased as well. As we will see, even when the United States had a wide overall economic and technological lead, U.S. companies used to license high-level overseas know-how, to a nonnegligible degree. Now, with a narrower overall gap between the United States and the rest of the world, the fields in which the rest of the world leads have expanded. The Internet revolution has also increased the capacity of U.S. innovators to locate and license overseas know-how.*

The increase in the globalization of innovative activities of large companies, which I did not study, has probably been greater than in VC-backed businesses. As we have seen, large companies have many advantages in exploiting cross-border opportunities. These include ample capital, surplus managerial capacity, an international infrastructure, and a broad range of activities that make it likely some can be moved overseas. Therefore, as the climate for undertaking cross-border activities has improved, large companies have been at the forefront. Their efforts have significantly contributed to a rise in the number of R&D labs that do cutting-edge research abroad,

---

* Many biotech companies in my sample—which, as I have mentioned, often "developed" someone else's molecules—had licensed these molecules from pharmaceutical companies abroad. Indeed, some of these CEOs told us it was easier to secure licenses from overseas providers than domestic ones because competition was less intense. The "good stuff" in the United States, as one of our interviewees said, is much more "picked over" and less available for a small VC-backed business.

as well as of offshoring centers that focus on mundane developmental tasks. In fact, large firms have often catalyzed offshoring through their pioneering initiatives, and sustained it through extensive use.

Unless there is a significant political backlash in the United States or unexpected instability abroad, the globalization of innovation is likely to continue to expand. The evidence and analysis in book 1 merely suggest that it is not likely to accelerate at the rates we have experienced in all fields, for example, in some light-manufacturing and assembly operations. In other words, cataclysmic disruptions are not imminent.

But even small changes can lead to great transformations. For this reason I now examine the question of whether, in the long run, these changes threaten U.S. prosperity. As we will see in the next chapter, techno-nationalists claim that the expansion of scientific and engineering research abroad will impair living standards in the United States unless the country takes steps to maintain its lead in cutting-edge science and technology. In the chapters that follow, I argue that though the expansion of cutting-edge research abroad of course reduces the U.S. share, as long as the United States maintains its capacity to harness the high-level know-how to improve the performance of its mid- and ground-level industries, the expansion of the global supply of cutting-edge research, regardless of where it originates, is a good thing for the United States. Moreover, techno-nationalist prescriptions to "maintain the U.S. lead" will tend to impair rather than enhance the U.S. capacity to harness high-level research and are therefore likely to do more harm than good.*

---

* In advancing this argument, I will rely on observations about mid- and ground-level know-how and products (including their portability across national borders) that I have made in Book 1. In addition, I will expand my case to include the "expert testimony," as it were, of many other researchers who have studied the phenomena of globalization and innovation.

7

■ Alarmist Arguments

When the United States secured independence, its economy was dominated by the production of agricultural and other commodities. Alexander Hamilton, the first secretary of the U.S. Treasury, produced, in 1791, *The Report on Manufactures,* which proposed a system of tariffs and subsidies to nurture "infant industries" that would not otherwise survive in the face of more established competitors from Britain and continental Europe. Although there was debate about the desirability of moving away from an agricultural economy and the protection of infant industries, Hamilton's *Report* was profoundly influential, and many of its ideas were later incorporated into Senator Henry Clay's program for an "American system." By 1914, however, the United States had surpassed the UK as the world's leading economic and industrial power. The question of whether to protect infant industries then became more or less moot.

Today a doctrine of preeminence has nourished techno-nationalism. The goal of catching up has been replaced by the concern that others will catch up, particularly in cutting-edge science and technology. This concern is based on the premise that prosperity requires staying ahead—on all fronts, and the further the better. Preeminence is crucial; mere eminence won't do. Any diminution of the U.S. technological lead, never mind any falling behind in any field, will lead to absolute decline in living standards. Therefore, instead of nurturing infant industries through tariffs and subsidies, techno-nationalists seek to protect or increase the U.S. lead by promoting a particular activity: cutting-edge scientific and technological research.

Techno-nationalism does not have a single voice, and it is not even a banner many would march behind. Rather, it is my characterization of a way of thinking, appealing to those who regard technological advances abroad with (in my view misplaced) anxiety but are loath to (in my view correctly) embrace old-fashioned protectionism or other mercantilist policies. In this chapter, I will review some arguments and prescriptions that reflect this mind-set.

■ A Preoccupation with Leadership

In the fall of 1957, the Soviet Union launched *Sputnik 1*, the first artificial satellite, producing what might be called shock and awe in the United States and the fear of a "missile gap" with the Soviet Union. As it happened, the gap "turned out to be a myth."[1] But, a common belief took hold, according to a National Academy of Sciences report, that the United States was "quickly falling behind the USSR in science education and research." This led to "major policy reforms in education, civilian and military research, and federal support for researchers. Within a year, the National Aeronautics and Space Administration and DARPA [Defense Advanced Research Projects Agency] were founded. In that era, science and technology became a major focus of the public, and a presidential science adviser was appointed."[2] The initiatives produced noteworthy advances—NASA landed a man on the moon, for instance. But we cannot know the counterfactual: what kinds of advances were preempted by the resources diverted to the Apollo program, and in what direction scientific research and education might otherwise have evolved.

In the 1970s and 1980s, the outbreak of what Robert Samuelson calls the "competitiveness crisis" engendered the belief that Germany and Japan were poised to "surge ahead" of the United States. Again, the neglect of science and engineering was fingered as the culprit. In their celebrated 1980 article, "Managing Our Way to Economic Decline," Harvard Business School professors Robert Hayes and William Abernathy noted that the 2.8 percent annual growth of manufacturing productivity in the United States between 1960 and 1978 was well below Germany's 5.4 percent and Japan's 8.2 percent. They also asserted that the United States had "lost its leadership position" in "many high-technology as well as mature industries."

Why had this happened? According to Hayes and Abernathy, in the United States overall expenditures on R&D as measured in constant dollars and as a percentage of GNP had peaked in the mid-1960s, whereas they had continued to rise in West Germany and Japan. Worse, U.S. spending on R&D as a percentage of sales in "critical research-intensive industries" had "dropped by the mid-1970s to about half its level in the early 1960s."

"Success in most industries" required "an organizational commitment to compete in the marketplace on technological grounds," the authors asserted. But by their "devotion to short-term returns and 'management by the numbers,'" many U.S. managers had "effectively forsworn long-term technological superiority as a competitive weapon." Those managers' preoccupation with finance, as well as their "market-driven behavior," derived from a "new management orthodoxy" and the changing backgrounds of top managers: "Since the mid-1950s, there ha[d] been a rather substantial increase in the percentage of new company presidents whose primary interests and expertise [lay] in the financial and legal areas and not in production." In contrast, "gaining competitive success through technological superiority" was "a skill much valued by . . . seasoned European (and Japanese) managers" who were "painstakingly attentive to the means for keeping their companies technologically competitive."

In 1991, three distinguished economists—Kevin M. Murphy, Andrei Shleifer, and Robert W. Vishny (Murphy and Shleifer won the prestigious Clark medal in 1997 and 1999 respectively)—published an article, "The Allocation of Talent: Implications for Growth," in which they suggested that "the flow of some of the most talented people in the United States today into law and financial services" could be "one of the sources of our low productivity growth." To test this hypothesis, they ran regressions (using the traditional assumptions discussed in chapter 6) of the growth of real GDP per capita between 1970 and 1985 in 55 countries, using college enrollment in engineering and the law as independent variables. According to their regressions, countries with high proportions of engineering enrollments grew faster, whereas countries with high proportions of law enrollments grew more slowly.*

---

* Shleifer and Vishny went on to do seminal studies of the relationship of common law and economic growth. Japan reportedly tried to expand its supply of lawyers to facilitate the growth of its financial markets; the number of lawyers passing the bar exam in Japan more than tripled between 1990 and 2005, and the restrictions on foreign lawyers practicing in Japan were erased by amendment of the Gaikoku Bengoshi Hou (Foreign Lawyers Law) in 2003.

Like the *Sputnik* scare, the threat from Japan and Germany was rooted in a fear of coming in second. As the economist Paul David wrote in 1986, success in the United States was "equated with 'leadership' . . . with pioneering on the technological frontiers. To be an assiduous 'follower' seem[ed] somehow to have acquiesced in defeat, abandoning adventure for the haven of routine." At that time, however, possibly because Japan and Germany could not be linked to a national security problem, and because the Soviet bloc was imploding, U.S. policymakers made no significant effort to direct resources to scientific and technological research, train more scientists and engineers, or create new NASAs and DARPAs. U.S. managers continued to emphasize financial targets (except during the Internet bubble), and law schools continued to expand their enrollments. What changed—and quite sharply so—was that, in the 1990s, the much-vaunted Japanese and German economies, with their farsighted managers, legions of engineers, and the blessed absence of lawyers, lost their sparkle. The absence of plausible candidates who might surge past the United States took away the visceral appeal of the techno-nationalist argument. This was, however, a temporary reprieve.

The rapid economic growth in China and India has now reenergized the "lead or lose" camp. Thomas Friedman is one of the many who see "doing unto others before they do unto us" as the only alternative to protectionism. A preoccupation with technological leadership, as the examples below illustrate, overtakes popular writers, academics, the scientific establishment, and policymakers.

Consider, for instance, recent writing by Clyde Prestowitz, founder and president of the Economic Policy Institute. Prestowitz has extensive first-hand knowledge of trade issues. According to a bio posted on his institute's website, Prestowitz worked in the Commerce Department in the Reagan administration and "led many U.S. trade and investment negotiations with Japan, China, Latin America and Europe. Before joining the Commerce Department, he was a senior businessman in the United States, Europe, Japan and throughout Asia and Latin America." Later, he "played key roles in achieving congressional passage of NAFTA and in shaping the final content of the Uruguay Round, as well as providing the intellectual basis for current U.S. trade policies toward Japan, China and Korea." He is fluent in Japanese, Dutch, German, and French and has studied at Keio University in Tokyo.[3] Quite the opposite, obviously, of the insular American.

In 1988, Prestowitz published *Trading Places: How We Allowed Japan to Take the Lead*. His book shared the prevailing preoccupation with Japan, and declared, "The United States is being tested now as it has been tested only a few times before in its history."[4] Its trade negotiators have been "outclassed" by their Japanese counterparts, he wrote.[5] A reviewer of *Trading Places* commented that Prestowitz had "style[d] himself as a sort of latter-day Paul Revere of the West coast, flogging a half-dead horse and alerting America to the terrible peril that Japan represents. . . . Prestowitz goes so far as to end his book with the Benjamin Franklin option of hanging together or separately."[6]

Fast forward about 20 years: Prestowitz now warns about a loss of U.S. technological preeminence. In *America's Technology Future at Risk*, published in 2006, Prestowitz writes: "American wealth, economic growth and national security have long been based on technological leadership. . . . [T]he United States has always focused on new technology as the main engine of economic welfare. For more than half a century, America's broad technological leadership has been unchallenged."

Prestowitz is especially concerned with the U.S. position in the telecommunications industry, which "has long been an indispensable element of America's technological leadership and economic success." Now, however, the United States is "well on its way to surrendering leadership in advanced telecom products and services." Prestowitz points to several other alarming developments: In 2005, the United States had a "$55 billion trade deficit in Advanced Technology Products." Venture capitalists are "pressing the start-up firms they finance to move R&D to Asia. . . . Many telecom and technology companies [have] cut vital R&D spending by 10 to 40%. At the same time, government R&D spending in these areas has also fallen by over 30%."

He continues: "Foreign companies make up the majority of the top 10 recipients of U.S. patents each year, and the United States has fallen behind the EU and lost ground to Asian countries in the publication of scientific articles. The United States is awarding fewer Bachelor of Science degrees than it did in 1985, and far fewer than Japan, the E.U., China, India and even Korea."[7]

The Harvard labor economist Richard Freeman uses different arguments but reaches similar conclusions. Freeman's 2005 NBER working paper, like Prestowitz's article, asserts the significance of leadership: *leader* or *leadership* appear in the title once and five times on just the first page. Shorn of their qualifying clauses and sentences, Freeman's concerns can be stated as follows.

"Leadership in science and technology gives the U.S. its comparative advantage," which "in a knowledge-based economy, contributes substantially to economic success." Unfortunately for the United States, its "global economic leadership" is under threat. "Changes in the global job market" are "eroding U.S. dominance in science and engineering." Freeman forecasts that "the erosion will continue into the foreseeable future." By "increasing the number of scientists and engineers, highly populous low-income countries such as China and India can compete with the U.S. in technically advanced industries" and "undo the traditional 'North-South' pattern of trade in which advanced countries dominate high-tech while developing countries specialize in less skilled manufacturing."

Freeman offers the following evidence to support his claim that U.S. dominance in science and engineering is eroding and will continue to erode: In 1970, "over half of science and engineering doctorates were granted by U.S. institutions of higher education." Since then, the U.S. share has steadily declined. As shown in table 7.1a, countries in the European Union produced 7 percent fewer PhDs than the United States in 1975. By 2001, EU institutions granted 54 percent more PhDs, and by 2010 they will probably grant nearly twice the number of PhDs as U.S. institutions. Japanese institutions produced just 11 percent of the PhDs produced by U.S. institutions in 1975. By 2001, that percentage had more than doubled, to 29 percent. China produced virtually no doctorates in 1975. By 2001, it was producing nearly a third as many as the United States, and by 2010 it was expected to produce more than the United States. Overall, according to Freeman's projections, the U.S. share of the world's science and engineering doctorates is likely to fall to about 15 percent in 2010.

Like Prestowitz, Freeman also points to a fall in the U.S. shares of scientific publications, patents, and engineering degrees, and to the expansion of R&D establishments in Asia. "Data on publications and citations by country of investigator show that the U.S. predominance has already begun to drop," writes Freeman. "In spring 2004, the front page of *The New York Times* reported a fall in the U.S. share of papers in physics journals, while *Nature* reported a rise in the share of papers in China. The NSF records a drop in the U.S. share of scientific papers from 38% in 1988 to 31% in 2001 and a drop in the U.S. share of citations from 52 percent in 1992 to 44 percent. The share of papers counted in the Chemical Abstract Service fell from 73% in 1980 to 40% in 2003."

"Many high-tech companies," continues Freeman, "have begun to locate major research installations outside the U.S. In 2004, the CEO of Cisco declared that 'Cisco is a Chinese company' when he announced that the firm was setting up its newest R&D facility in China. One of Microsoft's major research facilities is in Beijing. OECD data shows a large increase in U.S.-outward R&D investment from 1994 to 2000. . . . As of mid- 2004, the Chinese government registered over 600 multinational research facilities in the country, many from large U.S. multinationals. By contrast, in 1997 China registered less than 50 multinational corporation research centers."

Freeman also highlights what he believes are dangers (which Prestowitz does not emphasize) of depending on foreign-born researchers: "If U.S. economic growth and comparative advantage depend substantially on the work of scientific and engineering workers, relying so much on foreign-born supplies could be risky [because] any interruption or change in the flow of immigrant scientists and engineers would certainly harm U.S. research and development." Moreover, adds Freeman, the very presence of these foreign-born researchers discourages U.S. natives from pursuing careers in science and engineering: "[T]o attract more U.S. citizens, earnings and employment opportunities have to get better, which is difficult to effectuate as long as the country can attract many scientists and engineers from overseas at current wages and employment opportunities."[8]

Alarm about the erosion of U.S. technological leadership has also been expressed by numerous blue-ribbon committees. A December 2005 article in *Physics Today* (the flagship publication of the American Institute of Physics) notes that more than a dozen reports by the likes of the U.S. Council on Competitiveness, the Electronic Industries Alliance, and the Business Roundtable all carry "the same basic message: The U.S. is losing its competitive edge because of a lack of investment in education and research."[9] An especially high-profile exemplar (and the subject of the *Physics Today* story) is *Rising Above the Gathering Storm*, produced by a 20-person committee comprising luminaries from the academy and the business world. Presenting the report to Congress, Norman Augustine, chair of the committee, testified, "It is the unanimous view of our committee that America today faces a serious and intensifying challenge with regard to its future competitiveness and standard of living. Further, we appear to be on a losing path."[10]

The report itself warned that the "scientific and technical building blocks of our economic leadership are eroding at a time when many other nations are gathering strength. . . . Although many people assume that the United States will always be a world leader in science and technology, this may not continue to be the case inasmuch as great minds and ideas exist throughout the world. We fear the abruptness with which a lead in science and technology can be lost—and the difficulty of recovering a lead once [it is] lost, if indeed it can be regained at all." It also quoted a "blunt" letter from the leadership of the National Science Foundation to the President's Council of Advisors:

> Civilization is on the brink of a new industrial order. The big winners in the increasingly fierce global scramble for supremacy will not be those who simply make commodities faster and cheaper than the competition. They will be those who develop talent, techniques and tools so advanced that there is no competition.

Concerns about the erosion of U.S. leadership have apparently resonated with the Bush administration. Noting the "uncertainty" engendered by "new competitors, like India and China," President Bush, in his 2006 State of the Union speech, announced American Competitiveness Initiative, which would (according to a White House press release) "help the United States remain a world leader in science and technology." The initiative included proposals to double the federal commitment to "critical basic research programs in the physical sciences," make permanent the research and development tax credit (to encourage "bolder private-sector initiatives in technology"), and support universities that "provide world-class education and research opportunities."

The United States is not the only advanced economy where policymakers argue that scientific and technological leadership is essential. In the UK, then Chancellor of the Exchequer Gordon Brown's 2006 budget statement noted that China and India had "4 million graduates a year to Britain's 400,000" as well as more computer scientists and engineers. "Every advanced industrial country knows that falling behind in science," he said, "means falling behind in commerce and prosperity." He proposed the government "do more to support the dynamism and enterprise of business . . . start[ing] with the importance of Britain leading in scientific invention and discovery." Brown's budget included increased expenditures on scientific discovery, simplified allocation of research funding for universities, and an expanded scope for R&D credits.

In like manner, the European Council set out in 2000 its so-called Lisbon Agenda.[11] The Agenda commits the European Union to raising research spending in member countries to at least 3 percent of GDP by 2010. According to a European Commission (EC) website devoted to the agenda, "The EU invests less of its GDP in research and development than its main competitors"—just 1.96 percent of its GDP compared to 2.59 percent for the United States, 3.12 percent for Japan, and 2.91 percent for Korea. Europe also "does not have enough scientists and researchers—5.3 per 1000 in the workforce compared to 9 per 1000 in the U.S. and 9.7 per 1000 in Japan." The solutions proposed in the Agenda included creating a "European Institute of Technology" and making "science a more attractive career option."[12]

The Agenda didn't advance rapidly, however. In July 2005, the European Commission issued a report showing that "the growth rate of R&D intensity (R&D expenditure as a percentage of GDP) [had] been declining since 2000 and [was] now close to zero. Europe [was] on track to miss the objective it set itself to boost spending on R&D from 1.9 to 3% by 2010." Europe was "becoming a less attractive place to carry out research. . . . R&D expenditure by EU companies in the U.S. [had] increased much faster than R&D expenditure by U.S. firms in the EU. . . . Additionally, U.S. investment ha[d] been growing at a much greater rate in areas outside the EU—about 8% per year in the EU and 25% per year in China."

Following this report the EC launched new initiatives to "boost the 'Europe of knowledge.' "[13] These too did not bear fruit: two years later, the Commission was reporting that Europe's "R&D investment deficit against the U.S." had "remained constant over recent years," and that "low business R&D [continued to be] a major threat to the European knowledge-based economy."[14]

■ Why Does It Matter?

European alarmists and U.S. alarmists, such as Messrs. Prestowitz and Freeman, can't both be right. Is the United States "falling behind" Europe or not? Putting that aside, why does scientific and technological *leadership* matter to a country or region in the first place? For Prestowitz, the historical correlation of U.S. leadership with prosperity makes it self-evident that any erosion of leadership must impair standards of living: if the United States became rich when it led, leadership caused prosperity, and other countries' catching up will erode standards of living in the United States.

Freeman relies on models of North-South (or rich country–poor country) trade to reach the same conclusion that Prestowitz asserts as a given. Freeman's reasoning may be paraphrased as follows:

1. According to highly simplified, classical or neoclassical models, trade always benefits both parties; but more modern models of trade that include complications such as first-mover advantages or increasing returns to scale show that gains to one country may come at the expense of another.

2. Modern trade models also predict that technological advances in a country may help—or hurt—its trading partners, depending on the sector in which they occur. In particular, "a country benefits when a trading partner or potential trading partner improves technology in a sector in which the country does not compete, but loses when a country improves its technology in the country's export sector. [In other words] it is good for Alaska if El Salvador improves its technology for banana production but bad for Nicaragua."

3. North-South trade is mutually beneficial when "the South competes with the North for production of older products through low wages but is unable to compete in the newest technology." If however, the South starts competing with the North in "the high-tech vanguard sectors," the South gains at the expense of the North. Thus, as China increases its supply of scientific and engineering workers and competes with the United States for high-level innovations instead of just trinkets and toys, the United States begins to lose rather than benefit from trade. As Freeman puts it, "The loss of comparative advantage can substantially harm an advanced country."

To further simplify this kind of North-South argument, imagine the following scenario: New Yorker "North" meets up with his country cousin "South." North has a high-paying sales job that South would also like to have, but can't because he lacks the requisite panache and city smarts. Instead, he moves in with North and does housework in return for a modest allowance and room and board. As in the classical trade models, both parties benefit: North gets more time to make lucrative sales calls and South gets a chance to live in New York. In the fullness of time, South acquires the know-how needed for a sales job and moves out. Now only South benefits—North suffers a net loss.*

---

* Some theorists, not including Freeman, disingenuously interpret North's loss as the "consequence of free trade" when it is in fact purely the consequence of the upgrading of South's know-how. North would gain nothing from terminating trade (i.e., kicking out South) before South has upgraded his know-how. In fact, even though North loses when South moves out, measured from start to finish, both cousins benefit from their interactions.

However, it is not difficult to create an economic model that makes North a net winner in this imagined scenario. As trade economist James Markusen remarks, "I am confident that I can concoct a model to generate any result desired by a reader with a deep pocketbook."[15] Freeman acknowledges that there are models showing that "under some circumstances; the loss of technological advantage *could* benefit the advanced country," but he dismisses such a scenario as "more of a theoretical curiosum than a realistic representation of the current economic world." In Freeman's judgment, the "loss of technological superiority overall is likely to be disastrous for U.S. workers and firms." Trends like the "multinational movement of R&D facilities to developing countries are harbingers" of the difficult "adjustment problems" that await U.S. workers.

■ A Puzzle

History does not, however, seem to bear out the claim that the erosion of technological leadership is likely to be a disaster for the United States. Recall Freeman's evidence about the loss of U.S. shares in scientific publications, citations, and patent counts. Look again at the data in table 7.1a on the ratios of scientific and engineering (S&E) PhDs. Toward the end of his article, Freeman says that the increase in S&E workers in Europe and Japan is "recent," whereas the table points to a trend that has been in place for more than two decades (and has been widely bemoaned for that long). Yet table 7.1b shows that during this period there has been no decline in U.S. per capita incomes in either absolute or relative terms. PPP-adjusted per capita income in EU countries was about 75 percent of U.S. per capita income in 1975, and the gap has remained more or less at that level since.* Japanese per capita incomes reached 80 percent of the per capita incomes in the United States by 1989; after that, relative incomes in Japan actually fell a bit.

According to "convergence theories," European and Japanese incomes should naturally catch up with U.S. incomes; with substantial increases in their share of PhDs, scientific articles, and other markers of leadership, why didn't Europe and Japan roar ahead? Why, instead, was the growth rate in output per hour between 1995 and 2003 in Europe just half that in the United States?[16]

---

* Using a different comparative methodology, Gordon (2006) suggests that per capita GDP in Europe fell from about 75% of U.S. per capita GDP in 1975 to 69% in 2004.

Japan's reconstruction- and export- led boom after World War II, also doesn't square with Freeman's prognostication. As is well known, for nearly four decades Japan grew at miraculous rates as it moved from the "South" to the "North," and the composition of its exports changed from low-end trinkets to cutting-edge goods. U.S. per capita income and productivity, which started at a much higher base, did grow more slowly than Japan's, but grow they did. Indeed, prosperity increased in most Western countries, all of which could not possibly have been leaders in science and technology.

What accounts for the gap between the "technical leadership is a must" claim on the one hand and many decades of actual experience on the other? It certainly is possible that, had the United States maintained its technological lead, it could have achieved even greater prosperity. This, in fact, seems to be the position taken by Paul Samuelson's recent (and according to Leamer, somewhat "elliptical")[17] critique of "popular, polemical untruths" of the benefits of "dynamic fair free trade."[18] Using a model of the North-South type described above, Samuelson arrives at the following historical analysis: U.S. workers once had monopoly access to "superlative" U.S. know-how and capital, but after World War II, the know-how and capital "began to spread faster away from the United States." The U.S. share of total global output then steadily dropped from almost 50 percent at the end of the war to about 20 to 25 percent now. "Although these trends did not mean an absolute decline in U.S. affluence, they arguably did reflect a headwind slowing down the U.S. post-Keynes rate of real growth in the last half of the twentieth century."[19]

Samuelson's interpretation will surprise those who believe that the rebuilding of Europe and Japan was an economic boon rather than a headwind for the United States. A more plausible reconciliation of continued U.S. prosperity in the face of its diminishing share of cutting-edge research is that the North-South models that predict an inverse relationship are flawed. Even where the deductive reasoning is sound—and the refereeing process of academic journals almost guarantees that it will be—models can be practically useless if they mischaracterize reality in some fundamental way. To draw an analogy from the physical world: a model may prove that automobile brakes would fail in a world without friction. In such a world, the model would instruct engineers to devise alternatives (such as magnetic brakes); but given the reality of friction, the utility of such an "improvement" would be limited. Similarly, as I will argue, the North-South models invoked by Freeman omit or mischaracterize vital features of modern innovation and trading systems; these omissions and mischaracterizations are at the heart of predictions of the disastrous consequences of an erosion of the U.S. lead in cutting-edge science.

My counterargument starts with what I believe is the uncontroversial observation that *commercially successful innovations usually enrich more than just the innovator.* For instance, new products and services also generate a consumer surplus—value to their users in excess of the price. If they didn't, why would customers ever take a chance on a new product or service? The distribution of value between innovators and users also is noteworthy. Successful innovators (and their investors) can secure extraordinary wealth, whereas the total dollar value of an innovation secured by a user is often quite small; therefore, it is tempting to think that innovators are the main beneficiaries. But users outnumber innovators by a wide margin. Moreover, according to Baumol's analysis,[20] a competitive, free market system of innovation provides a positive but small share of the gains to the innovator, whereas users get the rest.

This proposition makes intuitive sense but is difficult to prove. The profits of the producers can provide at least a crude handle on what they get, but we cannot directly observe the "surplus" secured by the users. Researchers have tried several ways of getting around this problem, and although estimates vary with the method used and the industry studied, they all support the Baumol conjecture, that consumers rather than producers secure the lion's share of the benefit. For instance, Nordhaus (2005) analyzed data for the nonfarm business economy and for major industries in the United States. He found that producers captured a "minuscule" fraction of returns (on the order of 3 percent) from technological advances over the 1948 to 2000 period, "indicating that most of the benefits of technological change are passed on to consumers."[21]

An obvious but important implication of this is the following: *Innovation can only sustain widespread prosperity if it benefits many users rather than a few innovators.*

The question raised by the techno-nationalist thesis is whether and how it matters where cutting-edge research is undertaken. Do U.S. consumers benefit from breakthroughs that originate abroad, or could they, as in the North-South models invoked by Freeman, actually suffer? "Economists worry about another place owning the very next big thing—the next groundbreaking technology," says Stanford's Dan Siciliano. "If the heart and mind of the next great thing emerges somewhere else . . . then we will be hurt."[22] Are such concerns well founded? Would Texans, New Yorkers, Ohioans, or

Michiganders have been better off if the protocols for the World Wide Web had been invented at Stanford rather than CERN in Switzerland? Does it matter if French scientists at the Institut Pasteur isolated HIV before U.S. scientists did?

An important determinant of whether breakthroughs abroad help or hurt consumers at home is if the know-how is internationally "tradable." Suppose (as is the case with scientific research) that the ideas are published online or in a journal that anyone can subscribe to or (in the case of commercial R&D) the know-how is licensed all over the world at the same, low price compared to its value. Then it would not matter much where the breakthrough originated. In fact, if international financiers provided the capital and shared in the returns, the geographic origin would be particularly inconsequential.

Suppose, instead, that research is all domestically financed and that the products that embody breakthroughs can be exported, but not the know-how itself. Now the country of origin secures both the profits from the breakthrough and all the wage income associated with the production of related goods and services. Conversely, the receiving country has to generate exports not just to pay for the know-how but also for the production costs of the goods and services.

The North-South models that Freeman relies on for his alarming predictions make the latter assumption, that only final goods and services are tradable: cutting-edge research is joined at the hip, as it were, with every stage of the process used to produce goods and services derived from the research. I will argue that there are indeed a few industries (such as movies and music) where nearly everything—from the core idea to the final product—is produced in one location and then exported all over the world. But overall, the assumptions of the North-South models only scantly correspond to modern realities: contrary to the stipulations of those models, high-level know-how is now highly geographically mobile and *is* used to produce goods and services far from where it originates.

■ Concluding Comments

For nearly half a century, the U.S. lead in the development of high-level know-how has been eroding: as other countries have stepped up their research efforts and increased the total produced, the U.S. share has quite naturally declined. Through about the 1980s, this phenomenon was driven mainly by countries that had advanced economies before World War II, which were then regaining their scientific and industrial capabilities. Their ranks have now been joined by such countries as China and India, and it is likely that the share of high-level know-how produced by U.S.-based researchers will continue to decline.

This progressive erosion of the U.S. lead has led to periodic bouts of anguish and dire predictions about falling living standards. None of these bleak prognostications have come to pass. In fact, most people would say—notwithstanding Paul Samuelson's suggestion of "headwinds"—that the resurgence of Europe and Japan after World War II was a good thing for the United States, especially in light of what happened in Germany after World War I. History, then, is not on the side of the alarmists. But "past performance is no guarantee of future results," so we need to look into the reasoning and causal mechanisms underpinning the claim that the erosion of leadership will lead to bad consequences. Here we find that although more popular writers simply assert the result, economists such as Freeman point to sophisticated North-South models. I will argue that although the mathematics of the models are sound, their key assumptions, that cutting-edge know-how doesn't cross national borders and that only final goods are tradable, are unrealistic. A more accurate picture of cross-border flows leads to a very different view of what more cutting-edge R&D in China and India portends for prosperity in the United States and other countries of the North.

8

■ The Reassuring Realities
of Modern Cross-Border Flows

Once upon a time it might have been reasonable to assume that new technologies would only be used by domestic, vertically integrated firms (or "regional clusters") and that only the final goods and services they produced would cross national borders. This is not an accurate representation of cross-border flows today. Containers upon containers of "final" consumer goods arriving from China represent only the most visible and measurable manifestation of cross-border trade. As we will see in this chapter, globalization today also features substantial—although less vivid and hard to track—flows of capital, intermediate goods, and know-how. These background flows, I will argue, make it unlikely that the loss of U.S. share in the development of high-level scientific and technical knowledge has eroded (or in the future will erode) its prosperity.

■ Waves of Globalization: A Historical Recap

Before the Industrial Revolution, international trade was modest. Primitive modes of production did not offer significant economies of scale. This limited both the total quantities produced and the gains that could be realized from specializing in different kinds of production in different countries. Long-distance trade was also hampered by the high costs—and the physical dangers—of transportation. International commerce largely involved trade in commodities that could not be locally produced (e.g., spices for silver) and some goods for which natural endowments created comparative advantages that offset high transportation costs (e.g., wool for wine). Plunder and territorial conquest were the more salient forms of cross-border interactions.

The Industrial Revolution led to dramatic increases in both economic activity and international trade. World GDP growth per capita was virtually zero until the eighteenth century. In the nineteenth century, per capita incomes more than doubled, and then in the twentieth century increased more than eightfold. Growth was especially robust in the industrial nations of the West. The economist Bradford DeLong reports a ten-and-a-half-fold increase in real per capita GDP in the twentieth century.[1] The growth of international trade was even more explosive. According to estimates by the economic historian Angus Maddison, the share of exports in world GDP increased more than 13-fold between 1820 and 1992: exports increased 541-fold, whereas GDP increased a mere 40-fold.[*][2]

The rapid expansion reflected both technological and political changes. Most obviously, new forms of transportation reduced the costs of trading. In 1820, goods were carried mainly by "vehicles drawn by horses or other pack animals, by canal barge or by sailing vessels. In the nineteenth century, railways and steamships were very important substitutes. In the twentieth, motor and air transport developed on a large scale."[3] The faster and cheaper forms of transportation encouraged "interspatial specialization"; in other words, different places could focus on producing different things and buy what could be produced more efficiently elsewhere. The tendency toward trade and specialization was also promoted by technological innovations that led to economies of scale and economies of agglomeration. Manchester, for instance, with large-scale textile mills and locally available "complements" (such as trained mill workers) developed "technological" comparative advantages in producing textiles. The Rhine Valley similarly became a center for producing fine chemicals.

Political beliefs, particularly in Britain, turned from mercantilism and protectionism to free trade. Although Adam Smith promoted the idea much

---

* The acceleration of international trade attracted attention quite early in this period. In 1848, Marx and Engels wrote: "In the place of the old wants, satisfied by the production of the country, we find new wants, requiring for their satisfaction the products of distant land and climes. In the place of the old local and national seclusion and self sufficiency, we have intercourse in every direction, universal interdependence of nations"—*The Communist Manifesto* (1848), 84.

earlier, according to Baldwin and Martin, the "first sustained drive towards free trade" in Britain began in 1815. "Starting from a position of strict agricultural protectionism and manufacturing tariffs of about 50% . . . [industrialists] embraced free trade, since they believed it would boost exports by lowering wages (industrial wages were *de facto* tied to wheat prices) and by allowing foreign nations to earn the gold necessary to pay for British manufactures." Over the next few decades, industrial interests gained sufficient political strength "to push through across-the-board free trade in 1846 via the repeal of the Corn Laws." The continental ruling classes were much less enthusiastic, and in the United States Alexander Hamilton's advocacy of protection for "infant industry" "underpinned the U.S. protectionists' stance for more than a hundred years." But "British industrial productivity was unrivalled . . . and the sun never set on the Union Jack. Despite foreign protection, Britain chose to maintain its liberal policies and this allowed the world trading system to flourish, even as British dominance eroded."

The outbreak of World War I ended what Baldwin and Martin call the first "wave" of globalization, which they date from 1820 to 1914. The war brought about immediate and significant trade restrictions. It also "signaled the end of Pax Britannica and Britain's hegemonic support of the international trade system." When the war ended, some wartime trade restrictions remained in place, and through the 1920s protectionism continued to rise in Europe and elsewhere. The enactment of the Smoot-Hawley Tariff Act, in June 1930, proved to be the "straw that finally broke the back of the world trading system," as Baldwin and Martin write. The United States was by then an "economic super-power and the U.S. market mattered enormously." Italy, France, and other countries quickly responded with retaliatory tariffs, and Britain provided a second tariff "shock," passing the Abnormal Importation Act in November 1931 and the Import Duties Act in February 1932. Overall, according to Madsen's calculations, the world average of import duties (weighted by the volume of imports) almost doubled from 1929 to 1932. International trade contracted sharply, with import and export volumes in industrialized nations falling by nearly a third between 1929 and 1932.

The share of trade of overall economic activity stopped falling in most industrialized countries in the mid-1930s, but recovery to 1914 levels was interrupted by World War II and was only gradual even after the war. In

Baldwin and Martin's judgment, the "second" (and still ongoing) wave of globalization did not start until 1960. By the mid-1990s, trade-to-GDP ratios in most industrialized countries had passed their earlier peaks. In the case of the United States, which had not participated in the earlier wave and had in fact become "progressively more closed" between 1870 and 1910, trade-to-GDP ratios grew to twice their earlier peak. As in the previous wave, lower tariffs and transportation costs helped expand trade.[4]

Baldwin and Martin highlight some fundamental differences between the two waves. One was that the gap between the "have" and "have-not" countries (in terms of industrialization and income levels) was much greater in 1960, at the start of the second wave, than in 1820, at the start of the first wave. The composition and direction of trade was also different. In the first wave, the North exported manufactured goods to the South and imported raw materials and temperate and tropical foodstuffs in return. In the second wave, the North became a significant importer of manufactured goods from the South.* Finally, although the gap between the haves and the have-nots was wider to start with, as the second globalization wave progressed, differences between the advanced economies and their hitherto "backward" trading partners, such as China, narrowed. In the previous wave, differences had widened.

The mechanism of this convergence has an important, albeit subtle, bearing on techno-nationalistic assumptions about mobility of know-how and the composition of trade today.

UCLA economist Edward Leamer implies (in an insightful and readable critique of *The World Is Flat*) that ideas, traveling as "stowaways" along with traded goods, have raised productivity and standards of living in previously have-not countries such as China. My alternative to this anthropomorphized attribution of wanderlust to ideas is that the transmission of manufacturing know-how from advanced economies to places like China has *preceded* exports. In some instances, local entrepreneurs have copied or reverse-engineered know-how from advanced countries. More typically, overseas individuals and firms, ranging from individual entrepreneurs based in Hong Kong and Taiwan to giant multinational corporations, have taken their know-how to China through licenses and, more importantly, direct investments in subsidiaries and joint ventures.

---

* Moreover, North-South trade itself became less important in the second wave than North-North trade (i.e. between the already rich and industrialized countries).

The first globalization wave also featured significant foreign direct investment, but mainly in natural resources (e.g., mining), railways, and utilities rather than in manufacturing.[5] The mill owners of Manchester apparently preferred to export textiles to India rather than set up textile mills in India, in spite of the local availability of cotton, cheap labor, a large market, and the protection of a colonial government. I am not aware of any research about what made businesses more willing or able to undertake such investment in the second globalization wave, but the evidence suggests a few possibilities.

First, as documented by the late Alfred Chandler and other business historians, by 1960, large industrial corporations had developed the organizational structures and systems necessary to realize economies of scale and scope. With some modification, the same capabilities could be used to manage and coordinate remote manufacturing facilities. Second, many large U.S. companies were founded or came of age after the first globalization wave receded. According to a study published in the *Business History Review,* about half of the 1994 *Fortune* 500 companies were founded after 1910. When these companies sought to expand abroad, particularly to take advantage of opportunities created by the reconstruction of Europe after World War II, they faced the choice of either exporting to these markets or setting up local production facilities. Import tariffs and other trade barriers had begun to decline, but apparently were still sufficiently high to encourage significant local investing in local production to avoid the tariffs. U.S. multinationals therefore became a major local force in many countries abroad before the second globalization wave gathered force.*

Much of U.S. companies' direct investment was in Europe, and, even now, most such investment from the United States and other advanced economies still flows to other advanced economies. But the confidence and know-how that multinationals acquired in Europe could be used in other places as well. Therefore, as Asian countries such as Taiwan, Korea, Malaysia, Thailand, and eventually China opened up to foreign investment, these companies were willing and able to take advantage of the opportunity.

A third factor that likely encouraged direct investment in the second globalization wave was a decline in communications costs—a phenomenon

---

* The importance accorded to the role of U.S. companies in Europe in the early 1960s can be seen in many books, such as Servan-Schreiber's 1967 bestseller *Le Défi Américain* (*The American Challenge*).

extensively discussed in Frances Cairncross's *The Death of Distance*. As I have mentioned, a decline in transportation costs was an important stimulus to trade in the first globalization wave. Baldwin and Martin point out that the costs of sea freight declined sharply after World War II till about 1960, when they flattened out. Similarly, air-freight costs saw steep declines and then a flattening in the 1980s. The costs of communications, however, plunged, so, as Baldwin and Martin put it, the costs of trading ideas declined faster than the costs of trading goods.[6] It also transformed the capacity of businesses to coordinate and manage far-flung operations.

Access to technologies (through foreign direct investment and other mechanisms) previously developed in the North has allowed countries in the South to grow spectacularly.[7] Over the last 25 years, China's real GDP has grown nearly 10 percent a year. Such rates dwarf those of the North in the nineteenth century,[8] which themselves were historically unprecedented. Using tried-and-tested technologies previously developed abroad hastens growth, because acquiring wheel designs is cheaper and faster than reinventing the wheel from scratch.

Over the years, improvements in managerial know-how and communications infrastructures (and possibly some other factors) encouraged not just the simple replication of domestic production in international locations, but the dispersion of different stages of production to multiple locations. According to Baldwin, until about the mid-1980s, "production stages tended to be spatially clustered in a single facility, i.e. a factory, because this made it easier for managers and workers to co-ordinate their work. The innumerable small and large problems that arise during production could be settled directly with little interruption to the manufacturing process."

After the mid-1980s, as some backward countries' capacity to host manufacturing operations grew faster than their local wages, and communications costs declined, geographic separation of various production stages became more attractive: "In North America, the Maquiladora programme saw the widespread emergence of 'twin plants,' one on the U.S. side of the border and one on the Mexican side." At about the same time, Japanese manufacturers facing "phenomenal growth" in wages reacted

by offshoring labour-intensive production stages to nearby East Asian nations. . . . This tendency, which has been called the "hollowing out" of the Japanese economy, started so-called "triangle trade," where Japanese firms headquartered in Japan produce certain hi-tech parts in Japan, ship them to factories in East Asian nations for labour-intensive stages of production including assembly, and then ship the final products to Western markets or back to Japan. The division of East Asia into head-quarter (HQ) economies and factory economies strengthened as Taiwan, Korea, Singapore and Hong Kong experienced their own "hollowing out" and followed the lead of Japanese manufacturing companies in off-shoring the most labour-intensive manufacturing tasks.

An obvious implication of what has variously been called "unbundling," "disintegration of the production function," and the "slicing of the value chain" has been a considerable and well-documented increase in cross-border trade in intermediate goods, often occurring "within" multinational firms.[9] More importantly, for my purpose, is that unbundling drives a wedge between where the high-level technology or design for a new product originates and where it is manufactured. In the first globalization wave, production usually stayed close to the location of the invention. The Big Three automobile companies, for instance, developed new engines, radiators, brakes, and car models in Detroit and built them right there. Krugman describes Ford's River Rouge plant in the early 1930s as "a facility that ingested coke and iron ore at one end and extruded passenger cars from the other."[*][10]

In the early stages of the second globalization phase, in Raymond Vernon's "product life-cycle" theory, manufacturing migrated once a product and its production process matured. Now, the dispersion of manufacturing occurs very quickly or even from the get-go. There may still be some advantages in locating manufacturing close to the R&D or design center where a product originates; but this is just one of the many factors that influence the design of what is now called the "supply chain." Usually, other considerations—such as wage rates of production workers, tax regimes, proximity to markets, supplier networks, and complements—dictate that much of the manufacturing takes place in locations far removed from where the technology originates.

Certainly there are exceptions: we can still think of Hollywood studios as facilities that ingest scripts, stars, camera crew, and directors at one end and

---

* This was by no means the rule, however. The geographic separation of invention from production is an age-old phenomenon. For examples from the Second Industrial Revolution (including the textile, shoe, and electric industries), see Lamoreaux and Sokoloff 1996, 1997, and Sutthiphisal 2006.

extrude completed movies on the other. Similarly, biotechnology companies locate both their production facilities and their research centers in clusters such as Boston and San Francisco. But these are exceptions. Big pharmaceutical companies manufacture blockbuster drugs (on a scale much larger than niche biotechnology products) in places that, like Puerto Rico, have relatively low wages and attractive tax regimes. More often than not, locations that have a comparative advantage in cutting-edge research are palpably unsuited for manufacturing the products that result from the research. As Arora and Gambardella point out, the likelihood of the geographic separation of production from invention increases when the body of knowledge underlying the invention process has a strong scientific basis.[11]

Factors such as the low cost of communications that promoted the geographic dispersion of production have now also encouraged a similar unbundling of R&D. According to a 2007 report from the Economist Intelligence Unit:

Companies have long recognised that it is inefficient to keep the entire manufacturing process in-house. In order to compete effectively, they accept that they must distribute the work across multiple partners and geographies, with raw materials being sourced in one location, components in another and final assembly happening in a third. Until recently, however, R&D had largely escaped this trend and, in many companies, it was a centralised and jealously guarded department. Ideas sometimes trickled from production facilities in low-cost economies to R&D departments in the West, but the process was largely ad hoc. In the past few years, however, companies have started to implement a more systematic and integrated approach to spreading the load of R&D. . . . [C]ompanies are increasingly opening up R&D to external organizations and offshoring stages of the process to locations where it can be more efficiently handled.[12]

A senior manager of the research lab of a multinational industrial company provides a specific example:

We are developing a new engine technology that will be incorporated into a line of pumps with a research partner in Sweden. Once we take it through prototype testing in a laboratory environment, we will hand it off to a technology consulting company, probably in Germany or France, who will figure out how to integrate it into a pump. They will also test a large number of pumps equipped with the new engines under actual field conditions. If all our requirements are met, we will hand it off to our execution team in China who will do the industrial engineering necessary for mass production in Asia.[13]

This example illustrates another feature of the global development of innovation. As I stressed in book 1, high-level know-how coming out of R&D labs is only one part of the know-how required to develop and deploy new products. For example, we can think of new engine technology as high-level generalized know-how. Lower down, we have the design work of integrating the engine into a particular set of pumps, which in turn is followed by the industrial engineering necessary for production in a specific manufacturing facility. What we can see from this example is that the location (Sweden) where the high-level know-how is developed is not only separated from where the pumps are ultimately manufactured, but also from the locations where the mid- and ground-level know-how is developed. Securing the cutting-edge research, in other words, does not determine where the rest of the "intellectual" value-added occurs. (For a more expansive discussion of the levels of know-how, see the introduction.)

We can see the same phenomena in the low-tech apparel industry. Although apparel companies don't operate research labs, they do undertake many activities that in substance involve the development of the know-how necessary to design, produce, and sell a new line of clothes. A decade or so ago, most large U.S. apparel companies did all their know-how development at home and used contract manufacturing abroad. Now they are separating the levels of know-how development. Activities to develop high-level know-how such as market research and conceptual design are now often retained in the United States, but activities to develop lower-level know-how, such as design execution and technical engineering, are candidates for offshoring—either to reduce costs or to locate them close to manufacturing facilities.

■ Trends in IT Unbundling

The high-tech information technology apples of policymakers' and pundits' eyes have been at the forefront of the patterns I have described. Apart from some telephone companies, most of the businesses that now dominate the IT sector emerged after the first globalization wave. IBM, for example, started as the Computing-Tabulating-Recording (C-T-R) Company in 1911 through the merger of several small firms. Its product lines included scales, coffee grinders, meat slicers, time clocks, and a line of punch-card tabulating machines. In 1914, Charles Flint, the financier who put together C-T-R, hired Thomas J. Watson to run the company. According to the historian Rowena Olegario, Watson had "grandiose visions" for C-T-R. He eliminated the coffee grinders and meat slicers and, in 1924, renamed the company International Business Machines, "even though at the time the firm was not actually very international."[14]

According to historian Richard Tedlow, in the 1920s, Watson thought Europe was going to be a big deal and, in the 1930s, touted "World Peace through World Trade," while anticipating IBM would benefit from that trade.[15] IBM operated wholly owned manufacturing and marketing subsidiaries abroad—and some development labs.[16] IBM even opened an office in India in 1920, when the economy was both thoroughly backward and depressed.[17]

In 1948 Watson began "working on IBM's international business in a concentrated way," creating a wholly owned subsidiary, World Trade, to market and manufacture products outside the United States. Decades before "slicing up the value chain" came into vogue, World Trade's business was structured with a complicated system of shipping semifinished products across borders to reduce tariffs.[18] World Trade also proved to be a highly successfully enterprise, growing revenues from $51 million in 1950 to $788 million in 1963—when the second globalization wave was just starting—and profits from $7 million to $105 million. As Tedlow points out, if World Trade had been an independent company in 1963, its profits and sales would have placed it high on the *Fortune* 500 list for that year.[19]

World Trade's operations also included development centers. The first major product developed abroad was introduced in 1960. This was a low-priced accounting system "developed in the laboratories of the German company, for the worldwide market. Representatives from twelve countries had participated in setting its specifications."[20]

The company's unbundling of manufacturing started in an unplanned way: IBM's blockbuster success of the era, the now legendary System/360 (announced in April 1964), was developed in the United States, where all the manufacturing also took place. But huge demand for the 360 made it difficult for IBM to manufacture enough of some components, such as its ferrite core memories. The company built a plant in Boulder, Colorado, in mid-1965 to meet the demand, but this proved inadequate. "An experiment was undertaken to have people in Japan wire core frames by hand. So careful and meticulous were the Japanese workers, and so low were their wages, that memory arrays wired by hand in Japan had the same quality and a lower cost than those produced with automated wire-feed equipment" in the United States. Core wiring was then "quickly expanded throughout the Orient into what became known as the 'Hong Kong Core House.' "[21]

IBM is now an even more global company than it used to be. In 1960, the gross revenue of its World Trade subsidiary accounted for 20 percent of the company's total revenue.[22] In 2006, the company's international revenues accounted for 60 percent of the total. That year, CEO Samuel Palmisano wrote in *Foreign Affairs* that companies such as IBM were evolving into "globally integrated enterprises" comprising "arrays" of activities such as manufacturing, research, sales, and distribution with many choices about where these activities could be performed. While the number of places it can carry out its activities may have expanded dramatically, IBM's history suggests that a basic separation—of the location of high-level R&D or design, on the one hand, and the production and use of the resulting products, on the other—has been a feature of its business practices for at least half a century.

A similarly long-standing pattern of separation can be seen in a somewhat younger company whose name belies its international scope: Texas Instruments (TI). TI's antecedents go back to the acquisition of Geophysical Service Incorporated in 1941 by three entrepreneurs; it adopted its current name in 1951. Unlike IBM, which focused on providing customers with end-to-end systems and "solutions," TI evolved into a developer of high-level components and some stand-alone ground-level products. In 1954, TI designed the first transistor radio; in the same decade, TI's Jack Kilby and Fairchild Semi-Conductor's Robert Noyce independently developed the integrated circuit. TI also developed transistor-transistor logic (TTL) chips, the first hand-held computer (1967), and the first single-chip microcomputer (1971); it also secured the first patent on a single-chip microprocessor.

Starting in the 1950s, TI started setting up manufacturing facilities abroad to get on the right side of tariff barriers—to "compete from inside growing markets."[23] TI opened a plant in England in 1957, while a merger with Metals and Controls Corporation added more sites in Mexico, Argentina, Italy, Holland, and Australia. According to Richard Alm, "For a time, TI resisted production in low-wage countries," but then in the late 1960s the company sought to "slice production costs by putting labor-intensive assembly operations in Singapore and Taiwan, followed by Malaysia and the Philippines."

Alm's article on TI, published more than 20 years ago, could be the template for many an article today. TI, Alm wrote in 1987, has "an international division of labor . . . based largely on costs. The highly sophisticated, expensive silicon-wafer fabrication takes place in Japan, England, France, West Germany and the United States. Factories in Asia, Latin America and Oporto, Portugal, concentrate on assembly. There's further specialization among plants by product. For example, Singapore assembles basic data-storage chips, while Malaysia puts the final touches on more advanced bipolar chips. . . . All the time, TI is juggling its global assets with an eye on market needs and costs. . . . The company abandoned . . . semiconductor assembly in San Salvador, El Salvador in 1985 and in Plymouth this month. . . . This year it consolidated its worldwide calculator production in Reatti, Italy, deciding to import into the United States rather than produce in Lubbock."[24]

Also highly contemporary is Mitchell's characterization of the role of TI's communications infrastructure in 1987: "For TI, running a 40-nation global empire of 77,000 employees means dealing with customers and workers a world apart, sometimes in a matter of minutes. [Its communication] network is the linchpin of TI's global organization, the key to its ability to manage far-flung outposts." Mitchell quoted TI's CEO, Mark Shepherd: "You've got to have management systems and control systems that are computer-based and let you have communications ability anyplace in the world. We couldn't operate the company as big as it is today if we didn't have that capability." According to Mitchell, TI's "38,000 computer terminals—one for every two TI employees—tie together a private network that ranks as one of the most sophisticated in the world. . . . Satellites, desktop computers, 1,250 minicomputers and 40 mainframe computers at 20 sites link TI activities from ordering to designing to manufacturing to quality control to distributing."[25]

A node in TI's network in Bangalore, India, established a year before the Mitchell article appeared, has particular historical significance for our story. According to a TI vice president, the company "started to look at India seriously in 1984 as a potential site for software development." In 1985, the Indian government began allowing foreign companies to establish wholly owned subsidiaries if their production was all for export. TI immediately established a software development center with 35 software engineers and a $5 million investment.[26] TI wanted to transmit chip designs using a private earth station connected to a satellite using data encryption to keep designs secure. The Indian government wanted to own and operate the communications facility, but because TI was concerned about delays, it "imported a satellite, handed it over to the government and rented back the service."[27] The "uplink" was then also used by a number of other companies that established software-development centers in Bangalore and thus helped catalyze the phenomenon of offshoring.

Also noteworthy is what didn't happen. Over the years, TI expanded its design staff in Bangalore—by 2002 it had approximately 700 employees.[28] TI's example was followed by other semiconductor companies that also started chip-design centers in India. Nevertheless, for reasons that are not germane to this discussion, India did not provide a suitable location for manufacturing semiconductors, and the country did not participate in the rapid expansion of silicon foundries and semiconductor packaging and testing facilities in the Far East. Apparently, the very communications infrastructure and organizational capabilities that allowed semiconductor companies to undertake design work in India also allowed them to manufacture somewhere else.

Large IT companies have also been at the forefront of "horizontal" and "vertical" distribution of developmental activities—rather than just manufacturing—across geographies. I have already provided an example of horizontal (or "product") distribution—IBM's development (in 1960) of a low-cost accounting system in its German labs. IBM (like many other high-tech companies) now increasingly favors vertical specialization, whereby different levels of development (of the same product) are undertaken at different facilities. According to Dr. Subramanian Iyer, the chief technologist at IBM's microelectronics division:

> There is now a well-established devolution of R&D functions, not just within IBM but also through what we call the collaborative model. In the semiconductor industry, R&D expenses have been growing at nearly twice the rate of revenues; the cost of developing and ramping up a new generation of complementary metal oxide semiconductor (CMOS) technology is now about $1.6 billion. We are using collabo-

rative technology consortia across many firms and in many countries to reduce the development costs.[29]

The geographic separation of the development of different levels of know-how is also a long-standing practice at TI. Nearly 12 years ago, Burrows reported how Texas Instruments had developed its TCM 9055 high-speed telecommunications chip: The basic concept (the high-level idea) was developed in a brainstorming session with Ericsson's engineers in Sweden. TI's designers in Nice, France, "turn[ed] Ericsson's vision into electronic blueprints" using software tools developed in Houston, Texas. For the last stage of development, namely making a prototype, "TI tap[ped] Japan's manufacturing expertise through its 31-year-old Japanese subsidiary." Ultimately, the chip was produced in Japan and Dallas, and tested in Japan.[30]

■ Concluding Comments

If consumers capture the lion's share of the value of new products and services, why should the United States lose if its share of the high-level research declines? The North-South models invoked by techno-nationalists raise the specter of loss of national incomes derived from mid- and ground-level know-how development and the ongoing production of new products. The models implicitly assume that all these activities—mid- and ground-level development and ongoing production—are undertaken in the same place as the high-level research. Such co-location may have been common long ago (and may remain so in some industries), but it is no longer the norm in a wide range of industries, including most sectors of the high-tech industry. For many decades, high-level breakthroughs have nourished the development and ongoing production of innovative products in remote locations. Why, then, should an erosion in the U.S. share of high-level breakthroughs that results from an expansion in the world's supply of such breakthroughs reduce incomes or employment in the United States? How does it matter if a seminal invention to produce faster, cheaper, or cooler microprocessors originates in a research facility located in Silicon Valley, Israel, Britain, or India if the chips that embody this invention are subsequently manufactured in a plant located in China or Taiwan? In other words, techno-nationalists are implicitly trying to secure a horse that left the stable decades ago—and hasn't really been missed.

So far, so good—so far, the story is relatively straightforward. But we haven't come to the end: even if the United States need not fear the erosion of its lead in high-level innovation, should it embrace this decline? "Don't worry" doesn't necessarily imply "be happy." In the next three chapters I make a more complex case for the *benefit* that will accrue to the United States from the erosion of its lead in cutting-edge science and technology.

9

■ Valuable Differences

A first cut at explaining how the expansion of cutting-edge research in China and India could make the world as a whole more prosperous is now at hand: the development of more high-level know-how has modest economic value on its own, but it does provide raw material for developers of mid- and ground-level products who combine and extend the high-level know-how. Those lower-level innovations help increase overall productivity and incomes.

This analysis assumes that the high-level research does not usurp resources that would otherwise have been more fruitfully used to develop and deploy mid- and base-level innovations. Indeed, I am skeptical whether public policies in China and India to promote high-level research do these countries much good, given the enormous challenges they face in implementing and adapting know-how (at all levels) that has long been used in the West. But that is not the issue here: we are interested in how the expansion of R&D in China and India affects standards of living in the United States.

Developers of mid- and ground-level products obviously stand to gain from an expanded supply of high-level inputs, but that accounts for only a small part of the potential benefit. As I have discussed, innovators (aggregated across all levels) receive a small share of the value they create. The total profit and employment generated through the development of new products is, relative to the size of a large economy, small. An inventor, a business, or a university may do well selling or licensing breakthroughs, but not the citizens of a populous economy.* Rather, innovations sustain *widespread* prosperity only if they improve the productivity and incomes of a large proportion of the workforce and increase the "surplus" enjoyed by a large number of consumers.

In this chapter, I discuss an important but subtle reason why an increase in high-level research abroad is likely to stimulate innovations that disproportionately benefit consumers in the United States. I first argue that high-level know-how and products are much more geographically mobile than mid- and ground-level know-how and products; I then go on to show that, because of these differences, more high-level research abroad will tend to increase innovations that have been optimized to benefit U.S. consumers. (I defer to the next chapter the question of whether those innovations also increase the productivity and wages of U.S. *workers*).

■ Variations by Level

High-level know-how—general principles, theories, and big ideas—are by nature mobile, because they are universal and codified. In preindustrial times, know-how often traveled as a "stowaway" along trade routes, explorations, or conquests, to borrow Leamer's metaphor. By many accounts the use of the base-10 numeral system originated in India between the seventh and ninth centuries, came to the Iberian peninsula via North Africa in the eleventh century, and was then popularized by the Italian mathematician Fibonacci.[1] Since then, technological developments, from Gutenberg's invention of the printing press in 1450 to the Internet, have vastly reduced the time and cost of transmitting and receiving high-level know-how. Today, ideas no longer travel as mere stowaways: the pursuit of professional recognition and advancement or financial reward encourages producers of knowledge to widely disseminate their work, while it also encourages consumers to search for that knowledge. In between sit easily searchable repositories

---

* A 2005 *Economist* report places annual technology-licensing revenue in the United States at approximately $45 billion and worldwide at around $100 billion (Cukier 2005). Forty-five billion (which includes both domestic and cross-border earnings) is little more than a rounding error in a $13 trillion dollar economy, which generates $1.5 trillion in corporate profits and disburses over $6 trillion in wage and salary compensation.

of knowledge, such as electronic journals and databases, which facilitate connections that just a few decades ago would have been unimaginable.*

Legal changes in the United States and abroad have facilitated trade in high-level know-how. As previously mentioned, changes such as the patentability of software and methods of doing business led to increases in patenting in the United States. Inventors who might otherwise have relied on protecting their IP through laws covering trade secrets apparently were encouraged to codify their intellectual property, which then opened the door to its licensing or sale. The patent system thus helped "liquefy" knowledge and promoted a "market in technology."[2] Internationally, according to Branstetter, Fisman, and Foley, "over the past twenty years, there has been a global trend toward stronger intellectual property rights. By the mid-1990s, a minimum global standard had been enshrined in the WTO [World Trade Organization] Charter through the incorporation of the Agreement on Trade-Related Aspects of Intellectual Property Rights [commonly known as TRIPS]."[3] These changes helped make the market for IP more global. But note: liquid markets require goods or contracts that are well specified, so legal changes have favored the licensing or sale of high-level IP that is easily codifiable.

Although the mobility of mid- and ground-level know-how has also increased, it is still less mobile than high-level know-how. This is partly because knowledge at the lower levels is usually more difficult to codify. Archimedes' high-level principle—that a body will float if it weighs less than the liquid it displaces—has an unambiguous representation that easily traverses physical, cultural, and linguistic differences. But it takes more than knowledge of Archimedes' principle to design and build a seaworthy ship. The lower-level knowledge that is necessary cannot be fully specified in a voluminous handbook, much less a concise formula: much of it is learned by doing. For instance, to realize his dream of making Russia a naval power, Peter the Great personally studied shipbuilding in Deptford, Britain, and in Amsterdam. While in Amsterdam, Peter I worked four months in the largest private shipyard in the world, belonging to the Dutch East India Company. He also hired many skilled shipwrights, whom he took back to Russia.

---

* Some of the companies I studied had searched patent databases and subsequently licensed technology from unlikely and faraway places: one from the estate of a deceased doctor in the U.K., another from an inventor in Wellington, New Zealand.

Mid- and ground-level know-how may now be better codified, but it remains difficult to transmit. Consider, for example, Sun Microsystems—started in 1982 to produce workstations based on prototypes developed by Andy Bechtolsheim, a graduate student who had been working on the Stanford University Network (SUN) project. According to cofounder Vinod Khosla, Stanford had assigned the (mid-level) technology to Bechtolsheim because "in their wisdom they had decided it had no value." Bechtolsheim had in turn licensed the IP "to six or seven companies" at "$10,000 a pop." But the licensees "did not understand" Bechtolsheim's technology and "did not know what do with it" "even though they had all the details." Bechtolsheim's "frustration" with the failure of licensees to produce a good product led him to join forces with Khosla to start a new company. Khosla adds:

> You really have to conceptually understand something. It's got to be in your gut. . . . Otherwise, almost all technology licenses fail to work. In fact, if you look at the history of technology licensing, by and large, it has failed. People never, never believe how important it is to have that understanding.[4]

Contracting problems can also impede the free flow of mid- and ground-level know-how, especially to countries with weak legal regimes. High-level scientific knowledge is usually developed by researchers impelled to "publish or perish"—and publication obviously increases the mobility of the ideas. Businesses that develop high-level know-how for commercial purposes often secure its value through patents that can be licensed across national borders. In contrast, mid- and ground-level know-how is typically not developed for academic advancement, and is therefore not published. As discussed in chapter 12, because such know-how is often difficult to patent, businesses tend to rely on alternative legal protections such as those covering trade secrets. Unlike patent-protected intellectual property, which can be licensed to third parties, trade secrets are generally not transmitted across firms. They travel abroad mainly within firms, to wholly owned or controlled subsidiaries, and even then not freely: businesses are loath to transfer important trade secrets to subsidiaries located in countries where employees can steal trade secrets without much fear of prosecution.

Finally, mid- and ground-level know-how doesn't travel well because—in contrast to general principles—its utility tends to be context specific.

Subtle differences in physical conditions, for instance, can cause a technology that works in one location to fail in another. Polyani recalls that "in Hungary a new, imported machine for blowing electric lamp bulbs, the exact counterpart of which was operating successfully in Germany, failing for a whole year to produce a single flawless bulb."[5] I have also encountered the same phenomenon: my father had a business making thermos flasks, whose glass bottles were mouth blown by a relay of three workers. To increase production capacity, the company imported an automated glass-blowing machine from a Japanese manufacturer who also sent a team of engineers to commission the unit. But try as they might, they could not get the machine to produce bottles of acceptable quality. Something was obviously different in the Indian factory, but no one could figure out what. After two years, the effort was abandoned and the machine sold for scrap.

Such problems are not limited to differences in physical conditions. Differences in language, tastes, practices, and laws also make the same mid- or ground-level know-how difficult to use in different locations. Consider the chocolates sold in many markets by large multinationals such as Nestle, Hershey, and Cadbury's. These companies may use the same high-level concept—in terms of shape, color, consistency and so on—across multiple markets, but as these companies have discovered, the specific recipes, manufacturing processes, and marketing campaigns—mid- and ground-level know-how, in other words—have to be tailored to suit local tastes. For instance, according to Kim Severson:

> According to the label, a British Cadbury Dairy Milk bar contains milk, sugar, cocoa mass, cocoa butter, vegetable fat and emulsifiers. The version made by the Hershey Company, which holds the license from Cadbury-Schweppes to produce the candy in the United States under the British company's direction, starts its ingredient list with sugar. It lists lactose and the emulsifier soy lecithin, which keeps the cocoa butter from separating from the cocoa. The American product also lists "natural and artificial flavorings."

Cadbury-Schweppes ships the same mash of dried milk and chocolate to all its licensees, but it also tries to replicate "the taste that people grew up with" in each country: "In the United States, that means a bar that is more akin to a Hershey bar, which to many British palates tastes sour."[6]

Similarly, John Ruff, then senior vice president for technology, research, and scientific relations at Kraft Foods International, writes that establishing "a global brand"—a "product that is marketed actively in numerous countries around the world, usually under the same name and trademark" is challenging because consumers are often

> vastly different from one another in culture, language, consumption behavior and habits. . . . Coffee, for instance, is prepared by the consumer in a variety of different ways—with milk, cream or sugar (and, in the U.K., with boiled milk); strong or diluted; and in different combinations of these. . . . There are very few truly global food or beverage products that carry the same name and that taste exactly the same all around the world. Most successful "global" (that is, globally marketed) brands are really strong "multilocal" brands that satisfy local demands but share a powerful core image that is carefully maintained worldwide.[7]

The limited transferability of mid- and ground-level know-how helps explain why companies that dominate one market may be behind in another. A striking recent example is the case of Google, which has built an enormously successful business around a patented algorithm and other proprietary search technologies. In spite of its early start, enormous financial resources, and worldwide name recognition, Google has not been successful in all markets. According to Pankaj Ghemawat:

> Google boasts of supporting more than 100 languages and, partly as a result, has recently been rated the top global website. But Google's reach in Russia—cofounder Sergey Brin's country of origin—is only 28 percent as of this writing, versus 64 percent for the market leader in search services, Yandex, and 53 percent for Rambler—and these two local competitors account for 91 percent of the Russian market for ads linked to Web searches. Google's problems reflect, in part, linguistic complexities: Russian nouns have three genders and up to six cases, verbs are very irregular, and the meaning of words can depend on their endings or on the context. In addition, local competitors have adapted better to the local context by, for example, developing payment mechanisms through traditional banks to compensate for the dearth of credit cards and online payment infrastructure.[8]

In my terminology, Google's mid- and ground-level know-how has not been sufficiently well adapted to the Russian market to achieve a preeminent position.

High-level products (like high-level know-how) can also travel across national boundaries more easily than mid- or ground-level products. One important reason is that the value of high-level products tends to be less context specific or localized. For example, virtually identical sugar or cocoa is used to make chocolates that are designed to appeal to different national tastes. Or think of moviemaking: on the high-level side, the polyester that comprises the base of the film stock or the silver halide and other chemicals that go into the emulsion applied to the base are the same regardless of where the stock is made or used. The appeal of the final product—the movie—can vary significantly with geography, and not just because of differences in language. A movie that is highly popular in the United States may flop in the UK, and vice versa.

Some movies (or packaged "food" products such as chewing gum) of course do have universal appeal; I am merely suggesting that geographic variations in the attractiveness of ground-level products tend to be greater, possibly because they depend on many, often intangible, attributes. As discussed in book 1, the attractiveness of high-level products such as polyester and silver halide depends on a small number of well-defined characteristics, such as their purity or stability. In contrast, a ground-level product such as a movie has many ineffable elements deriving from the plot, direction, cast, editing, sets, and special effects that jointly and severally determine its appeal. A bundle of attributes that has been well-crafted for one market may have elements or deficiencies that make it unsuitable for another.

The same pattern exists in the software industry. Developers all over the world use nearly identical high-level inputs—the same computer languages (such as C++ or Java), operating systems (such as Windows or Linux) and the other building blocks discussed in book 1—especially if these blocks are developed by the global open-source community. The mid- and ground-level products derived from these inputs are, however, usually much more localized, most obviously in the languages of the interfaces. Software with English pull-down menus is of limited use to someone who speaks only Swahili. Search-engine algorithms, as we saw in the case of Google, also have to be more extensively modified. Similarly e-commerce applications have to reflect local shopping habits and the business practices of local banks, credit card companies, merchants, and privacy regulators. There are certainly some ground-level applications, such as online or video games, that are identical across geographies, but their existence does not negate my general point that differences across countries tend to be greater in ground-level products—including software—than in higher-level components.

■ *Vive la Différence!*

The mobility of high-level innovations alongside impediments to the free flow of mid- and ground-level innovations has the following significance for my argument about the benefits the United States is likely to derive from the expansion of cutting-edge research in China and India. First, it means that innovators in the United States have more high-level inputs available to combine and extend. This would obviously not be the case if cutting-edge research developed in China and India could not be used in the United States. Moreover, U.S. innovators have a comparative advantage in developing mid- and ground-level innovation, because (as discussed in book 1) proximity to customers matters more in developing such innovations than it does in developing high-level innovations. This creates incentives for developers in the United States to focus attention and resources on mid- and ground-level innovations rather than on their high-level innovations. Moreover, U.S.-based innovators tend to optimize mid- and ground-level products for use in the United States. In other words, resources that might otherwise have been devoted to research that benefits the world at large are deployed into innovations that "disproportionately" benefit U.S. consumers and workers.

The difficulty of exporting mid- and ground-level products optimized for the U.S. market has another subtle significance: it encourages U.S. innovators (as we saw in book 1) to focus their efforts on domestic markets. The innovators may, for instance, make more of an effort to win over U.S. customers who need more persuasion, ongoing support, or lower prices than they would if they could easily sell their innovations to customers abroad. Although this tends to reduce innovators' profits, it also increases the domestic use of their products.

For the economy as a whole, the greater domestic use of innovations has enormous value, even if it is secured at the expense of lower exports. It is a mistake to liken innovations to oil wells in a desert kingdom, extracted by few but providing a good living for all: recall the relatively paltry sums generated by the licensing of technology mentioned at the start of this chapter.

Rather, as I have repeatedly stressed, the innovation benefits the common good mainly by increasing overall productivity and consumer welfare. Such increases depend on the degree to which the innovations are effectively used. A miracle strain of rice won't increase agricultural output unless farmers plant it, and a new drug won't cure disease unless doctors prescribe it. And miracle seeds and drugs don't sell themselves. As mentioned in book 1, innovators usually must devote considerable effort to persuade customers to purchase and use their new products and services. Therefore, adoption of innovations by domestic customers tends to increase when innovators put more effort into marketing in their home markets rather than abroad.

■ Concluding Comments

North-South models (and, as we will see later, influential economic theories of endogenous growth) do not distinguish between different types of technologies or know-how. In this book, differences between different levels of know-how—ranging from high-level principles to situation-specific, ground-level knowledge—have been crucial. In book 1, I argued that different organizations specialize in developing different levels of knowledge (with VC-backed businesses focusing on lower-level know-how than scientific labs), using different processes (with more iterative user dialogue for lower-level knowledge) and employing different kinds of personnel (with fewer PhDs in lower-level development). In this chapter, I focused on the differences in the mobility of different levels of know-how. I argued that high-level know-how tends to be more geographically mobile; therefore, an expansion in high-level research capacity abroad helps innovators in the United States to develop and disseminate more mid- and ground-level products tailored to the needs of their domestic users. While this may reduce the U.S. share of patent counts and scientific articles, it increases the country's overall economic prosperity.

10

■ Serving the Service Economy

In the last chapter, I discussed how high-level know-how developed abroad benefits the U.S. economy by stimulating the development of mid- and ground-level products tailored for the U.S. markets. Obviously such products generate a larger surplus for U.S. consumers than they do for consumers abroad. In this chapter we will see why the growing role of the service sector means that the expansion of mid- and ground-level innovation "disproportionately" benefits domestic workers as well as domestic consumers.

Recall the assumption made by the North-South models that some techno-nationalists invoke: where cutting-edge research originates determines where all subsequent development and the manufacture of products derived from that research take place. By that logic, "losing" R&D wipes out all related jobs. To rebut this assumption, in chapter 8 I argued that in the modern world, cutting-edge research and production need not occur in the same place. A reduced share of R&D is therefore not likely to have a significant impact on U.S. employment.

But shouldn't the same argument undermine my claim that more mid- and ground-level innovation at home is *good* for the United States? Won't innovations increase the productivity and employment opportunities for overseas rather than domestic workers? To understand why this is not the case, we must take into account services such as retailing and health care, which are not exposed to international competition. As we will see in this chapter, such services have steadily increased their share of U.S. economic activity and now employ a substantial proportion of the workforce. Because services are both produced and consumed in the United States, innovations in the service sector benefit domestic workers and consumers more than they do workers and consumers abroad.

■ Countervailing Trends

The large expansion of international trade has fostered an illusion that all goods are tradable. Technological advances have certainly increased the tradability of some products: cheap air freight and refrigeration, for instance, allow vegetables and flowers from Latin America to appear on the shelves of U.S. florists. But this cost advantage does not apply to all goods. The cost of long-distance transportation compared to the value of freshness for bread have kept bread-making a local business, even though its ingredients, such as wheat and sugar, are globally traded commodities. Similarly, Coca-Cola is locally bottled (using a secret syrup produced in Atlanta); Frito-Lay fries its potato chips close to where they are sold, using locally grown spuds (where available), and cement is rarely transported more than a few hundred miles from where it is produced. In more technical language, while these goods can be transported across national borders, the high cost of doing so limits the international "contestability" of their markets.

Contestability is out of the question in many "tertiary," or service, activities. In contrast to "primary" (mining, agriculture, and fishing) and "secondary" (manufacturing) industries, the outputs of many tertiary businesses are by their nature not transportable. Consider iPods—secondary products— as an example. They are produced by a manufacturing network in the Far East, but once they arrive at a U.S. port, tertiary activities account for subsequent value-added. That value-added is, of course, domestic: domestic dockworkers unload the containers, domestic truck drivers transport the iPods to a domestic warehouse and from there to a domestic retail store, where domestic staff sell the product and provide after-sales service. Similarly, we can't choose international suppliers for the services provided by restaurants, cinemas, barbers, supermarkets, home builders, repair shops, hospitals, police forces, and schools.

According to Edward Leamer's estimates, only about 17.5 percent of U.S. GDP in 2004 was globally "contestable," that is, exposed to competition from imports. The rest was produced in "mostly non-traded sectors" including real estate; local, state, and federal government; construction; retail trade; hospitals; and ambulatory care. Even in contestable sectors, exposure to imports was not uniform. Apparel and leather and allied products were most exposed, with the value of imports nearly 350 percent greater than total domestic value-added. Motion pictures and sound-recording industries had the least exposure, with imports amounting to just 4 percent of the domestic value-added. In between were 20 sectors including plastics and rubber products, with imports amounting to 194 percent of domestic value-added; computer and electronic products (147 percent); chemical products (80 percent); food and beverage and tobacco products (13 percent); and insurance carriers and related activities (13 percent).

Taking the broad view, we see that the net growth of international trade is the result of two offsetting trends—the effect of a large increase in imports and exports of tradable goods has been dampened by growth in the nontraded sector's share of total GDP. As Bordo, Eichengreen, and Irwin note, only three sectors of the economy—agriculture, mining, and manufacturing—produce most of the goods included in standard merchandise trade statistics. These sectors have become active participants in international trade in the course of the two waves of globalization. In 1900, the United States exported a little more than 15 percent of the merchandise it produced. By 1950, the ratio had fallen to less than 10 percent. The rate returned to its 1900 level in 1970 and then shot up to over 40 percent in 1997. The ratio of merchandise exports to total GDP (rather than to merchandise produced) is, however, much lower. In 1997 the ratio of merchandise exports to GDP was about what it was 1900, because the share of the sectors producing "tradable" merchandise in GDP had declined sharply. "In both 1899–1903 and 1950," write Bordo and his coauthors, "agriculture, mining and manufacturing comprised about 40 percent of GNP; the comparable figure for 1997 was 20 percent."[1] In other words, the nontraded sector had increased from 60 percent to about 80 percent of GDP.

The growth of services accounts for much of the expansion of the nontraded sector.* According to the Bureau of Economic Analysis, in 2004,

---

* The categorization is not exact: as we have seen, some of the output of the manufacturing sector comprises goods (e.g., baked goods and cement) that are usually not traded, and some kinds of services (e.g., shipping, tourism, and insurance) do generate imports and exports.

service-producing industries accounted for 67.9 percent of GDP (value-added, in current dollars), whereas the government—the other nontraded sector—accounted for 12.6 percent of GDP. By contrast, in 1974 (when nontraded components accounted for 68.5 percent of GDP), service-producing sectors accounted for a much lower 53.7 percent of GDP, and the government sector a slightly higher 14.8 percent.[2] The distribution of employment reflects the same pattern. In 2004, there were about 132 million employees on nonagricultural payrolls. Of these, 67 percent were employed by service-producing industries, 16 percent by the government, and the remaining 17 percent by goods-producing industries (the tradable sector). In 1974, when there were 78.3 million employees on nonagricultural payrolls, 52 percent were employed by service-producing industries, 18 percent by the government, and the remaining 30 percent by goods-producing industries.

Other advanced economies have undergone a similar evolution. "Since the 1970s, the service sector has become the quantitatively most important sector in almost all OECD [Organisation for Economic Co-operation and Development] economies," writes the OECD's Anita Wölfl. (The OECD's members are, more or less, the world's advanced economies.) "The share of the service sector has strongly increased since the 1970s and, by 2000, amounted to about 60% or 70% of total value added in most OECD economies."[3] As countries get richer, the share of the service sector increases. For example, there is a strong correlation between per capita incomes and the service-employment share in every decade during the twentieth and late nineteenth century for 14 OECD countries.[4] The service sector's share of employment in poorer countries tends to be lower, but it is by no means negligible. For instance, the service sector accounted for 30 percent of employment growth in India in 2000—virtually all the jobs created in the prior six years—and about half of the country's GDP.[5]

The sizable opportunities provided by the servicing of products (regardless of where they are manufactured) have attracted the attention of astute managers of old-economy businesses. General Electric (GE) is a case in point. After Jack Welch became CEO in 1981, he instituted a sharp retrenchment, "shutting factories, paring payrolls and hacking mercilessly at its lackluster old-line units."[6] Welch writes in his 2001 memoir: "We went from 411,000 employees at the end of 1980 to 299,000 by the end of 1985. Of the 112,000 people who left the company payroll, about 37,000 were in businesses we sold, but 81,000 people—or one in every five in our industrial businesses—lost their jobs for productivity reasons."[7]

In the 1990s, when Welch turned his attention to growth opportunities, "the importance of services was self-evident." GE had become "a new-socket company to a fault." Executives would debate "whether we'd sell 50 or 58 gas turbines or several hundred aircraft engines a year" while neglecting "service opportunities for an installed base of 10,000 existing turbines and 9,000 jet engines."[8] In 1995, Welch launched a company-wide initiative to increase service revenues. A *BusinessWeek* cover story in 1996 noted that Welch foresaw "tremendous growth providing sophisticated services that spring from GE's core industrial strength." He told employees that GE could "no longer prosper on manufactured goods alone. 'Our job is to sell more than just the box.' " Company executives "hatched plans to do everything from helping utilities run power plants more efficiently to running engine service shops for airlines. GE even wants to set up and run corporate computer networks."[9]

GE's product services business grew from $8 billion in 1995 to $19 billion in 2000, and the long-term service backlog increased 10-fold from $6 billion to $62 billion.[10] GE continued to build its service revenues after Welch's retirement. A *Forbes* story in May 2007 reported that two-thirds of the company's revenue came from services—four times the percentage when Welch became CEO in 1981. "Lucrative service deals" were likely to "make infrastructure, already GE's largest division with over $30 billion in annual revenue, the company's biggest profit driver going forward."[11]

The growth of the (largely untraded) service sector has important implications for my argument. First, continued prosperity in advanced economies crucially depends on innovations that increase the productivity of the services sector. Higher productivity (in any sector) is rarely fully passed on to employees as higher wages—the gains have to be shared with both consumers and the owners of businesses. But without productivity increases, there is nothing to share, and if the service-productivity sector in an advanced economy stagnates, so will the wages of many workers and the well-being of many consumers. Conversely, innovations that increase the productivity of the services sector have enormous impact; the United States should therefore welcome the expansion of research in China and India that can be used to develop and deploy such innovations.

It is also important that, because most services are not traded, innovations that enhance productivity of services in the United States do not harm, except possibly in the most limited and indirect way, the well-being of other countries. Recall that in the North-South models, when the South learns to make advanced goods, the North is hurt because it had hitherto been able to export these goods to the South. In contrast, if the South improves the efficiency of its hospitals or supermarkets, the North is not made worse off.

Little more needs to be said about these two implications. A third may need more elaboration, however: in principle, innovative mid- and ground-level combinations that enhance U.S. service productivity may use high-level know-how developed abroad. But, as I will discuss in the next section, this requires *domestic* enterprise: productivity-enhancing innovations usually have to be tailored to U.S. conditions *and* must be deployed by U.S.-based service providers. Maintaining a strong indigenous capacity for developing and deploying lower level innovations in the service sector is therefore critical for the prosperity of an advanced economy (whereas pursuing self-sufficiency or dominance in high-level know-how is pointless).

■ Home Cooking (and Eating)

In the last chapter, I argued that recipes for mid- and ground-level combinations don't travel well across national borders. This also seems to be the case with many business-to-business ("wholesale") and business-to-consumer ("retail") services, because successful innovations have to fit several local conditions; combinations developed for markets abroad usually don't work out at home without extensive retooling.

We can see the importance of matching service innovations to indigenous conditions by looking at efforts to develop end-to-end hospital management systems. According to one expert, an effective system would incorporate the "back office" part of a hospital (e.g., data storage and information processing) and "a huge number of processes that take place between people," such as the discharging of patients, which "get done in a relatively *ad hoc* way." These processes vary widely from hospital to hospital and from region to region. It is hard to imagine a single system that could be used in hospitals in many countries. And indeed, efforts to develop global software solutions in hospital management have, according to one of my interviewees, been "miserable failures."

Similarly, innovations to improve the productivity of banking, insurance, transportation, real estate management, and a host of other such service businesses have to be tailored to local regulations, customs, infrastructure, business practices, and consumer preferences. As we saw in book 1, the cost and difficulty of retooling packages initially optimized for the U.S. market discourages many small innovators from attempting to secure customers abroad.

The difficulty of transporting know-how across borders can also be seen in the relatively low share of revenues that large companies in the service sector derive from their international operations. As compared to start-ups, large, mature corporations have a strong incentive to look for growth opportunities abroad: they have ample managerial capacity and the financial wherewithal to invest in international expansion. Yet in 2005, the median international share of retailers and wholesalers of consumer products (such companies as Safeway, Sysco, McKesson, and Wal-Mart) was just 10 percent (compared to the 33 percent share for the *Fortune* 100 as a whole) and the largest reported share by companies in health-care services was just 2.8 percent (for Cardinal Health).

The case of Wal-Mart is especially noteworthy. It has established a formidable international supply chain. In the 1990s, it undertook a "Buy American" campaign that it abandoned to become a major importer of Chinese goods. In 2006, Wal-Mart accounted for 10 percent of total U.S. imports from China and a much larger fraction of consumer good imports. Wal-Mart's capacity to source products from China has contributed significantly to its phenomenal growth in the United States.[12] Wal-Mart, however, has had much less success exporting its retail model abroad. In 1997, it shuttered retail operations in Indonesia. Its ventures in China and Japan have not been particularly successful.[13] In 2006, Wal-Mart gave up on the German market, selling its 85 stores to a German retailer and taking a loss of $1 billion.[14]

Wal-Mart's problem apparently did not arise from the immobility of high-level retailing concepts. According to Jonathan Reynolds, director of Oxford University's Institute of Retail Management, the phenomenon of "format internationalization" is commonplace. That is, concepts such as Home Depot's and Best Buy's category killers (high-volume discount retailing devoted to one category), developed in one country, are rapidly copied in other markets. The CEO of a UK supermarket chain has claimed that "the average dwell time for an innovation in food retailing before emulation is around six weeks."[15] The problem faced by companies such as Wal-Mart is that having the right big idea isn't good enough—overseas success also requires lower-level know-how tailored to local conditions. The difficulty of developing this know-how helps explain the dominance of domestic retailing: "Half of the biggest retailers in the world are still purely domestic, and the remaining half are, in reality, predominantly domestic. Most retailers, where they are international at all, are very regionally concentrated. Even those with substantial absolute volumes of international sales tend to be focused in a very few countries, and are far less global than the FMCG [fast moving consumer goods]* suppliers."[16]

Local deployment of innovations in nontraded services is also crucial: even if an innovation is perfectly tailored for the local market, it will not produce much domestic benefit without its effective use by local service providers. A great system for managing health-care records, restocking supermarket shelves, or tracking mail-order shipments does not create much domestic value unless it is properly deployed by local hospitals, supermarkets, and parcel-delivery companies. In contrast, an innovation to produce tradable goods can create at least some domestic benefit even if all development and manufacturing takes place abroad. For instance, more efficient looms for weaving textiles will benefit consumers in the United States even if those looms are developed in Japan and used in factories in China.

This is not to suggest that resources abroad (other than high-level know-how) cannot enhance U.S. service-sector productivity. The offshoring of standardized IT-related activities has promoted the development and use of mid- and ground-level service sector innovations. As discussed in chapter 4, VC-backed businesses are increasing their use of offshore personnel for such activities as software testing and the development of utilities and drivers.† Large IT hardware and software vendors, such as Hewlett-Packard, IBM, Oracle, and Texas Instruments, are doing so on an even larger scale. Such offshoring helps reduce the cost (and presumably increases the supply) of innovations used by the service sector in the United States.

---

* E.g., multinational companies such as Reckitt Benckiser, Sara Lee, Nestlé, Unilever, Procter & Gamble, Coca-Cola, Carlsberg, Kleenex, General Mills, Pepsi,and Mars. As we have seen, these companies also often tailor their products to local tastes, but this is apparently easier than adapting retailing formats.

† Utilities are programs that add to the capabilities provided by the operating system; drivers are programs that interact with a particular device.

■ An Encouraging Record

As it happens, innovation in the service sector needs all the help it can get, but it is not, as once supposed, a hopeless case. Productivity improvement in many parts of the service sector is a very big nut (in terms of the employees and consumers it affects), and has long been a tough nut to crack. William Baumol and William Bowen's pioneering 1966 book, *Performing Arts: The Economic Dilemma*, provides an influential analysis of the problem of service-sector productivity and its implications. Baumol and Bowen argued that productivity in performing arts (and other labor-intensive services) grows more slowly than in manufacturing. In manufacturing, output per employee can be readily achieved by using more machinery, or new equipment that embodies a new technology. In the live performing arts however, machinery, equipment, and technology do not play much of a role in the production process and do not change much over time. Their famous example was of a Mozart string quartet: it takes exactly the same four musicians the same 40 minutes to play the music now that it took in 1780. Extending this example to other service activities led to a gloomy inference about economic growth (now known as "Baumol's disease"): a faster rate of growth in manufacturing leads to a shift in the proportion of the workforce that provides services, and the innately slow growth of productivity in services reduces the overall rate of growth of productivity and increases inflation.

Manufacturing productivity did indeed grow faster than service productivity in the United States for about half a century after World War II. From 1946 to 1970, manufacturing productivity grew at 3 percent per year, while service productivity grew by 2.5 percent per year. From 1970 to 1980, both rates fell, but manufacturing productivity growth (1.4 percent per year) remained ahead of service productivity growth (0.7 percent). From 1980 to 1990, manufacturing productivity rebounded strongly (to an annual rate of growth of 3.3 percent), but service productivity did not (remaining at a low 0.8 percent a year).[17]

While service productivity may have grown relatively slowly, it wasn't stagnant. Productivity-enhancing innovations may be hard to come by in many services, but they aren't absent. As Tyler Cowen points out, even artistic production has "a progressive nature." Writes Cowen: "Electronic reproduction, in the forms of recording and radio, has improved the productivity of musicians by allowing them to reach larger audiences. Today's string quartet travels by airplane rather than by stagecoach or train. A string quartet in 1780 could play Mozart, but today's string quartet can play Beethoven, Bartok and the Beatles' 'Eleanor Rigby' as well."[18]

Some sectors of the service economy have meanwhile been more hospitable to productivity-enhancing innovations than others. According to Anita Wölfl, "At the aggregate level, unbalanced growth can be observed between a dynamic manufacturing sector on one hand and a rather stagnant service sector on the other. The service sector itself is, however, composed of a set of heterogeneous industries with productivity growth rates ranging from low or negative rates to growth rates exceeding those of high-growth manufacturing industries."[19]

The U.S. experience after the mid-1990s is especially encouraging. According to a 2003 study by two Brookings Institution economists, Jack E. Triplett and Barry P. Bosworth, the annual rate of labor productivity growth in services between 1995 and 2001 (2.6 percent), actually exceeded the rate in goods-producing sectors (2.3 percent). Furthermore, the productivity improvements were widespread. Productivity after 1995 grew in 24 of the 29 industry sectors they studied. In 17 of these sectors, productivity grew at an accelerated rate. The only sectors where (by conventional measures) productivity did not grow were hotels, health, education, and entertainment. These findings led Bosworth and Triplett to conclude that Baumol's disease "has been cured."

As we will see in later chapters, other advanced economies have also increased the productivity of their service sectors since the mid-1990s, but usually not to the same degree as the United States. Given the large share of services in the United States—and the domestic locus of their production—this has meant that overall productivity in the United States has also been more rapid. And, as we will also see, the development of IT innovations targeted at the services sector—and the willingness and ability of U.S. service providers to effectively use these innovations—has played a vital role in the exceptional growth of service sector productivity in the United States.

■ Looking Ahead

The use of IT-based innovations may or may not have permanently cured Baumol's disease, however. The gains in service productivity achieved after 1995 may be difficult to sustain, because the low-hanging fruit has already been plucked. Leamer points out that technology has, for example, helped make the architect's job more creative: "In 1970," he writes, "the time of a creative architect was partly consumed by the task of rendering the drawings. Some of this work could be done by assistants, but the communication costs were often so high that it made more sense to have the master do the drawings. The personal computer, however, allowed the architect to render the drawings with great efficiency, thus freeing up time to do the creative tasks that the computer cannot ever perform."[20] Presumably (whether or not this is fully reflected in standard measures), computers have increased the productivity of architects. But if architects now only undertake tasks that computers can never perform, any further gains from computerization will be difficult to achieve.

Similarly, research by Autor, Levy, and Murnane (published in 2003) and subsequently by Autor, Katz, and Kearney (in 2006) shows that the share of occupations in the United States involving "routine" cognitive tasks (such as bookkeeping and clerical work) that could be displaced by computers has been declining since about the 1970s. Conversely, the share of occupations involving nonroutine cognitive jobs (such as architecture), in which computers serve as complements rather than substitutes, has been increasing. But what if these shifts (which have accelerated in recent years) and the productivity growth they have generated have run their course, or are about to run their course? Computers may yet increase productivity (e.g., by standardizing tasks that are now nonroutine or by serving as better "complements"), but this could be rougher sledding than the automation of tasks that were already well codified.

Notwithstanding these uncertainties, the enormous size of the U.S. service sector—in conjunction with (as I will discuss in the next chapter) its venturesome consumption of IT—has attracted the attention of many high-tech vendors both small and large. As we saw in book 1, in my sample of VC-backed businesses, more than three-quarters were either selling consumer services, selling to other businesses that provided a service, or facilitating a service function (such as marketing, IT, or tax optimization). Large IT companies (which develop and sell data-processing and management systems as opposed to hardware) also largely serve customers in the service sector (or in service functions). IBM, in particular, has deep roots here. For instance, after the Social Security Act was passed in 1935, IBM secured a government contract to maintain employment data for 25 million people—described in IBM's archive as the "biggest accounting operation of all time."[21] Companies in banking, insurance, telecommunications, and other such service sectors have long been its key customers for its computers. Now IBM is increasingly turning itself into a service provider—in 2004, for instance, services accounted for more than half the company's revenues, exceeding the combined sales of hardware and software.

■ Concluding Comments

The material in this and the previous chapters shows why the United States stands to gain from an increase in high-level research abroad: such research is very mobile and, compared to its value, cheap. An increase in the overseas supply of such research encourages innovators in the United States to develop and market mid- and ground-level innovations that (in contrast to high-level research) usually must be optimized for local use. The local benefit is amplified by a growing share of nontraded services that are domestically produced and consumed. Innovations therefore not only create value for U.S. consumers, they also contribute to the well-being of the large number of workers employed by this sector. At the same time, to the extent that services aren't exported, the United States does not benefit at the expense of some other country.

We are not yet done with the optimistic case, however. The next chapter addresses the following question: if the increased supply of high-level research is available to all, is there a distinctive feature of the United States, particularly in the service sector, that encourages innovators to use the increased supply to develop and sell mid- and ground-level products optimized for U.S. customers?

11

■ Venturesome Consumption

*The customer is king, right? Most of us who came from India, Taiwan, or China
to the U.S. have been much more successful than if we had stayed at home,
because we are close to the market here. We understand the market problem:
I would understand what Bank of America's servers need better than
someone sitting in Bangalore or Shanghai. And as long as the market is here,
the U.S. will continue to be the place to innovate.*
—Founder and CEO of a VC-backed business

Why is the United States a good place to innovate? The question has attracted considerable attention in recent years, particularly in Europe and
Japan. Much of the writing on this topic emphasizes "supply side" factors
such as the availability of venture capital, the IPO (initial public offering)
market, the rule of law, and the enforcement of intellectual property rights.
In this chapter, I will offer a complementary, "demand side" perspective,
focusing on the frequently neglected role that consumers play in the multiplayer innovation game.

My interest in the purchase and use of new technologies dates to 1982,
when, as an employee of the consulting firm McKinsey & Co., I worked on
a study to help the European Union promote the IT industry. The team
focused almost entirely on what the EU could do to help the producers of
IT equipment through grants, subsidies, and tax breaks. Among the questions extensively debated was who was friend or foe: were U.S. companies
that had extensive operations in Europe sufficiently European to deserve
the EU's largesse? My efforts to broaden the scope of the study to include
the behavior and needs of IT users—who were *all* in Europe—were futile.
I was the lowest-ranking consultant on the team, and the clients for the
study had no interest. I then wrote a *Harvard Business Review* article about
the the nature of the demand for innovative products, but it had a similarly
negligible impact.[1]

My views have subsequently been informed by my studies over the last 20 years of new and emerging ("entrepreneurial") businesses. Obviously, entrepreneurs are more willing to innovate—and devote resources to marketing and selling their innovations—if they anticipate a large market for their product. Developers of products that have to be tailored for a particular market or require costly sales efforts are naturally concerned about whether customers will be receptive. But that's not all: I have observed the subtle role of customers, which goes beyond the decision whether or not to buy. As we will see in this chapter, they play an important "venturesome" role, rather like the one played by the developers of the products they use.

Although users' role in the innovation game is often neglected, my overall thesis is not new. Several economic historians have examined the close relationship between technology adoption and economic development. Among them are Mokyr[2] and Rosenberg and Birdzell,[3] who argue that the West grew rich first because people there were more open to new technologies than elsewhere. I use contemporary examples to argue that adopting technology, especially of IT by the service sector, continues to play a critical role in maintaining the prosperity of the United States and other advanced countries.

My argument also incorporates the notion of what is often now called "absorptive capacity" for innovations. The term has been used in the economic-development literature at least since the early 1960s to refer to the limited capacity of "backward" countries to put new investments (and the innovations they may embody) into productive use. Cohen and Levinthal[4] applied the term to the ability of individual firms to effectively absorb new technologies, and this usage has since become commonplace. Although their definition is broad, Cohen and Levinthal and subsequent researchers focus mainly on high-tech firms, examining, for instance, how internal R&D efforts help firms use research produced in university labs. I focus on organizations (and individual consumers) that have no formal R&D efforts and who use mid- and ground-level products rather than high-level scientific knowledge.

■ Contributions to Product Development

MIT's Eric Von Hippel has been a leading proponent of the view that innovation often starts with users, particularly the so-called lead users, rather than the manufacturers of products. In 1988 Von Hippel reported that users had developed about 80 percent of the most important innovations in scientific instruments, as well as most of the major innovations in semiconductor processing. In *Democratizing Innovation*, published in 2005, Von Hippel writes that "a growing body of empirical work shows that users are the first to develop many and perhaps most new industrial and consumer products."

The book recalls Adam Smith's observation that many labor-saving machines were invented by "common workmen" who "naturally turned their thoughts towards finding out easier and readier methods of performing" simple operations.[5] Von Hippel cites other examples of important innovations led by users: basic machine tools such as lathes and milling machines, oil refining, and the most widely licensed chemical processes.

In consumer products, Von Hippel provides examples from sports such as snow boarding, mountain biking, and high-performance wind surfing, which got its start when competitors in traditional wind-surfing events modified standard boards to do jumps. Their modifications were then used in boards used for normal wind surfing. Similarly, Von Hippel reports that mountain biking started in the early 1970s with young cyclists who built their own bicycles out of strong frames, balloon tires, and drum brakes from motorcycles for rough, off-road use. A fragmented cottage industry began supplying such cycles for those who didn't want to assemble their own machines: it wasn't until mountain biking had grown to a sport with half a million adherents that mainstream suppliers got into the act. Von Hippel also argues that, in general, "the contribution of users is growing steadily larger as a result of continuing advances in computer and communications capabilities."

In my research of entrepreneurial businesses over the last 20 years, I have not found user-led innovation to be widespread. At the same time I have observed that users do often play an important, "ventursome" role in the development of new products even if they don't lead or initiate the development.

In the current study of VC-backed businesses I saw virtually no evidence of user-led innovation except in the very broad sense that most innovators do put themselves in the shoes of users (but if we were to count that as user-led innovation, the category would mean nothing). Nor did I encounter much user-led innovation in my previous research on *Inc.* 500 companies, nor in several hundred other ad-hoc studies I have undertaken. This could be an artifact of my samples, of course. Or it could be that claims about the ubiquity of user-led innovation may be pushed by a "man bites dog" bias in the academic literature—studies of *producer*-led innovation would not excite much interest.

The current study of venture-backed businesses did, however, reveal other important roles that users play in the innovation game. In book 1 we saw that developers, especially developers of mid-level products, engaged closely with so-called alpha or beta users. The engagement was far more intense than is common in focus groups and market research questionnaires (which involve hypothetical questions) or even in taste tests (with actual products). Recall that users participated in ongoing dialogue with development teams that helped determine the attributes of the product or service that was ultimately sold.

As we saw, developers might start with the core component of a solution to an important problem faced by potential customers, but in their dialogue with users learn about complementary functions that must be added to the core to make it work. Or developers might conceive of a product with many functions, but learn that some features add more cost than value. Similarly, customer dialogue can contribute to designing an effective user interface; as the success of Google's search engine and Apple's iPod shows, the look and feel of a product can be as important to its utility as the technical features that lie "under the hood." According to many of our interviewees, many things learned from interactions with customers were incorporated into their products rather than their core idea (or patent), and this was the most valuable source of their intellectual property.

The contribution of customers to the development process tends to continue after the first commercial launch. As Rosenberg (and others) have pointed out, products can evolve so much over time that their relationship to antecedents may be unrecognizable. The first automobiles were so rudimentary that they could only be used by a "few buffs riding around the countryside terrifying horses."[6] Today's personal computers have come a long way from the pioneering Altair; its aficionados derived less practical use from their machines than did turn-of-the century automobile buffs. Lacking basic input or output devices (such as keyboards and printers), Altairs could not even scare horses. According to Rosenberg, "learning by using" by customers often plays a significant role in transforming products from rudimentary to refined.[7]

Users may also find new applications for existing technologies. A typical automobile, for instance, now contains scores of embedded microprocessors.

Similarly, consumer electronics companies have also embedded microprocessors in household appliances, sound systems, and telephones. Producers of laptops, PDAs, and electric vehicles have found new uses for innovative battery technologies. As users try to adapt new technologies for their specific applications, the technologies may gain new features (in addition to a larger market) that make them more versatile and less expensive. In other words, the initiative of users can make technologies developed for a few markets into more general purpose platforms.*

■ Bearing "Unmeasurable and Unquantifiable" Risks

According to Knight's theory, the essence of entrepreneurship involves responsibility for uncertainty—facing unmeasurable and unquantifiable risks rather than betting on situations where the odds have been well established by prior trials. But it is not just the producers of an innovation who face Knightian uncertainty—purchasers also cannot form objective estimates of their risks and returns.

One source of uncertainty lies in whether an innovation actually does what it is supposed to do. A product that works in the lab or in a few beta sites may not work for all users because of differences in the conditions of its implementation; a product that works fine at the outset may fail later. An innovation, like a theory, can never be proven to be "good"—at any moment, we can only observe the absence of evidence of unsoundness. Repeated use of a product may bring to the surface hidden defects that cause malfunctions, increase operating costs, or pose health and safety hazards to the user or the environment.

Unanticipated technical failures injure not only developers but users of innovations. In many products and services, failures can cost users many times the purchase price. Defects in a word-processing or email package that costs just a few hundred dollars may wipe out many years of invaluable files and correspondence. Even if data isn't lost, the costs of transferring files to a new software package—and learning how to use it—can be substantial. Similarly, a defective battery in a laptop can start a fire that burns

---

* I don't want to exaggerate this effect, however—many, possibly most, of the new critical applications for crucial general-purpose technologies such as steam engines and electric dynamos were not initiated by users (except in some all-inclusive sense of the term).

down a house (this did, in fact, happen to a friend). Tires that wear badly can have fatal consequences. A security hole in its servers can cripple an online brokerage, and the belated discovery of the hazards of asbestos can lead to tens of billions of dollars in removal costs.

Consumers face risk if they invest in new products that work perfectly well for them but fail to attract a critical mass of other users. If that happens, vendors (and providers of complementary add-ons) often abandon the product and stop providing critical maintenance, upgrades, and spare parts. Or vendors may go out of business entirely—a common occurrence in IT. Customers may be left stranded if upgrades and new releases don't have "backward compatibility" with their forebears, or if a new technology makes an old product obsolete.

Customers also face Knightian uncertainty about the value of an innovation in relation to its price. In the schema of neoclassical economics, consumers have a gigantic, well-specified utility function for all goods, extant as well as not yet invented. Therefore, when an innovation that serves a new want (or a new combination of old wants) appears, consumers consult their utility functions, as they might a tax table, and know exactly its worth to them. To my knowledge, there is no empirical basis for such an assumption. In fact, evidence from "behavioral" researchers such as George Lowenstein points in exactly the opposite direction: people don't have a clue about the value of things they have never experienced. When researchers ask subjects how much they would pay for some novel experience, such as kissing their favorite movie star, they receive whimsical responses, anchored to some irrelevant piece of data just planted in the subject's mind by the researcher, such as Social Security numbers. One interpretation of these behavioral experiments is that people are irrational; another is that they simply don't know and blurt out the first thing that comes to mind to earn their five dollars for participating in the experiment. ("Snappy answers to stupid questions," a long-ago feature from *Mad* magazine, comes to mind.)

Behavioral research has been criticized for experiments in which subjects, unlike actors in the real world, have no stake in the outcome, but in this instance the experiments do seem to correspond to reality. It is improbable, for instance, that anyone who wears glasses or contact lenses has a firm grasp of the economic value of (successful) corrective laser surgery, or that someone who has a conventional TV can gauge the value of switching to a higher-definition digital product. Indeed, I am skeptical that people who actually have laser surgery or buy a digital TV can quantify the value. Before or after a purchase, the enhanced utility is a shot in the dark, much like the value of the pleasure Lowenstein's subjects anticipate from kissing movie stars. I personally have not seriously considered either laser surgery or buying a high-definition TV, but I have been enticed by the latest in personal computer hardware and software for more than two decades. I have no idea of the value of my numerous upgrades (or for that matter, a good estimate of the time and opportunity costs I have incurred).

Similarly, although I have worried about—and periodically endured—the consequences of technical defects and abandonment of favorite programs by vendors, I have never actually made an effort to quantify the probability distributions. I cannot imagine being able to enumerate all the dire possibilities. People who have corrective eye surgery may ask about the probability that something might go wrong or that the operation won't give them 20/20 vision. But what basis could they possibly have for evaluating the consequences 20 or 30 years later?

Organizations that purchase expensive systems do often expend many person-years' effort to evaluate their costs and benefits. For example, Columbia Business School recently acquired a new "courseware" platform. A committee was formed, long Requests for Proposals issued, shortlists made, vendor proposals studied, consultants retained . . . but for all the effort and availability of the finest analytical minds, the value of the new courseware was—and will remain—elusive. The monetary value of enhancing student satisfaction and learning and of saving faculty time can only be a blind guess. Similarly, although the out-of-pocket costs of purchasing a system played a role in picking a vendor, the magnitude of the much larger "all in" opportunity costs (e.g., the time of faculty and staff) of switching to any new courseware platform were unfathomable.

Assessing the costs and benefits of enterprise-wide software and systems used by corporations that are many times the size of the Columbia Business School is even more difficult. As the box "Evaluating ERP Systems" indicates, off-the-shelf enterprise software rarely matches the practices and processes that it is supposed to facilitate or automate. Rather, organizations have to extensively modify and adapt both the software and their practices. The costs of modifying the software, and the frequently more problematic "reengineering" of the practices, are very hard to pin down. So are the benefits: these are supposed to include not just the improvements realized through automation, but also the adoption of superior practices.

Evaluating ERP Systems

According to the current Wikipedia entry on the topic, ERP (enterprise re-source planning) software is used for the "control of many business activities, like sales, delivery, billing, production, inventory management, quality man-agement, and human resources management." The systems are supposed to integrate many functions, including "manufacturing, warehousing, logistics, Information Technology, accounting, human resources, marketing and strate-gic management." In principle, all these activities and functions use a single database rather than, for instance, the human resources department and the payroll department maintaining records on the same employee in two dif-ferent and incompatible databases.

Most ERP systems are not built to suit—rather, they are based on pack-ages provided by software companies such as Oracle and SAP. The premise of such systems, according to Eric Roberts, professor of computer science at Stanford, is that "software systems are expensive and complex. What's more, the expense of a software system lies almost entirely in its development; once a system is built and tested, the marginal cost of delivering that same system to other users is typically quite small. The concentration of cost in the development phase creates a strong incentive to share development expenses over a large user base. If it costs $10 million to develop a system, it seems foolish for a single institution to bear that cost alone. Given that the bulk of that $10 million represents development, it makes far more sense—at least in theory—for a consortium of institutions to purchase software from a vendor that can then distribute those costs over the community of users."[8]

There is, however, a catch, writes Roberts: "The success of any enterprise system depends on refashioning the business practices of the institution to match the software rather than trying to change the software to accommo-date the idiosyncrasies of the institution. Changing the software violates the underlying economic assumption that allows for the reduction in cost. If each institution tailors the system to suit its needs, the cost advantage vanishes."

Enterprise software vendors claim that their systems incorporate the best possible business practices. Therefore, customers gain significant advantages if they refashion their business practices to fit the standard packages. But in fact, although the packages draw their "best practices" from a variety of industries and situations, there can be a considerable gap between the best-practice configuration available in the package and the practice that works best for a particular organization. In *The ABCs of ERP*, Christopher Koch comments, "While most packages are exhaustively comprehensive, each industry has quirks that make it unique. Most ERP systems were designed to be used by discrete manufacturing companies (that make physical things that can be counted), which immediately left all the process manufacturers (oil, chemical and utility companies that measure their products by flow rather than individual units) out in the cold."

In fact, it is simply infeasible for organizations to adopt all of the specified best practices. Therefore, they usually compromise: organizations change some of their practices to suit the system, but they also "struggle" to "modify" core ERP programs to their needs, writes Koch. All this makes it extremely difficult to assess the value or the costs. Koch writes that "the value of the systems is hard to pin down because . . . the software is less important than the changes companies make in the ways they do business. If you use ERP to improve the ways your people take orders and manufacture, ship and bill for goods, you will see value from the software. If you simply install the software without trying to improve the ways people do their jobs, you may not see any value at all—indeed, the new software could slow you down by simply replacing the old software that everyone knew with new software that no one does."

Similarly, there "aren't any good numbers to predict the costs" because

the software installation has so many variables, such as: the number of divisions it will serve, the number of modules installed, the amount of integration that will be required with existing systems, the readiness of the company to change, and the ambition of the project—if the project is truly meant to be a battering ram for reengineering how the company does its most important work, the project will cost much more and take much longer than one in which ERP is simply replacing an old transaction system. There is a sketchy rule of thumb that experts have used for years to predict ERP installation costs, which is that the installation will cost about six times as much as the software license. But this has become increasingly less relevant. . . . Research companies don't even bother trying to predict costs anymore.

■ Ground-level Development

The effective use of innovations usually requires acquiring or developing ground-level know-how. There are very few products that humans can use immediately: we have to acquire the knowledge, and sometimes the taste, for almost everything that we consume in our daily lives—we must learn how to brush our teeth, tie our shoelaces, knot ties, savor espressos, and drive cars. An innovative biometric lock opened by swiping one's fingers over a sensor eliminates losing or fumbling with keys, but there is a catch. As Anne Eisenberg (who reviewed the product for the *New York Times*) discovered, after installing the lock, she could not recall the finger-swiping technique the next day. "I swiped and swiped," she writes, "but the door wouldn't budge. Many speeds and angles can be used in swiping a finger, I gradually realized, and I could no longer recapture the technique I'd used the night before." Swiping a finger isn't necessarily harder than turning a physical key in a conventional lock; but as Stephanie Schuckers, a professor of electrical and computer engineering points out, people have already learned to use standard locks: "We are all trained how to use keys, from when we are young."[9]

Differences in how products are used require consumers to do more than just acquire the knowledge of a "standard technique"—they have to develop ground-level know-how tailored to their specific requirements. For instance, users of spreadsheets don't just acquire the knowledge of standard pull-down menus and commands; they also have to develop, or at least modify, their own templates and models. Furthermore, mid-level products that are jointly used by several individuals often require the development of ground-level organizational know-how as well as technical know-how—as previously mentioned, the use of enterprise software requires the development of new processes and practices as well as adaptation of the software itself. And because processes and practices can vary considerably, each organization has to develop its own.

Research[10] on the adoption of client/server technology documents the importance of developing multifaceted ground-level know-how (which Bresnahan and Greenstein call "co-invention").* Bresnahan and Greenstein

---

* Bresnahan and Greenstein distinguish between "invention" by producers and "co-invention" by users. Their distinction corresponds to higher and lower levels of know-how in my framework. In principle, I ought to defer to Bresnahan and Greenstein's prior terminology, especially since virtually everything in their paper is congruent with my thesis. Their language makes me uncomfortable, however: as I have said (and as Bresnahan and Greenstein note), innovations such as client/server technology are also "co-invented" by producers and users.

found that companies in the vanguard of adoption were in science- and engineering-based industries that were "least tied to complex business procedures." The slowest adopters were in industries with great "organizational complexity," where "organizational adjustment costs" were highest. Adjustment costs, rather than the benefits of client/server systems, seemed to drive the adoption of the technology.

As mentioned in book 1, innovators who develop mid-level "combinations" require different skills and human capital than do researchers who work on high-level scientific problems. Similarly, users who have to develop ground-level know-how require yet another set of skills—while technical knowledge is certainly necessary, managerial and organizational knowledge is crucial. In chapter 16, I will examine the policy implications of these differences. Here I want to emphasize the following similarity: both the developers and users of innovations often require a high degree of venturesome or entrepreneurial resourcefulness in problem solving.

Developers of innovations often face situations that require such resourcefulness in the following sense: although the situation may be similar to ones the innovator has faced before, it also contains novel elements, so the innovator cannot simply repeat what has worked in the past. Experience (or "human capital"), which we may think of as the accumulated knowledge of similar past situations, helps, but it is not enough. An innovator is more than just a skilled and knowledgeable surgeon performing difficult but routine arthroscopic knee surgery. The innovator must also act resourcefully in the face of novel situations with a can-do attitude, imagination, willingness to experiment, and so on.

Consuming something novel does not always require resourceful problem solving. Drinking a new soft drink or showing up for an appointment for corrective surgery is not especially demanding. Other kinds of consumption—such as assembling a model airplane—may require patience, dexterity, and experience, but as long as the instructions are clear and complete, they do not require resourcefulness or creativity. Indeed, creative deviations from prescribed instructions can lead to undesirable outcomes. But not all innovations come with clear and complete instructions. High-tech products, especially those with complex architectures and features, rarely do, and deriving utility from them requires a great deal of resourceful problem solving.

Manuals for Windows-based personal computers and software, for instance, are famously bewildering. This is not mainly because of the incompetence of the authors of the manuals. In considerable measure, the sometimes bewildering instructions reflect the complexity of the internal architectures of the systems, the many options and features they contain, and the difficulty of anticipating how the components will interact. But whatever the cause of that impenetrability, my experience has been that the alluring features of new products rarely work "out of the box" if one simply follows the instruction manual. I have spent countless hours getting new gizmos to work, or trying to stop inexplicable crashes. And the toil is far from mechanical: I have to guess what might be wrong, conduct experiments, and troll through postings of user groups on the Internet trying to find solutions to similar problems. Moreover, figuring out how something is supposed to work is often only half the battle: in many innovations, users have to figure out how to make the product work well *for them*. In the case of innovations such as enterprise software, the figuring out involves the solving of technical and organizational problems. Experience and effort is helpful, even necessary. But as the box "Using ERP Systems" indicates, because the problems tend to be idiosyncratic, the solutions require a great deal of resourcefulness as well.

Using ERP Systems

The effective use of complex enterprise software requires solving both technical and organizational problems. As Koch writes:

> The inherent difficulties of implementing something as complex as ERP is like, well, teaching an elephant to do the hootchy-kootchy. The packages are built from database tables, thousands of them, that IS programmers and end users must set to match their business processes; each table has a decision "switch" that leads the software down one decision path or another ... [F]iguring out precisely how to set all the switches in the tables requires a deep understanding of the ... processes being used to operate the business.

> Inevitably, business processes themselves have to be "reengineered." Users who want to take advantage of off-the-shelf software packages must align their processes with the "best practices" built into the software. To have a system that is truly enterprise-wide, organizations have to figure out

processes that work best across their different units. Inevitably, individuals and organizational subunits resist changing the way they do things; and even if they don't, business processes and their associated information systems cannot be changed overnight. Therefore, in addition to figuring out what their businesses processes should ultimately look like (and how the "switches" in the software need to be set to match the processes), organizations also need to resolve how they will overcome resistance to change and make the transition from "legacy" processes and systems.

Consultants who have implemented ERP systems in the past can help ameliorate these problems. However, the issues facing different organizations are never identical, so the consultants and their clients have to solve many novel problems. Moreover, ERP packages and the other applications—for instance supply-chain, customer-relationship-management (CRM), and e-commerce software—that ERP is supposed to complement also change frequently, which adds to the difficulty of deriving a tried-and-tested formula for implementation. Researchers and industry experts who have expended considerable effort to investigate what works and what doesn't have been unable to get beyond long and wooly lists. Somers and Nelson formulated a list of 24 "critical success factors," starting with "top management support" and including items such as "project team competence," "interdepartmental cooperation," and "clear goals and objectives."[11] For obvious reasons, such lists do little to obviate the need for situation-specific problem solving.

The mixed record of ERP systems also points to the difficult problems users must solve to realize the potential benefits. Holland and Light point out that successful implementations at Pioneer New Media Technologies and Monsanto have been well publicized, but "less successful projects have led to bankruptcy proceedings and litigation."[12] Similarly, Plant and Wilcocks note the success of ERP at companies such as Cisco as well as "spectacular" failures at Hershey Foods and FoxMeyer and disappointments at Volkswagen, Whirlpool, and W. L. Gore.[13]

■ Not Quite Free

Economists often believe that innovations are a gift to consumers. Stanford's Paul Romer writes that innovators "have brought the cost of a transistor down to less than a millionth of its former level. Yet, most of the benefits from those discoveries have been reaped not by the innovating firms, but by the users of the transistors. In 1985, I paid a thousand dollars per million transistors for memory in my computer. In 2005, I paid less than ten dollars per million, and yet I did nothing to deserve or help pay for this windfall."

My analysis suggests a slightly different view. In all likelihood, users do secure the lion's share of the benefit of successful innovations. But not all innovations are successful. Apple's iPod has been a resounding success for both the company and its customers—its Lisa and Newton were not. When products fail, the downside faced by users in the aggregate (and sometimes even individually) in innovations ranging from corrective laser surgery to enterprise software matches or exceeds the downside of the innovator. Indeed, one important challenge faced by innovators is to persuade entrepreneurs to take a chance on innovations in the absence of any hard demonstration that the returns are worth the risks (as discussed in chapter 3).

One of the notable features of the modern innovation system lies in the great many individuals and organizations that are willing to be so persuaded. At the dawn of the automobile era, only a few very rich buffs served as guinea pigs. Now, the not-so-well-off borrow against their credits cards—or spend what they "save" by buying paper napkins in bulk at Wal-Mart—to take their chances on laser surgery and flat panel TVs without much foreknowledge of the utility of their purchase. Similarly, large corporations run by the book with the help of squadrons of financial analysts will spend tens of millions of dollars on enterprise software based on the crudest of guesses of costs and benefits.

Even late adopters who only buy tried-and-tested products don't get a free ride. Romer sells himself—and other computer users—short in declaring that they have "done nothing" to deserve the windfall of lower prices. Large markets and the prospect of their continued growth have helped drive down prices. And markets have grown because individuals and companies have invested in learning how to use computers and developing ground-level know-how. The investment is not trivial. The prices of computers have declined, but their complexity hasn't. Feature bloat may, in fact, have made computers and programs harder to use. Yet the number of people who have made the effort—possibly incurring opportunity costs many times the purchase price of their equipment and software—has over the years continued to grow. Users who build their own templates and models for spreadsheet and database programs now number in the tens of millions, whereas the teams at Microsoft who develop such products number in the thousands (see box).

A Multitude of User Programmers

Scaffidi, Shaw, and Myers (from Carnegie Mellon's school of computer science) use a variety of sources to estimate the number of end users of computers and end-user programmers in the United States. They get a lower bound estimate of 55 million computer users in 2005 by multiplying the number of individuals in different occupational categories in 2005 by the percentage of computer users in that category in 1989. For instance, in 2005, there were about 36.7 million workers in the "managerial and professional" category, and 56.2 percent of such workers used computers in 1989, leading to an estimate of 20.6 million "managers and professionals" using computers in 2005. But as Scaffidi and coauthors point out, the percentage of computer usage in the different categories has increased significantly since 1989. For instance, the percentage of managers and professionals using computers grew from 56.2 percent in 1989 to over 70 percent in 1997. Extrapolating from these trends (because actual data for 2005 are unavailable), the researchers arrive at an estimate of 81 million users of computers at work in 2005. They note that other estimates are even higher—for instance, a Forrester Research survey commissioned by Microsoft estimated that 129 million people in the United States between the ages of 18 and 64 used computers at home or at work in 2003.

Scaffidi and coauthors also highlight the growth of some kind of programming by end users. Since 1989, the Current Population Survey (CPS) conducted by the Bureau of Census has included questions such as "Do you do programming?" and "Do you use spreadsheets or databases?" Here too we find substantial increases: The percentage of U.S. workers who said they used spreadsheets grew from about 10 percent in 1989 to over 30 percent in 1997. Similar increases were reported in the usage of databases. Between 1997 and 2001, "Usage of end user programming environments continued to explode, with over 60 percent of American end user workers reporting that they 'used spreadsheets or databases' in 2001. This amounted to over 45 million end users of spreadsheets or databases." Increases in the proportion of workers who reported they "did programming" were relatively modest, rising from about 10 percent of the workforce in 1989 to 15 percent in 2001. Nonetheless, the estimated 11 million workers who reported that they did programming was more than five times less than the 2 million programmers in the United States in 2001.[14] Of these software professionals, two-thirds worked for IT-using companies rather than IT-producing companies.[15]

■ Concluding Comments

In the North-South trade models—as in most mainstream economic theories—users of new technologies are at once passive and omniscient. They play no role in the development of innovations, but once innovations appear, users know whether they should buy the offering and what they should pay. Even in Schumpeter's theories (which in other ways challenge mainstream models), the innovator is the star, while those who imitate or modify have secondary parts. Consumers don't appear in the cast.

The neoclassical and Schumpeterian models both fail to do justice to the role of users. In a system where innovations are carried out by numerous players, the producers of innovations are, except for the end consumers, also users of higher-level or "adjacent" innovations. As I argued in this chapter, users—including those at the end of the line—often play a venturesome or "entrepreneurial" role in the design of new products, bearing "unmeasurable and unquantifiable" risks and developing ground-level knowledge. Therefore, contrary to the high-level research-centric view, the willingness and ability of users to undertake a venturesome part plays a critical role in determining the ultimate value of innovations. The venturesomeness of customers also encourages innovators to optimize their offerings for customers' needs and to invest in marketing to them.

In the next chapter, we look at evidence suggesting that IT users in the United States are exceptionally venturesome, and that their willingness and ability to deploy innovations has made a significant contribution to the nation's continued prosperity.

12

■ Winning by Using

Rich countries tend to make greater and more effective use of IT and other advanced technologies than do poor countries. But even within rich countries (as defined by membership in the OECD), we find considerable variation in "venturesome consumption" of new technologies. An OECD research team reports that "although ICT [information and communication technology] is a 'general purpose' technology and readily available in worldwide markets, only a limited number of OECD countries have been reaping its significant potential benefits to the full."[1] As we will see in this chapter, the United States happens to be one of those countries, and it is very likely the leading one. Relative to the size of its economy, its spending on IT products and services is exceptionally large, and U.S. companies also seem to be unusually good at deriving value from their IT spending. In this chapter I will review evidence suggesting that the extensive and effective use of IT, especially in the services sector, has made a significant contribution to the high growth of U.S. productivity and thus to sustaining the country's prosperity.

■ Comparisons of IT Use

The United States is the leading user for a wide range of new IT products and services. As Edward Leamer points out, "The U.S. is the primary home of the Internet, and in many ways is the center of the New Economy. Fully 67% of Internet hosts reside in the U.S., [as do] 23% of Internet users compared with a population fraction of 4.6%." According to Leamer's data, the number of Internet hosts per capita in the United States (0.39) is about four times the number in Japan, seven times the number in the UK, nearly 10 times the number in France, and 12 times the number in Germany.[2] The United States's lead in Internet hosting isn't simply a function of its greater wealth. The lead is also substantial when hosting is measured relative to gross domestic product: the United States's share of the world's Internet hosting is more than three times its share of world GDP.

Shipments of another "core" component of IT—operating systems— follow the same pattern. Tables 12.1 and 12.2 contain data on the sales of Windows, Linux, and other operating systems for personal computers and servers by selected regions and selected countries for 2001.[3] To construct these tables, I divided sales of operating systems (as available, in terms of units and revenues) by GDP for the region or country. Then I scaled each sales-to-GDP ratio by the sales-to-GDP ratio for the United States. The tables show that Windows operating systems sales-to-GDP ratios for Western Europe were about 25 percent lower than in the United States and more than 10 percent lower in Japan. Within Western Europe, only two countries, Sweden and Denmark, had higher sales-to-GDP ratios than the United States (see figure 12.1) (The GDPs of these two countries are, however, small, so their total sales amounted to only about one-twentieth of U.S. sales). German, French, and Italian GDP to sales ratios were about a third lower than in the United States. In the UK they were about 10 percent lower.

There is one caveat: The United States isn't the leading user of IT in every category. According to Prestowitz,[4] the United States now lags in broadband deployment. As of 2005, the United States was behind 15 other countries in terms of the number of broadband subscribers per 100 inhabitants. Prestowitz also cites data showing that the United States is forty-second in the world in cell-phone usage: in 2003, cell-phone subscriptions per 100 inhabitants in the United States were about half the subscriptions in Italy. The United States has also lagged behind Korea, Japan, and many countries in Europe in the deployment of 3G high-speed wireless data systems.

But exceptions apart, the United States leads in terms of overall IT consumption, just as it does in web hosting and the purchases of operating systems. Table 12.3 compares total IT expenditures (as estimated by the

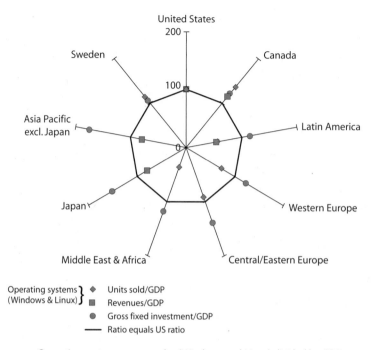

Figure 12.1. Operating system systems sales (Windows and Linux) divided by GDP compared to gross fixed investments GDP ratio.

Gartner Group in its *Market Data* books) across selected regions and countries for 2001 to 2004. As in the previous tables, I divided total expenditures by GDP. Here, too, we find that the IT expenditure–to-GDP ratio in Western Europe is 15 to 20 percent lower than in the United States, and in Japan it ranges from 10 to 30 percent lower than in the United States over the same period. (See figure 12.2 for 2004 data.)

As also shown in the tables and figures, U.S. purchases of IT are much higher than might be expected from the overall rate of investment and capital formation. The United States *does not* have a generally higher propensity to invest in fixed capital because of some general economy-wide factors like low interest or discount rates or tax breaks for long-term investment. The United States in fact *lags* in overall fixed investment-to-GDP ratios by about the same degree as it leads in IT spending. The ratio of gross fixed investment to GDP is about 50 percent higher in Japan than in the United States, and it is about 25 percent higher in Western Europe. Table 12.2 also shows that there is not a single country in Europe where the ratio of gross fixed investment to GDP is lower than in the United States.[5] In other words, U.S. businesses

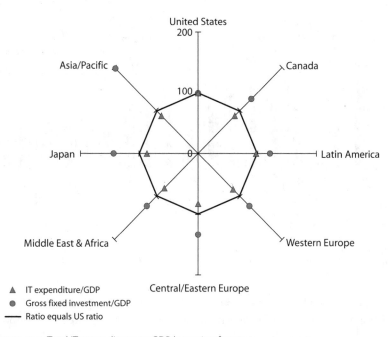

Figure 12.2. Total IT expenditures to GDP by region for 2004
See table 12.3 for sources and more details.

are relatively stingy in their conventional investments but are exceptionally venturesome when it comes to IT. (This propensity is also reflected in IT to total investment ratios as, shown in figure 12.3.)

The exceptional willingness of U.S. individuals and businesses to buy and use IT apparently encourages innovators to develop products optimized for the United States and to devote significant resources in marketing to U.S. customers. As we saw in book 1, except for some companies in segments such as mobile phones that "had to sell abroad," the default option for most VC-backed businesses is to build a base in the U.S. market first. The U.S. market also holds a strong attraction for innovators abroad: I recently attended a conference in Cambridge, England, on how entrepreneurs could "grow big gorillas." Speaker after speaker emphasized the importance of securing U.S. sales—but there was virtually no mention of the equally populous and more proximate market in continental Europe. Two reasons for this preference were the size of the U.S. market and its use of English. But the United States is more than just large and rich: the data we have just reviewed suggest that its consumption of IT is high even when scaled for the size of its economy. And just as the buying habits of U.S.

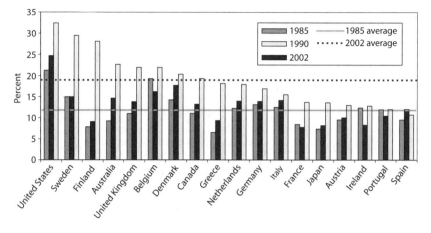

Figure 12.3. Share of IT investment in total nonresidential fixed capital formation
Source: Conway et al. 2006, 43.

customers attract IT innovators from all over the world, reciprocally, the attention that the innovators lavish on the U.S. market reinforces the propensity of U.S. companies to use IT.

One other feature of IT usage in the United States is noteworthy: as shown in table 12.4, the sectors normally considered "nontraded" account for roughly the same large proportion of U.S. IT usage as they do of overall economic activity. As we can see from the first column in the table, construction, services, and government—the nontraded sectors—account for more than 80 percent of the total value-added in the U.S. economy. The second column contains the percentage of IT hardware used as intermediate inputs (rather than by individuals as "final consumption") by traded and untraded sectors. The column seems to show that the manufacturing sector accounts for an exceptionally high share of the use of hardware intermediates. However (and not surprisingly), makers of computers and electronic products account for nearly 60 percent of the manufacturing sector's use of hardware intermediates; excluding the makers of computers and electronic products, the share of the manufacturing sector is much lower (although still high compared to its share of value-added).

The third column contains the distribution of IT services used as intermediates by the various sectors of the economy. Here we see that the traded sectors' use of IT services is slightly lower than their share of total value-added (and the share of the nontraded sectors is correspondingly higher).

The fourth column contains the distribution of IT occupations—programmers, database administrators, network administrators, and so on. Here we see that the service sector accounts for more than 80 percent of IT occupations. But about half of the IT jobs in the service sector are in "business services," in other words, in some form of outsourcing; it is impossible to know how many of these "outsourced" IT staff are actually working on projects for manufacturing clients. Nevertheless, looking at the data in all the columns, we may reasonably conclude that services and other nontraded sectors make a significant contribution to the unusually high use of IT in the United States.

If service industries use the IT they purchase effectively, this has a dual benefit for the U.S. economy overall. As mentioned in the last chapter, both the production and consumption of most *services* takes place domestically; therefore the effective use of innovative IT helps provide U.S. consumers with cheaper or better services while also improving the productivity of U.S.-based employees.* But has the deployment of IT, in fact, materially improved the productivity of the service sector in the United States? As we will see next, the evidence suggests that since about the mid-1990s, service sector productivity has grown exceptionally fast in the United States, and the high use of IT has indeed made an important contribution to this rapid productivity growth.

■ Service Sector Productivity Growth

The simplest measure of productivity—and the one that seems to track most closely with per capita wages and incomes, is value-added ("output," or GDP, in the national accounts) per employed person per year. This simple measure is not precise, because of uncertainties in controlling for inflation and other such complications, so estimates are prone to considerable revision over time. However, more sophisticated measures are even more uncertain and imprecise. For instance, estimates of labor productivity measured as value-added per hour worked involve the additional problem of accurately estimating hours worked (since workers don't punch a time clock maintained by government statisticians).[6]

---

* At the same time, because most services are not internationally traded, the capacity of U.S. service industries to use IT does not harm—at least in any direct way—the performance of other countries.

Although different estimation procedures produce somewhat different results, there seems to be agreement about the following general pattern: at the end of World War II, the United States led the world in labor productivity. Over the next several decades, productivity in Japan and Europe grew faster than in the United States, so their productivity levels appeared set to reach and then possibly exceed U.S. levels. According to Robert Gordon's estimates, by 1995, value-added per hour of labor in Europe reached 97.5 percent of the United States. In three countries, France, Belgium, and Holland, it surpassed the United States. But after the mid-1990s, the catch-up process ceased and, in fact, reversed. According to Gordon's estimates, by 2004, value-added per hour in Europe fell back to 89.7 percent of the U.S. level.

By 2006, according to the International Labor Organization's (ILO) estimates, the United States had the highest value-added per person employed. It was in second place after Norway in terms of value-added per hour worked. (Norwegians employees worked fewer hours but produced more). France, Belgium, and Holland, according to ILO, had all fallen behind.

Cross-country comparisons of productivity by sector, especially of services, are particularly challenging.[7] Nevertheless, it is hard to imagine how the United States could have expanded its overall lead in productivity after the mid-1990s without a significant contribution by the service sector (which, as mentioned, accounts for about 70 percent of the output of most advanced countries). Indeed, most estimates give considerable credit to the exceptional acceleration of productivity that occurred in the U.S. service sector after the 1990s (see box).

Differences between Productivity Growth in the United States and the EU

According to Van Ark's data,[8] between 1987 and 1995 productivity grew more rapidly in the EU than it did in the United States. "Other industries" (see the list below)—principally old-line manufacturing—accounted for more than 100 percent of the absolute difference in annualized productivity (in favor of the EU). Slower productivity growth in IT-producing sectors, wholesale trade, retail trade, and banking helped pare back the EU lead.

- Contribution, by sector, of the EU-U.S. growth differential (1987–95), percentage of total

IT-producing industries	−12
Wholesale and retail trade	−10
Banking	−1
Business services	4
Other industries and adjustments	119

Note that the absolute difference in annualized productivity growth was 1.13 percent per annum in favor of the EU. Productivity in the EU grew faster than in the United States in the sectors showing positive percentages, and more slowly in the sectors showing negative percentages.

Productivity in the United States grew faster than in the EU between 1995 and 2000, and then again between 2000 and 2003. This time IT production accounted for about a third of the U.S. lead and wholesale trade, retail trade and banking and business services accounted for more than half of the U.S. lead

- Contribution, by sector, to the EU-U.S. growth differential (1995–2000), percentage of total

IT-producing industries	31
Wholesale and retail trade	128
Banking	−49
Business services	83
Other industries and adjustments	−91

Note that the absolute difference in annualized productivity growth was .35 percent per annum in favor of the United States. Productivity in the EU grew faster than in the United States in the sectors showing negative percentages, however.

- Contribution, by sector, to the EU-U.S. growth differential (2000–2003), percentage of total

IT-producing industries	33
Wholesale and retail trade	19
Banking	19
Business Services	15
Other industries and adjustments	16

Note that the absolute difference in annualized productivity growth was 1.03 percent per annum in favor of the United States (which was "ahead" in all sectors).

McKinsey Global Institute (MGI) research has also found that service industries made a significant contribution to overall U.S. productivity growth after the mid-1990s. In 2002, an MGI study reported that just six of the economy's 59 sectors[9] accounted for virtually all the net productivity growth in the United States from 1995 through 1999. One sector comprised the producers of computers and electronic products, and the other five were in services (finance and insurance; real estate, rental, and leasing; professional, scientific, and technical services; utilities; and wholesale trade). In the following three years, the contribution of computers and electronic products declined in the wake of the technology bust. Nonetheless, U.S. overall productivity continued its rapid growth between 2000 and 2003. One reason was the continued strong growth of productivity in retail and wholesale trade; another was that productivity increased "in a much broader set of the service industry, including administrative support, scientific and technical services, construction and restaurants."[10]

■ The IT Contribution

Although the U.S. service industries have been world leaders in their use of IT, the share of IT in the overall inputs used by these industries—and in the economy as a whole—is small. According to data compiled by Brandeis economist Catherine Mann, IT hardware and services accounted for just 4.9 percent of all intermediates used in the U.S. economy in 2004 and 4.4 percent in 1998. In the 37 sectors in the services category, the median share of IT of intermediates used was 2.8 percent (in 1998, as well as in 2004). Besides three sectors that were also producers of IT, no service sector had a share greater than 10 percent. Retail trade, banking, and insurance—which are all large users of IT—nonetheless had shares of 3 percent or less.[11]

A small share of total inputs used does not, however, preclude a large impact on productivity. For instance, a new strain of seeds that represent a small fraction of a farmer's total costs may significantly increase crop yields; likewise, a small amount of fuel additive can coax many more miles out of a car's gas tank. But estimating the impact of adding IT to the service sector's input mix is problematic.

One reason already mentioned is that measuring the "outputs" of service activity is tricky: we cannot physically measure changes in output the way we can measure crop yields or fuel efficiency—and although we may be able to count the billings of a service enterprise, they have to be adjusted for changes in quality and inflation. This is hard to do: as Zvi Griliches and others have pointed out,[12] IT helps provide many benefits—such as greater variety, convenience, or quality—that are missed in standard GDP accounting.

For obvious reasons, it is also virtually impossible to run controlled experiments, as we could for a new seed or fuel additive. With the use of IT, we have to infer the counterfactual—what productivity would have been if IT had not been used. Under standard operating procedures, economists typically make such inferences using a regression model, which means, as discussed in chapter 6, the inference relies on arbitrary and often implausible assumptions.[13]

Another problem in estimating the impact of IT involves accounting for the changes that accompany its use. As I have mentioned, the use of ERP systems usually forces companies to adopt new—and often improved—business processes, just as the use of a new strain of seeds may stimulate farmers to change their soil management or pest-control techniques. But this raises the question: in the successful implementation of an ERP system, how much credit is due to the reengineered business process, and how much to the software? Or in the case of a failure, how should one allocate blame?

For many years, there was a disconnect between the inferences many economists made about the value of IT (see box "Productivity Paradox?") and what businesses executives did. James Cortada, historian and author of the three-volume study *The Digital Hand*, writes: "In the 1980s, as economists began debating whether computers improved a nation's productivity, managers of firms did not hesitate to acquire ever more amounts of IT and telecommunications. Apparently, they knew something that the economists did not. At the most basic level, the technology delivered the performance that these managers wanted, or needed. Over time, they relied so much on IT that it became part of the normal operations of industry."[14]

We don't know the counterfactual—what would have happened if businesses had invested in something other than IT. It is possible that many business executives made big mistakes for many years—or, as some theories suggest, they may have had such long time horizons that the returns on their IT investments could not be observed in short-term results. But how likely is this? Apart from the days of the Internet bubble, businesses did not systematically make pie-in-the-sky IT investments. According to Cortada's study (which encompassed virtually all IT-using sectors):

> Overwhelmingly across all industries in each decade, management adopted IT in order to improve internal business operations and to lower operating costs. While much of the literature advocating computer use focused on expanding marketing and distribution and selling more goods and services, managers treated those activities as welcome, but nonessential, benefits that were not required to justify the cost of projects. Companies preferred to implement computer use in small, incremental ways that fit the size of their budgets and minimized the risk of failure to firm and managers alike.[15]

The more likely possibility is that the models used to estimate the impact of IT were wrong, not the spending decisions. As I argue in the box, some of the most prominent studies relied on assumptions that are prima facie implausible; it is not surprising, therefore, that they suggested a result that was "too freaky to be true"—namely that nearly half a trillion dollars of IT expenditure was misspent.

In any event, the debate seems to be largely over. As Dedrick, Gurbaxani, and Kraemer conclude in a review of the literature, "The productivity paradox as first formulated has been effectively refuted. At both the firm and the country level, greater investment in IT is associated with greater productivity growth." Moreover, they write, at the firm level, "IT is not simply a tool for automating existing processes, but is more importantly an enabler of organizational changes that can lead to additional productivity gains."[16]

The literature also suggests that the United States is at the forefront of realizing productivity gains from IT. As I mentioned previously, the United States has enjoyed exceptionally high rates of productivity growth in the service sector. Research also suggests that the U.S. lead is most pronounced among the heavy users of IT, such as retail, wholesale, and financial intermediation. Robert Gordon wrote in 1999 that there was virtually "*no* productivity growth acceleration in the 99 percent of the [U.S.] economy located outside the sector which manufactures computer hardware." By 2004, Gordon was convinced that "after fifty years of catching up to the U.S. level of productivity, since 1995, Europe has been falling behind . . . studies of industrial sectors[17] suggest that the main difference between Europe and the U. S. is in [IT] using industries."[18]

The lead isn't simply the consequence of buying more IT. As I have said, U.S. companies do have a higher propensity to invest in IT even though the overall rate of business investment in the United States is relatively low. This propensity may, in part, reflect a greater willingness to take chances on new technologies, but this is tempered by competitive and financial-market pressures businesses face to extract value from their investments. Comparative research (which I review in chapter 15) suggests that the U.S. service sector has developed an exceptional capacity to effectively deploy IT. To a considerable degree, U.S. companies buy more IT because they get more bang for their buck.

Productivity Paradox?

Until not so long ago, there was debate among economists about whether IT investment had done the U.S. economy much good. In 1987, Robert Solow wrote: "We see the computer age everywhere, except in the productivity statistics." The following year, Steven Roach of Morgan Stanley dubbed this the "productivity paradox." In 1991, the *Economist* pointed out that returns from IT investments were so low that firms "would have done better to have invested their money in almost any other part of their business." On the other side, Paul David argued (in 1990) that it was too early to judge the value of computers—it took decades for the productivity benefits of the electric dynamo (whose technical development had been largely completed by 1880) to be realized. Brynjolfsson (in 1993), Griliches (in 1994), and others also suggested that the productivity paradox reflected deficiencies in measurements and methodological tool kits.[19]

By 1996, annual IT spending by U.S. firms had crossed the half-trillion-dollar level, and some organizations, such as Nations Bank, had annual IT budgets of $2 billion.[20] Yet in 1999 Robert Gordon suggested this was all for naught so far as the economy was concerned. According to Gordon, the acceleration of productivity in the United States after the mid-1990s was almost entirely due to more efficient production of IT, particularly computers, rather than to the *use* of IT.[21] In an oft-cited study, Jorgenson and Stiroh came to similar conclusions: the acceleration of productivity growth after 1995 could be "traced in substantial part" to improvements in the *production* of IT. On the user side, there had been some "capital deepening"—as computers got cheaper, firms bought more of them. The evidence was clear, they wrote, that "computer-using industries like finance, insurance, and real estate (FIRE) and services" had "continued to lag in productivity growth. Reconciliation of massive high-tech investment and relatively slow productivity growth in service industries remains an important task for proponents of the new economy position."[22]

In my view, the mismatch between "massive high-tech investment" and the Jorgenson and Stiroh finding of "slow productivity growth" very likely derives from the assumptions of their estimation procedure. Crucially, they assume perfectly competitive product and factor markets. Now there are some service businesses—the neighborhood florist or laundry, for instance—where "perfect competition" is a plausible approximation. But this is not the case in service industries, which are the major users of IT. There is often a lot of rivalry, and competitive advantages are usually under threat, but these businesses are far from perfectly competitive in the classic microeconomic way. In fact, if banking markets were nearly perfectly competitive, how could banks have the profits (or borrowing capacity) needed to make large investments in IT? Similarly, if the computer market was perfectly competitive, why or how could computer companies have made the sizable investments necessary to develop and market their products? In other words, the Jorgenson and Stiroh assumptions preclude the very phenomenon that their procedure purports to assess.*

Making simplifying assumptions is necessary for any analysis, and even gross simplifications can lead to useful corroborative insights. But it is hard to take seriously results that are not only based on implausible assumptions but sharply contradict easily observable features of the world. In my view, the Jorgenson and Stiroh claims are in conflict with the real world in three ways.

First, by the year 2000, computer-using industries had undergone vast changes over nearly two decades. The rise of new big-box retailers, most notably Wal-Mart, had displaced many traditional players. Similarly, small regional banks had been merged into megasized national institutions such as Citicorp and the Bank of America or had disappeared. With the new players came new ways of doing business—Wal-Mart established global supply chains and regional distribution centers, for instance. The old players and

* Their procedure further assumes that all industries have the same kind of production function, that there is a single equation according to which all inputs—labor, machinery, capital. and so on—are combined. This too flies in the face of the visibly different ways businesses are structured.

ways of doing business didn't fall like trees stricken with Dutch elm disease. The old order was pushed out only after competitive struggle in the marketplace. How could this have happened unless, in some way, shape, or form, the new was more "productive" than the old?

Second, could businesses facing relentless pressure from rivals and the capital market simply have thrown away the greater part of half a trillion dollars in IT spending a year? I once suggested that banks and other financial institutions overestimate the sustainability of the competitive advantages they can derive from investing in technologies because they overlook the possibility of imitation: if one bank builds ATMs that customers value, others soon will as well.[23] But this simply means that customers, not banks, derive most of the benefit. For the technological "arms race" to have no productivity benefit, competitors must all invest in innovations that even customers don't value. Much of the half a trillion dollars invested in IT would have to have been totally wasted.

Third, could IT-using industries really improve their output per worker from capital deepening alone, without finding new ways to use that capital? It is one thing to say that as the costs of vacuum cleaners and dishwashers decline, less labor will be required to clean floors and dishes because more capital equipment will be used. But I don't think that my writing will go faster if I have two computers on my desk instead of one (or get a computer with twice the processor speed). The idea of simply plugging more IT gear into the existing production function of a large organization becomes particularly far-fetched in light of the extensive reengineering that the implementation of new systems actually entails.

■ Norway versus Japan

Contrasts between Norway and Japan provide additional support to my argument that in an advanced economy, the effective use of IT in the service sector is as important as—if not more important than—the capacity to develop new products (and of course high-level research).

Norway is hardly a world leader in developing new technologies. According to an OECD policy brief published in 2007, "R&D intensity [in Norway] appears weak, patenting is moderate and business surveys report a limited interest for innovative activity." Similarly, according to a 2003 EU report, Norway was not in the top 20 countries ranked by their share of scientific papers published between 1995 and 1999. In fact, Norway's share actually declined over that period, and at the end of the period was lower than its Scandinavian neighbors' as well as that of countries such as Austria, Belgium, and the Ukraine. According to the report, the productivity of Norway's researchers also ranked below its Scandinavian neighbors (and Turkey and Hungary) as measured by publications per total R&D personnel.[24]

Yet Norway has the highest labor productivity (per working hour) in the world.[25] According to a report published by the Norwegian Central Bank in February 2007, "Even though some indicators suggest relatively limited innovation in Norwegian companies," labor productivity grew rapidly because "Norway has been quick to integrate new technology and reap the associated benefits." The report credited the service sector with "a considerable contribution to higher productivity growth since 1990." In retail trade, this reflected a combination of "structural changes" and "the introduction of [IT]". Similarly, in the financial sector, productivity increased through the implementation of "efficiency measures" and the increased use of IT in banking and payment services. "Productivity growth in the postal and telecommunications sector was also high" thanks "to deregulation, successful restructuring, rationalisation, automation and technological advances."[26]

Like Norway, Japan does not lack financial resources. Unlike Norway, however, Japan has shown great prowess in developing new technologies, but not in *using* new technologies in the services sector, according to an OECD study.

> Although Japan has kept its relatively strong position in [IT] investment by international standards, its contribution to productivity growth is significantly lower than what could be expected from the large asset that Japan has. For example, Japan holds many [IT] patents compared to other OECD countries. In an international comparison of [IT] patents at the EPO, Japan's share amounts to almost one quarter, which is the second largest share following the United States. On the other hand, Internet use and electronic commerce by enterprise in Japan is much lower than in other OECD countries; and in data on Web sites by country per 1,000 inhabitants, Japan is ranked almost last. These data indicate that Japan does not use its [IT] assets effectively. As a result, in data showing the contribution of [IT]-using services to annual average labour productivity growth, Japan is categorised among the "countries where productivity growth in [IT]-using services deteriorated," showing a sharp decrease during 1990s.[27]

Famously, Japan is a world leader in using robotics and other advanced technologies in its manufacturing plants and in developing the complementary organizational practices needed to exploit these technologies. But excellence in manufacturing has apparently not been enough to outweigh the low productivity of its services sector, which, in 2002, employed twice as many workers as the goods-producing sectors. So for more than a decade the overall economic performance of the country has been disappointing.

■ Concluding Comments

We rightly celebrate the accomplishments of IT innovators—and the researchers who develop the breakthroughs they incorporate in their products. But to achieve commercial success, innovations have to be effectively and widely deployed. Moreover, a highly innovative IT-producing industry cannot, by itself, produce widespread prosperity, because it just does not employ enough people. Silicon Valley[28] has the highest proportion of IT employees in the workforce of any metropolitan area in the United States. Yet even in Silicon Valley, only 8.3 percent of the workforce is employed by the IT industry.[29] The productivity and incomes of those IT workers have over time increased dramatically. But in the absence of a large and effective wealth-redistribution scheme, the incomes of the other 90-plus percent of the workforce cannot see any meaningful increases unless their productivity also grows.

As it happens, U.S. users, particularly those in the large services sector, have shown a great willingness and capacity to deploy innovative IT. As a result, the United States has been able to maintain or expand its productivity lead. Therefore, to go back to this study's primary question, whether the United States should worry about the increase in cutting-edge research being done in China and India: unless the United States somehow loses its capacity to harness innovations, any expansion of the supply of high-level knowledge used to develop innovations should be welcomed, regardless of where that new supply originates.

This analysis also suggests that, contrary to the arguments made by Prestowitz, the U.S. trade deficit in IT and other advanced technology products is not a symptom of a faltering economy. In my interpretation this deficit is an indicator of economic strength and dynamism: the United States has a voracious appetite for IT goods and services, many of which are made in countries where wages and manufacturing costs are relatively low.

A high propensity to use IT generates trade deficits, but it also enhances productivity in IT-using service industries, which account for a much larger share of economic activity than the IT industry itself.

But couldn't IT and other innovative technologies that have increased the productivity of U.S. workers in service industries also help move these jobs offshore? Indeed, one of the great concerns about globalization is that IT innovations are exposing hitherto-sheltered service jobs to competition from low-wage providers in India and China. Further stimulation of innovation by an increase in high-level inputs and know-how could therefore be a dubious blessing: while it might reduce the prices that U.S. consumers pay for their services, it could also erode employment opportunities—or the wage rates—of U.S. workers. In the next chapter I will assess the likelihood of such an outcome.

13

■ Nondestructive Creation

In the last two hundred years or so, innovative technologies have reduced labor costs through a combination of automation and specialization (as in Adam Smith's famous pin factory) and by facilitating the relocation of production to low-wage locations.* For instance, according to Edward Leamer, starting in the 1850s, "high-skilled, high-priced Boston craftsmen in artisan shops were replaced by low-skilled, low-paid workers in shoe factories in New York and points west, thanks to the standardization of shoes by size and shape, the mechanization of the factory floor (especially the McKay stitcher in the 1860s) and the division of labor. Mechanization and the division of labor allowed one relatively unskilled worker to perform a single task with productivity levels many tens of times the productivity in the artisan shops."[1]

Service jobs are considered harder to automate, specialize, and relocate. Nevertheless, many service jobs have been "industrialized" for decades. Burgers are produced by workers who are not necessarily well versed in the culinary arts, following a highly standardized process. Bank tellers have been replaced by a combination of cash machines and ethereal voices on telephone help-lines (which initially connected to staff in low-wage locations in the United States and now to call-center staff in places such as

* This chapter is based on a lecture given at the Royal Society of Arts (RSA) in London in 2004.

India). Similarly, computers have automated countless clerical jobs—and, as we saw in chapter 10—led to large reductions in employment in occupations involving mundane cognitive work.

In the future, technological and managerial innovations could automate tasks that now involve a high level of skill and judgment and allow them to be performed offshore. Moreover, prior innovations may have already created a backlog of service jobs that could easily be moved offshore. According to several alarmists (not necessarily of the techno-nationalist persuasion), a large number of service jobs are on the verge of such a journey. This would help increase productivity and reduce the costs that U.S. consumers pay for services. But it could also sharply reduce the demand for labor in the United States.

In this chapter, I will first contrast projections of widespread job loss through offshoring with the more modest degree to which jobs have, in fact, been lost. I will then argue that innovation is characterized not just by "creative destruction" (which reduces the demand for labor), but also by "non-destructive creation," which helps explain why innovation has not led to widespread unemployment (or declining wages) in the past and is unlikely to do so in the future.

■ Projections versus Reality

It was a report by Forrester Research in 2002 that "triggered public concern about the impact that offshoring would have on U.S. lives."[2] Forrester had estimated that 3.3 million U.S. service jobs would be lost to offshoring by 2015. In numerous additional studies "produced by private consulting firms, federal agencies, and economists from academia and think tanks," numbers differed by as much as a factor of 10.[3]

For example, Bardhan and Kroll estimated (in 2003) that about 10 percent of the labor force in the United States was employed in occupations (such as financial analysts, medical technicians, paralegals, and computer and math professionals) that could be offshored.[4] Using different criteria (such as IT intensity, codifiability of tasks, and the need for face-to-face interaction), Van Welsum and Reif (in 2005) and Van Welsum and Vickory (in 2006) estimated that 20 percent of U.S. jobs could be offshored.[5] McKinsey & Co.'s 2005 projections were more modest. They projected that for 2008, no more than 11 percent of the 1.46 billion service jobs worldwide could even theoretically be performed in an overseas location. They also estimated that actual offshore employment in 2008 would amount to just 3 percent of the theoretical maximum, or less than one-quarter of 1 percent of total service jobs worldwide.[6]

Princeton economist Alan S. Blinder's 2006 estimates are the ones that have received the most publicity (after Forrester's), possibly because of Blinder's standing (he is a former vice chairman of the U.S. Federal Reserve) and the magnitude of his figures. Blinder claimed that 40 million service jobs were vulnerable to offshoring, including those in high-skill occupations such as radiology, engineering, and (heaven forefend!) college teaching.[7] Unlike Forrester and McKinsey (but following the Wall Street dictum: "Never predict both a price and a date"), Blinder did not provide a time frame for the exodus. According to *Barrons's* Gene Epstein, Blinder subsequently "responded to critics by saying his scenario is at least 10 years away."[8]

As Epstein points out, however, "even such a distant prospect" ought to "leave a few . . . tangible traces in the present." And these traces are hard to find. According to one report, "It is difficult to be certain of the extent of offshoring. Federal data is not very helpful, and most of the existing data comes from consulting firms."[9] Whereas 12 to 14 million jobs are often believed to be "vulnerable to relocation," the estimates suggest that less than 300,000 service jobs per year have actually been lost.[10]

For an economy marked by considerable churn, these numbers are not particularly significant. As Epstein points out, according to the Bureau of Labor Statistics, the U.S. economy "created" 7.7 million new jobs and "lost" 7.2 million jobs in the last three months of 2006. Forrester's estimates of the more than three million jobs that would move offshore between 2000 and 2015, writes Epstein, amount to "little more than half the jobs created and lost in a single quarter. And even if we believe Forrester's estimate that approximately 800,000 service jobs moved offshore between 2002 and 2006, that's only a little over the 10% of the jobs created and lost in a single quarter."

Other factors have been far more responsible for job destruction. Many businesses that close and lay off their employees shouldn't have been started (or expanded) in the first place. Other businesses and jobs (especially in sectors such as housing) succumb to downturns in the economy. In the long run, innovations that improve efficiency play a particularly significant role. The service sector has shed many more jobs because of automation and consolidation than because of offshoring. Even in manufacturing, apart from a few specific industries such as toys and bicycles, efficiency improvements have had at least as much influence on job loss as offshoring. For instance, manufacturing employment in the United States in 2005 was nearly 10 percent lower than in 1960,[11] but thanks to a tripling in the output per worker over this period, total manufacturing output was roughly three times larger.

Stagnant or declining employment isn't, however, more palatable because it arises through efficiency improvements rather than offshoring. Fortunately, for all the noise about offshoring, large net increases in service sector jobs in the United States have more than offset the decline in manufacturing jobs. What is especially striking, according to Epstein, is that net employment has increased at an especially rapid rate in those jobs claimed by Forrester Research to be most vulnerable to offshoring. For his analysis, Epstein started with Forrester Research's May 2004 report, "Near-Term Growth of Offshoring Accelerating," which contains a five-tier ranking of job categories "most likely to move." Epstein found (using BLS data) that from 2002 through 2006, U.S. employment in the top two most "vulnerable" categories had actually *increased* by 7.7 percent, while overall service sector employment increased by 4.5 percent.[12]

But past performance is no guarantee of future results, as another Wall Street caution goes, and it is possible that a combination of efficiency and offshoring could indeed still cause services to follow the lead of manufacturing. To allay such concerns, I now examine the phenomena of "nondestructive creation," which helps the U.S. economy create more service sector jobs than it loses in manufacturing.

■ An Essential Symbiosis

According to Schumpeter, "a perennial gale of creative destruction" is an "essential fact about capitalism. It is what capitalism consists in and what every capitalist concern has got to live with."[13] Destruction is the price of innovation: the automobile must displace the buggy; and mass merchandisers must put country stores out of business. The innovator combines the roles of Shiva the Destroyer and Brahma the creator, of the mobs of the French Revolution who overthrew the ancien régime and Napoleon who founded an empire on its remains.

Schumpeter's vivid metaphor has become commonplace. Krugman writes that Schumpeter's "canonization as a patron saint of economic growth" is "based largely on his famous phrase, 'creative destruction.' "[14] The phrase is also central to the glum predictions of North-South models: if the South starts to innovate, incomes in the North are reduced, because if southern innovators win, northern competitors lose. In fact, as I will argue next, creative destruction is only half the story. Many innovations do not displace existing products and services, because they create and satisfy entirely *new* wants. This nondestructive form of entrepreneurship is as necessary for economic prosperity as creative destruction.

Over the long run, economic growth, of course, requires productivity growth—for per capita living standards to increase, per capita output must increase. But we often mistakenly believe that productivity growth comes only from improved efficiency—using fewer resources to satisfy our current wants. We fail to recognize that the creation and satisfaction of new wants can also increase per capita output. An artist may increase her productivity by developing new techniques that speed up her output of paintings. Alternatively, she may develop a new oeuvre that commands higher prices. She may produce exactly the same number of canvases as before, but if her work sells at higher prices, her *economic* output and productivity increases. Moreover, the new oeuvre may substitute for more traditional paintings, so this innovative artist's productivity gain comes at the expense of other artists who face reduced demand. But it doesn't have to: the new oeuvre may appeal to completely new sensibilities and find a place on walls that otherwise would have remained bare.

In fact, economies cannot sustain increases in productivity and living standards just by more efficiently satisfying existing wants. In the short run, increased efficiencies reduce costs, and, as costs decline, people consume more of the good or service. But eventually the law of diminishing utilities sets in. Sated consumers won't buy more, even if prices continue to decline. After that, further increases in efficiencies reduce the demand for labor.

In principle, societies could accommodate reductions in the demand for labor by increasing everyone's leisure. Over the last century, economic growth has indeed helped reduce working hours and increase vacations. But somehow, beyond a certain point, societies seem unable to accommodate reductions in the demand for labor by spreading around the work. Efforts to control unemployment by mandating reductions in workweeks or increasing the number of holidays seem to be ineffective.

Rather, it is the entrepreneurial activity of creating and satisfying new wants that keeps the system humming. This activity uses the labor and purchasing power released by increased efficiency in the satisfaction of old wants. It also stimulates continued increases in efficiencies even after demand for old wants has been fully satisfied: Producers who satisfy old wants have to keep economizing on their use of labor, because they must compete for employees (and share of consumers' wallets) against innovators who satisfy new wants.

Offshoring to low-wage countries resembles efficiency improvement in its symbiotic relationship to the satisfaction of new wants. It improves living standards in wealthy countries, provided the human capital released can be used to make new goods and services. Otherwise, like improvements in efficiency, offshoring will tend to reduce the demand for domestic labor.

■ The Historical Record

Improvements in efficiency as well as in the satisfaction of new wants played a significant role in the economic growth of the twentieth century. As I mentioned in chapter 8, the Industrial Revolution led to a surge in incomes. The growth resulted in part from more efficient methods for producing existing goods. Innovations such as tractors, threshing machines, fertilizers, pesticides, and hybrid seeds, for example, led to vast improvements in agricultural productivity. As higher productivity reduced the costs and increased the affordability of food, per capita consumption grew. But the increase in the consumption of food or other existing goods doesn't come close to accounting for the 10-fold increase in overall per capita GDP in the United States in the twentieth century. According to William Nordhaus's estimate,[15] less than 30 percent of the goods and services consumed in 1991 bear much resemblance to the goods and services of the late nineteenth century. "Most of the goods we consume today," Nordhaus writes, "were not produced a century ago. We travel in vehicles that were not yet invented, that are powered by fuels not yet produced, communicate through devices not yet manufactured, enjoy cool air on the hottest days, are entertained by electronic wizardry that was not dreamed of and receive medical treatments that were unheard of."

Some of the new goods replaced goods consumed by our forebears. Cars and buses replaced horses and stagecoaches. Steamships grounded sailing ships, and ready-to-eat cereal pushed homemade porridge off breakfast tables. As did the improvements in agricultural productivity, many of the new products reduced prices and costs. For instance, candles provided the primary source of artificial light until about the early 1800s. They were followed by lamps that used, successively, whale oil, town gas, kerosene, and electricity. Nordhaus calculates that these innovations reduced the price of light by 99 percent—from 40 cents per 1,000 lumen hours in 1800 to a tenth of a cent today.

But many new twentieth-century products did not displace existing products—rather, they created new markets and satisfied new wants. They were like a new oeuvre of art purchased for spaces that would otherwise remain bare. Air conditioners reduced temperatures in previously uncooled factories, stores, and office buildings. Airplanes did not reduce the demand for automobiles—people flew when they would not have driven. New drugs and vaccines offered cures for diseases for which treatments did not previously exist. In 1938, the *New York Times* observed that the typewriter was "driving out writing with one's own hand," yet Petroski reports the sale of 14 billion pencils in 1990.[16]

Moreover, even those apparently destructive new products also created new markets, because they had features that the products they displaced did not. Automobiles provided much faster, and not just cheaper, transportation than did horse carriages, so people could live in spacious houses located at some distance from their workplaces. This helped create demand for suburban housing that did not previously exist. Similarly, incandescent lamps didn't merely replace candles and kerosene lamps: their intense luminosity helped create a market for football and baseball games played at night.

Innovations in information technology of the late twentieth century have followed the pattern of the electromechanical innovations of earlier decades. According to a U.S. Department of Commerce report (1998), the share of the IT sector (computing and communications) grew from 4.2 percent of U.S. gross domestic product in 1977 to 6.1 percent in 1990 and 8.2 percent in 1998. This is not because computers displaced traditional goods and services. Rather, IT has accounted for a disproportionate share of growth: according to the Department of Commerce, IT industries have been responsible for more than one-quarter of real economic growth, or about three times their share of the economy.

The digital revolution has certainly involved some substitution. For instance, calculators displaced slide rules, microprocessor-based workstations displaced minicomputers, and CDs displaced cassette tapes. But there has also been at least as much nondestructive creation. The personal computer (PC) did not blow away the traditional mainframe computer in a gale of creative destruction. The PC's killer application, the spreadsheet, did not displace any existing mainframe-based applications. Rather, it allowed users, many of whom had not previously used computers extensively, to perform analyses and simulations that they would not otherwise have performed. Similarly, the enormous growth of the home market for PCs did not reduce the demand for mainframe computers.

Over 30 years after the introduction of minicomputers, and more than 20 years after the introduction of microcomputers, the mainframe remained an important category. Because total demand grew from $38 billion to $183 billion, mainframes' *share* of the total computer market dropped considerably, from 42 percent in 1982 to about 9 percent in 1997.[17] But total worldwide revenues of mainframes barely changed—from $16.2 billion in 1982 to $16 billion in 1997. IBM continues to invest in its mainframe business, which, all told, provides a quarter of the company's revenues and nearly half its profit.[18] In February 2008, IBM announced the model Z-10, with a base price of $1 million, which is said to be more energy efficient and take less floor space in crowded corporate computer rooms.[19]

The role of PCs in expanding the pie rather than destroying existing markets apparently represents a common feature of the digital revolution. New communications services—email, newsgroups, and "chat"—provided a critical mass of users for the Internet and online services such as AOL. These services did not, however, abate the demand for traditional phone lines—U.S. cities continue to require new area codes. New products that have displaced old products have often done so *after* they have created a new market. For instance, as I discovered in the course of a consulting study for a now defunct typewriter manufacturer, shipments of word-processing units increased 14-fold between 1977 and 1981. But because word processors increased primary demand by satisfying some hitherto unmet want, the sales for typewriters in the United States remained steady at around a million units a year during this period.

Similarly, one day (after standards and coverage issues have been resolved) cell phones may make landline phones obsolete. But not before consumers have purchased hundreds of millions of units in applications where landline phones had not been used. For now, most U.S. households have both. Mediamark Research, which has been monitoring phone usage in U.S. households since the mid-1980s, reported in 2007 "a glacially slow decline since 2000 in the percentage of households with landlines, and a steep rise in the number of households with cell phones. But overall, according to its 2007 report, only 14 percent of U.S. adults lived in households with a cell phone but no landlines. Twelve percent lived in households with a landline but no cell phone, and 73.7 percent in households with both cell phones and landlines.[20] Similarly, whereas many employers now routinely provide their employees with cell phones, no business or nonprofit of any size that I know of has dispensed with landlines.

In the 25 countries of the European Union in 2006, there were 95 mobile phones for every 100 Europeans, but just 18 percent of households had mobile phones and no landlines. The percentage of mobile-only homes was higher in formerly Communist countries where many households had never had landlines, and lower in West European countries. Even though the share of landlines had decreased, the total number had increased—from 43 lines per hundred people in 1995 to 48 in 2005.[21]

Innovations that created markets for new goods and services gave the lie to predictions that mechanization and mass production would create mass unemployment. Productivity improvements on the farm, which would ultimately allow about 2 percent of the workforce to feed the entire population, reduced agricultural employment in the United States from 11.7 million in 1900 to 5.9 million in 1960. Changes in production technologies also put many highly skilled artisans out of work. But total employment more than doubled—from 29 million in 1900 to 68 million in 1960. The labor released by the farm and workshop was quickly absorbed by factories established to serve new markets. And the assembly-line workers earned more than the farmer or skilled artisan. For instance, by 1900, the average annual manufacturing wage was more than twice the agricultural wage. This gap continued to widen, as real wages in manufacturing increased at 1.7 percent per year through the first seven decades of the twentieth century.

Although wages in the manufacturing sector stagnated after the 1970s, and manufacturing jobs topped out at about 20 million in 1980, overall employment and incomes in the United States continued to rise. The number of gainfully employed Americans in 2000, for instance, was 135 million—a nearly 35 percent increase over the 99 million employed individuals in 1980. Real U.S. GDP per capita during this period rose by 57 percent, and disposable personal incomes by nearly 50 percent. Apparently, the growth of businesses in sectors such as information technology that satisfied new wants more than compensated for the lack of growth in manufacturing. For example, the production of computers, semiconductors, and communications equipment increased 13-fold between 1992 and 2000. Employment in IT services nearly doubled in this period, from just over 2 million to 3.6 million. Wages in this sector were about 85 percent higher than in the economy as a whole. The growth in IT wages had likewise been about 1.6 times faster.

In the "second wave of globalization" discussed in chapter 8, the expansion of markets for new goods and services encouraged—and was facilitated by—imports from low-wage countries. The resources released by imports fostered the growth of industries that satisfied new wants in the United States. Cheap TV sets from the Far East allowed U.S. households the wherewithal to purchase PCs powered by Intel microprocessors and Microsoft software. Similarly, engineering graduates who would have otherwise been employed by U.S. TV manufacturers were available for employment by U.S. IT companies. Conversely, the growth in incomes and employment in the new industries helped U.S. consumers pay for goods produced overseas.

■ Incentives for Nondestructive Creation

Innovators don't undertake nondestructive innovations because of altruistic concern about the instability of a system that relies only on creative destruction; rather, creating and satisfying new wants often provides more attractive returns. The early technical deficiencies of new products like automobiles and personal computers make them unsuitable substitutes for existing tried-and-tested substitutes. Therefore, as Clay Christenson has pointed out,[22] innovative products usually start up serving a function that existing products do not serve.

Even when a new product is technically superior, displacing an existing product is expensive. The innovator has to overcome competition from the businesses that face the threat of substitution, as well as resistance from users who have invested in the old regime. For example, theaters that now use projectors for celluloid film have been unwilling to incur the costs of switching to higher-quality digital projection systems. Theater owners also face the costs of developing new ground-level know-how—for instance, training operators to use new projection equipment and figuring out the optimal environment for their theaters.

As previously mentioned, in many "enterprise-wide" systems and innovations, ground-level know-how has both technical and organizational facets. The cost and difficulty of developing such a combination makes users extremely reluctant to replace their existing systems. According to Bresnahan and Greenstein's research, for example, client/server systems could not easily replace mainframes because mainframe vendors and users had over many decades "improved and refined applications such as corporate accounting systems, bank automatic teller machine networks and inventory-control or reservation systems." It was also "difficult to reinvent organizations around a new computing platform, even a platform with large potential benefits."[23]

On the other side, the "venturesomeness" of some users encourages them to try innovations that solve a problem or satisfy a want that isn't solved or satisfied by existing technologies. If the innovation works, less venturesome users will be more willing to follow if they don't have to scrap their existing equipment and know-how.

The costs of displacing existing technologies can make the funding requirements of "destructive" innovations prohibitive for many entrepreneurs. For large companies, the incentive to favor nondestructive creation is weaker, but not absent. They do have the resources to overcome the unwillingness of consumers to incur switching costs. Where they are the incumbent oligopolists, the issue of competitive retaliation does not arise. But large companies also face pressure from stock markets and employees to increase their revenues. This encourages large companies to develop new sources of revenues rather than substitutes for their existing revenues. For instance, Robert Cringely suggests that IBM executives backed its PC initiative in 1980 because they thought personal computers would not reduce demand for IBM's other products, so "every sales dollar brought in to buy a microcomputer would be a dollar that would not otherwise have come to IBM."[24] Similarly the "rational drug discovery approach" established by Roy Vagelos at Merck stipulated that the company would focus on areas "where there were no therapies or drugs available."[25]

The reader who recalls the discussion in chapter 8 of mobility of the factors of production may now well ask, how does nondestructive creation maintain productive employment in the United States if much of the production of new goods is undertaken in low-wage locations abroad? To address this question, I next examine the relationship between nondestructive creation and the expansion of the nontraded service sector.

■ Nexus of Nondestructive Creation and Service Sector Growth

Except, perhaps, in primitive economies based on barter, services have always been an important feature of productive employment. Society has long used the services of taverns and innkeepers, barbers, moneylenders, lawyers, and physicians. Some of these services have been stand-alone. Others have been derived from the production of tangible goods: things produced in a factory or grown on a farm have to be transported, marketed, and sold, and sometimes also installed and maintained.

The preeminence of service-sector employment in the United States today is well known, but what may come as a surprise to some is its share of the workforce even when the manufacturing sector was at its peak. According to Angus Maddison's data, the service sector's share was *never* lower than that of manufacturing, mining, construction, and utilities. In 1820, both sectors accounted for 15 percent of employment, with agriculture, forestry, and fisheries employing the remaining 70 percent. By 1870, the share of agriculture (and forestry and fisheries) had fallen to 50 percent, and services had risen to second place. By 1913, services held the top spot, with a 42.8 percent share. In 1950, even as the manufacturing sector was in full cry (with about a third of total employment), services had pulled even further ahead, with a 53.5 percent share of employment. In Europe, too, according to Maddison, services became the leading sector, even as the economies were becoming "industrialized."[26] (See table 13.1.)

In 1957, Colin Clark advanced a demand-side explanation for the growth of the share of the service sector in advanced economies: once societies have crossed a threshold level of development, their demand for services grows faster than their demand for products.[27] Baumol's 1967 theory, mentioned in chapter 10, emphasized the supply side: productivity grows more slowly in services than in manufacturing; therefore, even if there is no increase in the "volume" of demand for services, their prices will rise more quickly and thus will account for a larger share of national income.

My analysis suggests the following additional view: the nondestructive development of tangible products (such as air conditioners, automobiles, and aircraft) stimulates demand for new services to transport, advertise, market, sell, install, and maintain the new products. In many cases, the value-added and employment generated through these complementary services generates more economic value and employment than does the design and manufacture of the products themselves. Moreover, even if manufacturing (and to a lesser degree, product design) is progressively undertaken abroad, most of the service activity remains in the United States.

The personal computer industry illustrates the point. From the start, many of its key components were manufactured abroad, sometimes in plants owned by U.S. companies. But, the growth of the industry as a whole has utilized many U.S.-based service resources. For instance, IBM's launch of its PC in 1981, which legitimized the use of microcomputers in large corporations, involved a national advertising campaign (using the likeness of Charlie Chaplin's character from *The Little Tramp*), training of its in-house sales force, and the establishment of an office product dealer network. The success of the PC spawned myriad small value-added resellers and large retail chains such as CompUSA (started in 1984 as Soft Warehouse).

Moreover, the role of services doesn't end when customers take delivery of their personal computers—they have to be installed and maintained. The so-called total cost of ownership surveys for computers have to be taken with a pinch of salt, since they are often "sponsored" by rival hardware and software vendors. But regardless of their sponsorship, all the surveys I have seen suggest that, over a three- to five-year lifespan, the total cost of ownership amounts to several times the upfront cost of the hardware and software. The costs of support staff alone can amount to six times the upfront cost (and half the upfront cost itself is made up of distribution and sales costs). In other words, 80 to 90 percent of the lifetime "value-added" of a computer (which may be manufactured abroad) takes place within the United States.

■ Looking Ahead

The process of nondestructive creation does not unfold at a predictable rate or in a predictable direction. It does not produce jobs at exactly the same rate as increases in efficiency, offshoring, or cyclical downturns cause traditional industries to shed them. Indeed, there are times, most recently after the bursting of the Internet bubble, when the process fails to keep up. Moreover, standard macroeconomic policies cannot speed up the process. Tax cuts and easy money might stimulate "old"-economy demand for automobiles and housing, but they cannot overcome the unwillingness of U.S. consumers to use Short Messaging Services on their cell phones. Nor can powerful private sector patrons predict or ensure success. For instance,

Microsoft bet big and wrong on proprietary online services instead of on the Internet. Similarly, in the early 1980s, venture capitalists and entrepreneurs were much taken by the promise of artificial intelligence. They started so many companies around MIT that a portion of East Cambridge came to be known as Intelligence Alley. To my knowledge, none of these companies survive.

But, although it would be foolhardy to make predictions about what great new markets lurk around the corner, we have no reason to fear that we have exhausted the potential for nondestructive creation. It may be true that, because (as Bresnahan and Gordon put it) we have run out of "stomach space,"[28] new food products must replace old food products. We may also have exhausted our "free" time—cell phones that may not displace landlines do absorb the time that we might otherwise devote to quiet reverie. Nevertheless, the scope for satisfying other kinds of new wants remains ample.

New forms of health care, for instance, are almost certain to expand. Modern medicine found cures for many diseases in the twentieth century and increased life expectancies in the United States from 47 years in 1900 to 77 today. No treatments exist, however, for a great many other diseases and current life expectancies are well below any theoretical limit for the human life span. The aging of the population similarly provides ample opportunities for goods and services that enhance the quality of the lives of older citizens. Among the young (or would- be young), the desire to look and feel good has sustained many new businesses. The number of health clubs in the United States has tripled in the last 20 years, and 13 percent of Americans are now enrolled as members. Cool new ways for altering body parts continue to arise: a doctor in L.A. has apparently pioneered the implantation of tiny platinum jewels shaped like stars into the corners of the whites of the eyes.[29] Innovators keep finding new ways to tickle the senses—for instance, by selling ring tones and face plates for cellular phones. Such consumption might not please all tastes, but it has maintained the growth of the modern shopping basket in the past and, in all likelihood, will continue to do so in the future.

■ Concluding Comments

Prognosticating about which U.S. jobs could migrate to low-wage countries 10 years from now is of questionable value—apart from the publicity and other private benefits it offers the prognosticators. Technology and the up-grading of skills may well allow all X-rays to be read by radiologists abroad, but it is also possible that this offshoring could be preempted by pattern recognition technologies. Moreover, if history is any guide, new diagnostic techniques, body-part replacement procedures, and so on will create completely new demands for medical skills and specialties. Contemplate, for instance, the ever-increasing number of support staff employed by my employer (and presumably Professor Blinder's department at Princeton). Typing pools are long gone—thanks to personal computers and software, faculty do their own typing; voicemail and email have helped eliminate receptionists; and quite likely a number of clerical functions have been automated or outsourced, possibly to an offshore provider. But Columbia Business School has more than forty employees in its Information Technology Group doing jobs that didn't exist when the typing pool did. They support sophisticated audiovisual equipment and manage the local area network, the course platform, and other such technologies—none of which the school had before the 1990s. Who knows—10 years from now, these technologies and the jobs they support could succumb to creative destruction. But it's a good bet that unless the enterprise as a whole falls on hard times, its support staff isn't going to shrink.* As long as the new want-machine hums smoothly, the jobs that innovation takes away (through efficiency improvements and expanded opportunities for offshoring) more than give back. The real question is: what does it take to keep the machinery in good order?

---

* According to Richard Vedder (2004), since the 1970s the number of administrators in U.S. universities has doubled, from about three per student to six.

14

■ Immigrants:

Uppers or Downers?

Immigration—the cross-border flows of people—is a particularly contentious facet of globalization, often stirring up more emotion than the importing of goods and the offshoring of services. As with imports and offshoring, populists and techno-nationalists have different concerns about immigration. Populists decry the immigration of unskilled and often "undocumented" individuals, just as they bemoan imports of "old-economy" goods and the offshoring of low-end services. Techno-nationalists aren't as concerned with low-skill immigration, just as they don't worry about old-economy imports or low-end offshoring. Rather, as mentioned in chapter 7, techno-nationalists believe that the United States is excessively dependent on foreign-born scientists and engineers, just as the country is hooked on Middle Eastern oil. "Imagine NIH [the National Institutes of Health]," writes Richard Freeman for instance, "without foreign-born post-docs and scientists. Imagine the labs at any major university or high tech firm without foreign-born students. Half of the benches would be empty."[1]

Critics also express concern that poorly drafted and enforced immigration laws encourage employers to exploit foreign labor, drive down U.S. wages, and discourage the native-born from pursuing careers in science and engineering. The H-1B program is a common target of criticism. The U.S. Congress has mandated that employers pay individuals hired under the H1-B program the "prevailing wage." But according to critics like Ron Hira, the "prevailing wage legislation has so many loopholes that employers can and do pay below the prevailing market wage, and there is essentially no oversight of the program."[2]

IT companies obviously dispute the claim, and, in fact, they have lobbied for an expanded H1-B program on the grounds that the United States benefits from the contributions of the exceptionally talented and qualified individuals who come on H-1B visas.

Although many believe that the United States should nudge more of its native-born into science and engineering (S&E) professions, the risks of a precipitous departure of immigrant S&E workers (or possibly of an OPEC-style supply squeeze by the countries that supply them) have not been, to my knowledge, rigorously evaluated. Considerable econometric effort has been put into investigating whether immigrants depress local wages, but, for reasons discussed in chapters 5 and 6, I am skeptical of the reliability of the results.*

As with the other topics in this book, my assessment of the risks allegedly posed by an overreliance on immigrant S&E workers relies on a common-law style inquiry. Relying on historical trends, contemporary technological developments, and the inferences drawn in chapter 5, I first examine why the immigrant share of the U.S. S&E workforce has increased. Here I pay special attention to immigrants from India, because they comprise a large proportion of the foreign-born S&E workforce: the Indian share of H1-B visas, for example, is nearly three times Saudi Arabia's share of U.S. oil imports.[3] I then assess the long-term risks posed by relying on foreign-born S&E workers, and how the immigration of such workers affects U.S. wages and employment.

■ Overall Trends

Giovanni Peri[4] observes that the "distribution of skills" (or more accurately, in my view, of levels of education) of immigrants in the United States has

---

* Researchers cannot observe what wages would have been like with more or fewer immigrants—they can only "estimate" the counterfactual using a particular model. But, as I argued at in chapter 6, no one can know the "right" model, so the estimates are reliable only if the model somehow happens to be right. Moreover, a complex economy comprises a multitude of submarkets for labor, segmented (at least in the short term) by factors such as industry, skill, and geography. What confidence, then, can we have in estimates purporting to measure the effects of "immigration as a whole" based on *any* one model?

a V-shape. As shown in table 14.1, overall, immigrants accounted for 12.4 percent of the labor force in 2000. But their share of workers without a high school diploma (26 percent) was more than twice as large as their overall average; it was less than average (8.6 percent) for those with just a high school diploma, and very close to the average for workers with college degrees. The table also shows that the shape of the distribution has not materially changed since 1990, when immigrants accounted for smaller share (9.3 percent) of the overall labor force. Rather, each point of the V rose proportionately from 1990 to 2000—in other words, the United States apparently became more open or attractive to immigrants to the same extent, whether or not they had high school diplomas or college degrees.

If we look just at the S&E workforce, however, the pattern isn't V-shaped. Table 14.1 also contains data compiled by Freeman on the proportion of immigrants in S&E jobs categorized by their level of education.[5] We see that immigrants accounted for a higher proportion of scientists and engineers than they did of the overall labor force in 1990; the percentage grew faster among scientists and engineers than in the overall labor force; and the percentage of immigrants was higher among scientists and engineers with more advanced educations both in 1990 and (to about the same degree) in 2000.*

Census data also shows significant changes in the countries that supply immigrants. As described in the box, the proportion of European immigrants has declined, while the share of Mexican immigrants has increased sharply. But there are considerable differences between the overall pattern of immigration and the pattern for S&E workers. In particular, Indian immigrants account for a much higher proportion of S&E immigrants than they do of the total foreign-born population of the United States.

---

* The same table shows a similar relationship between qualifications and the proportion of immigrants in the medical profession. In 1990, immigrants represented a higher proportion of physicians (20.2 percent) than they did of the labor force as a whole. Immigrants, however, accounted for a lower proportion of registered nurses (8.8 percent) than of the overall labor force. By 2000, immigrants' share of nurses had almost caught up with their share of the overall labor force; however, because their share of physicians had continued to expand, the absolute physician-nurse difference grew from 11.4 percent to 13.7 percent.

The Changing Distribution of Countries of Origin—and How S&E Is Different

The overall trends in immigration to the United States can be summarized as follows. In 1850, the first year in which the census collected data on place of birth, 92 percent of the foreign-born population had emigrated from Europe and another 6.7 percent from Canada. Only 1 percent came from any other area. A national-origin quota system intended to favor immigrants from Canada and northern or western Europe enacted in the 1920s and reaffirmed in the Immigration and Nationality Act of 1952 maintained a high share for these two sources for over a century. In 1960, European immigrants accounted for 75 percent of the U.S. foreign-born population and Canadian immigrants for 9.8 percent.

Significant changes came about with the elimination of national quotas by the Immigration and Nationality Act in 1965, and other legislative changes[6]—along with post–World War II catch-up in Western Europe, which presumably reduced incentives to emigrate. The European share fell from 75 percent in 1960 to 15.3 percent in 2000, and the Canadian share from 9.8 percent to 2.5 percent. In the same period, immigrants from Latin America grew from 9.8 percent of the U.S. foreign-born population to 51 percent and, from Asia, from 9.4 percent to 25.5 percent.

Countries and regions that became leading sources of immigrants to the United States did not necessarily account for a proportionately significant share of immigrants in occupations requiring technical educations. Mexican immigrants, for instance, accounted for more than a quarter of the foreign-born population in the United States in March 2000. This proportion, according to a Census Bureau report, is "the largest recorded share any country has held since the decennial census in 1890, when about 30 percent of the foreign-born population was from Germany." But the distribution of Mexican immigrants includes a relatively high proportion of individuals without college degrees—and a low proportion in S&E jobs.

In contrast, scientists, doctors, and engineers comprise a disproportionate share of Indian immigrants. According to Alarcon's account,[7] the first sizable influx of Indians occurred in 1907, with the arrival of about a thousand agricultural workers who mostly settled on the West Coast. In the following year, pressure from the Asiatic Exclusion League of San Francisco led U.S. immigration officials to start denying admission to Indians. A 1917 law prohibited all immigration until 1946, when Indian immigrants were granted an annual quota of 100. Between 1946 and 1965, all of about 6,000 Indians were admitted, most as professional and technical workers. The number of Indian immigrants grew rapidly after immigration law was amended in 1965, and most continued to be professional and technical workers—comprising 91 percent of those admitted in 1971.

In the mid-1980s, the proportion of Indians immigrating under the so-called family preferences established under the 1965 Act surpassed those entering under "employment" visas. But even immigrants who came under family preference visas apparently found professional employment. Therefore, although Indians accounted for only 3.8 percent of overall immigration in the 1970s and 3.6 percent in the 1980s, they accounted for 19.5 percent of professional or highly skilled immigrants in the 1970s and 13.4 percent in the 1980s. The 1990 census recorded that 87 percent of Indian immigrants had high school educations and 65 percent had college degrees. About 30 percent of the 379,970 Indian immigrants in the labor force were professionals; of these, engineers accounted for 26 percent and physicians accounted for 19.6 percent. The number of well-educated Indian immigrants continued to grow rapidly in the 1990s; for instance, the number of immigrants with college degrees more than doubled from the 1990 census to the 2000 census, rising from 255,916 to 584,948 degree holders. Indian immigrants were the leading recipients of six-year H-1B visas, granted mainly to software engineers and programmers. For instance, Indians received 16 percent of all H-1B visas granted in 1994 (followed by UK citizens, who got 12.9 percent of the visas). In 2003, Indians accounted for 40 percent of H-1B visa holders.

■ The (Comparative) Advantage of "Backwardness"

In my view, the "backwardness" of the economy in India constitutes an important ingredient for the proportion of Indian natives among S&E immigrants in the United States. That backwardness dates back to nearly two centuries of British colonial rule, starting roughly in 1757 and ending with Indian independence in 1947 (see box).

An Era of Darkness[8]

Retro-thusiasts of the British Empire say it bestowed many blessings on India: the historian Niall Ferguson writes that it was "the British who introduced quinine as an anti-malarial prophylactic" and who "carried out public programs of vaccination against smallpox."[9] Ferguson's claim is technically accurate but disingenuous. The only government that *could* have introduced quinine or smallpox vaccination was the British government. Quinine wasn't widely used anywhere before the British secured control of India in 1757, and Edward Jenner first used his smallpox vaccine in 1796. And while the British didn't steal on any large scale (apart from individuals like Lord Clive), they also failed to create the conditions that led to unprecedented rates of economic growth in the West.

Under colonial rule, India more or less missed the Industrial Revolution. While the West adopted mass production techniques, most manufacturing in colonial India remained confined to handicrafts. in the absence of productivity improvements, economic growth rates in colonial India were close to zero. As Ferguson himself notes, between 1757 and 1947, GDP grew nearly *25 times* faster in Britain than in India.[10] This created a huge gap in living standards between Britain and India that had been roughly equal in 1757. In 1900, for instance, the per capita income of Great Britain was about 25 times that in India. Similarly, an extreme laissez-faire ideology (and possibly indifference) discouraged colonial rulers from collecting taxes or providing public goods, such as primary education, to a much greater degree than democratic governments back home in the UK did. For instance, in 1910, the primary-school enrollment rate in India per 10,000 people was almost one-fourth the rate in Mexico, less than one-eleventh the UK rate and one-twelfth the U.S. rate.[11]

By the time of Indian independence in 1947, the country had a comprehensively backward economy. Employment in large-scale factories accounted for less than 2% of the workforce.[12] Employment in processing and manufacturing (including small-scale artisanal production) declined by 15 percent between 1901 and 1951, when the total population had increased by nearly 40 percent. Most Indians had no access to education—in 1947, 88 percent of the population was illiterate. In 1950, the life expectancy of an Indian at birth was 32—less than half that of a newborn in the UK or the United States.*

* According to historian Mike Davis (2001), life expectancy in India actually fell by 20 percent from 1872 to 1928.

> Remarkably, even though it is hard to think of Japan as a more benevolent colonizer, Korea and Taiwan developed more rapidly under Japanese rule than did India under the British. Maddison's data suggests that in the last half-century of British rule in India (which covers roughly the same years as the period of Japanese colonization of Korea and Taiwan), real per capita incomes declined in India while they grew in Korea and Taiwan.[13] And, although it was low by Western standards, the rate of literacy was more than twice as high in Korea at the end of World War II than as it was in India.

Industrialization and economic growth in India did increase after independence. Nevertheless, for many decades, economic growth in India was far slower than in Japan, the European countries that were engaged in postwar reconstruction, and Korea and Taiwan, which were rapidly entering the ranks of the developed world. Perhaps India had not yet accumulated a critical mass of industry, infrastructure, education, and so on to reach what Rostow called the takeoff stage of development. The socialistic, autarkical policies adopted by postindependence governments almost certainly held back growth, (although economic progress was far superior[14] to what it had been under the laissez-faire British colonial regime). It wasn't until the early 1990s that a balance-of-payment crisis forced the government to adopt reforms, after which growth took off. And even after that, the rate of growth of the Indian economy remained below that of China, which had initiated more radical reforms in 1978. Today, India may be "emerging" quite rapidly but it has a very long way to go before it enters even the fringes of the industrialized world. This entrenched backwardness, as we will see next, creates powerful incentives for Indians to seek jobs abroad.

According to classical trade theory, economies tend to specialize in activities in which they have a comparative advantage, whether or not they have an absolute advantage in those activities. This theory suggests that exports from economically backward countries will be from sectors where their backwardness engenders the least *dis*advantage. For instance, economies that don't have or cannot implement advanced technologies will tend to specialize in products where the best practices in advanced economies are relatively rudimentary or easily transferred, such as footwear or apparel. Similarly, a poor transportation infrastructure will encourage the export of goods and services for which transportation inefficiencies are the least burdensome.

Backwardness creates strong incentives to export labor, because erratic supplies of electricity, clogged ports, poorly enforced property rights, corrupt administrations, and so on do not impede emigration to the same degree that they do other kinds of economic activity. Judged by the size of remittances by its overseas workers, India is the world's largest exporter of labor, followed by Mexico, China, and the Philippines.[15] The theory does not predict, however, whether an economy will export skilled or unskilled labor: backwardness can also engender comparative advantages in producing certain kinds of basic technical skills. Although wage differentials create incentives for all kinds of labor to migrate, a variety of factors affect the quantity and composition of labor that relocates. Politics, for instance, strongly influences the demand for different kinds of immigrant labor. Similarly, institutions, history, and natural endowments affect the kind of labor that is available to emigrate.

During the colonial era, supply and demand favored the large-scale migration of low-skilled workers from India to other British colonies—often, until its abolition in 1911, as indentured labor.[16] Indians had a large share of the clerical positions in many British colonies, and large communities of merchants formed in Malaya, East Africa, and South Africa.[17] There was no demand-side resistance to low-skilled migrants from India, because British colonialists wanted them in and the natives had no say.

There was virtually no outflow of professionals from India, however, because of the limited supply—the number of doctors and engineers available to migrate was negligible. In 1917, for instance, the entire country had four engineering colleges that had a total enrollment (*not* matriculates or graduates) of 1,319 students. In 1931, the number of colleges had grown to seven and enrollment to 2,171. No more colleges were added in the 1930s, but enrollment grew to 2,509. Similarly, there were eight medical colleges in 1917, with 2,511 students enrolled: 11 medical colleges in 1931, with 4,201 students enrolled; and 12 colleges in 1940, with 5,640 students.[18]

After Indian independence, although the supply of low-skilled workers remained ample, changes in overseas demand limited their outflow. Many of the traditional destinations for manual and agricultural workers, merchants, clerks, and so on had themselves become independent countries—and more prone to expel Indian immigrants than welcome them. The UK, Canada, and Australia did provide opportunities for immigrants in the manufacturing, retail, and low-end service sectors. But the relatively small size of the UK, Canadian, and Australian economies and populations—and the many impoverished former colonies that also had ample supplies of would-be migrants—limited the outflow from India.[19] The other large Western economies relied on more proximate and traditional sources of immigrants—Mexico for the United States, Turkey for Germany and their former African colonies for France and Italy. The boom in the Middle East after the oil shock in 1973 provided the only significant opportunity for Indians with low to intermediate skills to migrate.[20] As we will see next, however, the migration of engineers and doctors expanded considerably because of the growth of supply in India and of demand abroad—principally in the United States.

■ The Supply Side

The Indian government initiated the expansion of supply through a series of Five-Year Plans (starting in 1950) to invest in sectors considered crucial for the country's development. Education was an obvious target, and planners allocated a disproportionately high share of resources to engineering and medical schools.* By 1967, the number of engineering colleges had increased to 105 (from seven in 1940) and the number of medical colleges to 98 (from 12 in 1940).

In the next 12 years, growth of new colleges decreased a little, with the opening of one engineering and two medical colleges a year. This slower growth was apparently the result of the government's deteriorating financial situation and the high cost of equipping and operating engineering and medical schools, for which tuition fees were set well below operating costs.† In order to continue the expansion of engineering and medical education, the government tacitly encouraged the opening of private so-called capitation

---

* According to the prevailing ideology, India could not rely on imported goods or know-how and needed to quickly train a large cadre of engineers and scientists; universal primary education and literacy was regarded as a worthwhile goal, but one that could wait. Political calculations likely reinforced the economic beliefs. Local politicians thought they could get more credit for a new medical or engineering school than for the expansion of primary schooling. Although, in principle, more constituents might benefit from the increase in primary education, progress would be halting and slow, whereas opening a new medical or engineering school was relatively easy to establish, at least from an administrative point of view.

† For instance, according to Chandrakant (1986), the elite Indian Institute of Technology charged annual tuition of Rs. 250 while incurring annual variable expenses of Rs. 50,000 per student in 1986.

colleges. Whereas public colleges admitted students on the basis of their performance in a qualifying examination (in conjunction with quotas for "backward" castes) and charged low tuition, private colleges admitted students who had performed poorly in their qualifying exams, if they paid a "capitation" fee and, usually, an under-the-table "donation."

Although the colleges were organized as nonprofit societies, their promoters earned attractive financial returns. Fees in public colleges were so far below the market-clearing level that applicants were willing to pay substantial capitation fees and donations. Donations—payable in cash—provided tax-free incomes to promoters. Capitation and tuition fees covered the modest costs of barebones operations.[21] Well-connected promoters could also receive subsidized land from the government, because the enterprise ostensibly had a public purpose.

Low risk and high returns attracted a lot of new entry. According to informed observers, in some states, every rural district, no matter how backward, now has at least one engineering college promoted by a coalition of local politicians and businessmen. In 1960, private colleges accounted for just 15 percent of the enrollment in engineering colleges and 6.8 percent in medical colleges; in 2003, they accounted for 86.4 percent of engineering enrollment and 40.9 percent of medical enrollment.[22]

The demand for engineers and doctors in India did not, however, expand in line with the supply. Planners had assumed that rapid economic growth would both result from and require a large cadre of engineers and scientists. But until the 1990s, growth did not live up to planners' expectations—in a backward economy, it is easier to start an engineering college than to remedy the conditions that impair growth and limit employment opportunities for engineers. In fact, unemployment consistently turned out to be more common among engineers than among uneducated workers. Similarly, although there was no shortage of patients, low economic growth limited the incomes doctors could earn outside large cities. Here, too, there was unemployment or underemployment. Remarkably, the paucity of attractive employment opportunities was common knowledge *before* the great expansion of capacity in the private sector occurred. Nonetheless, parents were willing to pay up for places in medical colleges that had deservedly poor reputations.

What happened on the demand side in the United States that expanded immigration opportunities for Indian—and other foreign-born—engineers, scientists, and doctors is more complex. As we will see next, this part of the story involves both the provisions and enforcement of immigration laws as well as technological and other factors affecting the "actual" demand for labor.

■ Rules of the Game (or Gaming the Rules?)

Until about the mid-1960s, U.S. immigration laws were apparently designed to exclude immigrants of certain ethnicity or national origin. The Statue of Liberty welcomed poor, homeless, tempest-tossed, wretched refuse—as long as it had embarked from a European shore. Now discrimination based on race and national origin has largely disappeared and has been replaced by efforts to select immigrants based on their economic impact. In particular, laws favor skilled immigrants—individuals who arrive with a lot of human capital. More importantly, the criteria and procedures screen out immigrants who are likely to displace native-born workers. In order to secure a permanent employment visa, immigrants usually have to demonstrate that they are performing a function that an American is unavailable to perform.[23]

Curiously, even free-traders and pro-immigration groups go along with the idea that economically desirable immigrants complement, rather than compete with, native-born workers. In the case of goods and services, free-traders are willing to make a case for inflows that compete with domestic supply. Imports of garments and call-center services that may lead to job losses in the United States are commonly justified by the benefits they provide to consumers and the overall desirability of free trade. But the argument that the import of cheap labor benefits U.S. consumers is almost never made. Rather, advocates of liberal immigration policies cite the benefits of the inflow of complementary skills that don't depress local wages or cause job losses.

Labor unions (and other groups who oppose immigration on economic grounds) claim that whatever the intent of the rules might be, loopholes and poor enforcement do, in fact, enable employers to import labor that competes with the domestic workforce. There is an element of truth to the claim that immigration rules aren't strictly enforced. Just as no two individuals are exactly alike in their training and abilities, individuals who are obviously different can often perform each others' functions. In an emergency, a flight attendant may take over the controls of an airplane, and an explorer may perform a surgery. In less dire circumstances, substitutability becomes a matter of cost and effectiveness, whose acceptable limits cannot be easily specified or magnitudes measured. Short of a blanket exclusion of immigrants, it is hard to imagine a set of rules that would entirely preclude substitution. Inevitably, rules that regulate, rather than prohibit, immigration are open to subjective interpretation, and it is unlikely that many employment visas (including the one I received) would be granted under the strictest reading of U.S. immigration laws.

But does this explain the historical trend? Could the inflow of physicians, engineers, and scientists really have increased since 1990 because immigrants or their employers have become more adept or willing to circumvent the rules? Although the rules don't prevent all displacement, they certainly discourage the employment of immigrants. Employers have to go through a costly and time-consuming exercise of demonstrating their inability to hire local labor in order to secure an employment visa (such as an H1-B) for a foreigner. According to Anderson: "To hire a foreign national on an H-1B visa, a U.S. employer must incur the following costs: $1,500 to $2,500 in legal fees; $1,000 training/scholarship fee; $1,000 'premium processing' fee (not required but often used to overcome long processing times); and $125 or more in additional incidental costs (Federal Express, etc.). These combined costs total between $2,600 and $4,600. That does not include additional in-house human-resources costs associated with the extra work involved in the employment of foreign nationals. . . . Sponsoring a foreign national for permanent residence, which many large technology companies, in particular, will do, often costs $10,000 or more."[24] Moreover, the laws make it illegal to pay H1-B workers less than the prevailing wage. The combination of the costs of securing a visa, the legal risks, and the difficulty of administering a dual wage scale for immigrant and native-born workers make it improbable that employers of trained technical professionals would routinely hire immigrants merely to secure labor at a low wage.

An alternative explanation is that the spirit of the rules favoring complementary immigration is, in fact, being observed: most employers sponsor individuals for employment visas mainly because they cannot readily find workers in the local labor market who are willing and able to do the same job. Under this explanation, legal stratagems are used mainly because strict interpretations of the laws would treat immigrants and locals, whose skills and abilities were different, as close substitutes. This explanation is consistent with what we were told by our interviewees and my personal experience, but it does raise the question: why aren't native-born workers available for the kinds of jobs that immigrants from India and elsewhere have arrived in such large numbers to fill?

In the medical field, the answer seems straightforward and the facts consistent with complementary inflows of labor. As Wall writes, the "annual number of medical school graduates [in the United States] has remained almost constant since 1980, despite a population increase of 50 million. Over that same period, only one new medical school has opened its doors." Foreign medical school graduates helped satisfy the medical needs created by population growth. Two other facts are noteworthy here. First, 60 percent of immigrant doctors are from developing countries like India. These countries have a comparative *and* absolute cost advantage in starting medical schools vis-à-vis the United States. The quality of the education provided by these schools may not be up to U.S. standards, but this deficiency can be corrected by requiring immigrant doctors to take a tough qualifying exam. Second, as Wall points out, immigrants are generally hired by hospitals located in places that many U.S.-trained physicians do not consider desirable, such as in small towns or inner cities.[25] Thus, immigrants complement, rather than compete with, local physicians.

The situation with engineers (and scientists) is more complicated—as we will see next, allegations of visa abuse don't take into account the importance of matching rapidly the supply and demand for specific skills in a specific place (which was discussed in chapter 5).

The capacity for providing basic scientific and engineering skills is certainly more elastic than it is for training doctors. Engineering schools face less severe accreditation hurdles than medical schools—there is no requirement for attachment to a "teaching hospital," for instance. The costs of expanding capacity, through additional seats or even new departments and schools, is therefore smaller, and supply can more easily respond to changes in demand. In fact, according to Freeman, the job market for engineers in the United States has "shown cyclic oscillations of the cobweb variety. . . . Tight labor markets generate large increases in supply that depress the labor market approximately 4 to 5 years later."

Freeman also asserts that "every few years or so, the scientific establishment and/or the top executives from major high technology firms proclaim that the U.S. has a shortage of [scientific and engineering] workers," whereas in fact, "labor market measures show no evidence of shortages." Freeman suggests that the "continual claims of a shortage" may be "disingenuous." Forecasts of shortages are used to increase labor supply from overseas, so that U.S. firms can "hire scientists and engineers at lower wages."

Freeman's distinction between "shortages" (which he claims don't exist) and "tight labor markets" (which he says periodically stimulate large increases in enrollments in engineering schools) does not seem particularly sharp. Moreover, suggestions that employers concoct claims of shortages to drive down wages ignore how specialization and timing affect the demand for high-tech labor. Demand for different kinds of skill and experience within the same broad category (e.g. electrical engineer) can be sharply different, and a task that provides great value if completed today may have no utility tomorrow. These two factors (which Freeman does not mention) have played a significant role in encouraging employers to incur the costs of hiring immigrant engineers.

The massive effort mounted against millennial ("Y2K") software bugs in the late 1990s provides an important case in point. Recall that as the year 2000 approached, there was widespread concern about whether systems that had been written in the 1970s and 1980s would fail because the software had not anticipated the four-digit dates that would become necessary after 1999. Many of these programs had been written in COBOL, a programming language that had fallen into disuse. In other words, Y2K bug-control required individuals who could work in a nearly obsolete language *and* were available before December 31, 1999. Moreover, at the same time, the Internet bubble was creating another largely unexpected surge in the demand for programmers. Under these circumstances, few programmers in the United States had much interest in retooling themselves for the transient and tedious task of repairing old programs. India happened to have a stock of COBOL programmers and individuals who were willing to work on Y2K bugs, so the country became an important source of labor for them.*

■ Technological Developments

Although Y2K was a singular episode, trends that enhance the value of the timely availability of specialized skills and thus help pull in imported labor

---

* Indian outsourcing companies have continued to play this role. Infosys CEO Kris Gopalakrishnan (2008) writes that "a considerable part of our business comes from maintaining our clients' legacy systems. Often employees say to me, 'Kris this is boring. The software was written 25 years ago. All I do is patch it.' "

have been in place in the IT sector for many years. Changes in how software is developed have increased the importance of specialization. In the early years of the computer industry, programmers developed applications from scratch with machine language (which we can think of as comprising elemental ones and zeros) or using one of a few higher-level languages such as COBOL and FORTRAN. Now programmers start with a variety of specialized building blocks. These include languages like HTML and Java, tools like Visual Basic for creating user-interfaces, and platforms like Oracle databases and Excel spreadsheets.

As the Industrial Revolution did with tools and dies, the IT revolution has both harnessed and promoted the proliferation of building blocks and what Baldwin and Clark call a "modular" process of innovation.[26] Building blocks reduce the costs and thus increase the demand for software, because programmers don't have to develop each product from scratch. Building blocks also reduce the skills and innate abilities required—programmers don't have to be highly skilled master craftsmen to develop applications— thus increasing the supply of labor. Conversely, a huge surge in demand for software has stimulated the development of more building blocks. Rapid improvements in the price performance of hardware have also increased customers' tolerance for "bloated" building-block based applications and reduced the value of lean applications that used to be built from scratch by highly skilled and ingenious programmers. This has further promoted the use of the building-block approach.

Although building blocks may have reduced the role of master craftsmen, they have also diminished the interchangeability of journeymen program- mers. Many building blocks, like the software applications they are used to develop, are specialized,* and the tacit and codified knowledge used to de- velop applications with one building block may not be helpful for applica- tions based on another building block. In fact, it may be an impediment if the habits developed for work with one building block have to be unlearned for the other. Therefore, a programmer who has learned to develop applica- tions based on Access databases may not be ready to develop applications based on Oracle databases. The problems of substitution introduce imbal- ances in the labor market, because a surplus of Access programmers cannot

---

* For instance, Access databases provide a starting point for applications used by small organiza- tions, whereas Oracle and SAP provide platforms for applications used in large enterprises.

ameliorate shortages (or, depending on semantic tastes, "tight labor markets") in Oracle programmers.

Uncertainties in the popularity of building blocks exacerbate imbalances in the market for programmers. Java, which was commonly used in web browsers, was then almost completely superseded by Marcromedia Flash and Shockwave, but retained its popularity in applications for web servers. These uncertainties make it difficult to anticipate changes in supply and demand for specialized skills. Total demand for IT labor (aggregated across subspecialties) is also unpredictable. Although IT has increased its share of U.S. GDP in the last several decades, the growth has not been monotonic, and the apparent failure of suppliers in the product and labor markets to anticipate changes in demand has led to booms and busts. Booms tend to soak up labor in all specialties—one of the distinctive features of the IT industry is that many building blocks that fall out of favor live on in so-called legacy systems. Budgets for ongoing maintenance and upgrades of legacy systems also tend to follow the overall IT cycle. A generally high level of demand in boom times obviously limits the number of individuals who want to retrain themselves for a hot specialty.

More intense competition in product markets has made employers increasingly sensitive to the timely availability of labor. The IT industry has evolved from a vertically integrated, quasi-monopolistic structure to one marked by competition between many specialized firms.[27] According to the new rules of the game, speed to market—and not just costs, reliability, or performance of products—has become an important feature of competition. Speed leads employers to place a high premium on the immediate availability of the labor they need to develop new products; they prefer to pay the immigration-related costs of hiring migrants with the right skills rather than wait until local workers with the wrong skills can be retrained.

A similar pattern can be seen in industries like financial services and airlines that have traditionally been large purchasers of IT systems. Here, too, more competition (due to factors such as deregulation) and pressure from shareholders to raise profitability have created incentives to quicken the deployment of new systems. As previously discussed, the staff employed by users of IT is larger than the staff employed by vendors, so their sense of urgency represents an important source of imbalance in the labor market.

■ Evidence of Complementary Immigration

The hypothesis that employers seek immigrants to ameliorate skill- and time-specific shortages is supported by several pieces of evidence that, in isolation, may not seem compelling. First, we see that IT accounts for a disproportionately large share of labor inflows compared to occupations less prone to unexpected spikes in demand. Most immigrants with professional qualifications, including those who first enter the country as students, start their employment in the United States on an H-1B visa. For at least the last decade, half or more of H-1B visas have been granted for IT professionals. For the fiscal year 2000, the Immigration and Naturalization Service reported that 58.1 percent of the H1-B petitions it approved were for computer-related professions. Mechanical engineering occupations accounted for just 1.6 percent of approved petitions, and all other occupations in engineering, architecture, and surveying accounted for 10.7 percent.[28] In contrast, according to the National Science Foundation's database, occupations in computer hardware and software accounted for just 5 percent of total engineering employment in 1999, whereas mechanical engineering occupations accounted for 8 percent of engineering employment in the United States.[29] If immigrants were used principally as substitutes for native-born workers, we would expect to see occupations with stagnant or declining demand for labor to account for at least a pro-rata—or higher—share of H-1B visa approvals.

Second, the rate of IT-related immigration under the H1-B visa program does ebb and flow with the overall cycle. Through the first half of the 1990s, when the law placed an annual cap of 65,000, fewer than 60,000 actually obtained these visas each year, and it wasn't until shortly before the end of 1997 that the cap was actually reached. In the following year, writes Anderson, "The 'hot' high-tech economy made the 65,000 cap prove woefully inadequate, with the limit on hiring new individuals on H-1B visas reached by spring 1998." Lobbying by industry groups led Congress to legislate progressive increases in the cap: to 115,000 for 1999 and 2000, and ultimately to 195,000 for the years 2001, 2002, and 2003. In the event, the last increase coincided with an overall economic recession and a particularly sharp downturn in the IT sector. The actual number of visas issued during the downturn was well below the 195,000 cap, with 164,000 issued in 2001, and 79,100 in 2002. Then, as demand for IT labor recovered after 2004, applications for H-1B visas far exceeded the annual cap.[30]

It is also noteworthy that imports of manufactured goods from China and "outsourced" services from India *increased* during the recession. Apparently, U.S. trade laws allow more imports of goods and services in periods when buyers are more likely to demand low prices. The prevailing wage requirements of immigration laws, in contrast, do seem to deter employers from importing low-cost labor when they are particularly anxious to control their wage bills.[31]

A third piece of circumstantial evidence pertains to the wage differentials between native-born and immigrant workers. Peri has tried to estimate wage differentials after controlling for observable characteristics of individuals such as age, sex, race, and marital status. Peri's estimates cover four groups of workers—college graduates, holders of graduate degrees, graduate degree holders who are below 45, and holders of graduate degrees in the sciences, management, and engineering—from Europe, Canada, India, and China. In 15 of the 16 cases, Peri estimates that immigrants receive higher wages than native-born workers—the sole exception being graduate-degree holders in engineering, science, and management from China. For immigrants from India, Peri estimates an annual wage premium over native-born workers of 7.4 percent for college graduates, and for all three groups of workers. For workers with graduate degrees, the premiums exceeded 10 percent.* A National Science Foundation study reports similar results: after controlling for certain factors such as age, foreign-born science and engineering workers with bachelor's degrees earn a 6.7 percent wage premium, and those with PhDs earn a 7.8 percent premium.[32]

The absence of discounts undermines (although doesn't refute) the argument that immigrants provide a low-cost substitute for native-born workers. But why should immigrant wages be higher? Peri claims that differences in wages that cannot be explained by the "observable" factors of age, sex, race, and marital status reflect differences in "quality." Why, then, should immigrants from India and China—countries where, Peri concedes, the quality of education is not exemplary—have higher "quality" than the

---

* My use of Peri's estimates should not suggest I have a double standard vis-à-vis regressions. Rather, it fits what I see as the appropriate use of such analysis because of the following: (1) it is one of several pieces of evidence (and the results aren't too freaky to be true); (2) I emphasize the "signs" rather than the magnitudes of the estimates (although if the magnitudes were tiny, Peri would probably not have published his results); (3) the "simple" or "uncorrected" premia (as reported to me in personal correspondence with Peri) are not materially different from the regression estimates.

native-born? Peri argues that immigrants represent the cream of the output of their nation's education systems and are therefore of higher quality than the typical native-born U.S. worker, who by definition must be drawn from the middle of the national distribution.

An alternative explanation for these wage differentials is that apart from a small number of exceptional immigrants, who may indeed be of higher quality than the average native-born worker, the general quality of Indian education is so much lower that most immigrants are, at best, of the same quality as their U.S.-trained counterparts.* Whatever IT industry representatives may say in arguing for easier immigrations rules, the average H1-B applicant is just that—an average foot soldier. But ever changing technologies divide markets into many segments that have different supply-and-demand characteristics, with different degrees of unexpected tightness and slack. In segments with flat or declining demand, immigration rules preclude large-scale labor imports (overriding the comparative and absolute advantages of backward economies). Wages also tend to be relatively low. Conversely, immigration rates and wages are both higher in the subsegments prone to episodic shortages.

■ Assessing the Risks and Impact

Invoking the specter of a dangerous dependence on foreigners has been an age-old way of promoting a favored cause. In some cases, the arguments are plausible. Its high dependence on imported oil does make the U.S. economy vulnerable to disruptions in supplies from countries governed by unstable or hostile regimes and to the rapid growth in competing demand from China and India. More commonly, however, arguments exaggerate the risks. Notwithstanding the claims of domestic sugarcane growers, there would be very little risk to the U.S. economy if it imported more of the sugar it consumes: farmers in many countries all over the world can grow sugarcane. And unlike oil producers, sugarcane growers can rapidly increase supply by devoting more acreage to the crop. In fact, relying mainly

---

* Peri (2005) reports that "a stunning 26% (one out of four) of the Nobel laureates in the sciences that worked in the U.S. (in the decade 1990–2000) were foreign born." Interestingly, of these foreign-born laureates, none was a native of India. All but three (a Chinese, a Mexican, and an Egyptian) were natives of Europe or some other advanced (OECD) country.

on sugarcane grown in Florida increases the risk of supply disruptions caused by natural calamities or diseases.

The risks of importing S&E workers are more like those of importing sugar, than of oil. The proliferation of engineering and medical colleges in India shows how easy it is to add capacity. The country has no secret sauce for training engineers and doctors, or even a generally well-functioning educational system: along with lower per capita incomes, India has lower rates of literacy and lower enrollment ratios at the primary, secondary, and tertiary level of education than Mexico. Rather, its growth of engineering and medical schools has been driven by a combination of political calculation, rent-seeking, and the widespread belief that a technical education is a path to economic advancement.

Moreover, India is only one of many countries that have, sensibly or not, rapidly increased their capacity to train S&E workers. According to a National Science Foundation report published in 2006:

> [T]he education of young people in NS&E [natural sciences and engineering] has become increasingly important for many governments. Results vary widely for first university degrees in the NS&E from about 16 per 100 24-year-olds in Taiwan to 12–13 in Australia and South Korea and 10 in the United Kingdom. The United States ranks 32nd out of 90 countries for which such data are available, at just under 6 per 100. China and India have low ratios (1.6 and 1.0, respectively), reflecting low overall rates of access to higher education in those countries. . . . However, this trend appears to be changing: S&E-degree production in China doubled, and engineering degrees tripled over the past two decades.

As a result of rapid expansion abroad (see figure 14.1), according to the report, "in 2002, engineering degrees awarded in Asia were more than four times the amount of those awarded in North America, and the number of natural science degrees was nearly double. Europe graduated three times as many engineers as North America in 2002."

It so happens that a number of historical circumstances, such as IBM's exit from India in 1978 (which I won't discuss here), created a good pipeline for engineers, particularly in the software industry, to migrate from India to the United States. But if that pipeline somehow gets blocked, the data we have reviewed suggests that there are ample alternative sources of supply.

Degrees (thousands)

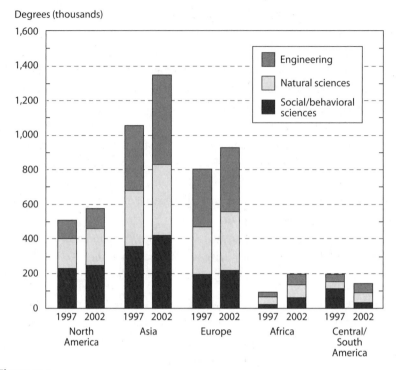

Figure 14.1.

Of course, the supply would not help satisfy the demand for labor in the United States if the S&E workers were unwilling to migrate to the United States or if the ones who were here got up and left. But why would they? Some individuals will work for lower wages in the country where they were born in order to live close to relatives or because they find the society and culture of their homeland more congenial. And indeed, the media has recently published many stories of Chinese and Indian immigrants who have gone back home for these reasons. If the Chinese and Indian economies continue to boom, we should expect the number of returnees to increase.

However, the economic opportunities in the United States remain a powerful draw for a multitude of immigrants. Queues outside U.S. consulates in many parts of the world remain long. Since 2005, annual quotas for H-1B visas have been exhausted on the first day of their availability. The number of skilled workers waiting for permanent resident visas is also many times larger than legislated annual quotas.[33] According to the 2006 NSF report, "stay rates" of overseas students getting S&E doctorates in the United States have not declined—and may well have increased. According to the report, about 61 percent of such students who received their doctorates in 1998 remained in the United States.* Moreover, the 2003 stay rate was higher than the 56 percent five-year stay rate found in 2001—in spite of a decline in the stay rate of Chinese students (from 96 percent to 90 percent).

Even if faster economic growth in China and India narrows wage differentials with the United States, there is a very long way to go before the gap shrinks sufficiently to erode incentives to migrate. Research shows that India was not the largest supplier of college-educated immigrants living in OECD countries in 2000. Rather, it was the UK (with 1.4 million emigrants) that had the largest college-educated diaspora.[34] UK per capita incomes are only 20 percent below U.S. incomes, whereas Indian incomes are less than one-tenth of U.S. incomes, and incomes in China are less than one-fifth of U.S. incomes.

The evidence we reviewed also suggests that, on the whole, employers of S&E workers do adhere to the spirit of U.S. immigration laws if not to the precise letter, in that they generally apply for a work visa for an immigrant only if they can't easily hire a U.S. citizen or permanent resident. But this does not preclude the possibility that immigrants who initially complement could eventually compete with the domestic workforce. And (as Freeman seems to suggest) the long-run wages that immigrants are willing to work for reduce the attractiveness of jobs in engineering and science vis-à-vis other opportunities open to natives of the United States. By implication, immigration discourages the native-born from enrolling in U.S. engineering schools.

The alternative possibility is that even in the long run, by continuing to play a complementary role, immigrants increase employment opportunities and wages for all S&E workers. This may seem far-fetched: shouldn't an increase in supply always reduce wages? But consider this simple example: 30 years ago, I played on a men's field hockey team that a Dutch student organized at Harvard. Most players were, like me, "international students," but if it hadn't been for us, and more importantly, the Dutchman, there would have been no men's field hockey team for any U.S.-born students on which to play. In fact, employment opportunities and wages for the native-born can increase

---

* Stay rates were higher than average in computer and electrical engineering (70 percent) compared to a well-below-average rate of 36 percent in economics.

even if there is some displacement by immigrants. Baseball players from the Caribbean and Central America have taken spots on baseball teams that might otherwise have gone to U.S.-born players. Nonetheless, the stellar quality of some of the immigrant players may well have expanded the total employment and wages of the native-born by encouraging the formation of additional teams and the payment of higher salaries.

Only an omniscient being could tell whether immigrants have actually increased or decreased the wages and employment opportunities for U.S. born S&E workers. What we can observe is that as the number and proportion of immigrants has increased, so have S&E jobs, incomes, and college enrollments. According to the 2006 NSF report, between the 1990 and 2000 censuses, employment in S&E occupations expanded at an average annual rate of 3.6 percent—more than triple the rate of growth of other occupations. Similarly, between 1993 and 2003, "Median real salary for recent S&E bachelor's-degree recipients increased more than that of recipients of non-S&E bachelor's degrees in all broad S&E fields." For example, median real salaries increased by 34.1 percent in engineering and 28 percent in computer and mathematical sciences, compared to just 7.7 percent in non-S&E fields. Unemployment rates in S&E occupations have also been "lower and less volatile" than the rates for all U.S. workers.[35]

The growing proportion of immigrant S&E workers obviously means that S&E college enrollments in the United States have grown more slowly than U.S. S&E jobs. But they have increased, not decreased—and in hot subfields, the growth has been explosive. According to data compiled by the NSF, bachelor's degrees granted by U.S. universities increased by 23 percent from 1991 to 2002, in all S&E fields: computer science and math degrees grew by more than 50 percent and, in the physical and biological sciences, degrees grew by 40.5 percent. The growth of U.S. S&E bachelor's degrees (more than 90 percent of which are awarded to U.S. citizens or permanent residents) was certainly slower than the growth of Asia's. But it is noteworthy that U.S. S&E degrees grew at a 48 percent faster rate (between 2002 and 1991) than did non-S&E bachelor's degrees granted in the United States.

■ Concluding Comments

We examined two (slightly contradictory) concerns about the increasing share of immigrants in the U.S. S&E workforce. First, is the United States dangerously addicted to imported S&E labor? And second, do immigrants reduce employment opportunities and wages in S&E fields for native-born workers?

On the dangerous addiction issue, I argued that if all of *Dilbert*'s mythical Asoks—the immigrants toiling away in their cubicles or lab benches— were really to disappear, this would indeed cause serious harm. But in the absence of a thoroughly perverse immigration policy or outbreak of xenophobia, this is unlikely. The overseas supply of would-be immigrants attracted by high U.S. wages is large, and continues to grow. The quality of workers can be questionable, but technological advances have made it acceptable. India and China account for large shares, but they are no Saudi Arabias capable of sustaining an OPEC-like cartel. Freeman's suggestion that the United States has "an adequate supply of scientists and engineers only because of the sizeable influx" of immigrants may well be true, but why is this any more alarming than its more widespread dependence on morning jolts of imported coffee?

On the issue of the impact of immigrants on wages and employment opportunities for the native born, I argued that most employers do, in fact, abide by the spirit of the immigration laws. Immigrants therefore tend to secure their U.S. working papers in positions that cannot be easily filled by domestic workers. Subsequently, immigrants may compete with the U.S.-born for S&E jobs, but they could also continue to play a complementary role.

The relatively high growth rate of S&E employment and wages favors the latter hypothesis, but it is not conclusive. It is impossible to divine how many more U.S.-born individuals might have been attracted to S&E jobs if those jobs had not been filled by immigrants. Let us suppose, for the sake of argument, that they would have been much more numerous. But would this have been a good thing for the U.S. economy as a whole? And should immigration laws (or other public policies) be used to increase the share of the native-born in S&E occupations? This is a question we will examine in chapter 16.

15

■ The Elusive Underpinnings

Let us return to the puzzle raised at the end of chapter 7 about why the United States has not fallen behind in economic growth. According to convergence theories, poorer countries naturally grow faster than richer countries. Even the mild version of the techno-nationalist argument suggests that any catch-up in their research capabilities by poorer countries will boost their naturally higher rates of growth. The tougher version takes this one step further, predicting that if the research gap is reduced, richer countries will suffer an absolute decline in living standards. But the alleged erosion of its lead in science and cutting-edge technologies has not kept the United States from maintaining (or even increasing) its lead in per capita income. What accounts for the discrepancy between the predicted and actual outcome?

The analysis in previous chapters suggests the following explanation: average per capita incomes depend on the *average* productivity of the workforce, rather than, say, the performance of a few star scientists or technologists. An abundance of IT-based innovations optimized for the United States—and, crucially, the ability and willingness of users to effectively deploy these innovations—has sustained exceptionally high growth in the productivity of the U.S. service sector, and thus of U.S. per capita incomes.*

---

* Parente and Prescott (1994) analyze a similar model. In it, all countries draw their technologies from a common pool that keeps getting bigger and better; however, the investments that

Therefore, the growth of high-level research abroad (which may have reduced the U.S. share of scientific articles, patents, and so on) has benefited the U.S. economy by providing more raw material for innovative combinations. Even the offshoring of mundane tasks and the immigration of journeyman programmers have helped, by increasing the resources available to deploy these innovations at home.

This explanation is more consistent with modern experience than the techno-nationalist version in an important respect: it is not zero-sum—the success of the United States in using technological innovations to increase productivity does not harm other countries. In fact, even if innovation hasn't raised all boats the same distance—and many countries in the South have been left far behind—it has elevated many boats to a significant extent. Taking the long view, we see that differences within the "northern" OECD countries in productivity and incomes are small compared to the gap between where these countries were in the nineteenth century and where they are today. In contrast to the huge advances the U.S. economy has made over the last century, the extent of its outperformance of other economies within the OECD in the last decade is but a trifle.

The explanation raises further questions, however, about the causes of differences across countries and eras. Why, for instance, is the level of IT deployment in the United States higher than in most countries in Europe, when its overall rate of conventional investment and capital formation is lower? More importantly, putting aside differences in individual countries, why has the North, as a whole, significantly improved its capacity to nurture and harness technological innovations?

These questions take us back to Adam Smith's 1776 classic, *An Inquiry into the Nature and Causes of the Wealth of Nations*. Several scholars have updated the *Inquiry* to encompass the now prominent role of technological progress. To name just a few of my favorites, Nathan Rosenberg and L. E. Bridzell's *How the West Grew Rich* (1986), Joel Mokyr's *The Lever of Riches* (1990), and several books by Alfred Chandler provide insightful historical

---

firms have to make to take advantage of the ever-improving pool depend on the "barriers to technology adoption" in their countries. According to Parente and Prescott's empirical findings, the differences in the magnitude of these barriers do not have to be "implausibly large" to account for the "huge observed income disparity" between rich and poor countries. Their paper does not, however, focus on the nature of the barriers to technology adoption (although they do mention "regulatory and legal constraints, bribes that must be paid, violence or threats of violence, outright sabotage, and worker strikes" as examples).

perspectives on the great technological advances that have been made after 1776. Baumol, Litan, and Schramm's, *Good Capitalism, Bad Capitalism, and the Economics of Growth and Prosperity* contains a contemporary analysis.

I will not attempt to summarize these books—that would cover a volume in itself. Nor can I analyze every important feature of the modern economy. Rather, in this chapter I provide a perspective based on the fieldwork described in book 1, the higher-level arguments of the subsequent chapters, and ideas drawn from the books I just mentioned. I will not have much to say, for instance, about the financial system. Conversely, and for obvious reasons, I place special emphasis on factors that promote the venturesome use of innovations.[1] I also highlight the distinctive features of the modern U.S. system, both because it seems to have produced above-average results (at least along the dimensions that I have analyzed), and because those features are what I have focused my research on. But I will not claim that the United States has the only possible system for "delivering the goods," nor will I suggest that blindly copying the U.S. system makes sense for countries whose economies have not performed as well.

■ Supply Side: A Point of Departure

What we may broadly think of as the "supply side" perspective is a useful point of departure for my hypotheses. Supply-side theories are relevant because they emphasize the importance of long-run economic growth (rather than the control of cyclical fluctuations) and the role of innovations in promoting growth. They also specify conditions that can preclude innovation and growth, such as excessive regulation, insecure property rights, and confiscatory taxes; and these conditions may explain *some* of the differences in the economic performance of OECD countries. Supply-side theories, however, fail to explain the even larger differences between nineteenth- and twentieth-century performances, as we will see. Analyzing the differences between the "old" and the "new" economies provides a more complete understanding of the conditions that now make technological innovation such a potent economic force than is provided by standard supply-side theories.

A 2006 OECD study of the effects of regulation on the productivity of the service industry exemplifies the nature and contribution of supply-side research. The study reports that productivity in the services sector is lower in countries where regulation is high, and this effect is concentrated in industries that use (or produce) IT. Regulations also seem to affect the degree to which IT is used. The study estimates that, from 1985 to 2003, about 12 percent of the cross-country differences in IT investment (as a percentage of total investment) could be attributed to variations in the rules. A low regulatory burden apparently added four percentage points to the IT share of investment in the United States compared to the OECD average. More onerous rules in France, Greece, Italy, and Portugal pulled down the IT percentages by 2.5 to 3.5 points.*[2]

Similarly, a paper by my colleagues Van Biema and Greenwald argues that "the most important contribution that government is likely to make to improving productivity growth is to minimize the attention demands it makes on business management." The paper supports this hypothesis by analyzing the impact of different presidential administrations on productivity growth. The authors find a "remarkably consistent" relationship between high regulatory activities (as measured by pages in the Federal Register) and declines in productivity growth.[3]

Although it seems plausible that excessive government regulation, confiscatory levels of taxation, insecure property rights, and a failure to maintain law and order—the principal bugaboos of the standard supply-side view of the economy—are bad for productivity growth, does their absence ensure rapid productivity growth? As mentioned in chapter 14, the colonial rulers of India imposed lower taxes and had fewer regulations than governments in Britain. Yet India's economy languished while Britain's leaped ahead.

Differences in the growth rates in the United States and other Western countries during the nineteenth and twentieth centuries also raise questions about the degree to which the basic supply-side formula is a sufficient (rather than a necessary) condition for rapid growth. By historical standards, economic growth in the nineteenth century—when per capita incomes doubled—was unprecedented. But then in the twentieth century, incomes increased four times as rapidly as they had in the nineteenth century. Given

---

* Although the overall results are consistent with other research (such as the paper discussed in the next paragraph) I am reluctant to attribute much significance to the numerical estimates. As discussed in chapter 6, they are based on the implausible assumption that the same model applies to all countries—when it is far more likely that regulations affect the use of IT differently in France than they do in the United States. As the Nobel laureate Robert Solow elegantly put it: "I confess to a chronic intellectual deficiency: I am not deeply devoted to cross-country regressions as a way of improving our understanding of economic growth. But I suppose they could suggest interesting topics for serious research" (Solow 2006).

the higher "base," one might have expected growth in the twentieth century to have been slower. Strikingly, the modern economy has also been less prone to lurch from exhilarating boom to devastating bust: In the nineteenth century, several depressions interrupted economic growth, whereas in the twentieth century, apart from the Great Depression, downturns were relatively mild and short-lived—in spite of two great wars.[4]

Yet conditions in the nineteenth century conformed to the basic supply-side formula more closely than those of the twentieth century. In the United States, government expenditures and taxes were extremely low—and, except during the Civil War, there was no income tax. There was no federal bureaucracy to impose minimum-wage laws, regulate health and safety standards, or resist monopolies and trusts. No Clean Water or Securities and Exchange acts had been passed. Medicare, Medicaid, and Social Security programs had not been conceived. And property rights—another mainstay of supply-side recommendations—were at least as secure, if not more so, in the nineteenth century.

Another puzzle: according to Solow's ground-breaking research, technical progress rather than capital accumulation was the source of nearly 90 percent of U.S. growth in the first half of the twentieth century. In the nineteenth century, capital accumulation made a larger contribution to growth than did technical change.[5] Yet the new products invented in the nineteenth century were extraordinary. Inventions between 1850 and 1900 include the monorail, telephone, microphone, cash register, phonograph, incandescent lamp, electric train, steam turbine, gasoline engine, and street car, as well as dynamite, movies, motorcycles, linotype printing, automobiles, refrigerators, concrete and steel construction, pneumatic tires, aspirin, and X-rays. These may well overshadow inventions credited to the entire twentieth century.

The smaller economic impact of nineteenth-century inventions suggests that they weren't effectively commercialized—their widespread use was hampered by some combination of inappropriate features, high costs, poor marketing, or a paucity of venturesome consumption. Why in spite of more congenial supply-side climate was this so? What changed in the twentieth century that allowed the United States (and other countries with advanced economies) to extract more value from technological and scientific breakthroughs?

A ready answer is that modern economies have better "institutions, or what Ohkawa and Rosovsky called "social capabilities."[6] But that just begs the question: in what specific ways have institutions improved? Although it is easy to talk about institutions in the abstract, it is difficult to pin down their specific elements—the composition of good institutions, as my colleague Richard Nelson has pointed out, is complex.[7] What I will do next, therefore, is to highlight six important ways (summarized in the box) in which the modern system of innovation is better than its nineteenth-century counterpart.* The broad strokes of my description could apply to advanced countries as a whole; I will however limit the "then" versus "now" comparison to the United States. Later in the chapter I discuss the (less striking) contrast between the United States and other developed countries along the same dimensions.

Why the Modern System for Nurturing and Deploying Technological Innovations Is Better Than Its Nineteenth-century Counterpart: A Summary

- Broader participation: the modern system draws on the contributions of more individuals both as developers and as users of new products.
- Greater organizational diversity and specialization: the evolution of new forms of organization enables the system to use the contributions of many individuals more effectively
- Changes in common beliefs and attitudes: such changes, for example about technological change and thrift, accelerate the adoption of new products.
- Intensified pressure to grow: the "grow or die" imperative faced by many businesses encourages them to look for help from new technologies.
- Professionalization of management and sales functions has improved the capacity of modern organizations to develop market and use new products.
- Expansion of higher education has increased the supply of individuals inculcated with the habits and attitudes that improve their ability to develop and use innovations.

---

* I do not, however, get into how or why the elements of the modern system coevolved in the manner in which they did: its "ultimate causes" I believe are impossible to fathom.

■ Broader Participation

One aspect of the modern system that has made it more successful at developing innovations suitable for widespread use is its capacity to harness the talent and effort of a large number of individuals. In the nineteenth century, new products were developed by a few individuals. Edison brought forth a remarkable cornucopia—incandescent bulbs, motion pictures, and gramophones—from a small facility in Menlo Park (New Jersey, not California) with fewer employees than the typical Silicon Valley start-up. Alexander Graham Bell had one assistant. Automobile pioneers were one- or two-man shows—Karl Benz and Gottlieb Daimler in Germany, Armand Peugeot in France, and the Duryea brothers of Springfield, Massachusetts. But small outfits couldn't develop products for mass consumption. The early automobiles were expensive contraptions that couldn't be used for day-to-day transportation because they broke down frequently and lacked a supporting network of service stations and paved roads. One or two brilliant inventors couldn't solve these problems on their own.

In the twentieth century, the task of converting inventions into mass-market products pervaded society. As often as not, pioneers paved the way for many followers who built on and refined the first offerings. Planned and unwitting collaborations, taking place simultaneously and in sequence, made products that initially worked imperfectly commercially viable. Over the last three decades numerous innovations—such as electronic spreadsheets, the mouse, graphical user interfaces, and local area networks—have changed the personal computer from a virtually useless oddity into a ubiquitous artifact. A procession of individuals—Ed Roberts, Gates and Allen, Jobs and Wozniak, Bricklin and Frankston, Mitch Kapor, Robert Metcalf—made all this happen. Few of their individual contributions were actually breakthroughs per se, but collectively they created an industry that changed the world.

Similarly, the Internet does not have a solitary Alexander Graham Bell. Some of its leading figures have not acquired fame—even if they've become wealthy. Mention Sir Timothy Berners-Lee, for instance, and you will often evoke a puzzled look. And it isn't just a few visionaries or researchers who have turned the Internet into a revolutionary medium of communication. Innumerable entrepreneurs, venture capitalists, executives of large companies, members of standard-setting institutions, researchers at universities and commercial and state-sponsored laboratories, programmers who have written and tested untold millions of lines of code, and even investment bankers and politicians have played important roles in the Internet revolution.

Venturesome consumption also now includes individuals from many walks of life. Some new products and services—the Telstra Roadster 100, an electric sports car that retails for $100,000, and Virgin Galactic, which is selling tickets for suborbital flights for $200,000—are out of the reach of all but the very well-to-do. But the rich don't dominate the ranks of leading-edge consumers for most other innovations. It wasn't mainly the very well-to-do who lined up to buy half a million iPhones in just the first weekend of the product's release,[8] in spite of high prices.[9] Within weeks, you could see them flaunted in New York's subways by people who didn't look like investment bankers or hedge fund managers. At Columbia Business School, the presumably heavily indebted students were far more likely to own an iPhone than the faculty.

Broad-based venturesome consumption has been crucial to the effective deployment of innovative mid-level products in the workplace. Personal computers and other IT products and services have helped raise U.S. productivity because of the effort and resourcefulness of a very large number of users. As previously mentioned, in 2001, 60 percent of U.S. workers reported they had learned to use spreadsheets or databases, and 11 million said they did some kind of programming but were not professional programmers.

As a rule, IT has raised the intellectual challenge to workers, even if some innovations (such as touch screens in the fast-food industry) have helped dumb-down certain jobs. The old-fashioned executive secretary typed on a manual or electric typewriter. The modern executive assistant not only has to have the same motor skills on a keyboard, but also the more cognitive skills and knowledge of using word-processing software. In addition, he may have to learn how to create PowerPoint presentations, coordinate meetings on an electronic calendar, make reservations for airlines and hotels online, or edit his boss's web page or blog.

■ **Greater Organizational Diversity and Specialization**

A second distinctive feature of the modern era has been an increase in the diversity of organizations that play in the innovation game. As a result, individuals now participate through many different specialized organizations and subunits and can select ones that are best matched to their abilities and interests. In contrast, in the nineteenth century, individuals made their contributions to innovation through simple partnerships or small firms.

One important source of organizational diversity has been the rise of large, professionally managed corporations. As the business historian Alfred Chandler has shown, this form of organization, which appeared in the last half of the nineteenth century,[10] become a major force for developing and deploying innovative products in the twentieth century. Companies such as DuPont, for instance, developed new materials, such as nylon, in their research labs, produced them on a mass scale at low cost, and created large markets for their use. By the 1960s, this organizational form became ubiquitous. In 1967, J. K. Galbraith observed that the 500 largest corporations produced nearly half the goods and services annually available in the United States.[11]

Contrary to predictions, however, large corporations did not wipe out traditional forms of organization. In fact, shortly after Galbraith's book was published, their share of economic activity stabilized. By the early 1980s, professionally managed venture-capital funds began to see explosive growth, and the firms they invested in came to be regarded as the new standard-bearers of innovative enterprise. The once-hot large corporation was regarded as passé and on the path to eventual extinction. In fact, the emergence of VC-backed businesses also represented an increase in the diversity of organizational forms rather than creative destruction. Just as large corporations did not make the classic self-financed entrepreneur obsolete, VC-backed businesses did not knock out large corporations.

Rather, different types of organizations now specialize in different innovative activities and complement each other's capabilities. Large publicly traded corporations, for instance, can undertake very large initiatives that require the coordination of many individuals and the pooling of many investors' capital. Self-financed entrepreneurs, in contrast, don't have either the capital or the organizational capacity to undertake such projects. But the same governance and control mechanisms that give big corporations an advantage in pooling capital and labor also discourage them from undertaking projects with high Knightian uncertainty. Self-financed entrepreneurs, in contrast, can pursue projects with high Knightian uncertainty because they aren't answerable to anyone.[12]

These differences often lead self-financed ventures and large corporations to build off each others' contributions in advancing the technological frontier. For instance, between 1975 and 1980, individual entrepreneurs, rather than large companies, tried to create useful applications for personal computers when the Knightian uncertainty about the utility of these quirky toys was high. But after these efforts bore fruit, it was the launch of IBM's PC in 1981(when IBM accounted for more than 60 percent of the world wide sales of mainframe computers) that "legitimized" the personal computer for the data-processing departments of large companies. Multi-billion-dollar investments by Intel and Microsoft after that helped carry the PC into virtually every home and office.

Moreover, Knightian uncertainty and capital requirements are just two dimensions that characterize an organization's specialization. Other factors may include choice of market (the options constantly expand because of nondestructive creation); levels of know-how and products (high level, mid-level, or ground level); functions (some organizations, such as Qualcomm, specialize in research, while others, such as PR and ad agencies, specialize in marketing; yet others, such as Intel, are vertically integrated); and geographic scope. The large number of dimensions of specialization helps give organizations distinctive roles in the innovation process.

The specialization of the players in the innovation game provides two kinds of benefits. First, specialized organizations can develop more effective capabilities than if they (like some nineteenth-century inventors) "did it all on their own." Whereas an Edison had to develop new technologies and create marketplace buzz largely on his own, a Jobs can draw on the services of specialized design-houses on the one side and PR and ad agencies on the other. Second, organizations can more effectively utilize the contributions of individuals with different abilities and dispositions: the "mad scientist" (who comes up with breakthrough research) can work at a dedicated lab; the methodical engineer (who figures out how to "scale up" an innovative prototype), in the production function of a large corporation; and the flamboyant marketer at an ad agency.

■ **Changes in Beliefs and Attitudes**

Several common beliefs and attitudes that undergird the modern system of innovation—expectations of technological change, gratification from buying cool new products first, and the desirability of job hopping—have distinctively modern, late twentieth century, features. Let us see how.

In earlier times, a relatively small number of people—mostly visionary inventors and scientists—believed in the inevitability and desirability of technological progress. Now popular magazines, TV shows, and management books are predicated on the assumption that scientific and technological progress is inevitable. Many believe they can prosper by pursuing the new New Thing, and that if they don't, they will fall behind.

The widespread acceptance of such beliefs has helped turn progress into a self-fulfilling prophecy. Consider Intel cofounder Gordon Moore's famous observation that the number of transistors built on a chip doubles every 18 months. Semiconductor companies who believe in this so-called law invest the resources needed to make it come true. Other players such as PC manufacturers and applications-software companies design products in anticipation of the 18-month cycle. So when new chips arrive, they find a ready market, which in turn validates beliefs in Moore's law and encourages even more investment in building and using new chips.

The fear of being left behind similarly helps explain the speed with which IT innovations are deployed. Cortada notes that a common pattern across many industries in the adoption of computers was that everyone would use "computers in the same way to perform the same functions. Thus, when bank[s] initiated ATM services, they seemed to do so all at once within a short period of time."[13] Although such herdlike behavior means that no competitor can rely on an exclusive use of IT as a sustainable source of profit, the behavior is still rational—a bank that doesn't install ATMs risks losing customers.

In principle, expectations of technological change can also slow change down.[14] Why buy the $3,000 flat panel TV set now if the price will drop and the reliability of the models increase? But apparently, many users derive utility not just from the functions new products provide but from early adoption. As Keynes pointed out, people have both "absolute" needs (health, survival) as well as "relative" needs that we experience "only if their satisfaction lifts us above, makes us feel superior to, our fellows."[15] Early purchasers of flat panel TVs apparently enter into a tacit bargain with other consumers: they incur the higher risks and costs, which drive down prices and improve the quality for the consumers who wait; in return, those who wait give early purchasers the gratification of being first.

The gratification that many modern consumers enjoy may be contrasted with the pleasure of "conspicuous consumption" of the Gilded Age that Thorstein Veblen wrote about in *The Theory of the Leisure Class*—consuming expensive goods for the sake of displaying status or wealth. Only the wealthy can indulge in conspicuous consumption. According to Veblen, to satisfy its purpose—the demonstration of wealth—conspicuous consumption must be wasteful. In contrast, many early purchasers of the latest gadgetry aren't flush with cash (or even pretending to be); they seek to display, to themselves and to others, their technological sophistication rather than their wealth. (The classic form of conspicuous consumption has certainly not disappeared, however.)

The widespread opening of hearts and wallets to new offerings also involves the dilution of prior beliefs in the moral and economic value of thrift. Through the end of the nineteenth century, according to Max Weber's thesis, religious convictions about thrift sustained the "spirit of capitalism." Weber argued that merchants and industrialists accumulated capital in the belief that they had a moral duty to strive for wealth as well as to lead austere lives. But today, because venturesome production requires venturesome consumption, excessive thrift can injure rather than help capitalism. As it happens, modern consumers have been more inclined to keep up with (if not stay ahead of) the recently acquired baubles of their neighbors than to display excessive thrift.

The utility individuals now derive from using cutting-edge technology can also stimulate business purchases of IT if the IT staff put their love for the latest toys ahead of their employers' interests. Top executives who are aware of this tendency can resist it—or they may be subject to it themselves and argue for the adoption of cutting-edge technology in the guise of demonstrating their farsighted vision. Even managers who have no love for technology per se may be concerned with keeping up with their competitors. If these competitors also have IT staff who are subject to techno-lust, the entire industry may be stampeded into adopting new technologies.

Along with thrift, the aspiration and expectation of long-term employment has also gone by the wayside, particularly in the last quarter-century. Although relatively few people actually enjoyed lifelong employment at high wages, it was once at least widely aspired to; starting and retiring at IBM or General Motors was a considered a good thing. Now employees often regard job hopping as necessary for getting ahead and building their personal "brands." Conversely, employers don't look down on well-traveled résumés or reward the loyalty of employees who don't leave: promoting from within is out, and the path to the top is rarely up one ladder.

Frequent job-hopping promotes the development and use of technological innovations. According to AnnaLee Saxenian, one important reason for Silicon Valley's "regional advantage" in innovation is the high propensity of IT workers to change jobs. According to one of her interview subjects, people could change jobs without changing parking lots. These "spontaneous regroupings of skill" are said to allow whoever comes up with the best technology to attract the best people.[16]

On the deployment side, job hopping helps disseminate the ground-level know-how necessary to effectively use innovations. Wal-Mart, for instance, has been a leader in the use of IT in managing its supply chain. Its alumni have helped propagate Wal-Mart's expertise not only to its direct competitors, but also to online retailers such as Amazon. In fact, Wal-Mart once sued Amazon and Drugstore.com in order to bring "an immediate stop" to "a wholesale raiding of its proprietary and highly confidential information systems . . . through the use of former Wal-Mart associates." The defendants had hired former Wal-Mart employees as chief information officer (at Amazon) and chief logistics officer.[17] Footloose employees of IT-using organizations are also more likely to support the purchase of unproven new products (for their private gratification or otherwise), because they don't expect to be around if it ultimately fails.

■ **Intensified Pressure to Grow**

In the modern era, I have previously argued, many businesses have to "grow or die" because of the demands placed by competitors, customers, capital markets, and labor markets.[18] The pressure to grow creates strong incentives for producers of IT to develop new products and for users to increase their deployment. HP illustrates the former. Cofounder David Packard writes in his memoir that, over the years, he and Bill Hewlett "speculated many times about the optimum size of a company." They "did not believe that growth was important for its own sake," but eventually concluded that "continuous growth was essential" for the company to remain competitive.[19] The goal, in turn, led HP, which was until 1964 just a developer of scientific instruments, to enter the computer industry.

Growth facilitates and encourages firms to use IT and other innovative technologies in several ways. First, the larger a business grows, the more it can support the fixed costs of deploying IT. Unlike Wal-Mart, a small retailer cannot afford to purchase a license for a sophisticated supply-chain management software package or pay for the in-house IT staff necessary to install and maintain the package. Moreover, since vendors' costs of marketing their packages also tends to be fixed, they tend to favor large customers who buy large (or many) packages.

Second, growing companies often start new facilities, in which it is both easier and more economical to adopt new technologies. While an old plant may be technologically obsolete, it may still cover its variable costs and make replacing it with a state-of-the-art plant irrational for its owners. Moreover, it can be operationally disruptive to pull out the old technology. Neither consideration applies with a greenfield facility.[20] It is worth noting here that the main differences in the productivity of European and U.S. retailing are in the arena of "big box" retailers (like Wal-Mart), and that within this category, the U.S. edge derives mainly from its newly opened retail outlets.[21]

Third, efforts to grow can stimulate searches for innovative technologies that help companies realize economies of scale and scope. For instance, in 1988, Physicians Sales and Services (a company I have written a case series about) was once an "itty bitty company in Florida." In 1989, founder Pat Kelly declared that PSS would become the first national distributor of medical products to physicians' offices in the United States. With just $20 million in revenues, it had no significant economies of scale that would justify nationwide operation. The goal of becoming a national company, however, provided the impetus to create such economies. For example, the company invested in an order-entry system based on handheld computers, which increased the speed of deliveries and enabled PSS to reduce the inventories it had to carry. These and other applications of IT allowed PSS to create national-level scale economies where none had previously existed.

■ Professionalization of Management and Sales

The professionalization of management and sales functions has been another hallmark of modern organizations that has improved their ability to develop, market, and use new products.

Let's start with how new management techniques have affected companies developing new products: In the first half of the twentieth century, as Alfred Chandler has documented, top managers of large companies such as General Motors evolved a systematic approach to decide what innovations to undertake, taking into account factors such as market opportunities, the firm's capabilities, expected capital requirements, and returns. Managers also developed techniques to control how the innovations were undertaken: large companies transformed innovation into a "routine and predictable process."[22] Baumol cites the example of Eastman Kodak, which uses computers to generate "pseudo photographs" with variation in contrasts, brightness, balance of colors, and so on. Kodak then polls panels of consumers and professional photographers to decide "which of the computer generated pseudo photographs promise to be the most saleable, and the company laboratories are assigned the task of inventing a film that will yield the desired results."[23]

As the digital revolution unfolded, IT producers followed in the footsteps of their "old economy" predecessors in adopting a disciplined approach to the development of their new products. For instance, according to cofounder Gordon Moore, Intel's process for R&D budgeting required each product group to "submit a project list ordered in decreasing priority, explain in sometimes excruciating detail why the list is ordered as it is, and indicate where the line ought to be drawn between projects to work on and projects to put off."[24]

Along the same lines, Cypress Semiconductor, according to CEO T. J. Rodgers, developed a "goal system" to monitor development projects. For example, designing and shipping the company's third generation of PROM chips was accomplished by completing 3,278 goals over roughly two years.[25] Cypress management reviewed project goals more or less continuously. After project teams met on Monday, goals were fed into a central computer. On Tuesday mornings, functional managers received printouts on the status of their direct reports' new goals. On Wednesday mornings, the vice presidents of the company received goal printouts for the people below them. On Wednesday afternoons, the CEO reviewed reports with the vice presidents.[26]

Critics of this managerial approach claim that it is excessively bureaucratic and stifles entrepreneurship; but unlike the inventions of solo inventors, complex development projects that use large teams simply cannot be undertaken without rules and organization. Below the apparently freewheeling open-source development of Linux lie elaborate processes and rules and, yes, a hierarchy. To play in the big leagues, even companies that start off with no management to speak of, such as Microsoft, have to routinize their approach to development—and hire managers from large companies to oversee the new routines. VC-backed companies hire executives from large companies to implement (albeit with suitable adaptation) systematic managerial processes from the get-go. Ad hoc improvisation certainly hasn't become obsolete, just as the self-financed entrepreneur hasn't become extinct; rather, modern management techniques have improved the development of certain kinds of products.

Large IT companies (and not just consumer-goods behemoths such as Coca-Cola and Procter & Gamble) have also applied management techniques to improve the efficiency of sales and marketing. As discussed in the box, IBM, under the leadership of Thomas J. Watson Sr., was a pioneer in this regard. More professional sales techniques increased the diffusion of IT products and the effectiveness of their use, and salespersons were trained to ensure that customers derived good value for their money. The development of an effective sales channel also encouraged IT companies to develop more products to utilize the channel to its fullest.

IBM: Achieving Greatness through Selling

According to Richard Tedlow, "Selling, even more than technology ... made IBM great during its glory days." IBM's sales techniques, he writes, can be traced back to what Watson learned in earlier jobs. Watson first started as a salesman at the Painted Post company in the 1890s, when the "job was as unsystematic and unscientific as it had been from time immemorial." Salesmen taught themselves "the tricks of the trade," and "there were plenty of tricks to learn."[27] Watson then joined National Cash Register (NCR) as a salesman in its Buffalo office. The company had codified its sales approach in a booklet, known as "the Primer," which was, according to Tedlow, "a classic of managerial advice" that instructed the reader "what to do and why, as well as what to avoid."[28] Everyone was "expected to know it and to abide by it" and was subjected to cross-examination if they deviated from it.[29] The NCR system "transformed" selling from a "sometimes sleazy method of operation into a systematic, quantifiable business assignment."[30]

At IBM, Watson "civilized" the NCR methods and made them "appropriate for the twentieth century."[31] Decades before IBM ever sold a computer, and when electric accounting (or "tabulating") machines comprised its main product line, Watson built a formidable sales system. Salesmen were recruited on college campuses (rather than from the school of hard knocks) and were put through an extended in-house training program (started in 1927 in Endicott, New York). Before attempting to make a sales call, salesmen were "expected to know more about the prospect's accounting" (IBM's machines were typically used in accounting departments) "than the prospect himself." The salesman would send a letter asking for an appointment (accompanied by a written testimonial from a satisfied customer). Usually, writes Tedlow, the salesman got the appointment "because IBM had the reputation for sending people 'to serve,' not to sell. Once inside the organization, the salesman was expected to learn every aspect of the prospect's accounting system" and help identify "deviations from best practice."

The salesman then met with the chief accountant or head bookkeeper (who might be offered the opportunity to attend a training program at Endicott). The chief accountant was persuaded to let the salesman undertake a survey. The goal of the survey, which could take up to six months to complete, "was to show how IBM's equipment could provide more accurate information at greater speed and lower cost than was otherwise possible." According to Tedlow, because this was invariably true, "IBM had genuine advantages over the manual methods it was replacing." The survey eliminated "all the puffery which so often has surrounded selling."

With the survey complete, the IBM salesman took prospects for a demonstration at the local IBM branch office. By then, the salesman had the prospective customer "in his grip." The salesman would know "as much about the customers business as the customer himself, and a lot more about the latest systems in the customer's industry." Instead of "a drummer or a Willy Loman figure," the IBM salesman was "an expert selling an expert system to a man who had the option of buying it or being left behind by the rest of the business world."[32]

IBM's sales methods helped the company dominate its markets, but they also promoted the development and effective use of its products. "The sales force," according to Tedlow, "pulled new products out of the laboratories because they wanted more to sell. Because of the success of his motivation and management, Watson put more pressure on his inventors and engineers than he may have intended."[33] Because as the dominant player IBM needed to expand its markets to increase its sales—and because its sales process relied heavily on testimonials from satisfied customers—the company had a strong incentive to ensure that the benefits it promised were actually realized. Thus, the company not only had to sell its equipment, but also ensure it was effectively used. IBM's salesmen couldn't be "knockers-on-doors"; they were "efficiency engineers."[34]

If we turn to the user side, the adoption of modern management techniques has enhanced the capacity of buyers to effectively deploy the products they purchase. In the case of IBM's accounting machines: the machines cut costs dramatically, eliminated work that was "boring, repetitive and mind-numbing," and "limited expensive accounting and actuarial mistakes."[35] IBM's salesmen analyzed their prospects' operations and informed them about "best practices." Ultimately, of course, it was customers who had to implement these best practices to effectively use their purchases.

In recent decades, "good management" has become particularly crucial in treating the service sector's "Baumol disease." IT companies have developed many products that can potentially improve the productivity of services. But realizing their value, according to Van Biema and Greenwald's research, is "above all a *management* issue." Their case studies "demonstrated without exception that consistent and effective management intervention is the decisive factor in obtaining significant productivity gains."[36] Although "management challenges in the service sector are in many ways more severe that those confronting manufacturing," the high productivity of "leading edge service companies strongly argues that proper management attention can produce vastly improved performance throughout the service economy."[37]

Now, 10 years after Van Biema and Greenwald's study, the performance of the service sector has apparently "vastly improved"; it is reasonable to infer, then, that the overall level of management in the service sector has improved,[38] possibly through the growth of the better-managed service companies such as Wal-Mart (which are good at leveraging available technologies) at the expense of their less-well-managed rivals.

■ Expansion of Higher Education

Tertiary education (or more simply, "attending college") became much more widespread in the United States and other rich countries in the twentieth century, especially after World War II. But has the expansion of college enrollments contributed to the growth of productivity and prosperity? It could be that the concurrent expansion of college enrollments and prosperity is just a coincidence. Or perhaps greater prosperity has allowed societies to underwrite the pleasures of a college education for more of its young, without realizing any economic benefit for the outlay. Making this argument, Charles Murray, coauthor of *The Bell Curve*, asserts that "far too many" (even of those in the upper half of the IQ distribution) "are going to four-year colleges."

Murray argues that many students whose intelligence is at or just above average may cope with high school but can't survive college-level coursework in engineering or natural sciences—though in the humanities and the social sciences they can, unfortunately, squeak by. "It is possible for someone with an IQ of 100 to sit in the lectures of Economics 1, read the textbook, and write answers in an examination book," writes Murray. "But students who cannot follow complex arguments accurately are not really learning economics. They are taking away a mishmash of half-understood information and outright misunderstandings that probably leave them under the illusion that they know something they do not." A college education "makes sense for only about 15% of the population," or at a stretch 25 percent, he states. Yet "more than 45% of recent high school graduates enroll," in large measure because of the "false premium that our culture has put on a college degree." Government policy has also made "college scholarships and loans too easy to get."

Murray (a graduate of Harvard College with a PhD in political science from MIT) favors more training of short duration in "practical specialties" offered by vocational schools and two-year colleges. "For learning many technical specialties," writes Murray, "four years is unnecessarily long." Even in many high-tech occupations, a four-year college education is "no more important" than for "NBA basketball players or cabinetmakers. Walk into Microsoft or Google with evidence that you are a brilliant hacker, and the job interviewer is not going to fret if you lack a college transcript."[39]

What is the counterargument? Earlier in this chapter, I argued that in the twentieth century innovation was much more inclusive than it was in the nineteenth century and that it now draws on the contributions of not just a few brilliant inventors but a wide swath of individuals—many of whom, by definition, have average IQs. Obviously some individuals—those doing cutting-edge research in nano-technology, or chief scientists at firms using such research to develop new products—benefit from knowledge that they accumulated by attending college and graduate school. But not everyone involved in developing or marketing new products makes much direct use of the knowledge acquired in a four-year college. As Murray points out, Steve Jobs and Bill Gates dropped out of college, and their enormously successful enterprises, Apple and Microsoft, have benefited from the services of programmers with similarly abbreviated educational careers.

Similar questions arise about the value of college educations for the "average" individual involved in the use of new technologies. In their classic 1966 paper, Richard Nelson and Edmund Phelps offered the general (i.e., economy-wide) hypothesis that "education speeds the process of technological diffusion."[40] Decades later, Phelps suggested (in several papers) that continental Europe had been unable to adequately capitalize on the Internet revolution because of "a scarcity of university educations." In 2006, Phelps cited the example of a manager of a vineyard "who might have no idea" of what the costs and benefits of a new insecticide would be "if he lacked an education in basic science and the humanities." A "modicum of knowledge of engineering, chemistry and other fields" goes a long way, Phelps suggested, in helping individuals evaluate new products and techniques.[41] But why does this modicum require a university education? And just how does the knowledge acquired in Economics (or Sociology) 101 actually help a manager evaluate or implement an ERP system?

In my view, attending college (instead of a vocational school) can indeed help many individuals play a more effective role in developing and using innovations, but in a subtle way. Personal experience (in a *five*-year engineering program) makes me skeptical of how much basic knowledge is actually retained by students after they graduate; and knowledge of "technical specialties" (programming in FORTRAN, in my case) often becomes obsolete. But college curricula, which are invariably more kaleidoscopic than those at vocational schools or in technical apprenticeships, do offer other kinds of benefits: they require students to quickly familiarize themselves with a wide range of often unrelated subjects. This can improve both the ability—and equally importantly the confidence*—to learn new things. Good colleges also require students to apply new knowledge for resourceful problem solving, and, because the costs of things going wrong are relatively low (compared to apprenticeships), students can take more risks.

Going to college (especially on a residential campus) also has value because it provides extracurricular social experiences. Students generally have to communicate and cooperate with a more diverse set of fellow students than they had previously encountered in their high schools or who they might encounter in a vocational school, especially if the admissions office puts some weight on diversity. This kind of socialization can also be valuable in modern innovative activity, which often involves the teamwork of a changing cast of characters.

I do not have any hard data for my conjectures, but they are based on more than just personal experience and observation. In 2006, as a judge in the Kauffman Foundation's $25 million Campuses Initiative grant program, I asked nearly a dozen university presidents and chancellors how colleges in the United States contributed to the dynamism of its economy. Rather than touting specific knowledge, they spoke of the value of "learning how to learn," and developing confidence and socialization. Moreover, there was nothing in their remarks that would indicate that only individuals in the top 15 to 25 percent of the IQ distribution benefited from that value.

What Colleges Add

Here I select (and condense) some of the responses to the question posed to university chancellors and presidents about how U.S. colleges enhance their graduates' economical contribution to society:

> "The best American universities do three fundamental things. One is social-capital networking. Individual students learn from each other— and learn that relying on each other is, in fact, the way to go, that doing it alone doesn't work in this world. Second, universities embed what might

---

* Learning about something entirely new poses Knightian uncertainty about whether the effort will be successful. Repeated prior success in learning new things reduces the uncertainty.

traditionally be called a technical education—the components of knowledge—in an agile, broad inquiry that comes at questions from multiple directions. Third, we pose problems for our students to solve in order to make them feel that is a pressing issue."—Chancellor Nancy Cantor, Syracuse University

"Education in this country teaches you that you own what you learn and what you do on the basis of your learning. You have to participate: you're going to have to do projects, you're going to have to defend what you're doing, and so on. At [my university], every student, from the moment they come through the gates, believes that they are empowered to challenge the worth of our ideas. That allows students to go one step further and say, 'I have the creativity and the ability to advance my own ideas.' They own their ideas. Well, if you own your ideas, you're willing to push them; you're willing to do all kinds of things.

"I actually think learning this begins when children are quite young, in grade school. People ask me, How were you able to go from where you were to where you are today? To me, it's very simple. I grew up in circumstances that were not particularly robust in terms of education. But as soon as I stepped into grade school in a very impoverished area when I was six years old, I understood my agency right then."—President of an Ivy League university.[42]

"One of the great pieces of value-added that residential universities provide is the socialization that occurs by being mixed together with lots of people from different backgrounds, races, ethnicities, religions, countries of origin, disciplines, interests, and talents—and having to learn to get along and do things together in these 650 student organizations, and in their class projects, and so on. That really is every bit as valuable as what takes place in the classroom."—Chancellor John Wiley, University of Wisconsin–Madison

"All the evidence is that the more educated you are, the higher your income is. One element is that people who are well educated probably have been parented well and, statistically at least, probably come from higher income levels. But it's not only that: people who are well educated are both empowered to take control of their lives and are better equipped to learn and contribute things that the society is prepared to reward. I'm a first-generation college student. Nobody in my family went to college before I did, and certainly nobody before me has had a graduate degree, a PhD, or been a president of a university. The impact of that education in my own life is utterly profound.

"For instance, we have an experiential learning program. It's less about imparting deep knowledge and making students more expert in something than about motivating students, giving them some sense of the consequences of their education and, more importantly, giving them the self-confidence that they can do it."—President Martin Jischke, Purdue University

"We've repeatedly heard from employers that our students are self-starters: they can be given a task and don't need a lot of directions to pursue this task. One important reason is that we have a kind of technical professional approach that fosters independent problem-solving, drawing on lots of domains. For instance, you can be an English major but specialize in technical writing and learn about science and technology."—President Jared Cohon, Carnegie-Mellon University

■ U.S. Exceptionalism?

I now turn from the "then" versus "now" contrast to the "here" versus "there." Although the latter is not as sharp as the former, there are, as we will see next, some modest similarities: the differences between the economies of the United States and other OECD countries are in manner but not in magnitude like the differences we have just reviewed between the nineteenth-century U.S. economy and its modern incarnation.

Consumers in the United States seem more willing to splurge on new things. This is not true across all products—the Japanese are famously more adventurous in their purchases of consumer electronics, and European youngsters embraced text messaging on their mobile phones long before their U.S. counterparts. But figures on aggregate consumer spending and borrowing suggest that, overall, U.S. consumers lead the pack in spending on new gizmos—whether they have the current financial means at hand or not.*

My interviews suggest that prospective customers in the United States are more willing take chances on unproven innovations developed by fledgling companies—and to provide candid feedback that helps refine those innovations (see box "Attitudinal Differences"). According to my interviewees, this was not because buyers abroad are less technically qualified. Rather, even if they are more knowledgeable, they are less willing to stick their necks out, possibly because of some combination of cultural norms (my interviewees' favored explanation), organizational rules, and the lower incidence of job hopping (which decreases concern about bad investments).

Attitudinal Differences

CEOs who all happened to be immigrants to the United States made the following comments about differences in the attitudes of U.S. and non-U.S. customers.

> "U.S. customers are more willing to spend several hundred thousand dollars on unproven products from unproven companies. They worry less about the company going bankrupt, and they relish the idea of being on the cutting edge. It's fun to be on the cutting edge, but it's challenging too. Early products don't work properly—nothing works as advertised for an early-stage product. You have to like the idea that, 'Hey, I get to give feedback. They listen to what I say. I say "jump" and these guys jump.' In Europe and Japan, people are more concerned about making a mistake."

> "In Germany, people expect everything to work perfectly. If it doesn't work, it's a problem. When somebody in the U.S. says, 'This is broken,' you

---

* Steven Currall, from University College London, who has studied public attitudes toward new technologies (such as GMO and nanotechnology), wrote in an email to me: "In the United States versus Europe, public attitudes toward emerging technologies (e.g., nanotechnology or GMO) appear to differ with respect to perception of the tradeoff of risk and benefit. In the U.S., the public seems more inclined to assess the level of risk in terms of not only potential negative consequences of the technology, but simultaneously in terms of potential benefits. In Europe, by contrast, the public places greater emphasis on first understanding the risks and then considering potential benefits. This orientation may make Europeans less likely to embrace emerging technologies until they feel that they have full information on possible risks."

ask them, 'How often do you use it?' They say, 'Well, maybe once a year. Come to think of it, don't worry about it.' In Germany, if it's broken, it doesn't matter how often they are going to use it: it's broken. In the U.S., there is a focus on being simple, and people don't want to waste time going through manuals. In Germany, they will invest the time to read manuals and fully understand your product. But then they expect it to work perfectly. Sales teams in Germany have the same approach. They are technically sophisticated, but if you ask them to sell something, they insist it has to be perfect.

"European IT people are more conservative. The mentality in the U.S. is, 'We'll give it a try, and if it works, great, and if it doesn't, we'll stop.' In Europe it's, 'We talk about it—we talk a lot about it—and when we feel good about it, we do it.' It isn't a trial-and-error type of culture. I came from France to business school in the U.S. In one of our first case studies, we had a group discussion to resolve a problem. Very quickly, the Americans said, 'We think we've got it. Let's just do it, then we can figure out whether it works.' As a European, I had a problem with that. I said, 'Guys, we really haven't looked at all the pros and cons. How can we make a decision?' "

"When I came to the States, I was amazed by the degree of openness of Americans to share even personal things. Consider money: money is very important in the States, but you ask to borrow someone's car, people say yes, very easily. In Europe, people say money is not important, but then try borrowing their car. The same thing happens with customers and their knowledge. In Europe, they see knowledge as an asset that they need to protect. There's also risk aversion. It's a very hierarchical structure in Europe. They may not know if they can share with you or not, but their instinct is to say no. In the U.S., people will say, 'What the heck, let me just tell you.' "

"When you go proactively for information to customers, the U.S. is better. When you are looking for reactive feedback, sometimes the Europeans are better. Why? Because a lot of Europeans in our market have a higher level of education than their American counterparts. If you ask for suggestions, they can become resistant, but if you don't ask them, they can be very vocal. It's funny. So they may not be good beta customers at the very early stage, but later on, they may give you better feedback."

The United States seems to offer more incentives and opportunities to grow businesses and turn them into megacorporations. According to some historians, the United States has spawned many large companies because of a favorable legal and regulatory environment. In the formative years of the country, leaders such as Jefferson directed their fear of concentrated power toward government—the issue of corporate power was moot. When the Second Industrial Revolution started, around 1880, a "tiny" government, according to business historian Thomas McCraw, left a "vacuum of power" that allowed American companies to attain "gigantic" size.[43]

Subsequently, "trust-busting" politicians did attempt to curb the power of large corporations, but as McCraw points out, antitrust legislation was "not synonymous with anti-bigness law." The "most conspicuous targets" of antitrust were giant companies, but "the majority of prosecutions" had been against groups of small firms engaging in collusive behavior.[44] Financial and labor markets—and customers—in the United States favor "winners" (including "up-and-comers") and shun losers. So winners get the capital, talent, and revenues that help them grow even more quickly. This tendency enabled Wal-Mart (which was founded in 1962 and went public in 1972) to rise to the top of the *Fortune* 500 list in 2002—and not coincidentally to become one of the largest users of IT in the world.

Growth rates of firms outside the United States are lower. This may be in part because the "system" doesn't feed winners and starve losers to the same degree. According to a McKinsey & Co. analysis, the top quartiles of U.S. firms—which are considerably more productive and larger than their European counterparts—also "attract resources and gain market share considerably faster than in the EU."[45] Similarly, regulations (and possibly opportunities for tax avoidance) encourage small firms outside the United States to remain small. As shown in figure 15.1, start-ups (that survive) grow many times more rapidly in the United States. And in service sectors such as retailing in Europe, a range of policies directly and indirectly discourages the growth of behemoths such as Wal-Mart[46] (even though the *hypermarché* concept supposedly originated in France with an outlet opened by Carrefour in 1963).

The "development of modern sales management," according to historian Walter Friedman, "is a uniquely American story. The intense efforts to standardize salesmanship distinguished the growth of capitalism in America

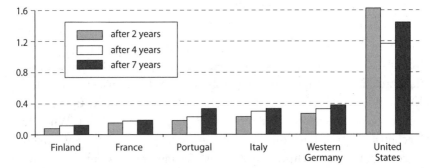

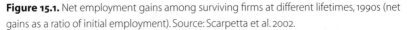

Figure 15.1. Net employment gains among surviving firms at different lifetimes, 1990s (net gains as a ratio of initial employment). Source: Scarpetta et al. 2002.

from that in other countries." Although "all European nations had peddling networks," none "created organized sales forces to the same degree." An important reason for this was (as discussed above) that "the scale of American firms was greater than elsewhere. The massive manufacturing concerns of the early twentieth century hired salesmen in the hundreds (and even thousands)."[47] Sales efforts were "central to the growth of the U.S. economy." Sales and marketing were not "afterthoughts to the coming of industrialization, but were part and parcel of the same phenomenon. Large firms were capable not only of producing on a great scale, but also of persuasion, pressure and the fostering of an evangelical exuberance. The 'visible hand' of management . . . could not have succeeded . . . without the 'visible handshake' of a team of salesmen out on the road."[48]

In contrast, British companies, which operated on a smaller scale, and German manufacturers, who "were rooted in craftwork traditions," did not exhibit an interest in mass selling campaigns. In addition, "Organized selling in America flourished for cultural reasons." For instance, the United States had "more fluid class boundaries" than Europe, and salesmanship "seemed to offer a path to personal success [to] Americans [who] read know-how-to-sell books and turned Bruce Barton's *The Man Nobody Knows* (1925), which portrayed Jesus Christ as a successful sales and advertising executive, into a bestseller."[49]

As previously mentioned, purchases of IT by mainstream users (and not just by early adopters) in the service sector is exceptionally high in the United States, possibly because those users derive more value from their IT investments than their counterparts in many countries abroad. In part, this may be the result of U.S. policies (such as fewer restrictions on big-box retailing) that permit the effective use of IT. But the exceptional capacity of U.S. managers also apparently plays an important role. Bloom, Sadun, and Van Reenen's research suggests that the managerial capacity of U.S.-based service companies to derive value from their IT investments was strong when those companies operated in countries where the environment for using IT might be less favorable. They compared establishments based in the UK that were owned by U.S. multinationals, non-U.S. multinationals, and domestic (i.e., UK-based) companies, and found that establishments owned by U.S. multinationals invested about 41 percent more per employee in IT than the average for the industry; non-U.S. multinationals invested about 20 percent more than the industry average, while domestic companies invested about 15 percent *less*. U.S. multinationals also apparently got more for their IT buck; they enjoyed "significantly higher productivity of IT capital." This effect accounted for "almost all the difference" between the overall productivity of resources used by "U.S. owned and all other establishments." The researchers also found that the "IT edge" of U.S. multinationals was "confined to the same 'IT using intensive' industries that largely accounted for U.S. productivity growth acceleration since the mid 1990s."[50]

The researchers further argue that U.S. multinationals can use IT more effectively because of their greater "devolution"—they operate "with flatter hierarchies with more control passed down to lower level employees."[51]

I find it unlikely that decentralization is the whole story. Even as a conceptual matter, many IT systems cannot be adopted and implemented by decentralized employees. The decision to use a company-wide ERP system has to be made centrally—and its implementation also requires individual members of the organization to follow common rules and procedures.[52] In fact, some interviewees told me that one problem with selling enterprise systems to large European companies was that they operated as a collection of independent fiefdoms who would not easily agree on any corporate-wide purchase.

But my observations (both as a former management consultant and now as a field-based researcher) also lead me to believe that some "big decisions" apart, U.S. companies do give individual employees more responsibility and opportunity to exercise personal initiative than many European or Japanese companies. This ought to provide the benefit of giving decision rights to individuals with the necessary "specific knowledge," as well as of motivating employees to do their best (even if they don't expect to work in the organization for the long haul).

In other words, it isn't just that U.S. businesses are more decentralized. Notwithstanding the self-image of "rugged individualism," my impression is that people who live in the United States, or work for U.S. organizations, in fact more wholeheartedly submit to authority and rules than, say, Italians or Indians.* Moreover, individuals in the United States are more than just compliant—they are less cynical and more willing to identify with the good of the organizations. In my view, all this is secured because organizations are, paradoxically, willing to treat their members more as individuals than as interchangeable automatons—and to specify rules, curiously enough, that provide opportunities for individual initiative. To use a phrase popularized by Peters and Waterman, U.S. businesses have figured out the right balance of "loose-tight" controls. For example, a CEO may dictate the choice of an ERP system and may even closely monitor its implementation, but also leave ample scope for employees to exercise individual initiative and creativity.

On the higher-education front, according to most sources that I have reviewed, the United States is at or near the top of advanced countries in college enrollment (or the percentage of the adult population with college degrees.) According to UNESCO, the gross enrollment ratios in tertiary education (i.e., the percentage of the college-age population that actually enrolls) in the United States was 72.6 percent (in 2000)—higher than the 56.4 percent average for all developed countries. Similarly, according to OECD data, the United States had (by one definition) the highest percentage of the population aged 25 to 64 with a tertiary education.[53]

U.S. universities charge higher tuitions than those of any other country, but this may have helped them develop relatively robust financing structures. For instance, according to the *Economist*, by mobilizing private resources, the United States can spend twice as much on higher education (as a proportion of its GDP) as Germany. German universities (nearly all of which are state run) stopped charging tuition in October 1970, "in the

---

* This should come as no surprise to anyone who has observed the traffic on the roads of Rome or Mumbai. Indian driving and car-maintenance habits also ought to give pause to those who believe that people living in the United States have an unusually large appetite for risk or low fear of the consequences of failure.

name of access for all." Unfortunately, "ever-rising student numbers" stoked by free tuition "then met ever-shrinking budgets, so the reforms backfired. Today, the number of college drop-outs is among the highest in the rich world, making tertiary education an elite activity: only 22% of young Germans obtain a degree, compared with 31% in Britain and 39% in America. German universities come low in world rankings, so good students often go abroad."[54]

U.S. colleges, according to some observers, also seem more able to cultivate learning habits and attitudes that enhance graduates' capacity to contribute to innovative activity. As the president of an Ivy League university put it: "In the U.S., you become a participant in education, not a victim of education, not a passenger. My experience in studying in Mexico, in France and in Germany is that it's highly passive. You can go into a classroom and sit there and not have to do anything or say anything. You certainly never do one thing that's very important in the United States: you never challenge the professors, the thought leaders."[55] According to the *Economist*, the Japanese educational system was designed 60 years ago to train children for "long, uncomplaining hours on production lines." Now the economy has "changed out of all recognition," but the educational system has retained its "emphasis on facts and figures and drilling of mental arithmetic."[56]

■ Concluding Comments

In previous chapters, we saw that useful innovations combine many different kinds—and levels—of know-how. Here we examined some of the elements of the modern U.S. system that have underpinned its exceptional capacity for developing and deploying useful innovations: a high level of inclusiveness and participation; a wide diversity of organizational forms; venturesome beliefs that embrace new technologies and goods, sometimes at the expense of thrift; a premium on growth; the capacity to systematically manage the development marketing and use of new technologies; and tertiary education that promotes the skills and attitudes necessary to develop and acquire new knowledge.

Although I did not discuss how the elements interact, they surely reinforce each other: high enrollment in colleges promotes wide participation in the innovation system, which then improves economic opportunities for college graduates. Attractive prospects in turn encourage many to incur the high costs of a college education. Similarly, professional sales techniques help users deploy new products effectively, which then nurture a predisposition to buy new products. The predisposition, in turn, encourages innovators to develop new products—and to invest in sales and marketing. In other words, modern innovation is sustained by a system of interconnected elements rather than through the simple addition of causal factors.

The system is elusive in that we cannot fully understand how all the elements interact or what their ultimate sources are. It is highly likely that my list of elements is incomplete; even with the elements listed I cannot provide a sensible scheme for their measurement or quantification. More importantly, in thinking about how public policies might nurture or advance innovation, it is crucial to keep in mind these elusive and systemic underpinnings. This is what techno-nationalists and techno-fetishists fail to do, as I will argue in the next and concluding chapter. As a consequence, their prescriptions are liable to do more harm than good.

16

■ First Do No Harm

In previous chapters, I disputed the techno-nationalist prediction that disastrous consequences await the United States should its lead in cutting-edge science diminish. However overly dire forecasts can lead to desirable outcomes, particularly given the human tendency toward optimism and inertia, and people can make good choices for the wrong reasons. "Paranoid" executives like Intel's Andy Grove, for instance, can drive their businesses to exceptional performance partly by exaggerating the threat their rivals pose. Smokers who take fright from false signs of a heart attack may actually quit. Similarly, even if their analysis of globalization is wrong, the techno-nationalist remedies could, in principle, increase prosperity.

In fact, even though techno-nationalists use the competitive threat from China and India as a rallying cry, they do offer other justifications for their prescriptions. As mentioned in the introduction and chapter 7, the formula for maintaining the U.S. (or European or British) lead vis-à-vis Chinese and Indian upstarts has two main ingredients: expand subsidies and tax incentives to undertake cutting-edge research; and increase public funding for training more scientists and engineers to do this research. Apart from the competitive advantages these policies are supposed to bestow, advocates also claim that they represent a worthwhile investment of public funds because of externalities and spillover effects, regardless of what might happen because of globalization. Economists from the hot new field of "endogenous growth theory" also espouse these measures, again without relying on arguments about globalization.

One possible reason these policies have emotional appeal is that they evoke memories of the vigorous U.S. response to the *Sputnik* scare five decades ago. Politicians and the media vastly exaggerated the Soviet space lead, but it is now widely asserted—by the National Academies' *Gathering Storm* report among others—that the shock was a galvanizing event that gave science and technology in the United States funding and attention that ultimately had a huge economic payoff. The subtext to the popular narrative is that even if the Chinese and Indian threat turns out to be a false alarm, only good can come out of more investment in scientific research.

In this concluding chapter, I argue that, notwithstanding this apparent consensus, increasing subsidies for scientific education and research will not serve up a free lunch. Constituencies that benefited from the *Sputnik* scare are happy to advertise what they achieved with the resources they secured, but a proper accounting must also include the opportunity costs; in the view of some observers, these have exceeded the benefits. Walter McDougall, for example, says it is wrong to believe "that the American people need 'another Sputnik' to increase U.S. competitiveness in space or technology." The country "does not need another ill-conceived spasmodic reaction to some humiliation that does not pose an immediate threat."[1]

Modern societies have undeniably derived great benefit from cutting-edge research; but ever more of a good thing doesn't make it great. Up to a point, proteins are good for you, but an all-protein diet isn't the most nutritious. More than four decades ago, British economists, Carter and Williams, cautioned that "it is easy to impede growth by excessive research, by having too high a percentage of scientific manpower engaged in adding to the stock of knowledge and too small a percentage engaged in using it. This is the position in Britain today."[2] Similarly, I will argue there is little evidence of an "undersupply" or a need for public polices to stimulate the production of more high-level know-how or to subsidize the training of more homegrown scientists and engineers. Rather, given the realities of modern innovation, there is a good argument for *reversing* policy biases against the development—and even more importantly—the effective use of mid- and ground-level innovations. Public policies should stop trying to rob mid- and ground-level Peters to pay high-level Pauls.

■ An Inevitable Expansion

My skepticism does not derive from any dogmatic belief that the state has no business interfering with business. It is all very well to say that that government is best which governs least; but what's the least? The legal and regulatory role of governments—at all levels—in the United States and the resources they control have increased vastly since the founding of the Republic. Many public choice theorists suggest that the expansion is the inevitable and unfortunate consequence of special interests politics. Does this mean then that the Founding Fathers made a mistake in their initial design, or does democracy inevitably lead to overbearing government?

My more benign explanation for some of the expansion in the role of government is that the great technological advances that occurred after the eighteenth century increased what most people would consider the minimal roles of government on a variety of fronts.

Consider property rights. These are sometimes considered natural, but they have features that do not occur in nature—territories in the animal kingdom cannot be rented or sold, for instance. Rather, it is the state that permits transactions in land by recording deeds, maintaining land records, settling disputes, and evicting trespassers.* The transformation of U.S. society from agrarian to industrial created the need to define and enforce new kinds of intellectual property. Initially, this effort comprised patents on "inventions"; then as economic activity became more specialized and diverse, the scope of what could be regarded as intellectual property expanded to include brand names, logos, designs, software code, and even customer lists. Legal protections had to be defined and enforced for such property through new state interventions such as copyright legislation, the policing of counterfeiting, and the expansion of common laws governing trade secrets.

New technologies created the need for new rules to coordinate interactions between individuals or groups. The invention of the automobile, for example, necessitated the formulation and enforcement of driving rules and a system of vehicle inspections. The growth of air travel required a system to control traffic and certify the air worthiness of aircraft. Similarly, radio and television required a system to regulate the use of the airwaves in order to avoid the collision of signals by competing broadcasters.

---

* The idea that state power is necessary for individual rights to property goes back to at least Thomas Hobbes's writings in the mid–seventeenth century.

Modern technology created new forms of pollution that didn't exist in agrarian economies. Governments had to step in, in one way or the other, making it unrewarding to pollute. Similarly, antitrust laws to control commercial interactions and conduct emerged after new technologies created opportunities to realize economies of scale and scope—and realize oligopoly or monopoly profits. These opportunities were largely absent in preindustrial economies.

Government action has facilitated the provision of "positive" externalities (or public goods) that support the development and use of new technologies. Governments have, for example, financed, built, and operated interstate highways that have catalyzed the use of automobiles and a network of airports that have sustained the expansion of air travel. In principle, private enterprise could have been harnessed for the highways and airports, but it is hard to imagine how such efforts could have been accomplished without a government more active than were governments in the United States in the eighteenth century. For instance, such projects could have been "privately" financed through bond issues rather than through budgetary appropriations. But large-scale bond issuance also requires more extensive legal machinery for enforcing contracts than is necessary for the much simpler and localized process of credit in an agrarian economy.

Similarly, the expansion of higher education has supported technological progress. To a degree (unlike, say, traffic rules), private initiatives can support some level of higher education without government involvement. But many believe that availability of higher education to anyone who is capable of doing the work, regardless of parental income, is a valuable public good that governments ought to support. Therefore, even though the private delivery and financing of higher education is unusually high in the United States, college enrollments have almost certainly been raised by direct grants to state universities and by indirect government support through student loan programs.

Technological advances have also stimulated the expansion of the U.S. government's role in redistributing income, through progressive taxation and a variety of income-maintenance programs. This has occurred in two ways. First, technology amplifies differences in economic rewards that can result from differences in individual talent and temperament—and even luck. When agricultural technology was relatively primitive, one settler who received title to 160 acres under the Homestead Act could expect to make roughly the same living from farming the land as his neighbor. With modern technology, however, farmers who have the ability to use tractors, harvesters, hybrid seeds, crop rotation techniques, and futures markets to hedge their output—or have good fortune in their choices—can earn significantly higher returns than those who don't. Like it or not, in democratic societies differences in outcomes create irresistible political pressure to create equal opportunities for the offspring of the less well-to-do.

Second, technology changes workers from undifferentiated providers of simple effort to individuals with specialized skills and knowledge who are not interchangeable. This encourages employers to value continuity—it is costly to replace a programmer who quits in the middle of a project. And, since Henry Ford's audacious five dollars a day in pay was shown to do the trick,[3] U.S. employers have learned to pay "efficiency wages"—a premium over what the worker can earn elsewhere. However, although efficiency wages provide high earnings as long as workers keep their jobs, workers also experience a commensurate drop in earnings if they get laid off. Moreover, in a technologically advanced economy, matching a specific worker's skills and knowledge with a specific employer's requirements can be difficult; therefore, unemployment sometimes stretches on. In technologically backward economies (as I observed in my recent field research in India), labor turnover is high, and many employers regard the very notion of efficiency wages as madness (just as other employers in the United States did at the time of Henry Ford). Therefore, quitting or being fired is of much less consequence.[4] Long-lived bonds of community and family that can provide a cushion during hard times also seem to be weaker in technologically advanced societies. Therefore, there is strong political pressure on governments in modern economies to provide safety nets for workers who face a sharp drop in income when they lose their jobs.

■ Warranted Interventions?

Even if the "least" that governments should do tends to increase with technological progress, this does not mean that we should embrace the opposite principle, that that government governs best which governs most. It's one thing for the Federal Aviation Administration to manage the air traffic control system, but quite another for the Civil Aeronautics Board (b. 1938, d. 1985) to regulate airfares, routes, and schedules. The Founding Fathers' mistrust of excessive concentration of power remains apt for the modern U.S. economy, especially when it comes to policies to promote innovation.

First, innovation is an uncertain process whose direction is extremely hard to predict. "Markets" can get it wrong, but when many individuals and firms exercise independent judgments, there is a higher probability that *someone* will get it right than when a single judgment is made by a centralized authority. Second, as Hayek pointed out in 1945, centralized authorities lack the specific knowledge of the "man on the spot." Hayek wrote that when "rapid adaptation to changes in the particular circumstances of time and place" is necessary, "decisions must be left to the people who are familiar with these circumstances, who know directly of the relevant changes and of the resources immediately available to meet them."[5] Third, power corrupts, and special interests hijack the good interventions of government for dubious ends. The construction of the interstate highway system may have been a great boon to the U.S. economy, for example, but it did not take long for Congress to start appropriating funds for bridges to nowhere.

Entrepreneurial "leaps into the dark" are therefore best sustained by great caution in expanding the scope of government intervention—the private virtue of daring can be a public vice. The U.S. chief justice has often repeated the maxim: "If it is not necessary to decide an issue to resolve a case, then it is necessary *not* to decide that issue." Similarly, if it is not necessary to intervene to promote innovation, it should be considered necessary *not* to intervene. Among other things, such a maxim makes more attention and time available for interventions that are necessary or at least more useful. Federal regulation of air traffic control and safety is likely to be better if the government avoids expending resources on regulating ticket prices, for instance.

I find it helpful to make a distinction between two kinds of interventions: one in which autonomous private initiative (or Hayek's "spontaneous order") completely fails to coordinate joint activities (as in the case of traffic laws) or control negative externalities (as in the case of pollution); and the other, when private enterprise does supply desirable goods, but allegedly not in socially desirable quantities. In the latter case, it is very hard for anyone to know what the right quantity is, especially in a complex interconnected system where bottlenecks are difficult to identify and unintended consequence difficult to predict. It is also relatively easy for special interests to exaggerate the need. In my view, therefore, advocates of expanding the supply of their favored good should be required to make a strong case for why it would otherwise be undersupplied (or if the good is subsidized, why the amounts are inadequate).

The two kinds of interventions usually proposed by techno-nationalists are intended to correct an alleged *undersupply*—of cutting-edge research and of scientists and engineers—rather than an *absence* of research and scientists. In fact, in absolute terms, more research is being done than ever before, and the number of scientists and engineers trained in the United States has grown, albeit slowly, over the last decade. How strong is the case that they are not enough—that it would behoove society to move money and people from the activity they would otherwise be engaged in to producing more scientific and engineering know-how, preferably of the cutting-edge variety?

As we will see next, it's much less than compelling.

According to the National Academies' *Gathering Storm* report, "The economic value of investing in science and technology has been thoroughly investigated. Published estimates of return on investment (ROI) for publicly funded R&D range from 20% to 67%." The report apparently relies on 11 studies it lists in a table. A footnote records that many of the authors of the studies "caution about the reliability of the numerical results obtained";[6] this is in spite of the authors' presumably not sharing my skepticism about the robustness of econometric methods discussed in chapter 6. That's not all the doubt one can muster, either.

Only one of the studies, by Cockburn and Henderson, published in 2000, tells us anything about the returns earned over the last decade. All the others are more than 13 years old: seven were published in the 1950s, 1960s, and 1970s, and three between 1981 and 1993. Of course, a critical assumption of the natural sciences is that what's happened in the past will also happen in the future. But in human affairs, this is a precarious stipulation. There has been a great expansion in public funding of R&D and significant changes in the nature of the research funded in the last decade. It's a leap to believe that studies undertaken before that expansion are representative of what happened afterward, much less of what any further expansion of funding will achieve.

Then there is the cherry-picking problem: all but one of the 11 studies cover public spending in specific sectors rather than of the overall public expenditures on R&D. The bias against negative results in academic research is well known. It would be easy to compile extensive lists of projects that almost certainly did not produce an economic return, but it would be virtually impossible to get such lists published—at least in a reputable academic journal. Note also what kind of research the studies cover: nine of the 11 estimate the returns from publicly funded research of hybrid corn, poultry, tomato harvesters, and other agricultural subjects. The 2000 study covered pharmaceuticals. Only Mansfield's 1991 study was broad—it covered all academic science research—but the data on which it was based is now practically ancient history.*

Finally, why should we expect the now much broader portfolio of publicly financed scientific research to yield measurable economic returns? Most proposals aren't evaluated on the basis of their economic returns and rarely contain claims that they will have any such impact—federally funded agricultural research with clear practical goals is the exception rather than the rule. Some kinds of scientific research may end up producing economic returns by accident, but that's not its goal. I have personally reviewed fine National Science Foundation proposals that were likely to produce interesting insights but no economic return to taxpayers.

I'm not arguing for reducing public funding of science. Rich countries ought to give serious consideration to supporting activities such as public gardens, art, museums, theaters, and broadcasts—and scientific research—that can enrich the lives of their own citizens (or even those of other countries) and of future generations, without regard to their measurable economic payoffs. But equally, I believe it is disingenuous to argue for an expansion of public funding for scientific research on the grounds that it will produce high economic returns or other material benefits.

In a thoughtful essay, "The Many Purposes of Science," Dick Teresi recounts the appearance of physicist Robert Wilson's congressional testimony to secure $250 million for building Fermilab, the largest particle accelerator in the world. A friendly congressman tossed a softball question that gave Wilson the opportunity to justify the new atom smasher using national defense. Wilson insisted that it had "nothing at all" to do with national security. Rather, Wilson said, "It has only to do with the respect with which we regard one another, the dignity of men, and our love of culture. It has to do with, are

---

* A similar cherry-picking can be seen in the glowing reviews of post-*Sputnik* policies: they focus on the initiatives that apparently did some good, such as the National Defense Education Act, rather than perform a cost-benefit analysis of the full package of policies.

we good painters, good sculptors, great poets? I mean all the things we really venerate and honor in our country and are patriotic about. It has nothing to do directly with defending our country except to make it worth defending."[7] Similarly, public funding for most scientific research should be justified principally on how it enriches our lives, not how it will increase GDP.

The *Gathering Storm* report also cites studies compiled by the President's Council of Economic Advisors in 1995,[8] of the rates of return on private (rather than publicly funded) investment in research and development. A table summarizes the results of eight studies, each of which shows that "the ROI [return on investment] to the nation is generally higher than is the return to individual investors," typically by a factor of at least two. Again, the research is not current—the most recent study was published in 1993—and the estimation procedure turns on arbitrary assumptions.[9] But let us grant that private R&D investment has indeed produced much higher returns for society than it has for the investors, through some combination of a consumer surplus or through spillovers of technical knowledge that reduced the costs of someone else's research.

So what? Techno-nationalists would have us believe that a gap between social and private returns indicates money that was left on the table: if individuals and firms had been able to appropriate more of the returns that "leaked" into society, for instance, through a subsidy or tax credit, they would have undertaken more R&D, and everyone would have been better off. This logic, as I argued in the introduction, turns on some heroic assumptions.

First off, greater financial incentives don't always elicit more effort, and more effort doesn't always produce better results. To illustrate: I am highly confident that Roger Federer's superb performances at Wimbledon have produced a huge consumer surplus for fans—very likely (if we could somehow quantify it) far in excess of Federer's prize money and the pleasure he derived from winning the tournament. In technical language, the social return to Federer's effort has probably been much higher than his private return. I am highly doubtful that the expectation of larger financial reward (because of more prize money, or tax breaks on his earnings) would have induced Federer to train or play harder and thus brought even more joy to fans. More likely, the existing level of prize money and prestige, in conjunction with fierce competition from players such as Rafael Nadal, make Federer play as well as he knows how. Similarly, it is far from obvious that providing greater incentives for R&D would actually have generated more useful know-how. It might be easier for a pharmaceutical company to increase its research budgets than it is for Federer to devote more effort to playing tennis at Wimbledon; but as recent experience shows, in the absence of good targets and good compounds to attack these targets, companies can spend billions of dollars without developing a single successful drug.

In addition, as I have repeatedly emphasized, the development and effective deployment of new products entails the development and use of many different levels (high, middle, and ground) and kinds (scientific, engineering, managerial, sales, and marketing) of know-how. R&D investments cannot produce the full range of this know-how; and, if the kind of know-how produced by R&D is not the bottleneck, increasing such know-how may do little good. On the contrary, it could do harm. Returning to the Federer example, inducing Federer to play better through more prize money (even if it could be done) might do less to increase the surplus of viewers than, for instance, buying better courtside TV cameras. Moreover, if paying more prize money requires skimping on cameras, viewers could be worse off rather than better off.

Similarly, the development of other kinds of know-how, and not just technical knowledge, can generate valuable spillovers. As discussed in chapter 15, the professionalization of IBM's marketing and sales processes helped promote wider and more effective use of its computers. But this professionalization didn't benefit IBM alone and its direct customers. The know-how was widely disseminated throughout the high-tech industry to the benefit of a large number of innovators and their customers. Indeed, one of the advantages that upstart innovators enjoy today is an ample supply (a "thick market") of professional sales personnel; so a business that develops an attractive product can ramp up revenues quickly and efficiently. Similarly, as also discussed in chapter 15, developers of the managerial know-how necessary to effectively deploy IT cannot prevent its leakage. As much as companies such as Wal-Mart would like to keep such knowledge to themselves, it inevitably spills over to other companies through employees, consultants who help install the systems, and vendors of the systems.

In other words, the historical difference between private and social returns on R&D investments does not justify even the retroactive claim that policies to divert resources to R&D would have improved the common good. To be true, such a claim would require at least the following conditions: the resources would have been productively used, and more R&D would not have reduced some other activity that played a more critical role in generating consumer surplus or in producing more valuable spillovers. But such a determination is simply impossible to make; studies on the social return of R&D can at best provide an account of what transpired; they are not scientifically controlled experiments: they cannot tell us what would have happened if more resources had been deployed in R&D. Therefore, under the principle that governments should not make wild gambles with taxpayers' funds, the research cited by *Gathering Storm* does not sustain an argument for increasing subsidies to private R&D any more than it does the funding of more scientific research.

The now fashionable "endogenous growth" theory's case for intervention derives from mathematical models rather than empirical research. At the risk of extreme oversimplification, the origins of this theory can be traced back to pioneering work in economist Paul Romer's doctoral dissertation. In what is widely regarded as brilliant mathematical coup, Romer constructed a model of the economy with a revolutionary feature: economic growth was driven by new ideas and advances in technology, and, more importantly, governments could establish incentives to stimulate such advances and thus economic growth. Older growth theories (such as Robert Solow's) also attributed economic growth to technological progress, but they could not mathematically model a role for public policy. Therefore, these theorists were forced to assume that technological advances arrived like manna from heaven—their quantity was "exogenous" rather than "endogenously" determined by government intervention.

But what was the cash value, as the pragmatist philosopher William James might have called it, of this breakthrough? Would the treatments derived from it meet an FDA test of greater efficacy vis-à-vis current therapies? Outside the never-never land of closed-form mathematical models, the ideas do not appear to be especially revelatory. Rulers in the Middle Ages knew the value of know-how and were prepared to provide financial incentives to secure it. The U.S. Constitution contained the Copyright and Patent Clause, empowering Congress to "promote the Progress of Science and useful Arts, by securing for limited Times to Authors and Inventors the exclusive Right to their respective Writings and Discoveries."

Around 2002, Romer, by then (and as now) a professor at Stanford's business school, proposed a scheme to boost the number of undergraduates majoring in science, mathematics, and engineering. Under Romer's scheme, the government would provide grants to universities based on their success in increasing the proportion of students majoring in these fields. "The United States should lead the world in the fraction of 24-year-olds who receive science and engineering degrees," said Romer. "Unfortunately, by this measure, we now lag far behind many other nations." Romer also proposed a $1 billion program to provide 50,000 fellowships for graduate work in the natural sciences and engineering.[10]

Romer argues that his scheme for subsidizing the supply of scientists and engineers is more market-friendly than is subsidizing research projects. It is also less vulnerable to cronyism and pork barrel politicking—congressional R&D "earmarks" in the 2008 budget amounted to about $2 billion, including more than $500 million for "performer-specific" projects.[11] Nonetheless, the Romer scheme is inarguably interventionist—it assumes that labor markets tend to get it wrong, so that too many students who should do graduate work in physics or engineering wind up going to business schools (such as Stanford), or law schools, or don't go to graduate school at all and become salespersons.

But why is it in society's interest to bribe them to do otherwise? Romer argues, in an eloquent essay on economic growth, that scientists and engineers "are the basic input into the discovery process, the fuel that fires the innovation engine. No one can know where newly trained young people will end up working, but nations that are willing to educate more of them and let them follow their instincts can be confident that they will accomplish amazing things."[12]

How much more though, and what's enough? Filling up the "innovation engine" with scientific and engineering fuel is fine, but not if this means driving with poorly inflated tires. Recall the paper, coauthored by Romer's colleague Bresnahan, about how the problem of co-invention (developing ground-level know-how in my terminology) held up the adoption of client-server architectures. "Technological progress," the paper concluded, "is not just bits and bytes," and it isn't limited simply by technical difficulties. In the case of many IT systems, because the technology advances more quickly and easily than ground-level managerial know-how, "the co-invention of organizational change" becomes the bottleneck.[13] It is reasonable to infer that such bottlenecks are more likely to be eased by a more ample supply of managers, rather than by scientists or engineers. But this is precisely what Romer's scheme to train 50,000 more scientists and engineers tilts against.

The share of managerial and professional jobs in the United States has increased from about one in six in 1940, to about one in three today.[14] In the last couple of decades, the growth has taken place in a climate of cost-cutting, restructuring, and reengineering, and probably does not reflect a spontaneous increase in bureaucratization of U.S. companies. More likely, it follows from the growth of activities, particularly in the expanding service sector, that are difficult to coordinate and in which economies of scale and scope are difficult to come by. These managers have been responsible for efforts to improve productivity through the use of technologies such as ERP (or client-server computing) that may require a much higher ratio of managerial to technical personnel than did productivity-increasing technologies in the manufacturing sector. In other words, the labor market may not have gotten it monumentally wrong. Interventions to train more scientists and engineers may well impair, rather than increase, productivity growth.

Other endogenous-growth theorists have different proposals to promote cutting-edge research, but none that I'm aware of provides a convincing rationale for their favored scheme for putting the government finger on the market scale. My conjecture is that the prescriptions of growth theorists reflect the assumptions of their models. In order to be mathematically tractable, the models lump all knowledge into a single category, like land, labor, or capital, without making distinctions between the levels or kinds of knowledge or how it is generated. At least some of the theorists fully understand the many forms that knowledge can assume: Romer's essay on economic growth acknowledges that "it takes more than scientists in universities to generate progress and growth," and that the "seemingly mundane . . . development of new business models can have huge benefits."[15]

The mathematical models used by the growth theorists, however, do not—and in fact cannot—accommodate many distinctions between different kinds of know-how. At the same time, it is hard to imagine policy instruments that could stimulate the production of all the various forms of knowledge generated by the massively multiplayer innovations game that sustains economic growth. Therefore, when theorists try to apply their finding (that it is good for society to invest in knowledge), they conflate knowledge with just one thing—namely, technical knowledge produced by engineers and scientists. The end result is that a theory that is inherently harmless (and without practical implications) can generate negative "cash value," by suggesting policies that may do more harm than good.

■ Against the Tide

The prescription to subsidize more U.S. science and train more home-grown scientists and engineers also fails to take into account the growing share of the service sector in the U.S. economy; the emergence of China and India as new sources of research, and, finally, technological and managerial developments. As I will argue in this section, these three trends reduce, rather than increase, the value of expanding the domestic supply of research and researchers.

A report by the National Association of Manufacturers points out that the manufacturing sector, which produces just 12 percent of U.S. GDP, accounts for 42 percent of R&D undertaken in the country and "employs 25% of scientists and related technicians and 40% of engineers and engineering technicians."[16] The service sector, which produces about 70 percent of U.S. GDP, presumably accounts for a disproportionately low share of R&D and scientific and engineering employment. But this doesn't mean that the service sector shuns innovation. Rather, as Dirk Pilat notes: "R&D in services is often different in character from R&D in manufacturing. It is less oriented toward technological developments and more at co-development, with hardware and software suppliers, of ways to apply technology, in particular ICT, to deliver services. The research may, for example, be aimed at improving interfaces with customers, and also increasingly involve human factors, psychology and design."

"Most service innovations," continues Pilat, "are non-technical and mostly involve small and incremental changes in processes and procedures [and] often do not meet the criteria for patenting." Patent counts therefore understate the true extent of service-sector innovation. Moreover, "Expenditure on R&D is only one element of firms' expenditure on innovation. For manufacturing, R&D generally amounts to about half of total investment in innovation," whereas "R&D expenditure captures only a small part of the total innovative effort of service firms" that typically "involves changes in processes, organisational arrangements and markets."

In other words, whatever might be the level of resources a manufacturing-dominated economy should devote to formal research and the education of scientists, we should expect this level to be lower in a predominantly services-based economy.

The growth of research capabilities in China and India also dampens the need for governments in the United States (and other rich countries) to direct more resources to science and engineering. As I have argued in several chapters of this book, cutting-edge research, regardless of where it is produced, is either a free public good for the world at large or available at a low cost to users everywhere. Similarly, less well-to-do countries such as India have arguably over invested in engineering education and trained many individuals who, given the opportunity, would eagerly migrate to the United States.

Moreover, U.S. industry would not have to learn any new tricks to capitalize on overseas research and technology. Technologies used in the United States have never been fully or even largely homegrown—there is a long history of adapting for domestic use technologies developed abroad. According to the British economist Von Tunzelmann, the United States "borrowed British industrial products and technologies in the nineteenth century, but wasted little time before re-engineering them to suit American conditions. While the new technologies developed in the USA were rather modest contributions to the sum total of human technological knowledge before the twentieth century, it would also be inaccurate to describe those used in U.S. industry as simple copies of the British. It was less a case of imitation than of re-invention in the eyes of Marshall. A major element in that re-invention procedure was speeding up British practices; examples include the ring spindle in place of the mule in the U.S. cotton spinning industry, and hard driving in the U.S. steel industry."

That reinvention also involved a greater focus on mass markets: "Whereas many British items were customized for wealthy purchasers, Americans concentrated on cheaper, more standardized items for the whole community—an example much referred to in the mid-nineteenth century was guns, where (military purposes aside) the British concentrated on sporting pieces for the aristocracy, while the Americans produced rifles and, later, pistols in large quantities for the small farmers and cowboys." A mass-market focus favored adapting technologies for standardization and high-volume production: "Even items that might be expected to be individually tailored were vastly more standardized in the USA, such as boots and shoes."[17]

By the end of World War I, according to Maddison, the United States had become the leading developer of new technologies. Yet considerable technological give-and-take with other advanced economies continued. Eaton and Kortum examined the growth in productivity in West Germany, France, the

UK, and the United States between 1950 and 1990. According to their analysis, the growth of the first four countries, which started far behind the United States at the start of the period, was "primarily the result of research performed abroad." Notwithstanding its overall lead, "even the United States obtain[ed] over 40% of its growth from foreign innovations." These findings, according to Eaton and Kortum, are "consistent with historical accounts" of the importance of foreign technology to the United States, such as Mueller's[18] description of "the foreign inventions underlying DuPont's innovations."[19]

We have no reason to suppose that the U.S. capacity to use technologies developed abroad declined after 1990. Rather, because of factors such as the increasing flows of information, ("the death of [communications] distance") and the growing operations of U.S. firms abroad (and of foreign multinationals in the United States), it has very likely increased.

This is not to suggest that, either from an economic or moral point of view, the United States should become a freeloader and rely exclusively on research (or researchers) produced abroad. Rather, my argument is that just as the rich make larger contributions to the arts than the not-so-well-off, prosperous countries can and should contribute more to research on string theory or the decoding of the genome than poor countries. As prosperity becomes more widespread, we should expect more countries to contribute to the world's stock of scientific knowledge. This helps, rather than hurts, the countries that once took the main responsibility. The declining share of U.S. scientific research and researchers that so alarms economists such as Romer and Freeman does not, in fact, require the U.S. government to increase its funding for these activities. Rather, the expansion of the overseas supply of research and researchers should make the U.S. government *more*, not less, willing to let markets determine what kind of innovative activities secure capital and talent.

Finally, new technologies and better management techniques contribute to reducing the proportion of the workforce that needs deep scientific and engineering training. As mentioned (in chapter 14), new programming tools and techniques and cheap hardware allow individuals of modest technical ability or training to write code. In fact, for many programming tasks, it is not even necessary to have formal training in computer science. Similarly, as mentioned (in chapter 11), in 2005, an estimated 80 million individuals in the United States used computers in the workplace. While most users likely made a significant investment in learning to use computers, the great majority weren't trained programmers. Yet, they could "develop applications" to suit their needs because spreadsheet and database programs (with increasingly easy-to-use interfaces) have made it possible for them to do so.

Better management techniques have also helped individuals without deep technical training harness new technologies. The legendary architect Frank Gehry provides an interesting (if extreme) example. According to an article in the *Wall Street Journal*, "Mr. Gehry's buildings are as much feats of engineering as they are of architecture," but there are no computers in his office. Gehry told Sharma (the article's author) that he didn't know how to turn on a DVD and could "barely use the technology" in his car. "The actual physics and engineering of Mr. Gehry's buildings," Sharma wrote, "are managed by teams of employees. Some 150 people work for him, and when Mr. Gehry talks about what exactly he does that leads to a building, it seems that he is almost more a manager of personalities and processes than he is someone who sits down with pencil and paper."[20] Similarly, Wal-Mart's founder, Sam Walton, was also very far from a computer whiz; he was nonetheless able to use IT to build the world's largest retailing chain by hiring and supervising IT executives, who in turn built a large IT staff.

Here, too, I'm not suggesting that technological advances have made training in computer science obsolete. To a great degree, Google has become a valuable and universal tool because of the contributions of superbly trained engineers and scientists. My argument is simply that new technologies and management know-how provide much more leverage: the talents of a few great programmers go a much longer way than they once did, so a smaller proportion of users need to actually learn how to program.

■ Redressing the High-level Bias

If increasing government support for high-level research is unwarranted, are there any other changes or policy adjustments that the modern U.S. economy would benefit from? I argue next that there is a worthy case for reversing long-standing policy bias in favor of high-level innovation and against the development, and even more importantly, deployment of innovative mid- and ground-level products.

A useful starting point is a paper that Stanford economist Paul David wrote in 1986, in the midst of high anxiety about the Japanese threat to U.S. competitiveness. David wrote that innovation had become a "cherished child, doted upon by all concerned with maintaining competitiveness . . . whereas diffusion has fallen into the woeful role of Cinderella, a drudge like creature who tends to be overlooked when the summons arrives to attend the Technology Policy Ball."[21] Pointing out that diffusion (the use of new technologies) was at least as important, David made the following points about how this was affected by public policies.

1. Overt efforts to promote the diffusion of innovations are modest in terms both of money and attention devoted to them. They usually comprise efforts to disseminate information (such as agricultural extension or "technology transfer" programs in the United States) or the payment of subsidies to adopters of new technologies (such as those offered to purchasers of robots in Japan).

2. The range of policies that actually affect the adoption of new technologies is quite broad. These include the "tax treatment of investment, the funding of R&D, the education of scientists and engineers, regulation and standard setting, as well as the monetary and fiscal measures shaping the macroeconomic environment."

3. Speeding up the rate of technology adoption isn't always in the public interest; sometimes, slowing it down could be more beneficial.

4. Policies to quicken or retard the adoption of new technologies should only be undertaken after "explicit assessments" of the varied and changing environments of different industries: an "absolutely indispensable ingredient in the formulation of rational economic policies" vis-à-vis diffusion is "detailed assessments on an industry-by-industry basis."

5. The processes of the development and diffusion of new technologies are closely intertwined; therefore, "intelligent" policymaking would take a more "integrated" approach to designing innovation and diffusion policies.[22]

My analysis suggests implications that are in many ways similar to David's observations, save in two respects. First, I question the utility of a case-by-case approach. I have little doubt that the binding constraints or pinch points vary significantly from situation to situation, but the record of case-by-case interventions is not inspiring. The approach obviously invites efforts, both overt and covert, by lobbies to secure results that suit their private ends. The process of public policymaking is also slow, and, indeed, to secure the legitimacy of openness and the accommodation of many points of view, public policy ought to be formulated with all due deliberation in most cases. But technologies and their associated bottlenecks keep changing, so interventions that might have been apropos yesterday may be irrelevant tomorrow. There is no point, for instance, in promoting "hardwired" broadband connections to the Internet if we are on the verge of a cheaper or better wireless alternative.

Moreover, suppose policymakers could identify the "right" bottlenecks across all industries in a timely manner: they would face the problem of formulating effective responses. As I have argued in this book, the development and the use of new technologies has entrepreneurial features that lie outside the domain of mainstream economics, and, while we may crudely describe their manifestations, their underpinnings are elusive. But economic and policy analysts tend to focus on measurable indicators and relationships. The danger is that such an orientation may not only fail to touch the larger and more elusive barriers to progress, but may actually increase them.

Second, the same concerns about our profound ignorance of the underlying factors make me skeptical about "integrated approaches" to promoting technology development and diffusion. Integrated approaches may be fine in principle, but do we know enough to implement them?

A proper appreciation of the complexity and elusiveness of the modern innovation systems does not lead to new interventions but rather suggests the removal of a long-standing bias in favor of high-level research and the neglect or even impairment of other activities involved in the development and use of lower-level innovations. One obvious example is the provision of subsidies and grants for R&D but not for the marketing of products or the development of ground-level know-how by their users. As we have seen, sales and marketing play a crucial role in realizing the value of innovations. Buyers of new products face significant Knightian uncertainty about the utility of their purchases, and in addition to good information they need some persuasion. In fact, persuasion is an essential ingredient of technological progress—and even when done in the most professional way, often involves the use of smoke and mirrors or psychological manipulation. But far from providing tax credits or subsidies for this important activity, policymakers (and others)* often treat it with indifference or disdain.

---

* I once attended a seminar where a leading developmental economist presented the results of a research project to study why farmers in Africa did not use fertilizer when it was obviously in their interest to do so. The research team had tried a large number of "interventions"—except the use of a commissioned sales force. In any real-world, for-profit business, such an omission would be inconceivable.

Similarly, companies like Wal-Mart may have very large IT budgets and staff who have to develop a great deal of ground-level know-how—and may even develop some in-house systems. But none of this qualifies for R&D incentives. Even mid-level innovators, such as the VC-backed firms I studied, often miss out. They may in principle qualify for R&D subsidies, but in practice, many such firms not only lack the earnings needed to take advantage of tax credits, but often cannot easily segregate R&D outlays and activities from their other functions, such as marketing and sales.

Subsidies to train more scientists and engineers obviously have the same—and in my view unwarranted—bias. They increase the supply of labor for producers of high-level know-how and reduce it for other players in the innovations game.

Other biases against the development and use of mid- and ground-level products that need to be reevaluated are more subtle.

One is the effort to stimulate savings and investment. There appears to be a consensus among policymakers of many stripes that, except possibly in recessions, saving is always virtuous and consumption always undermines long-term growth—a mind-set exemplified by Prestowitz's alarm that the United States "is building its economy into a giant consumption machine."[23] Mechanisms to mobilize savings, such as the stock market and retirement plans, are thus regarded with favor, while mechanisms that facilitate consumption—such as credit cards—are regarded with suspicion. But as I have argued, Max Weber's thesis that capitalism is synonymous with capital accumulation ignores the role of venturesome consumption of innovative goods in a modern economy. Moreover, the young and the impecunious are more likely to have the recklessness of spirit necessary to perform this role. At least up to a point, their spendthrift ways and the credit cards that sustain them are a boon to economic growth; and because there is no knowing what that point might be, there is no justification for promoting or discouraging their behavior.

Similarly, policies to promote long-term investment by providing tax credits for capital outlays also seem outdated. The modern knowledge economy appears to have erased the old boundaries between long-term investment and (supposedly undesirable) short-term spending. Much of what would traditionally have been categorized as spending by users of mid- and ground-level products is, in fact, risky, long-term investment. For instance, as discussed, the purchase price of an ERP system is a fraction of the total cost of ERP projects, but businesses eligible for investment-tax credits for their purchases of computer hardware or software don't receive a tax break for the costs of training users, adapting the system to their needs or reengineering their business processes. It may be that a tax credit for computer hardware also encourages the other, larger outlays. But to the extent that promoting long-term investment is in fact a worthy goal for tax policy, this seems like a roundabout and inefficient way to achieve this purpose. (The tax credit may, for instance, encourage a business to invest more in computers and less in user training and reengineering.)

Immigration policies favor high-level research by preferring highly trained engineers and scientists (i.e. those with PhDs and master's degrees) to individuals with just a bachelor's degree. Supposedly, highly trained individuals required to undertake cutting-edge R&D are scarce, whereas engineering and scientific jobs that don't require advanced degrees can easily be filled in the local labor market. In fact, as I have argued, the highest valued use of talented, native-born individuals may not be scientific and engineering jobs at all; therefore, immigrants who don't have advanced degrees probably make as valuable a contribution as those who have advanced degrees by, for instance, working in the IT departments of, say, retailers and banks. As we also saw in book 1, unlike the R&D labs of large companies, the technical staff of mid-level innovators employ high proportions of immigrants without advanced degrees.

A liberal patent system seems more attuned to the needs of R&D labs than to those of innovators developing mid- and ground-level products. As we saw in book 1, the latter often do not produce patentable IP, whereas patents are the stock in trade of R&D labs. Easily obtained patents by high-level players also pose significant legal risks for developers of mid- and ground-level products whose innovations often combine high-level know-how and inputs. Such a bias would seem particularly perverse in a globalizing economy where the United States has an absolute and comparative advantage in using high-level know-how in lower-level products. Nevertheless, the reflexive high-level bias—the dogma that technological strengths depend on patentable cutting-edge research—is so strong that recent bipartisan efforts to make life easier for users of IP (by making it harder to secure and protect patents) hit "resistance because of concerns that the United States might be exposed to greater foreign competition."*

■ Treating Health Care

The health-care industry provides an important illustration of the high-level bias of public policy—and of the large potential benefits of paying more attention to the development and use of mid- and ground-level innovations. The United States spends more of its national income on health care—about 15.3 percent of 2003 GDP—than any other country in the world. In 1999, U.S. health-care spending stood at 13.1 percent[24] of GDP and, by 2016, is expected to rise to about 19.6 percent. This is not necessarily bad: for instance, if the "nondestructive" development and use of innovations is greater in health care than in the rest of the economy, we should expect health care's share of GDP to increase over time. Similarly, if U.S. citizens prefer to spend more on health—and receive care commensurate with their greater expenditures—than the citizens of other countries, what's the harm?

The development of many treatments for previously untreatable diseases and conditions does point to a high level of "nondestructive creation." Similarly, at the top end, the "best health care that money can buy" in the United States is stellar. Premier institutions (such as the Mayo Clinic) attract wealthy patients from all over the world (including those from countries that have advanced health-care systems). But the overall picture suggests that the United States isn't, on average, getting good value for money spent on health care. According to a 2000 World Health Organization study, the performance of the U.S. health-care system ranked forty-seventh in the world. Such rankings are sensitive to what indicators are included, but even if we consider only the most basic of indicators, the U.S. performance rank is far below its spending rank. According to the *CIA World Factbook*, in 2007, 40 countries had lower infant mortality rates than the United States,[25] and 44 countries had higher total life expectancy.[26]

---

* Rep. Howard Berman, the lead sponsor of the patent reform, said it is "hard for me to understand" how it would hurt the United States. "To the contrary," he argued, "it is the weakness and abuses of the current system that are impeding American innovation." Nonetheless, in the teeth of opposition from the producers of high-level research like the pharmaceutical companies and large research universities, Berman's view did not carry (and, as of this writing, has not carried) the day (Hitt 2007, A3).

The problem most certainly doesn't lie in skimpy government support for high-level medical research. The U.S. government doubled its funding for the National Institutes of Health between 1998 and 2003. According to an OECD study, "Health R&D in government budgets, as a percentage of GDP in 2004" in the United States, was six times the level in Japan and more than 10 times the levels in Austria, Sweden, and Switzerland[27]—all of which had lower infant mortality and higher life expectancy. For-profit companies and foundations like the Howard Hughes Medical Institute put up even more funds: in 2003, tax-funded NIH paid for 28 percent of medical research,[28] while private sources accounted for most of the remaining 72 percent.

But while the U.S. government provides handsome support to research—through direct grants and tax credits for R&D programs—pharmaceutical companies are pilloried by politicians (and other opinion leaders) for their marketing efforts. Big pharma is told to spend more on research and less on peddling "frivolous" drugs; but the frivolous drugs also start in a lab, and even useful drugs can only be effective if they are properly incorporated in a therapeutic regime. As one study suggests, doctors may say they get their information from reading medical journals, but pharmaceutical company salesmen play a more important role in influencing their prescribing habits.[29]

As one salesperson who works for a biotech company told me: "Doctors sometimes dismiss me with 'I already know everything about your product.' But when a patient asks this same omniscient doctor for my product, I get a call needing immediate answers to questions like 'What dose do I use? How do I write the script? Is it IM or IV? Do I inject it in the arm or the butt? Both butt cheeks or one? What does it interact with? What are the contraindications? Will insurance plan X cover it? How do I store it?' "

Without a marketing push, breakthrough treatments may fail to catch on. As Harvard economist David Cutler says, "The biggest failure of the American health care system is not that we overuse stuff, but that we underuse stuff."[30]

Consider the history of using antibiotics to treat ulcers, which suggests an important role for marketing beyond the passive dissemination of information. Warren and Marshall demonstrated a link between *helicobacter pylori* and peptic ulcers in the early 1980s. In 1987, an article published in *Lancet* reported that the eradication of *H. pylori* with antibiotics could effectively cure peptic ulcers. Medical opinion leaders took nearly a decade to be persuaded that ulcers could in fact be cured by antibiotics. Marshall went so far as to infect himself by drinking a Petri dish of *helicobacter pylori* to produce evidence for his theory. Eventually, the establishment was persuaded, and in 2005 Warren and Marshall were awarded the Nobel Prize in medicine.

All this is well known. Equally interesting is what happened after the opinion leaders were persuaded (in the first half of the 1990s) and national and international guidelines on the treatment of *H. pylori* were published. Although the consensus guidelines were clear, pharmaceutical companies did not have an incentive to promote the therapies. A literature review by O'Connor (2002) showed that although there was "widespread acceptance of *H. pylori* as a causal agent" among physicians in principle, there was "significant under-treatment" of peptic ulcers with *H. pylori* therapies. Furthermore, physicians who did use the therapies often used "treatment regimens of doubtful efficacy" instead of following the consensus guidelines.[31]*

Organizational, legal, and regulatory issues (in the "untraded" services subsector of health care) pose an even bigger problem for the health-care system. While the development and pricing of prescription drugs attract a great deal of attention, expenditures on pharmaceuticals in the United States accounted for just 12.9 percent of health-care costs in 2003. While the costs of drugs in the United States are higher than in other OECD countries (which often impose de facto price controls) and the per capita spending on drugs is also higher, the expenditures on pharmaceuticals as a percentage of health-care costs is lower in the United States than for the OECD as a whole. (In 2003, the OECD average was 17.7 percent). This suggests either that the United States gets more, or better, "nonpharmaceutical" health care, or—more likely, given the overall performance of the system—that the United States receives really poor value for nearly 90 percent of its health-care expenditures.

Health-care experts have different views about what needs to be done. Some advocate a broader role for the government, such as mandatory health-care coverage for all or a "single payer" government program to replace private insurance. Others favor more market-oriented solutions. What most

* This data led O'Connor to suggest the use of "some of the methods used by pharmaceutical manufacturers to educate physicians about their products, which are known to be effective and often overshadow the information available in the medical literature."

experts agree on, however, is that there is a very big problem, the solution of which has nothing to do with the quality or quantity of medical research. Rather, it has to do with changing the rules of the game so that hospitals will be better managed, IT will be used more effectively and extensively, and insurance schemes will be better organized. Regardless of whose script you read, the cast comprises hospital administrators, IT managers, entrepreneurs, lawyers, actuaries, and financiers, not MD PhDs decoding genomes.

Harvard's Regina Herzlinger notes that the United States spends $2.2 trillion on health care, yet "more than 40 million Americans lack health insurance, mostly because they cannot afford it." Hospitals account for $400 billion in excessive health-care costs but provide services of increasingly poor quality—hundreds of thousands of patients have been killed by hospital medical errors in the past few years. Innovative entrepreneurs have improved the productivity "in almost every sector" of the U.S. economy, but in the "bloated, inefficient health-care system," innovation has been restricted to medical technologies and health insurance. In health services "entrepreneurs are nowhere to be found," because "status quo providers, abetted by legislators and insurance companies, have made it virtually impossible for them to succeed." Herzlinger's solution (detailed in her book, *Who Killed Health Care?*) is a system that will "allow consumers to reward those entrepreneurs who lower costs by improving health."[32]

Medical research, which already accounts for a large share of taxpayer-funded research, would be a natural beneficiary of its expansion: program administrators can easily justify putting large amounts of money to work, because individual projects have large price tags; they are backed by real—and glamorous—science and often aimed at diseases crying out for a cure. Now proponents of funding more medical research can also evoke the fear of "losing out to the Chinese." According to *BusinessWeek,* in February 2006, "China's State Council announced a big boost in research and development spending," with biotech "as a top priority." The story highlights an experimental gene therapy for treating cancers in which China "is racing to a lead" with "substantial funding and encouragement" from the Chinese government.[33]

But should the U.S. government invest in making U.S. companies winners of every possible such race? How would it hurt U.S. health care (or economic prosperity) if the Chinese government subsidies enabled more cancers to be cured? A techno-nationalist obsession with staying ahead in every possible frontier of medical research, at least on the margin, takes away money and attention from reforming health services, solutions that would provide far greater payoffs and, to a very large degree, remain in the United States (because of the largely nontraded nature of these services).

■ And Finally . . .

In 1779, Adam Smith wrote in a letter to Lord Carlisle, head of the British Board of Trade: "Should the industry of Ireland, in consequence of freedom and good government, ever equal that of England, so much the better would it be not only for the whole British Empire, but for the particular province of England. As the wealth and industry of Lancashire does not obstruct but promote that of Yorkshire, so the wealth and industry of Ireland would not obstruct but promote that of England."[34]

At that time, the First Industrial Revolution had not yet broken out, or (according to some interpretations) may have just started. No one could have foreseen how technology, business, the organization of society, the legal system, and so on would evolve over the next centuries. They could have evolved along the lines of North-South models, in which the economic development of one country could injure well-being in another. As it happens, they didn't. Rather, as discussed in previous chapters (see box, "Why Embrace? A Summary"), as matters actually evolved, advances today, particularly technological ones, tend to raise—not reduce—living standards everywhere. Adam Smith's observation still holds, although for reasons that no one in 1779 could have anticipated.

Why Embrace? A Summary

■ The United States need not worry about an expansion of cutting-edge research (high-level know-how) produced abroad because high-level know-how is highly mobile and cheap: developed in country A, it can be put into production in country B and create a consumer surplus in country C.

The United States, in fact, stands to gain from such an expansion:

- More high-level research provides more raw material for developing mid- and ground-level products.
- A high level of venturesome consumption in the United States encourages innovators to develop products optimized for U.S. customers and to promote their widespread use in the United States.
- These products not only generate a large surplus for U.S. consumers, to the extent they are aimed at the service sector (which now comprises about 70 percent of its GDP), but they also increase the productivity and wages of the U.S. workers.

Moreover:

- Technological innovations could, in principle, upset the apple cart by promoting the offshoring of these service jobs, but nondestructive creation is likely to create new service-industry jobs that don't currently exist.
- Immigrant scientists and engineers don't depress U.S. wages; rather, they (even the nonstellar majority) are a valuable resource in the process of developing and deploying innovations.

This is not to say that the economic and technological development of populous and previously impoverished countries poses no threat to the West. Rapid growth in China and India significantly increases the demand for fossil fuels and may require U.S. consumers to pay much more to drive their cars and to heat their homes. Similarly, as per capita incomes of China and India rise, so does their capacity to pollute the planet. And to turn Mao's maxim around, gun barrels can grow out of economic power—and China's growing military strength naturally disturbs the prevailing geopolitical order.

These problems are neither insurmountable nor unprecedented. Poverty in India has denuded forests on a large scale, as those who could not afford any other source of fuel chopped down trees for firewood. While technology can increase pollution, it can also reduce it. Tractors may burn gasoline, but a plow-horse requires two acres of pasture to graze on, which could be a forest. Thanks to the tripling of its agricultural productivity in the last century, and starting in about 1920, the United States has progressively turned farmland back into forests. Globally, the land area it takes to feed the world is 20 percent less than in 1950, while the population has more than doubled from 2.5 billion to more than 6 billion.[35] New energy-efficient products allowed the U.S. economy to grow by 126 percent from 1973 to 2000, when energy use grew by just 30 percent. Who knows? With enterprise, the right incentives, and some luck, we could see growth with reduced carbon-releasing energy.

China's growing military changes the power balance, but does it necessarily make the world a more dangerous place? Recall that it fought three wars—in Korea, India, and Vietnam—*before* it undertook radical economic reforms. The real danger spots (such as North Korea) aren't the ones supposedly menacing U.S. technological primacy. Developing new approaches that reflect the reality of the new China would improve international security—and that's an investment well worth making. What is perverse and futile, from both an economic and moral point of view, is for the West to try to dial back to the old conditions—or to throw resources at maintaining the technology differential at its current level.

Complacency is dangerous, but jumpy reactions to false alarms can also do real harm. It is one thing to nip trouble in the bud, but going full tilt against imaginary dangers can consume blood, treasure, and attention that could be applied to meaningful threats.* The unduly paranoid can also miss out on attractive opportunities. Perennial pessimists who anticipated another Depression after the 1987 stock market crash missed out on an extraordinary two decades during which prices increased more than fivefold. For the United States to hunker down or to obsess about international technology races is folly. The world has changed and will continue to change, and perhaps one day nations may have to engage in economic combat. But that is not the case now. Today's conditions allow nations to gain from each other's advances, and our challenge lies in making the best of this good fortune.

---

* Not to carp, especially since the *Gathering Storm* has offered a fine foil for me, but might the common interest have been better served if the National Academies had produced a study of carbon taxes that might have helped stiffen some political backbones instead of a report that gives politicians more cover for easy votes to expand research subsidies?

■ Acknowledgments

This book, like most ventures I study, integrates the contributions of many individuals and organizations.

A generous grant from the Kauffman Foundation gave me the time and the research assistance I needed to do the fieldwork and to write this book. I am especially grateful to the Foundation's Judith Cone, Robert Litan, Carl Schramm, and Robert Strom for their confidence that something good would emerge from the more than six-year-long effort.

Jim Robinson and Michel Orban of RRE Ventures started me off with introductions to the CEOs of their portfolio companies; without this help, the project might have been stillborn. Bruns Grayson (of ABS Ventures) and Jean-François Formela (of Atlas Ventures) provided the next tranche of introductions. Then I learned what it must be like to sell insurance door to door. But amid many rejections, former students, old friends, and some new acquaintances did come through. They were, in roughly chronological order: Bob Goodman, Tom Gillis, Scott Weiss, Jed Smith, Chris Winship, Jamie Goldstein, Stacey Lawson, Izhar Armony, Debra Peattie, Lyle Hohnke, Desh Deshpandé, Rich Aldrich, Anders Barsk, Michael Greeley, Zachary Wilhoit, Bob Batty, Tim Connors, Hemant Kanakia, Doug Cole, Michael Bego, Val Rayzman, Kranti Kapre, Andy Sack, Tom Policelli, Steven Kaplan, Tracey Pinsoneault, Marcia Radosevich, Mark Casey, and Paul Tierney.

The 106 CEOs who made time in their busy schedules for interviews played a pivotal role, of course. Unfortunately limitations of space and confidentiality issues preclude me from mentioning their names.

Elizabeth Gordon managed all aspects of the project with great patience, diligence, and skill and also provided excellent overall research support. Columbia undergraduates, including Debra Rudd, Massimo Cordella, John Grando, and Tim Jarvi, cheerfully performed tasks large and small. Hany Syed and Shira Cohen kindly helped out on a voluntary basis.

Tom Austin and Navi Radjou provided data from Gartner's and Forrester's research reports respectively. Jane Berentson and Katie Madden helped Shira Cohen and I conduct a "ministudy" of the cross-border interactions of companies on *Inc.* magazine's 2006 "500" list. Jeanne Batalova, Ronald Bird, and Diana Furchtgott-Roth provided useful leads to data on immigration. Nancy Carter mobilized Catalyst's research resources for me. Subramanian Iyer, Madhu Raghavan, and Raghu Raghavan provided background on the R&D efforts of large companies.

Catherine Mann provided me with source data from her fine book. Uday Karmarkar shared his deep knowledge of the service industry. Pankaj Ghemawat was, as always, a great tutor—on globalization and many other topics. Ashish Arora was responsive beyond the call of collegiality and friendship, providing leads, data, and insights.

Gene Zelazny and Brian McAlley of McKinsey & Co. created a striking illustration for the introduction (after a chance meeting with Gene at a McKinsey alumni event).

Scholars who provided feedback included Carliss Baldwin, William Baumol, Max Bazerman, Alain Bourdeau De Fontenay, Lee Branstetter, Fabrice Cavarretta, Aaron Chatterji, Glenn Hubbard, Walter Kuemmerle, Jerry Muller, Richard Nelson, Geoffrey Owen, Richard Robb, Gus Stuart, and especially Srikant Datar and Howard Stevenson (who read multiple drafts). Friends from business and government who provided a reality check and considerable editorial help included Stephen Adams, Yves De Balmann, Deaver Brown, David Chaffetz, James Dougherty, Don Gogel, Roger Kline, Bill Matassoni, Raymond McConaghy, Lars Östling, Jeff Sandefer, Susan Webber, and Mette Wikborg.

Gina Moucka repeatedly combed through drafts in her inimitably meticulous way—and this is just one of the innumerable kindnesses that she has bestowed over the years.

I have had the great privilege of having lunch with Ned Phelps practically every week from the time I arrived at Columbia in June 2000. The numerous lunches stimulated many ideas that have percolated into this book. Ned also provided me with a high-quality sounding board and the nerve to 'think big' and challenge the common wisdom.

Elizabeth Kadetsky edited the manuscript nearly nonstop from Thanksgiving through the first week of January 2008. How I couldn't say, but somehow she effected an amazing transformation. Richard Isomaki's thoughtful copyediting added both clarity and grace.

During fortnightly visits to Boston I saw Lila turn from tween to teen and enjoyed the warm hospitality of Iain and Johanna Cockburn and my sister Gauri and her husband Michael Romero. The visits provided a break from the pattern that Lila periodically remarked upon: "You should get a life, Daddy."

One day, I might. But I can never repay the enormous obligation I have incurred to you all. I hope that I can defray it a little; meanwhile, my most heartfelt thanks.

■ Appendix: Tables

Table 3.1
Current and Expected Shares of Revenues from Overseas Customers

Overseas Customers' Share of Revenues	Current		Expected after Five Years	
	Number of Companies	Percentage	Number of Companies	Percentage
More than 50%	3	4	20	25
More than 25%, less than 50%	16	22	38	48
More than 10%, less than 25%	10	14	8	10
10% or less	45	61	14	18
Total	74	100	80	100

Table 3.2
Average and Median International Revenues as a Percentage of Total Revenues

	Average %	Median %
All non-FDA-regulated companies ($N=84$)	16	10
By level of products developed		
High-level	30	30
Mid-level	15	10
Ground-level	10	0
By type of customer served		
Manufacturing	33	65
Service industry or function	11.5	0
By age of company		
0-5 years	12	0
6-9 years	17.5	10
10 years and older	24	25
By total revenues		
$0-5 million	8.1	0
$5-19 million	19	5
$20-49 million	23	21
$50 million and greater	23	25
By extent of localization necessary to serve customers abroad[a]		
Extensive (9 companies)	7	0
Modest (38 companies)	19	10
None (25 companies)	22	25
By whether company served customers abroad in first six months		
Yes (23 companies)	21	30
No (47 companies)	9.5	0[b]
By type of customer or function served		
Manufacturing	33	65
Service	11.5	0
By extent of patenting efforts		
No patents (22)	10	0
Token patenting (19)	11	5
Defensive patents (21)	15	5
Strong portfolio (22)	27	20
By funds raised from overseas investors		
Yes	25	21
No	9.5	0

[a] Twelve companies reported no overseas demand for their product or service.
[b] Only 15 companies had any international revenues.

Table 3.3
Number of Companies with Own Offices or Third-Party
Relationships Overseas for Marketing and Sales, by Location

Location	Own Office	Third-Party
UK	15	9
Japan	6	9
China	5	4
Germany	5	4
France	4	2
Scandinavia	4	3
Holland	2	
Hong Kong	2	
Taiwan	2	4
Australia	1	2
New Zealand	1	
Canada	1	
Brazil	1	
Korea	1	5
Israel	1	2
Italy	1	2
UAE		1
Belgium		1
Spain		1
Russia		1
Singapore		1
Switzerland		1
Thailand		1
Other	2	7

Note: No company in the study had both its own offices and a third-party relationship in the same country. However, some companies had their own offices and had third-party relationships in different countries.

Table 4.1
Distribution of Companies with Offshore Outsourcing Relationships, by Function

Function Performed[a]	Number of Companies	Location of Facilities
Product or infrastructure development	29	Bangladesh, Canada, China (2), Denmark, Germany (2), India (19), Indonesia, Ireland, Korea, Poland, Russia, Singapore (2), Ukraine (2)
Core products	5	Germany, India (3), Ukraine (2)
Infrastructure	1	India
Components	9	Canada, China (2), Germany, India (6), Russia, Singapore
Ancillary products	9	Bangladesh, China, Denmark, India (6), Ireland, Russia
Testing	14	China (2), Germany, India (9), Indonesia, Korea, Poland, Russia, Singapore, Ukraine
Ongoing inputs	14	Asia, Canada (2), China (5), Denmark, Europe, Germany (2), Japan, Korea (2), Mexico, Taiwan (4), India
Contract manufacturing	10	Asia, Canada, China (4), Denmark, Europe, Germany, Japan, Korea (2), Mexico, Taiwan (4)
Other	6	China, Germany, India, Japan, Korea, Taiwan, Western Europe
Ongoing services	4	Canada, China, India (2), worldwide
S/W maintenance	1	India
Technical support	0	
Transaction processing	1	Canada, India
Other	3	Canada, China, India, worldwide
Complements	6	China, Europe, France (3), Germany, Japan, Sweden, UK, Western Europe, worldwide
Services	3	France, Sweden, Western Europe, worldwide
Hardware	2	China, France (2), Germany, Japan, UK
Other	2	China, France, Japan, UK

[a] Some companies had more than one functional relationship in each category.

Table 4.2
Distribution of Companies with Own Offshore Facilities, by Function

Function Performed[a]	Number of Companies	Location of Facilities
Product or infrastructure development	19	Australia, Belgium, Canada (2), China (3), Denmark, India (5), Israel (3), Switzerland, UK (5), Ukraine
Core products	11	Australia, Canada (2), China, Denmark, India (2), Israel (2), UK (3)
Infrastructure	1	Ukraine
Ancillary products or components	6	Belgium, China (3), India (3), Israel (2), Switzerland, UK (3)
Testing	1	Belgium, India
Ongoing inputs	4	China, UK (2), Western Europe
Purchasing	1	Western Europe (various)
Manufacturing	2	China, UK
Ongoing services	8	UK (2)
S/W maintenance	3	UK (2)
Technical support	4	UK
Other	2	Denmark, Japan, UK

[a] Some companies had more than one functional relationship in each category

Table 5.1
Distribution of Immigrants on Founding Teams

Size of Founding Team	Companies with Immigrant Founders		Percentage of All (290) Founders	Percentage of All (104) Immigrant Founders
	Number	Percentage of All Companies with Founding Team of That Size		
1	6	40	5	6
2	22	54	28	29
3	15	68	23	24
4	7	58	17	14
5+	12	86	27	27
Total	62	60	100	100

Table 5.2
Distribution of Active Founders by Current Role and Country of Origin

	CEO	R&D	Mktg.	Sales	Ops.	CFO	Other	All Functions
Active founders	49	48	13	5	12	1	6	134
Immigrants	17	23	6	0	6	0	0	52
% Immigrants	35%	48%	46%	0%	50%	0%	0%	39%

By country of origin (as % of total immigrants in category)

	CEO	R&D	Mktg.	Sales	Ops.	CFO	Other	All Functions
India	35%	39%	33%					33%
UK	18%	9%	17%		33%			15%
Other West Europe		17%						8%
Other Asia		9%			17%			6%
Russia								4%
China		9%						4%
Canada	12%	4%						4%
Sri Lanka	6%				17%			4%
Israel	6%							2%
Australia, NZ								2%
Mexico	6%							2%
Belgium	6%							2%
Romania	6%							2%
Switzerland	6%							2%
France		4%						2%
Taiwan		4%						2%
Turkey		4%						2%
Latin America			17%					2%
Germany			17%					2%
Singapore			17%					2%
Brazil					17%			2%
Morocco					17%			2%

Table 5.3
Distribution of Top Managers by Functional Role and Country of Origin

	CEOs	CFOs	R&D	Marketing	Sales	Prod. Mgmt.	Operations	Other General Management	Legal & Regulatory Staff	All Top Managers
By functional role										
Number of managers	103	63	147	85	73	10	66	30	4	581
% of all managers	18%	11%	25%	15%	13%	2%	11%	5%	1%	100%
By country of origin (as % of total managers in function)										
United States	64	89	61	74	82	80	79	87	75	73
Immigrants (total)	36	11	39	26	18	20	21	13	25	27
Canada	8		5		23	50		25		7
UK	24	29	12	23	38	50	14			20
Ireland		14								1
France	3		5	5						3
Germany, Italy	3			5	8			25		3
Other West Europe			7	5						3
East Europe	3						7			1
Israel	3		2	14			7			4
India	34	29	23	27			14	25	100	24
South Africa	3									1
Australia, NZ			4	5				25		3
China		14	9	5			7			5
Korea, Taiwan, Japan			2				7			1
Other Asia			5				7			3
Latin America	3			5						1
Other	19	14	26	6	31		37			21

Table 5.4
Distribution of Immigrants by Function

Function	Total Number of Employees	Employees in Function as % of Total Employees	Immigrants	Immigrants in Function as % of Total Immigrants	Immigrants as % of All Employees Function
Technical	2,579	50%	800	74%	31%
Marketing	1,112	22%	69	6%	6%
Core Management	335	6%	68	6%	20%
Other	1,082	21%	141	13%	13%
All Functions	5,108	100%	1,078	100%	21%

Table 5.5
Active Founders by Highest Degree and Current Role

	CEO	R&D	Mktg.	Sales	Ops.	CFO	Other	All Functions
All active founders	49	48	13	5	12	1	4	132

Active founders with specified degree as percentage of all active founders in role

	CEO	R&D	Mktg.	Sales	Ops.	CFO	Other	All Functions
None	2%	2%						2%
Bachelor's	21%	21%	8%	50%[a]	33%	100%	33%	23%
MS	19%	26%	23%		8%		33%	20%
PhD	6%	45%	15%		42%			24%
MBA	40%	4%	54%	50%[a]	17%			25%
MD	4%	2%						2%
Law degree	8%						33%	4%

	CEO	R&D	Mktg.	Sales	Ops.	CFO	Other	All Functions
Active immigrant founders	17	23	6	0	6	0	0	52

Active immigrant founders with specified degree as percentage of all active immigrant founders in role

	CEO	R&D	Mktg.	Sales	Ops.	CFO	Other	All Functions
None								
Bachelor's	31%	14%	17%		33%			22%
MS	31%	23%	17%		17%			24%
PhD	13%	59%	17%					32%
MBA	13%	5%	50%		50%			18%
MD	6%							2%
Law degree	6%							2%

Note: We do not have educational information on two active founders.
[a] Information on education was not available for one of the five founders in this category

Table 5.6
Distribution of Top Managers by Highest Degree and Role

	CEO	CFO	R&D	Marketing	Sales	Prod. Mgmt.	Operations	Other General Management	Legal & Regulatory Staff	All Top Managers
All top managers	103	63	147	85	73	10	66	30	4	587
Managers with specified degree as percentage of all managers in role										
None	5%	0%	1%	2%	4%	0%	2%	0%	0%	2%
Bachelor's	25%	48%	22%	26%	64%	10%	33%	25%	0%	32%
MS	14%	2%	28%	11%	4%	40%	25%	4%	0%	16%
PhD	10%	0%	39%	5%	0%	10%	3%	7%	25%	14%
MBA	35%	45%	6%	51%	23%	40%	33%	25%	0%	29%
MD	5%	0%	4%	1%	1%	0%	0%	0%	0%	2%
Law degree	4%	3%	0%	2%	1%	0%	0%	39%	75%	4%
Other graduate degree	3%	2%	1%	1%	1%	0%	3%	0%	0%	2%
Immigrant top managers	35	7	57	13	10	2	15	4	1	144
Immigrant managers with specified degree as percentage of all immigrant managers in role										
None	6%	0%	2%	8%	10%	0%	0%	0%	0%	3%
Bachelor's	24%	43%	11%	23%	60%	0%	20%	0%	0%	20%
MS	18%	14%	32%	23%	0%	100%	27%	0%	0%	24%
PhD	18%	0%	49%	8%	0%	0%	7%	25%	100%	26%
MBA	21%	14%	4%	38%	30%	0%	47%	25%	0%	18%
MD	6%	0%	4%	0%	0%	0%	0%	0%	0%	3%
Law degree	3%	14%	0%	0%	0%	0%	0%	50%	0%	3%
Other graduate degree	3%	14%	0%	0%	0%	0%	0%	0%	0%	1%

Note: Includes only MS and PhD degrees in engineering or science.

Table 5.7
Distribution of Immigrants in Comparison to All Employees, by Highest Degree

Highest Degree Earned	Total Number of Employees	Degree Holders as % of Total Employees	Number of Immigrants	Degree Holders as % of Immigrants	Immigrants as % of Degree Holders
None	349	7%	47	6%	13%
Bachelor's	3,053	61%	264	32%	9%
MS	672	14%	274	34%	41%
PhD	406	8%	151	19%	37%
MBA	365	7%	52	6%	14%
MD	29	1%	11	1%	38%
Law degree	49	1%	5	1%	10%
Other graduate degree	52	1%	10	1%	19%
Total	4,975	100%	814	100%	

Table 5.8
Country of Origin for Immigrant Employees

	Total	% of All Immigrant Employees
India	296	30
China	171	17
East Europe (except Russia)	66	7
Latin America	60	6
UK	52	5
Other Western Europe	47	5
Canada	46	5
Other Asia	35	4
Russia	34	3
France	22	2
Israel	20	2
Korea	19	2
Australia, NZ	16	2
Ireland	11	1
Germany	11	1
Scandinavia	11	1
Japan	11	1
Taiwan	10	1
South Africa	4	0.4
Other	43	4
Total	985	100

Table 7.1a
Ratio of S&E PhDs Awarded in Selected Countries
to S&E PhDs Awarded in United States

	All EU Countries	France, Germany, and UK	Japan	China
1975	0.93	0.64	0.11	na
1989	1.22	0.84	0.16	0.05
2001	1.54	1.07	0.29	0.32
2003	1.62			0.49
2010	1.92			1.26

Source: R. Freeman 2005.

Table 7.1b
PPP-Adjusted Per Capita GDP in Selected Countries as Ratio of U.S. Per Capita GDP

	U.S Per Capita GDP (constant 2000 dollars)	All EU Countries	France, Germany, and UK	Japan	China
1975	19,830	0.74	0.76	0.72	0.03
1989	28,090	0.72	0.75	0.80	0.06
1995	30,165	0.74	0.77	0.83	0.09
2001	33,983	0.75	0.77	0.77	0.12
2003	35,373	0.73	0.75	0.74	0.14

Source: World Development Indicators Online.

Table 7.1c
Annualized Growth Rates of PPP-Adjusted Per Capita GDP, Selected Countries

	U.S	All EU Countries	France, Germany, and UK	Japan	China
1975–1989	2.52%	2.36%	2.39%	3.25%	7.15%
1989–2003	1.66%	1.76%	1.66%	1.10%	8.00%
1989–1995	1.20%	1.46%	1.62%	1.80%	9.75%
1995–2003	2.01%	1.84%	1.68%	0.56%	7.80%

Source: World Development Indicators Online.

Table 12.1

Ratios of Sales of Operating Systems (in units and revenues) to GDP and of Gross Fixed Investment to GDP in 2001

Country or Region	Units Sold / GDP			Revenues/GDP			Gross Fixed Investment/GDP
	Windows	Linux	All Systems	Windows	Linux	All Systems	
United States	100	100	100	100	100	100	100
Canada	141	106	137	116	102	115	121
Latin America	60	36	57	58	36	55	116
Western Europe	74	65	73	NA	NA	NA	123
Central/Eastern Europe	96	54	91	NA	NA	NA	139
Middle East and Africa	38	23	36	NA	NA	NA	118[a]
Japan	NA	NA	NA	87	34	80	152
Asia Pacific excl. Japan	NA	NA	NA	88	24	80	175

Source: GDP data from World Development Indicators Online; operating system sales data generously provided by Pankaj Ghemawat and Ramon Casadesus-Masanell; gross fixed investment to GDP ratios from Economic Intelligence Unit database.

[a] Calculation is the weighted average of two regional aggregates provided by EIU:"Middle East and North Africa" and "Sub-Saharan Africa."

Table 12.2
Ratios of Sales of Operating Systems (in units) to GDP and of Gross Fixed Investment to GDP in 2001

Country	Units Sold / GDP			Gross Fixed Investment/GDP
	Windows	Linux	All Systems	
United States	100	100	100	100
Austria	71	53	69	136
Belgium	86	65	83	125
Denmark	127	92	123	122
Finland	100	73	97	125
France	68	65	68	120
Germany	65	63	64	123
Greece	72	36	68	146
Ireland	92	56	88	143
Italy	63	42	60	125
Netherlands	93	80	92	130
Norway	87	62	84	112
Portugal	94	54	89	163
Spain	47	29	45	160
Sweden	117	91	114	106
Switzerland	92	73	90	137
UK	87	93	87	102

Source: Same as in table 12.1.

Table 12.3
Ratios of IT Expenditures to GDP, and Gross Fixed Investment to GDP

Country or Region	2001		2002		2003		2004	
	IT Ratio	GFI Ratio	IT Ratio	GFI Ratio	IT Ratio	GFI Ratio	IT Ratio	GFI Ratio
United States	100	100	100	100	100	100	100	100
Canada	90	121	90	130	90	130	88	126
Latin America	83	116	89	123	93	120	98	121
Western Europe	83	123	81	129	81	127	84	122
Central/Eastern Europe	98	139	105	144	90	143	83	134
Middle East and Africa	64	118[a]	68	133[a]	76	133[a]	81	123[a]
Japan	71	152	74	155	84	152	87	143
Asia/Pacific excl. Japan	83	175	85	193	88	200	88	198

Source: IT spending estimates from Gartner Dataquest Market Databook for December 2005 and December 2003, GDP data from World Development Indicators Online, Gross Fixed Investment to GDP ratios from Economic Intelligence Unit database.

[a] Calculation is the weighted average of two regional aggregates provided by EIU: "Middle East and North Africa" and "Sub-Saharan Africa."

Table 12.4

Percentage of Value-Added, IT Intermediates Used, and Computer Professionals Employed, by Sector, 2004

Sector	Total Value-Added	IT Hardware Intermediates Used	IT Service Intermediates Used	Computer Professionals Employed (2001)
Agriculture and mining	2.70	0.11	1.17	0.13
Manufacturing	12.10	58.49	13.53	10.77
Computer and electronic products	*1.13*	*34.41*	*4.08*	*1.81*
Construction	4.70	1.82	1.12	0.26
Services	67.90	30.29	55.43	84.26
Government	12.60	9.29	28.75	4.32
Total	100.00	100.00	100.00	100.00
Excluding computer and electronic products				
Agriculture and Mining	2.73	0.17	1.22	0.13
Manufacturing	11.10	36.71	9.85	9.12
Construction	4.75	2.77	1.17	0.26
Services:	68.68	46.18	57.79	85.82
Government	12.74	14.16	29.97	4.40
Total	100.00	100.00	100.00	100.00

Sources: Total value-added shares are from Economic Report of the President, 2006, table B-12. IT hardware and service intermediates are from Bureau of Economic Analysis input-output data underpinning table 3.1 in Mann 2006,75. Computer professionals employed are from Bureau of Labor Statistics data kindly provided by Ashish Arora.

Note: 48.9% of computer professionals in 2001 were employed in the "Computer Programming, Data Processing, and Other Computer Related Services" category.

Table 13.1
Shares of Employment by Sector and by Country, Selected Years, 1820-1992

	U.S.	France	Germany	Netherlands	UK	Japan	China	Russia
Agriculture, Forestry, and Fisheries								
1820	70.0				37.6			
1870	50.0	49.2	49.5	37.0	22.7			
1913	27.5	41.1	34.6	26.5	11.7	60.1	n.a.	70.0
1950	12.9	28.3	22.2	13.9	5.1	48.3	77.0	46.0
1992	2.8	5.1	3.1	3.9	2.2	6.4	58.6	17.0
Mining, Manufacturing, Construction, and Utilities								
1820	15.0	n.a.	n.a.	n.a.	32.9	n.a.	n.a.	n.a.
1870	24.4	27.8	28.7	29.0	42.3	n.a.	n.a.	n.a.
1913	29.7	32.3	41.1	33.8	44.1	17.5	n.a.	n.a.
1950	33.6	34.9	43.0	40.2	44.9	22.6	7.0	29.0
1992	23.3	28.1	37.8	24.3	26.2	34.6	22.0	36.0
Services								
1820	15.0				29.5			
1870	25.6	23.0	21.8	34.0	35.0	n.a.	n.a.	n.a.
1913	42.8	26.6	24.3	39.7	44.2	22.4	n.a.	n.a.
1950	53.5	36.8	34.8	45.9	50.0	29.1	16.0	25.0
1992	74.0	66.8	59.1	71.8	71.6	59.0	20.0	47.0

Source: Maddison 1997, table 5.
Note: Blank cells indicate data not available.

Table 14.1
**Percentage of Immigrants in U.S. Labor Force, by Education
and in Selected Occupations**

	1990	2000
Total U.S. labor force	124,722,500	138,733,660
Total number of immigrants	11,984,585	17,154,417
As percentage of labor force	9.3%	12.4%
Without high school diploma	22.4%	16%
High school graduate	56.4%	59%
College graduate	21.3%	26%
Percentage of immigrants in labor force by educational level		
Without high school diploma	18.6%	26%
High School graduate	6.1%	8.6%
College graduate	9.4%	12.5%
Bachelor's	11%	17%
Master's	19%	29%
All PhDs	24%	38%
PhDs under age 45	27%	52%
Percentage of immigrants in science and engineering jobs, by highest degree		
Bachelor's	11%	17%
Master's	19%	29%
All PhDs	24%	38%
PhDs under 45	27%	52%
Percentage of immigrants in selected medical occupations		
All medical professions		13%
Physicians	20.2%	25.2%
Registered nurses	8.8%	11.5%
Occupational therapists		7.4%
Physical therapists		7.4%
Dental hygienists		4.6%

■ Notes

1 We have a similar result in the twentieth-century classical models where two countries have the same technologies, but are permanently endowed with different stocks of labor and capital. The country with more people exports the labor-intensive good and imports the capital-intensive good, and everybody wins. (Technically, after the two countries are opened up to trade, the wage may go down for workers in the rich country, and the return on capital may go down for capitalists in the poor country. But governments can ensure that everyone participates in the gains through redistributions.)

2 Bhidé and Phelps 2007.

3 Phelps 2007.

4 Edmund S. Phelps's (unsigned) summary of the Aims and Scope of *Capitalism and Society*, posted at http://www.bepress.com/cas/aimsandscope.html (February 27, 2007).

5 In principle, the efforts of researchers to model complex adaptive systems (at places like the Santa Fe Institute and MIT's Systems Dynamics Group) offer another possibility. Though the underlying concepts seem compelling, even after a couple of decades of work by brilliant minds the approach has not yet yielded many useful insights for assessing phenomena like international trade and innovation.

6 My study (Bhidé 2008), however, focused mainly on whether and how the boom had created opportunities for small local businesses in Bangalore.

7 The innovation game in the United States, of course, has many other important players that I have not studied in detail. That said, even a narrow probe from an unusual angle can provide a clearer view of new ideas or more accurate interpretations

of existing facts about what lies under the surface. I also hope that the inductive nature of the exercise will reassure my readers: As mentioned, I did not collect data in support of a point of view, and had no expectation about what I would observe or what the broader implications might be. If the sequence had been reversed—if I had used the interviews to test previously formulated hypotheses—I myself would be skeptical of the results.

Introduction

1 Lohr 2004.

2 Engardio and Einhorn 2005.

3 Pettus 2005.

4 Results posted at http://online.wsj.com/public/resources/documents/WSJ-POLL-20071003.pdf.

5 Ostry and Nelson 1995.

6 Friedman 2006.

7 Krugman 1994, 29. In a footnote Krugman provides a dozen examples.

8 The OECD's *Oslo Manual* defines technological innovation in the following way: "Technological product and process (TPP) innovations comprise implemented technologically new products and processes and significant technological improvements in products and processes. A TPP innovation has been implemented if it has been introduced on the market (product innovation) or used within a production process (process innovation). TPP innovations involve a series of scientific, technological, organisational, financial and commercial activities. The TPP innovating firm is one that has implemented technologically new or significantly technologically improved products or processes during the period under review" (OECD 1995, 31).

9 The three-level stratification of products evokes but does not exactly map into the traditional primary, secondary, and tertiary sectors.

10 Productivity is a crude proxy for innovative capacity, but consistent with the thesis of the "Solow residual."

11 Examples include the supersonic Concorde and the French government's effort to make Machine Bull a counter to IBM's dominance of the computer industry.

12 Sensible people nonetheless, adds Krugman (1994), "appropriate the rhetoric of competitiveness on behalf of desirable economic policies. Suppose that you believe that the United States needs to raise its savings rate and improve its educational system in order to raise productivity. Even if you know that the benefits of higher productivity have nothing to do with international competitiveness, why not describe this as a policy to enhance competitiveness if you think it can widen your audience. It's tempting to pander to popular prejudices on behalf of a good cause, and I have myself succumbed to that temptation." My extensive misuse of "national competitiveness" in a 1984 book resulted simply from the mindless repetition of a catchy phrase. Luckily the misuse does not undermine the thesis of that book, and a quick search of my subsequent work does not reveal subsequent lapses. Regardless, henceforth: never again!

13 Krugman 1994.

14 Economic Report of the President, 2006, table B-12, pp. 296–97.

15 Assuming that patent laws effectively restrict spillovers.

16 This may be an apocryphal attribution to Emerson.

17 Jaffe and Lerner 2004.

18 Bhidé and Phelps 2007.

19 As Krugman (1994) points out, obsessing about international competitiveness (technological or otherwise) can be "dangerous" because it can distort domestic policy making across a "broad range of issues, including some that are very far from trade policy per se." Writes Krugman: "A government wedded to the ideology of competitiveness is as unlikely to make good economic policy as a government committed to creationism is to make good scientific policy even in areas that have no direct relationship to the theory of evolution."

20 Pogue 2007.

21 Malone 2007.

22 Email from Susan Kevorkian, March 8, 2007.

23 Malone 2007.

24 Dvorak 2007.

25 Codecs are devices or programs that *encode* digital data for transmission or storage and then *decode* the encoded data for viewing, listening, or editing.

26 Malone 2007.

27 When measured at market exchange rates. At purchasing power parity rates, the U.S. share of the world's GDP is about 21 percent.

28 IDC estimate reported by CNN.com on March 30, 2001, posted at http://edition .cnn.com/2001/TECH/ptech/03/30/mp3.hotcakes.idg/index.html.

29 Morgan Stanley report by Richard Bilotti and Svetlana Ksenofontova, cited by Yoffie, Merrill, and Slind 2006.

30 According to an estimate cited in Yoffie, Merrill, and Slind 2006, the "bill of materials" for a video iPod in 2005 accounted for just under half of the $299 retail price. The bill of materials includes the difficult-to-estimate profit margins of the suppliers. The value-added in the distribution and logistics chain is also difficult to estimate, because of Apple's vertically integrated structure. According to industry experts, the distribution channels usually account for 30 to 40 percent of the retail price of consumer electronics goods.

31 Economic Report of the President, 2006, p. 294.

32 The best-known example is a paper by Kortum and Lerner (2000). Using a variety of methods, but then "focusing on a conservative middle ground," they estimate that "a dollar of venture capital appears to be three times more potent in stimulating patenting than a dollar of traditional corporate R&D." They then suggest that "venture capital, even though it averaged less than 3 percent of corporate R&D from 1983 to 1992, is responsible for a much greater share—about 8 percent—of U.S. industrial innovations during this decade."

33 VC investments have expanded manifold in the last two decades, but in the greater scheme of things the amounts are still underwhelming. According to the National

Venture Capital Association, VCs invested a total of $22.2 billion in 2005—less than what private equity firms often spend on a single acquisition and comparable to the sum of IBM's and Intel's capital and R&D expenditures.

34 Baldwin (2008) contrasts "thick" and "thin" transaction crossing points depending on the amount of information exchanged.

35 In Bayesian terms, priors are inevitable but they ought not to be "strong."

36 Elster 1993.

37 Rosenberg 1976.

38 Neither of us has been persuaded that theories of "asymmetric information" and "behavioral economics" have been much more enlightening in this regard either.

Book 1: Cautious Voyagers

1 Varian 2005.

2 I have accordingly not used the real names of the CEOs and their companies at several points in this book.

3 From Logispring website, http://www.logispring.com/index.php, downloaded April 14, 2007.

4 "Joie de Vivre," *Catalog Age*, March 1, 2005.

5 These are known as ASICs or application-specific integrated circuits.

6 Spot checks (with other VCs) suggest that the limited degree to which the companies we studied did business abroad is representative of the universe of venture-backed business, although if a researcher with a different personal network had conducted the study, the numbers would not be quite the same.

Chapter 1: VCs in New Ventureland

1 The number of new businesses with employees started every year is, however, lower. In 2005, for instance, an estimated 653,100 "employer" firms were started in the United States (Source: Office of Advocacy, U.S. Small Business Administration, from data provided by the U.S. Bureau of the Census, Statistics of U.S. Business).

2 Bhidé 2000.

3 Knight 1921.

4 Downloaded from http://www.crv.com/AboutCRV/WhatWeLookFor.html on February 19, 2007.

5 "Provisionals" aren't searched or examined by the Patent Office, do not start the 20-year patent term running, do not turn into "real" patents, and are automatically abandoned in one year. They can, however, be converted to a "real" patent within the year.

6 Flynn 2004. Page and Brin, did not, however, withdraw from overall management. When Google went public in 2004, in the registration document filed with the SEC Page and Brin wrote that they and Schmidt ran the company as a "triumvirate."

7 See, for instance, Scott Kirsner's profile of Kamen in *Wired* magazine's September 2000 issue.

8 Kawamoto 2003.

9 In an interview, Reeves said: "What we are doing now is building the foundation. We have some rough concepts in mind and now we're talking to engineers in Europe and Asia. . . . We want to conduct more research before we're ready to commit. We want to keep testing our concepts and make sure the technology is even achievable" (Silvestrini 2002).

10 Mangrove Press Release, "Mangrove System Secures Over \$20 M funding," PR Newswire, April 15, 2003.

11 Some of these companies, notably Apple, after they had been in business for a while did raise funding from VCs that made an important contribution to their subsequent growth.

12 Wikipedia entry as of February 21, 2007, on Dell Computers.

13 In recent years, the number of *Inc.* 500 companies that have patents appears to have increased because of a veritable explosion of patent filings and an increase in the proportion of VC-backed companies on the *Inc.* 500 lists since 1989. Shira Cohen and I attempted to estimate patent filings by companies on the 2006 *Inc.* 500 list. We contacted every fifth company (by rank) on the 2006 list over the telephone. In cases where we were not successful in getting responses, we relied on company websites and other online resources. According to our rough estimates, approximately 22 percent of the companies on the 2006 *Inc.* 500 list had filed for or received a patent; nearly half of these companies had received VC-financing. Excluding the VC-financed companies, the proportion of the 2006 *Inc.* 500 companies that had filed for or received patents was about 15 percent. In contrast (as previously mentioned), nearly half the VC-backed companies that I studied had filed for patents before they received VC funding (and another quarter or so had done so after funding).

14 Case 1989.

15 Entrepreneurs who initially rely on their personal hustle may, however, discover unanticipated competitive advantages that can sustain a large enterprise and then be able to attract professional VCs. These competitive advantages need not be technology based if they have a strong track record. For instance, Starbucks, whose profits and growth are mainly the function of its business model and reputation, was able to attract professional VCs some five years after it was launched with funding from individual investors. The later-stage funding provided to companies like Starbucks does dilute the proportion of "high-tech" companies in VC portfolios. But even with such dilution, overall VC investments (which include later-stage investments) are concentrated in high-technology industries.

Chapter 2: Advancing the Frontier

1 Innovations at the various stages are often interrelated: for instance, advances in flash memories (a "component") led to the development of the iPod Nano (a consumer good); and, in some unusual cases, all the innovations may occur within one large, vertically integrated organization. Nonetheless, as a conceptual matter, we can think of separate levels of new product development that are undertaken by different individuals or organizations.

2 Over time the uncertainty is resolved, but then the need for external financing also goes away.

3 To be sure, businesses whose focus is on developing mid-level know-how may be unable to outsource the development of all the ground-level knowledge needed to make their products useful. I am only suggesting that this does not constitute their raison d'être.

4 Downloaded from http://www.kpcb.com/portfolio/portfolio.php on March 17, 2007.

5 The MIT group teamed up with two business school students from Harvard to start Brontes. Initially they wrote a business plan to develop 3-D imaging for manufacturing applications but changed their focus to dentistry when they were unable to raise financing. One of the two students, Eric Paley, then became CEO of Brontes.

6 This is also the case as we saw in the introduction with developers of ground-level consumer products such as the iPod.

7 The extent of these changes came as a bit of a surprise. I observed the same phenomenon in the *Inc.* 500 companies I had studied. But I also then hypothesized that changes in basic strategies and business models would be less likely in VC-backed start-ups on the grounds that, because of the considerably larger up-front investment and the due-diligence of VCs, fewer businesses would be started on an incorrect premise. My current findings have not caused me to back away from this reasoning; rather, they point to two additional factors. First, many of the companies in my current sample received VC funding during the Internet bubble, when by all accounts VCs suspended their normal due diligence and screening procedures. Or perhaps those businesses made reasonable bets, but a collapse in the technology market forced a search for a new model. Second, many of the companies in my sample were started as self-financed or angel-financed ventures, and in several cases continued in this manner for several years. Then, after VCs entered the picture, they implemented, often in conjunction with new CEOs, significant changes in basic elements of the strategy and business model.

8 Interview with the then CEO.

9 From company website as of April 20, 2007.

10 Howe 2000.

11 Soundbite Press Release, "Soundbite Communications Closes Record Breaking 2002 with Strong Sales and Expanding Partner Relationships" Business Wire, February 10, 2003.

12 Sapias Press Release: "Sapias™ Emerges from Stealth Mode," PR Newswire October 29, 2002.

13 Sahlman 1990.

14 Could the high proportion of companies that made only a token effort to secure patents—or none at all—simply be an artifact of the CEOs that I happened to interview? Cockburn and Wagner's (2006) research suggests otherwise. Cockburn and Wagner studied 356 firms in Internet services (210), Internet software (82), and computer software (64) that had gone public between February 1998 and

August 2001. They note that the patentability of software had been firmly established in the United States by the mid-1990s and that court decisions had helped trigger "a flood of patents on methods of doing business, particularly those implemented in computers and networks." Yet more than half of the 356 firms they studied had not obtained or attempted to obtain a patent. Among the 205 firms that had received at least one round of venture capital financing, 55 percent had not filed for or secured a patent; in firms that did not receive VC financing, an even higher proportion, 62 percent, had not filed for or secured patents.

In other words, the proportion of nonfilers in Cockburn and Wagner's study is higher than in my sample. In fact, it may well be the case that my sample is biased toward companies that are more likely to invest in patents: as I have mentioned, several VCs who provided introductions screened CEOs for their interest in doing business abroad. One explicitly told me that half the companies in his portfolio were providers of services to U.S. customers who would have no interest in talking to me. The companies in his portfolio that had an interest in globalization turned out to be (for reasons that we will explore in the next two chapters) predominantly developers of high-level hardware and software. But as mentioned in the main text, every single one of the companies that made little or no effort to secure a patent developed mid- or ground-level products. So, to the degree that such businesses are underrepresented in my sample, the extent of serious patenting that I observed may represent an upper bound of the true proportion.

15 Another CEO estimated that patenting costs were "$10,000 a pop."

16 Of the 13 health-care investments currently listed on the website of Highland Capital Partners (a leading VC firm in health-care ventures), seven appear to be developers of drugs or devices that would be regulated by the FDA. The remaining six include a provider of home care services to the elderly, a managed care company for nursing home residents, a developer of instruments and reagents for DNA sequencing, a provider of customized health benefits, and a chain of yoga centers. A similar distribution was reflected in my sample: 22 companies in health-care services regulated by the FDA and 6 in health-care services that were not. (Highland's portfolio downloaded from http://www.hcp.com/content3776.html on March 22, 2007.)

17 Nichols 1994, 107–8.

18 For at least as long as the company remains VC-backed and does not go public.

19 Large companies that tend to focus on treatments for widespread, chronic conditions such as hypertension and diabetes may not want to "develop" compounds that show promise in treating diseases that are not widespread and may therefore license such compounds to smaller companies.

20 Even drugs that may be used against more than one disease are prescribed for a single indication.

21 The agency (and Western pharmacology in general) have been hostile to herbs and other substances made up of many substances common in traditional Chinese and Indian medicine and "holistic" therapies such as homeopathy, which purport to offer a wide range of benefits rather than a cure for a specific disease. Thus, a company seeking FDA approval for a therapy based on an herbal extract, for instance,

has to identify the single active ingredient that is doing the job—and prove its safety and efficacy. In June 2004, the FDA did, however, issue guidelines that would make it easier to secure approval for botanical drugs that have not been "purified" to a single molecule.

22 Chatterji (2007) provides a more comprehensive overview of innovation and entrepreneurship in the U.S. medical products industry.

Chapter 3: Marketing

1 Disguised name.

2 The developers of high-level products also had more ambitious expectations for future international sales, although this is not shown in the box or tables.

3 Details are contained in table 3.2. The table and box only include companies that had started generating revenues. Most of the other "prerevenue" companies were FDA-regulated drug and device developers; I discuss the distinctive features of these companies in a separate section near the end of this chapter.

4 According to industry sources, Taiwanese ODMs produced slightly over 80 percent of the world's PCs in 2006.

5 The list of components needed to build an end item.

6 Disguised name.

7 Moreover, whether serving U.S. multinationals overseas had a meaningful effect on getting other overseas customers seemed to be related to whether the business also established a physical presence overseas. Overall, 44 percent of my sample reported serving U.S. customers abroad; the median percentage of international to total revenues for these companies was 21 percent, compared to 10 percent for the sample as a whole. But the median for the subgroup that served U.S. multinationals without having any offices abroad was exactly the same as the median for the overall sample. In other words, having just a virtual presence to serve U.S. customers abroad bore virtually no relationship to securing non-U.S. customers.

8 Disguised name.

9 Moreover, because the organizational structures and routines in VC-backed businesses haven't yet matured, management capacity cannot be easily increased simply by recruiting more executives.

10 Phil Gyford notes the absence of authoritative figures and comes up with a rough estimate of 22 percent (downloaded from his web page, http://www.gyford.com/phil/writing/2003/01/31/how_many_america.php, on May 13, 2007).

11 This is not to say that such conflicts are lower with U.S. strategic investors.

12 The CEO also said that the capital markets could also be considered customers (because the company could go public instead of being acquired). But because "it had become almost impossible to do a quality IPO," big pharma was now his sole customer.

13 Device makers also faced the localization, sales and marketing, and organizational issues that we have already discussed in this chapter.

14 Data was unavailable for 25 companies. These included four financial services companies (Bank of America, Goldman Sachs, Merrill Lynch, and Wells Fargo),

Delphi (auto parts), and Lockheed Martin (aircraft) that have a significant presence in overseas markets. Many of the other 19 companies almost certainly do very little if any business abroad. Therefore, the overall means and medians I report very likely have an upward bias.

15 As discussed in an earlier chapter, VCs tend to keep their companies on a tight financial leash.

16 Does this example suggest that the financing constraints imposed by VCs are too tight and that an inordinately high cost of capital induces unwarranted delays in the pursuit of international markets? In other words, is this an instance of "market failure"? Not according to my analysis. Certainly, large companies that have stabilized their organizational systems and structures and don't operate on a milestone-to-milestone financing scheme have more capital and managerial capacity and may therefore have a lower required rate of return for their overseas operations. But we should recall that VC-backed businesses' innovations involve trial and error. Regardless of capital constraints, it may be optimal for these businesses to figure out what works in one market first. It is also noteworthy that J&J applies its acquire-and then-globalize approach to products whose commercial viability has already been established in one market. Furthermore, as I have already mentioned, during the Internet bubble, some VCs pushed their companies to expand abroad before their U.S. model had been refined. This is no longer the case, suggesting that the iterative development and exploitation of innovations is often the right way to go.

Chapter 4: Offshoring

1 See Prestowitz's comments in chapter 7.

2 I include in this count a company started by Israeli founders that was incorporated in the United States and had some sales and marketing staff in New York. Everything else was in Israel.

3 Overall, about a quarter of the companies in my sample had acquired another company. The seemingly high proportion is explained by the bursting of the Internet bubble, after which a number of struggling companies were up for sale. In addition, the difficulty of going public (for companies that weren't struggling) meant that more companies remained under VC-ownership when they reached the "normal" stage for undertaking acquisitions.

4 Disguised name.

5 Although I am not aware of any research about this gain in mutual understanding, it is reasonable to assume that similar benefits help explain some of the effort that goes into negotiating contracts within the United States as well.

Chapter 5: Founders and Staff

1 According to the Bureau of Labor Statistics "News" released on April 14, 2006, USDL 06-640, "Foreign born workers made up about 15 percent of the U.S. civilian labor force, age 16 and over." The foreign-born includes undocumented immigrants. Estimates that exclude them put the foreign-born share at under 10 percent.

2 In 16 companies, all the immigrant founders had left.

3 Since we do not have the composition of the initial founding teams, we cannot say whether these teams had few founders in the other functions (such as finance, marketing, sales, etc.) or whether founders in these functions were more prone to leave their companies shortly after start-up. My experience suggests that the former is much more likely to have been the case.

4 These numbers exclude two outliers. One company, which provided outsourcing services, employed 325 immigrants out of a total of 350 employees, most of whom worked "on-site" for their clients. The other had 1,500 U.S. employees, 3 percent of whom were immigrants, and more than 1,400 of the company's total staff was engaged in clerical work.

5 These numbers refer to the founders who were still active in the business, and the only ones on whom we have such data.

6 Posted at http://www.nsf.gov/statistics/seind06/c3/c3h.htm.

7 The actual numbers are probably not "representative," however. The process through which I secured introductions to interviews very likely led to a greater representation of founders and CEOs of Indian origin and an underrepresentation of immigrants from China. By way of comparison, a study conducted by a team from Duke University of high-tech companies founded in the United States between 1995 and 2005 (Wadhwa, Saxenian, et al. 2007) estimates that about a quarter had at least one immigrant founder, compared to half the companies in my sample. A quarter of the immigrant founders in the Duke study were from India, compared to a third in my sample, and 7 percent were from the UK and China (each), compared to about 12 percent for each of those countries in my sample. My reading of the Duke methodology suggests, however, that the results of that study may have been affected by the same kind of response bias as my study.

8 Namely India, the UK, Canada, Sri Lanka, Australia, New Zealand, and Singapore.

9 This is the principal "nonimmigrant" visa category under which foreign-born individuals start working in the United States. The visa, which requires at least a bachelor's degree, is granted for a "temporary" period up to six years. Well over half of H1-B visas (in the most recent years for which data is available) were granted for individuals working in scientific and engineering jobs. We do not know, however, what proportion of H1-B holders from India worked in such jobs.

10 Posted at http://www.nsf.gov/statistics/seind06/c3/c3h.htm.

11 CFO magazine, June 2007, reported in "Informed Reader" section of the *Wall Street Journal*, May 24, 2007, B4.

12 The Association to Advance Collegiate Schools of Business (AACSB), Overview of U.S. Business Schools, 2004–2005 (2006). Cited in "2005 Catalyst Census of Women Corporate Officers and Top Earners of the *Fortune 500*."

13 The INS ceased to exist in March 2003. Its immigration functions are now handled by the U.S. Citizenship and Immigration Services (USCIS) within the Department of Homeland Security.

14 National Science Foundation 2006.

15 We have data on the national origins of the overall staff and the distribution of the overall staff by function. Our interviewees did not know (or easily find out) the national origins "within" each function.

16 For instance, whereas the median proportion of immigrants in the total technical staff for business whose founders were all U.S.-born was 16 percent lower than business with an immigrant on the founding team, the proportions in the former category ranged from zero immigrants to 57 percent immigrants.

17 In my prior research on *Inc.* 500 companies, I found that about three-quarters had been started by teams (rather than a "solo" entrepreneur) and that in every such case, the founders had previously been classmates or colleagues or had started a business together. In contrast, 86 percent of VC-backed businesses had been started by more than one founder, and in nearly a quarter of such cases, there had been no prior connection between the founders.

18 About half the teams included members who had previously been colleagues, just under a tenth were former classmates, and in 15 percent there had been some other prior connection. Perhaps coincidentally, the proportions of founders who knew each other were almost exactly the same whether or not a founding team had an immigrant on it.

19 Index of Silicon Valley 2006, published by Joint Venture Silicon Valley Network and posted at http://www.jointventure.org/PDF/Index%202006.pdf.

20 Another reason cited by the CEO was that "Microsoft recruits heavily on campuses, where it's much easier to recruit foreign-born people. We need experienced staff."

21 Press releases, bios, newspaper articles, etc., are more likely to mention countries of origin for foreign-born executives than for U.S.-born executives. For instance, we could find no record of such prominent executives such as Carter Cast, president of Wal-Mart. However, all the other evidence suggests that Mr. Cast is a U.S. native.

22 The lower number assumes that all the unknown values had the same distribution as the known values. The higher number assumes that all executives for whom we could not find any reference to their country of birth are U.S.-born.

23 In my previous study of companies on the *Inc.* 500 list for 1989, I found that about 20 percent of the founders were immigrants. This may have been a quirk of my sample or of the time: *Inc.* magazine reports that 15 percent of the founders on its 2000 "500" list[23] (and 12 percent on its 2006 list)[23] were born outside the United States. All three percentages are well below the 36 percent of the founders of VC-backed businesses who were immigrants in my current study. I did not collect any data in my previous study on the national origins, either of the top management of the companies or their rank-and-file staff of the 1989 *Inc.* 500 companies. As far as the former are concerned, the companies did not have much of a top management layer to speak of, and as for the latter, I have every reason to believe that (with one exception) the composition reflected the demographics of the local workforce.

24 *Inc.* magazine reports, for instance, that 14.85 percent of the founders on its 2001 list had an "advanced degree." (Source: Article posted at http://www.inc.com/magazine/20001015/20742.html.) According to my previous study, the proportions

were even lower for companies on the *Inc.* list for 1989. Although the founders I had then interviewed were better educated than the population at large—81 percent had college degrees—only a handful had advanced degrees in engineering or science (including one PhD from the UK and one from India).

Chapter 6: On Methods and Models

1 Wessel 2007.

2 Perhaps because of my formative years spent studying engineering—the prospect of an exploding reactor tends to concentrate the mind on the robustness of the assumptions used in its design.

3 Note this is *not* the standard "unobserved heterogeneity" problem and *cannot* be solved by tagging the cones and cylinders with "dummy variables."

4 Moreover, it is not enough to identify the firms (or professions) whose international sales (or wages) are more sensitive to localization costs (or years of work experience). To make a legitimate claim to "statistical significance at the 95 percent level" for an estimate, the researcher must have precisely the right equation for how international sales vary with localization costs (or wages vary with work experience) for every subgroup.

5 Interview with Jon Stewart on the *Daily Show*, September 18, 2007, reported on http://blogs.wsj.com/economics/2007/09/19/greenspan-cracks-a-joke-and-breaks-it-down/.

6 Doll et al. 2004.

7 Borjas 2005, 8.

8 "In electrical engineering," writes Borjas (2005, 4), "the immigrant share rose from 30.0 percent in the 1970s to about 48 percent in both the 1980s and 1990s. In biological sciences, the immigrant share hovered around 10 percent in the 1970s and 1980s, and rose to 27.5 percent in the 1990s."

9 National Science Foundation 2002 and 2006.

Book 2: Embrace or Resist?

1 National Science Foundation 2006, chap. 3, p. 19.

Chapter 7: Alarmist Arguments

1 R. Samuelson 2005.

2 National Academies 2005.

3 Posted at http://www.econstrat.org/.

4 Prestowitz 1988, 332, cited in N. Mitchell 1991, 346.

5 Prestowitz 1988, 260.

6 N. Mitchell 1991, 346.

7 Prestowitz 2006a.

8 R. Freeman 2005.

9 Dawson 2005, 25.

10 Statement of Norman Augustine, Chair, Committee on Prospering in the Global Economy of the 21st Century, Committee on Science, Engineering, and Public

Policy, Division on Policy and Global Affairs, National Academies, before the Committee on Science, U.S. House of Representatives, October 20, 2005.

11 Also known as the Lisbon Strategy or the Lisbon Process.

12 Posted at http://ec.europa.eu/growthandjobs/areas/fiche05_en.htm, downloaded on August 13, 2007.

13 Press release July 19, 2005, posted at http://europa.eu/rapid/pressReleasesAction. do?reference=IP/05/968&format=HTML&aged=0&language=EN&guiLanguage=en.

14 Press release, June 11, 2007, posted at http://europa.eu/rapid/pressReleasesAction. do?reference=IP/07/790&format=HTML&aged=0&language=EN&guiLanguage=en.

15 Quoted in "The Great Unbundling," *The Economist*, January 18, 2007.

16 Gordon 2004.

17 Leamer 2006.

18 P. Samuelson 2004.

19 P. Samuelson 2004.

20 Baumol 2002.

21 Other studies reporting (or implying) large consumer surpluses include Mansfield et al. 1977, Bresnahan 1986, Trajtenberg 1989, Hausman 1997, and Baumol 2002.

22 Interview with Kronholz (2006).

Chapter 8: The Reassuring Realities of Modern Cross-Border Flows

1 DeLong 2000.

2 Maddison 1995, 38, cited in Baumol, Blinder, and Wolff 2003, 87.

3 Maddison 1997.

4 The reductions of transportation costs in the current wave of globalization have not been quite as dramatic as in the previous wave.

5 Baldwin and Martin 1999, 10.

6 Baldwin and Martin further assert that "[i]n the 19th century, the high cost of transmitting knowledge favored long-term capital investments" abroad, whereas "the telecommunications revolution of the 20th century favors the rapid, almost frenetic movement of highly liquid assets." I do not question that the telecommunications revolution has facilitated the globalization of trading in foreign exchange, stocks, bonds, and commodities. However, it has also helped make the twenty-first century multinational a fundamentally different creature from its nineteenth-century counterpart. As will be apparent in the quotations that follow, one of the authors, Baldwin, endorses this view in a 2006 article.

7 Not all countries in the South were able to establish the necessary conditions to do this, however; in fact, more couldn't than could.

8 Baldwin and Martin 1999, 29.

9 In addition to Baldwin 2006, other recent studies include Grossman and Rossi-Hansberg 2006, Leamer 2006, and Hanson, Mataloni, and Slaughter 2005, to name just a few.

10 Krugman 1995, 333.

11 Arora and Gambardella 2005. Sutthiphisal (2006) provides a historical example of this tendency, and Mariani (2001) a contemporary one.

12 Economist Intelligence Unit, "Sharing the Idea: The Emergence of Global Innovation Networks," 3, http://a330.g.akamai.net/7/330/25828/20070323181759/graphics. eiu.com/files/ad_pdfs/eiu_IDA_INNOVATION_NETWORKS_WP.pdf.

13 Email correspondence with author: some facts disguised to protect confidentiality.

14 Olegario 1997, 356.

15 Tedlow 2003, 169.

16 IBM's international operations often started with the acquisition of local competitors. For instance, in 1922 IBM purchased a controlling interest in a German company, Dehomag (Pugh 1995, 258).

17 Document posted at http://www-03.ibm.com/ibm/history/documents/pdf/faq. pdf, 15.

18 Tedlow 2003, 170.

19 Tedlow 2003, 173–74.

20 Pugh 1995, 380–81. As it happened, Pugh adds, after initial success, the product "became an embarrassment in the marketplace, because it was introduced half a year after the more versatile and cost-effective IBM 1401."

21 Pugh 1995, 291.

22 Pugh 1995, 380.

23 Alm 1987.

24 Alm 1987.

25 Mitchell 1987.

26 "Texas Instruments Looks to Grab Fast-Growing Asian Markets," *Chicago Sun Times*, August 19, 1985, 50.

27 Economist Intelligence Unit, "Strategy—Texas Instruments Blazes Trail for Software Exports," March 5, 1998.

28 Goldstein and Harrison 2002.

29 Email correspondence with author.

30 Burrows 1995.

Chapter 9: Valuable Differences

1 Grimm 1973.

2 Arora, Fosfuri, and Gambardella's (2001) book contains a comprehensive analysis.

3 Branstetter, Fisman, and Foley 2005.

4 Quoted in Bhidé 1989.

5 Polyani 1964, 52, cited in Nelson and Winter 1982, 119.

6 Severson 2007.

7 Ruff 1996, 731.

8 Ghemawat 2007.

Chapter 10: Serving the Service Economy

1 Bordo, Eichengreen, and Irwin 1999, 7.

2 Economic Report of the President 2006, table B-12, 296–97.

3 Wölfl 2003, 10.

4 Messina 2004. Both Wölfl and Messina note that the correlation is not perfect, and Messina's paper in fact focuses on why, controlling for income, the relative size of the service sector might vary across countries and over time.

5 Indian Ministry of Finance 2003, table 10.9, cited in Walters, Stapleton, and Andrews 2007, 35.

6 Smart 1996.

7 Welch 2001, 129.

8 Welch 2001, 318.

9 Smart 1996.

10 Welch 2001, 323.

11 Van Riper 2007.

12 Basker and Pham 2006.

13 Civils 2006.

14 Landler 2006.

15 Jonathan Reynolds, personal correspondence.

16 Howard 2005.

17 Van Biema and Greenwald 1997.

18 Cowen 1998, 11.

19 Wölfl 2003, abstract.

20 Leamer 2006.

21 Posted at http://www-03.ibm.com/ibm/history/history/decade_1930.html.

Chapter 11: Venturesome Consumption

1 Bhidé 1983. Its in-apt title, "Beyond Keynes: Demand Side Economics," didn't help.

2 Mokyr 1990.

3 Rosenberg and Birdzell 1986.

4 Cohen and Levinthal 1989.

5 Smith 1937.

6 Rosenberg 1976, 72–73.

7 Rosenberg 1982.

8 Roberts 2004.

9 Eisenberg 2007.

10 Bresnahan and Greenstein 1996.

11 Somers and Nelson 2001.

12 Holland and Light 1999.

13 Plant and Wilcocks 2006.

14 Scaffidi, Shaw, and Myers 2005.

15 BLS Occupational Employment Statistics, cited in Arora, Forman, and Yoon n.d.

Chapter 12: Winning by Using

1 Conway et al. 2006.

2 Leamer 2006.

3 The data used to construct the tables was generously provided by Pankaj Ghemawat and Ramon Casadesus-Masanell.

4 Prestowitz 2006a. This characterization is, however, disputed by other observers.

5 Moreover, the gross fixed investment numbers in the tables include investments in residential real estate. The ratio of true "business" investment to GDP is likely to be even lower in the United States than in Japan and in Western Europe.

6 Matters get even more complicated when it comes to productivity comparisons between countries. For instance, value-added measured in local currencies has to be converted to a common currency. The conversion is typically done by using so-called purchasing power parity (PPP) rates rather than rates derived from the currency markets. But estimating the PPP rate, the amount of a country's currency required to purchase a standard set of goods and services, is far from an exact science.

7 As the ILO reports, in many economies, output for some sectors is estimated on the basis of inputs such as labor compensation, or it is projected based on previous productivity growth. In such cases, obviously, the comparisons are meaningless. Another factor making comparisons famously unreliable is differences in the procedures used in different countries to correct for quality changes or for the changing mix of outputs.

8 Van Ark 2006, 12.

9 Per the North American Industry Classification Scheme (NAICS).

10 Baily, Farrell, and Remes 2006, 7.

11 Mann 2006.

12 Griliches 1994.

13 It is highly implausible. for instance. that any one model could fit the wide range of circumstance in which IT is used.

14 Cortada 2006, 762.

15 Cortada 2006, 760.

16 Dedrick, Gurbaxani, and Kraemer 2003.

17 See O'Mahony and Van Ark 2003 for a comprehensive review.

18 Gordon 2004.

19 Brynjolfsson 1993; Griliches 1994.

20 Lucas 1999.

21 Gordon 1999.

22 Jorgenson and Stiroh 2000, 6–7.

23 Bhidé 1986. Carr's 2004 book also makes this point.

24 European Commission 2003, 281–82.

25 According to a Swedish reader, the higher productivity growth in Norway may reflect sectoral differences between the Swedish and Norwegian economies. Regardless, this does not undermine the main point of this section—that Norway, which does not "produce" as much high-tech innovation as Japan, nonetheless has higher productivity because of its more effective and extensive use of IT.

26 Norges Bank 2007, 3.

27 OECD 2005; citation within the quotation omitted.

28 Technically San Jose–Sunnyvale–Santa Clara.

29 U.S. Census Bureau, 2006 American Community Survey.

Chapter 13: Nondestructive Creation

1 Leamer 2004, 4. Leamer also notes that shoemaking became the first industry "to move abroad en masse," in the 1950s and 1960s.

2 Arora et al. 2006, 76.

3 Arora et al. 2006, 77.

4 Cited in R. Baldwin 2006, 38.

5 Cited in R. Baldwin 2006, 38.

6 Kirkegaard (2006) provides a comprehensive overview of the different estimates.

7 Blinder 2006.

8 Epstein 2007.

9 Arora et al. 2006, 24.

10 Aspray, Mayadas, and Vardi 2006, 26. See also Bhagwati, Panagariya, and Srinivasan 2004.

11 According to the 2006 *Economic Report of the President* (table B-46, p. 336), 15.438 million workers were employed in manufacturing in 1960, compared to 14.279 million in 2005.

12 Epstein 2007.

13 Schumpeter 1961, 81, 83–84.

14 Krugman 2006.

15 Nordhaus 1997.

16 Petroski 1990.

17 Bhidé 2000.

18 Lohr 2008.

19 Bulkeley 2008.

20 Mindlin 2007.

21 European Commission research posted at http://news.bbc.co.uk/2/hi/technology/7116599.stm (November 28, 2007).

22 Christenson 1997.

23 Bresnahan and Greenstein 1996, 2.

24 Cringely 1996.

25 Nichols 1994.

26 Maddision 1997.

27 Clark 1957.

28 Bresnahan and Gordon 1997, 16.

29 Rundle 2004.

Chapter 14: Immigrants

1 R. Freeman 2005.

2 Interview with Ron Hira, published in *IT BusinessEdge*, May 24, 2007, and posted at http://www.itbusinessedge.com/item/?ci=28785.

3 According to the latest Energy Information Administration data (for the month of October 2007) Saudi Arabia provided 14 percent of U.S. oil imports, whereas Indian applicants secured 40 percent of H1-B visas issued in 2003 (the latest year for which this data is available).

4 Peri 2005.

5 R. Freeman 2005.

6 These included the Immigration Reform and Control Act of 1986, which offered lawful permanent residence to some illegal aliens, and the Immigration Act of 1990, which increased the annual caps on immigration.

7 Alarcon 2000.

8 With apologies to Sir Vidiadhar of course.

9 Ferguson 2003, 180–81.

10 Ferguson 2003, 181.

11 Easterlin 1981.

12 Tomlinson 1993.

13 Maddison 1971.

14 Substantially more capital was mobilized and invested. For instance, between 1914 and 1946, net capital formation had averaged 2.27 percent of GNP, and net savings 2.75 percent of GNP. Between 1956 and 1960, the percentages averaged 12.5 percent (a five-and-a-half-fold increase) and 7.95 percent (a nearly threefold increase).

15 World Bank data cited by Varma (2007).

16 According to Ferguson (2003, 181): "Between the 1820s and 1920s, close to 1.6 million Indians left to work in a variety of Caribbean, African, Indian Ocean and Pacific colonies, ranging from the rubber plantations of Malaya to the sugar mills of Fiji. The conditions under which they traveled and worked were often little better than those which had been inflicted on African slaves in the century before."

17 The expatriate communities in turn attracted a few Indian professionals, famously Gandhi, who went to South Africa as a lawyer.

18 Mishra 1961.

19 For instance, during the 1960s, the U.K. received just over 634,000 migrants, of whom 125,600 (19.8 percent) were from India. In the 1970s, the U.K received just 83,040 Indian immigrants, and in the 1980s, 51,480, as the total level of migration to the U.K stabilized and then declined (to about 514,000 in the 1980s) and the Indian share fell to 11.3 percent in the 1970s, and 10 percent in the 1980s (Debabrata and Kapur 2003).

20 At the end of 1999, the stock of Indians in the Middle East was about 3 million strong. According to an estimate for 1986, about 40 percent were unskilled, 47 percent had vocational skills (for instance in construction), and only 5.2 percent had "high skills."

21 According to Kaul's (1993) study of private colleges in the state of Karnataka, more than half of their faculty did not have graduate degrees, compared to less than 10 percent of the faculty of public colleges in the state. Faculty of private colleges taught between 50 and 350 percent more students than did the faculty of public colleges and were paid lower salaries. Private colleges "save[d] on providing

infrastructural facilities like laboratory and workshop equipment"—the "computer departments in some colleges had no computers."

22 Kapur and Mehta 2004.

23 This is not the case, however, for "temporary" H1-B visas.

24 Anderson 2003.

25 Wall 2005.

26 According to Baldwin and Clark (2000), a modular process allows many players to focus on individual components without having to worry about how they will all fit together. They further argue that an especially high level of modularity in the computer industry has allowed for a high level of innovation.

27 See, for example, Bresnahan and Greenstein 1999.

28 Immigration and Naturalization Service 2002.

29 Abt Associates 2004.

30 Anderson 2003.

31 Kirkegaard 2005 provides a detailed evaluation of the degree to which employers might be "misusing" temporary H-1B and L-1 visas.

32 National Science Foundation 2002.

33 Wadhwa, Jasso, et al. 2007.

34 Docquier and Marfouk 2004, cited in National Science Foundation 2006.

35 National Science Foundation 2006.

Chapter 15: The Elusive Underpinnings

1 Paul David's (1986) review of the research on the economics of technology diffusion covers an adjacent territory. The review shows that a great deal of work has been done on the incentives that firms face and the costs they incur in adopting new technologies. These findings help explain differences in the rates of the adoption across industries and firms and help us analyze whether, from a social welfare point of view, the rates are too slow or too fast. The research does not, however, examine the sources of the differences in rates of new technology adoption across countries. Similarly, Cohen and Levinthal (1989 and 1990) and other researchers, such as Cockburn and Henderson (1998), who have worked on "absorptive capacity" peek "under the hood" of firms to examine how their strategies affect their adoption of new technologies, but not why such strategies might vary across countries.

2 Conway et al. 2006 and cited in "Economics Focus: Taped" section of the *Economist*, October 5, 2006, 84.

3 Van Biema and Greenwald 1997, 33–34.

4 This paragraph paraphrases the observations of DeLong 2000.

5 Crafts 2000.

6 Ohkawa and Rosovsky 1973.

7 Nelson 2006.

8 Piper Jaffrey estimate posted on July 1, 2007, at http://www.news.com/8301-10784_3-9738446-7.html.

9 Apple's iPhone, which was released in June 2007, was priced at $499 for a four-gigabyte model and $599 for an eight-gigabyte model. The steepness of the price

may be inferred from the magnitude of the subsequent price cuts: in September 2007 the price of the eight-gigabyte model was cut by about a third and the four-gigabyte model discontinued.

10 Chandler 1990, 1.

11 Galbraith 1967, 1.

12 Bhidé 2000, 2006.

13 Cortada 2006, 760.

14 According to Paul David (1986), "If it is expected that every one will quickly adopt the [new] technology, the inducements to bear the costs of adopting it early are reduced."

15 Keynes 1971–73, 326.

16 Saxenian 1994, cited in Postrel 2005.

17 http://www.news.com/Wal-Mart-sues-Amazon,-others/2100-1001_3-216812.html.

18 Bhidé 2000, chap. 9.

19 Packard 1996, 141.

20 David 1986.

21 Gordon 2004, citing research by McKinsey & Co.

22 Baumol 1993, 117.

23 Baumol 1993, 282.

24 Moore 1996, 169.

25 Rodgers, Taylor, and Foreman 1993, 105.

26 Rodgers 1990, 88–89.

27 Tedlow 2001, 230.

28 Tedlow 2001, 204–5.

29 Tedlow 2001, 204–5.

30 Tedlow 2001, 230.

31 Tedlow 2001, 204.

32 Tedlow 2001, 232–33.

33 Tedlow 2001, 228.

34 Tedlow 2001, 232.

35 Tedlow 2001, 226.

36 Van Biema and Greenwald 1997, 16.

37 Van Biema and Greenwald 1997, 8–9.

38 For a comprehensive discussion on the "industrialization" of services, see Karmarkar 2004.

39 Murray 2007, A19.

40 The "better educated farmer," write Nelson and Phelps (1966), will adopt a profitable process more quickly since "he is better able to discriminate between promising and unpromising ideas." In large industrial corporations, educated scientists keep abreast of technological improvements, and educated top managers make the final decision. Therefore, as a general principle, the "time lag between the creation of a new technique is a decreasing function of . . . average educational attainment."

41 Phelps 2007, 554.

42 Who declined to be identified.

43 McCraw 1997, 327.

44 McCraw 1997, 330.

45 Ministry of Economic Affairs, Netherlands, McKinsey & Co. 2004, 12.

46 See, for instance, Gordon 2004.

47 Friedman 2004, 4.

48 Friedman 2004, 7.

49 Friedman 2004, 5.

50 Bloom, Sadun, and Van Reenen 2005, abstract and 20.

51 Bloom, Sadun, and Van Reenen's 2005, 19.

52 Plant and Willcocks (2006), citing the work of Markus et al. (2003), argue that a decentralized global organizational structure can undermine the whole concept of ERP as appropriate for that organization.

53 Under different definitions, the OECD data show a lower ranking for the United States.

54 "Jacob's Ladder—German Higher Education," *The Economist*, December 16, 2006.

55 Response to author's question at Campuses Initiative event at the Kauffman Foundation.

56 "The Wrong Answer," *The Economist* , December 19, 2006.

Chapter 16: First Do No Harm

1 Quoted by Begley (2007).

2 Carter and Williams 1964.

3 Ford introduced the five-dollar day for his workers—more than twice the prevailing wage—in order to reduce worker turnover, which sometimes reached 300–400 percent per year (McCraw and Tedlow 1997, 275).

4 Bhidé 2004, 29.

5 Hayek 1945.

6 National Academies 2005, 2–8.

7 Teresi 2004.

8 Council of Economic Advisors 1995.

9 National Academies 2005, 2–9 and 2–10.

10 Stanford Graduate School of Business Press release, January 31, 2002 posted at http://www.gsb.stanford.edu/news/headlines/romer_subsidize_training.shtml.

11 See *Congressional Action on R&D in the FY 2003 Budget* and its accompanying preview, posted at http://www.aaas.org/spp/rd/earmo8s.htm.

12 Romer 2007.

13 Bresnahan and Greenstein 1996, 68.

14 Bird 2004.

15 Romer 2007.

16 Popkin and Kobe 2006.

17 Von Tunzelmann 1997.

18 Mueller 1962.

19 Eaton and Kortum 1995.

20 Sharma 2006, A8.

21 David 1986. David repeated this observation at a 2003 conference held in memory of Zvi Grilichches: "The political economy of growth policy has promoted excessive attention to innovation as a determinant of technological change and productivity growth, to the neglect of attention to the role of conditions affecting access to knowledge of innovation and their adoption" (David 2003). In that paper, David also remarked that Griliches's work, first on the diffusion of technology and then on sources of growth of total factor productivity, had been pathbreaking, yet Griliches did not pursue the connections between the two. Instead, in his later work, Griliches focused on the high-level sources of productivity growth, namely R&D efforts and patenting.

22 David 1986.

23 Prestowitz 2006b.

24 World Health Organization 2006, 184.

25 Downloaded from https://www.cia.gov/library/publications/the-world-factbook/rankorder/2091rank.html on October 22, 2007.

26 Downloaded from https://www.cia.gov/library/publications/the-world-factbook/rankorder/2102rank.html on October 22, 2007.

27 OECD 2005, 124.

28 Osterweil 2005.

29 McGettigan et al. 2001.

30 Porter 2006.

31 O'Connor 2002.

32 Herzlinger 2007, A15.

33 Einhorn 2006.

34 Letter of November 8, 1779, from Rae 1895, chap. 23, "Free Trade for Ireland 1779."

35 National Academies 2005, 2–20.

■ References

Abt Associates. 2004. *Engineers in the United States: An Overview of the Profession.* Engineering Workforce Project Report No. 2. Cambridge, MA: Abt Associates.

Alarcon, R. 2000. "Migrants of the Information Age: Indian and Mexican Engineers and Regional Development in Silicon Valley." Working Paper 16, Center for Comparative Immigration Studies, University of California, San Diego, May.

Alm, R. 1987. "The TI Empire: Company Stays in the Chips Despite Stiff Competition." *Dallas Morning News*, July 26, 1A.

Anderson, S. 2003. "The Global Battle for Talent and People." *Immigration Policy Focus* 2, no. 2 (September).

Arora, Ashish, William Aspray, B. Barnow, and V. Gurbaxani. 2006. "The Economics of Offshoring." In *Globalization and Offshoring of Software: A Report of the ACM Job Migration Task Force*, ed. William Aspray, Frank Mayadas, and Moshe Y. Vardi. New York: Association for Computing Machinery.

Arora, Ashish, Chris Forman, and Jiwoong Yoon. N.d. "Software." Forthcoming in *Globalization of Research* (tentative title), ed. Jeffrey Macher and David C. Mower. Washington, DC: National Academies Press.

Arora, Ashish, Andrea Fosfuri, and Alfonso Gambardella. 2001. *Markets for Technology: The Economics of Innovation and Corporate Strategy.* Cambridge: MIT Press.

Arora, Ashish, and A. Gambardella, eds. 2005. *From Underdog to Tigers: The Rise and Growth of the Software Industry in Some Emerging Economies.* Oxford: Oxford University Press.

Aspray, William, Frank Mayadas, and Moshe Y. Vardi. 2006. *Globalization and Offshoring of Software: A Report of the ACM Job Migration Task Force.* New York: Association for Computing Machinery.

Autor, David H., Lawrence F. Katz, and Melissa S. Kearney. 2006. "The Polarization of the U.S. Labor Market." NBER Working Paper No. 11986, January.

Autor, David H., Lawrence F. Katz, and Alan Krueger. 1998. "Computing Inequality: Have Computers Changed the Labor Market?" *Quarterly Journal of Economics* 113: 1169–1213.

Autor, David H., Frank Levy, and Richard Murnane. 2003. "The Skill Content of Recent Technological Change: An Empirical Exploration." *Quarterly Journal of Economics* 118:1279–1333.

Baily, Martin N., and Robert J. Gordon. 1988. "The Productivity Slowdown, Measurement Issues, and the Explosion of Computer Power." *Brookings Papers on Economic Activity* 2:347–431.

Baily, Martin N., Diana Farrell, and Jaana Remes. 2006. "Where US Productivity Is Growing." *McKinsey Quarterly* 2:6–8.

Baker, Unmesh, Simon Montlake, Hilary Hylton, Chris Daniels, and Jenn Holmes. 2006. "Outsourcing Your Heart Elective Surgery in India? Medical Tourism Is Booming, and U.S. Companies Trying to Contain Health-Care Costs Are Starting to Take Notice." *Time*, May 29.

Baldwin, Carliss Y 2008. "Where Do Transactions Come From? Modularity, Transactions, and the Boundaries of Firms." *Industrial and Corporate Change* 17:155–95.

Baldwin, Carliss Y., and Kim Clark. 2000. *Design Rules: The Power of Modularity.* Cambridge: MIT Press.

Baldwin, R. E. 2006. *Globalisation: A Great Unbundling.* Report to the Prime Minister's Office, Economic Council of Finland, September.

Baldwin, R. E., and P. Martin. 1999. "Two Waves of Globalization: Superficial Similarities, Fundamental Differences." NBER Working Paper No. 6904, January.

Basker, Emek, and Van H. Pham. 2006. "Putting a Smiley Face on the Dragon: Wal-Mart as Catalyst to U.S.-China Trade." University of Missouri–Columbia Working Paper, July. http://ssrn.com/abstract=765564.

Baumol, William J. 1967. "Macroeconomics of Unbalanced Growth: The Anatomy of Urban Crisis." *American Economic Review* 57:415–26.

———. 1993. *Entrepreneurship, Management, and the Structure of Payoffs.* Cambridge: MIT Press.

———. 2002. *The Free-Market Innovation Machine: Analyzing the Growth Miracle of Capitalism.* Princeton: Princeton University Press.

Baumol, William J., Alan S. Blinder, and Edward N. Wolff. 2003. *Downsizing in America: Reality, Causes, and Consequences.* New York: Russell Sage Foundation.

Baumol, William J., and William G. Bowen. 1966. *Performing Arts: The Economic Dilemma.* New York: Twentieth Century Fund.

Baumol, William J., Robert E. Litan, and Carl J. Schramm. 2007. *Good Capitalism, Bad Capitalism, and the Economics of Growth and Prosperity.* New Haven: Yale University Press.

Begley, S. 2007. "The Real Sputnik Story." *Newsweek*, October 8.

Bhagawati, Jagdish, A. Panagariya, and T. N. Srinivasan. 2004. "The Muddles over Outsourcing." *Journal of Economic Perspectives* 18, no. 4 (November): 93–114.

Bhidé, Amar. 1983. "Beyond Keynes: Demand Side Economics." *Harvard Business Review* 61, no. 4 (July–August): 100–110.

———. 1986. "Hustle as Strategy." *Harvard Business Review* 64, no. 5 (September-October): 59–65.

———. 1989. "Vinod Khosla and Sun Microsystems (A)." Harvard Business School Case No. 390–049.

———. 2000. *The Origin and Evolution of New Businesses.* New York: Oxford University Press.

———. 2004. "Non-destructive Creation: How Entrepreneurship Sustains Development." Lecture at the Royal Society of Arts, London, November 17.

———. 2006. "How Novelty Aversion Affects Financing Options." *Capitalism and Society* 1, no. 1, article 1. http://www.bepress.com/cas/vol1/iss1/art1.

———. 2008. "What Holds Back Bangalore Businesses?" *Asian Economic Papers* 7, no. 1 (Winter): 120–53.

Bhidé, Amar, and Edmund S. Phelps. 2007. "A Dynamic Theory of China-U.S. Trade: Making Sense of the Imbalances." *World Economics* 8, no. 3 (July–September).

Bhidé, Amar, and A. Puri. 1981. "The Crucial Weaknesses of Japan Inc." *Wall Street Journal*, June 8.

"A Bigger Private Role in Universities." 2006. *Economist*, December 16.

Bird, R. 2004. "The Department of Labor's Overtime Regulations Effect on Small Business Committee." Testimony before Committee on Small Business, Subcommittee on Workforce, Empowerment, and Government Programs, May 20. http://wwwc.house.gov/smbiz/hearings/databaseDrivenHearingsSystem/displayTestimony.asp?hearingIdDateFormat=040520a&testimonyId=172.

Blinder, Alan S. 2006. "Offshoring: The Next Industrial Revolution?" *Foreign Affairs* 85, no. 2: 113–28.

Bloom, Nick, Rafella Sadun, and John Van Reenen. 2005. "It Ain't What You Do It's the Way That You Do I.T.—Testing Explanations of Productivity Growth Using U.S. Affiliates." Working paper, Centre for Economic Performance, London School of Economics, September. http://www.statistics.gov.uk/articles/nojournal/sadun_bvr25.pdf.

Bordo, Michael D., Barry Eichengreen, and Douglas A. Irwin. 1999. "Is Globalization Today Really Different Than Globalization a Hundred Years Ago?" NBER Working Paper No. W7195, June.

Borjas, G. J. 2005. "The Labor Market Impact of High-Skill Immigration." NBER Working Paper No. 11217, March.

Branstetter, L., R. J. Fisman, and C. F. Foley. 2005. "Do Stronger Intellectual Property Rights Increase International Technology Transfer? Empirical Evidence from U.S. Firm-Level Data." NBER Working Paper No. W11516, August.

Bresnahan, Timothy F. 1986. "Measuring the Spillovers from Technical Advance: Mainframe Computers in Financial Services." *American Economic Review* 76:742–55.

Bresnahan, Timothy F., and Robert J. Gordon, eds. 1997. *The Economics of New Goods.* Chicago: University of Chicago Press.

Bresnahan, Timothy F., and Shane Greenstein. 1996. "Technical Progress and Co-invention in Computing and the Use of Computers." *Brookings Papers on Economic Activity: Microeconomics* 1996:1–78.

———. 1999. "Technological Competition and the Structure of the Computer Industry." *Journal of Industrial Ecconomics* 47, no. 1 (March): 1–40.

Brynjolfsson, Erik. 1993. "The Productivity Paradox of Information Technology: Review and Assessment." *Communications of the ACM* 36, no. 12 (December): 67–77.

Brynjolfsson, Erik, and Lorin M. Hitt. 1996. "Paradox Lost? Firm-Level Evidence on the Returns to Information Systems Spending." *Management Science* 42 (April): 541.

Burrows, Peter. 1995. "The Global Chip Payoff." *BusinessWeek*, August 7.

Bulkeley, W. M. 2008. "New IBM Mainframe Is Seen Lifting Sales." *Wall Street Journal*, February 26, B4.

Cairncross, F. 1997. *The Death of Distance: How the Communication Revolution Will Change Our Lives.* Boston: Harvard Business School Press.

Carr, Nicholas G. 2004. *Does IT Matter? Information Technology and the Corrosion of Competitive Advantage.* Boston: Harvard Business School Press.

Carter, C. F., and B. R. Williams. 1964. "Government Scientific Policy and the Growth of the British Economy." *The Manchester School*, September, 197–214.

Casadesus-Masanell, R., and Pankaj Ghemawat. 2006. "Dynamic Mixed Duopoly: A Model Motivated by Linux vs. Windows." *Management Science* 52, no. 7: 1072–84.

Case, J. 1995. "The Wonderland Economy." In "State of Small Business 1995." *Inc.* magazine special issue, 14–29.

Chandler, A. D., Jr. 1990. *Scale and Scope: The Dynamics of Industrial Capitalism.* Cambridge: Belknap Press of Harvard University Press.

Chandrakant, L. S. 1986. *Private Enterprise in Engineering Education.* Bangalore: Indian Institute of Management.

Chatterji, Aaron K. 2007. "Spawned with a Silver Spoon? Entrepreneurial Performance and Innovation in the Medical Device Industry." Working paper, Fuqua School of Business.

Chen, K., and A. D. Marcus. 2005. "Once-Touted Drug for Cancer Finds New Life in China." *Wall Street Journal*, December 22, A1.

Christensen, C. M. 1997. *The Innovator's Dilemma: When New Technologies Cause Great Firms to Fail.* Boston: Harvard Business School Press.

Civils, W. 2006. "Retail Retreat." *Wall Street Journal Online*, July 28. http://online.wsj.com/article_print/SB115408827169320321.html.

Clark, Colin. 1957. *The Conditions of Economic Progress.* London: Macmillan.

Cockburn, I. M., and R. M. Henderson. 1998. "Absorptive Capacity, Coauthoring Behavior, and the Organization of Research in Drug Discovery." *Journal of Industrial Economics* 46:157–82.

Cockburn, I. M., and S. Wagner. 2006. "Patents and the Survival of Internet-Related IPOs." Conference paper, NBER Entrepreneurship Meeting, March 10.

Cohen, W. M., and D. A. Levinthal. 1989. "Innovation and Learning: The Two Faces of R&D." *Economic Journal*, September, 369–96.

―――. 1990. "Absorptive Capacity: A New Perspective on Learning and Innovation." *Administrative Science Quarterly* 35:128–52.

Conway, P., D. de Rosa, G. Nicoletti, and F. Steiner. 2006. "Regulation, Competition and Productivity Convergence." OECD Economics Department Working Paper No. 509, September.

Cortada, J. W. 2006. "The Digital Hand: How Information Technology Changed the Way Industries Worked in the United States." *Business History Review*, Winter, 755–66.

Council of Economic Advisors. 1995. *Supporting Research and Development to Promote Economic Growth: The Federal Government's Role.* October.

Cowen, Tyler. 1998. "Is Our Culture in Decline?" *Cato Policy Report* 20, no. 5 (September–October).

Crafts, Nicholas. 2000. "Globalization and Growth in the Twentieth Century." IMF Working Paper.

Cringely, Robert X. 1996. *Accidental Empires: How the Boys of Silicon Valley Make Their Millions, Battle Foreign Competition, and Still Can't Get a Date.* New York: Harper Business.

Cukier, Kenneth. 2005. "A Market for Ideas." *The Economist*, October 22.

David, Paul A. 1986. "Technology Diffusion, Public Policy, and Industrial Competitiveness." In *The Positive Sum Strategy: Harnessing Technology for Economic Growth*, ed. Ralph Landau and Nathan Rosenberg, 373–91. Washington, DC: National Academy Press.

―――. 1990. "The Dynamo and the Computer: An Historical Perspective on the Modern Productivity Paradox." *American Economic Review Papers and Proceedings*, May, 355–61.

―――. 2003. "Zvi Griliches on Diffusion, Lags and Productivity Growth . . . Connecting the Dots." Paper prepared for the Conference on R&D, Education, and Productivity Held in Memory of Zvi Griliches, 1930–1999, August 25–27.

Davies, Stephen. 1979. *The Diffusion of Process Innovations.* London: Cambridge University Press.

Davis, Mike. 2001. *Late Victorian Holocausts: El Niño Famines and the Making of the Third World.* London: Verso.

Dawson, J. 2005. " 'Gathering Storm' Report Urges Strong Federal Action to Save US Science and Technology Leadership." *Physics Today* 58, no. 12 (December).

Debrarata, Michael, and Muneesh Kapur. 2003. "India's Worker Remittances: A Users' Lament about BOP Compilations." Paper presented at the Sixteenth Meeting of the IMF Committee on Balance of Payments Statistics, Washington, DC, December 1–5. BOPCOM-03/20.

Dedrick, J., V. Gurbaxani, and K. L. Kraemer. 2003. "Information Technology and Economic Performance: A Critical Review of the Empirical Evidence." *Computing Surveys* 35, no. 1 (March): 1–28.

DeLong, J. Bradford. 2000. "The Shape of Twentieth Century Economic History." NBER Working Paper No. 7569, February.

Docquier, Frédéric, and Abdeslam Marfouk. 2004. "International Migration by Educational Attainment, 1990–2000." In *International Migration, Remittances, and the Brain Drain*, ed. Caglar Özden and Maurice Schiff. New York: Palgrave Macmillan.

Doll, R., R. Peto, J. Boreham, and I. Sutherland. 2004. "Mortality in Relation to Smoking: 50 Years' Observations on Male British Doctors." *British Journal of Cancer* 92:426–29.

Donohue, John J., III, and Steven J. Levitt. 2001. "The Impact of Legalized Abortion on Crime." *Quarterly Journal of Economics* 116, no. 2: 379–420.

Dvorak, J. C. 2007. "Ballmer, iPhone and the Reality-Distortion Field." Posted on Dow-Jones Market Watch, January 17.

Easterlin, R. A. 1981. "Why Isn't the Whole World Developed?" *Journal of Economic History* 41, no. 1: 1–19.

Eaton, Jonathan, and Samuel S. Kortum. 1995. "Engines of Growth." NBER Working Paper No. 5207, August.

Einhorn, B. 2006. "A Cancer Treatment You Can't Get Here; China, with Lower Regulatory Hurdles, Is Racing to a Lead in Gene Therapy." *BusinessWeek*, March 6.

Eisenberg, A. 2007. "The Door Key That Can't Be Misplaced." *New York Times*, June 10.

Elster, Jon. 1993. *Explaining Technical Change: A Case Study in the Philosophy of Science.* Cambridge: Cambridge University Press.

Engardio, P., and B. Einhorn. 2005. "Outsourcing Innovation." *BusinessWeek*, March 21, 84.

Enos, John L. 1962. *Petroleum Progress and Profits: A History of Process Innovation.* Cambridge: MIT Press.

Epstein, Gene. 2006. *Econospinning: How to Read between the Lines When the Media Manipulates the Numbers.* New York: John Wiley.

———. 2007. "Static Disrupts the Bangalore Connection." *Barrons*, September 10.

Etherton, Sandra L. 2002. *Let's Talk Patents.* Tempe, AZ: Rocket Science Press.

European Commission. 2003. *Third European Report on Science & Technology Indicators, 2003.* ftp://ftp.cordis.europa.eu/pub/indicators/docs/3rd_report.pdf.

Ferguson, Niall. 2003. *Empire: The Rise and Demise of the British World Order and Its Lessons for Global Power.* New York: Basic Books.

Flynn, L. J. 2004. "2 Wild and Crazy Guys. Soon to Be Billionaires, and Hoping to Keep It That Way." *New York Times*, April 30.

Freeman, C. 1968. "Chemical Process Plant: Innovation and the World Market." *National Institute Economic Review* 45 (August): 29–57.

Freeman, Chris, and Luc Soete. 1997. *Economics of Industrial Innovation.* 3rd ed. Cambridge: MIT Press.

Freeman, Richard B. 2005. "Does Globalization of the Scientific/Engineering Workforce Threaten U.S. Economic Leadership?" NBER Working Paper No. 11457, July.

Friedman, Thomas L. 2006. "Big Ideas and No Boundaries." *New York Times*, October 6.

Friedman, Walter A. 2004. *Birth of a Salesman: The Transformation of Selling in America.* Cambridge: Harvard University Press.

Galbraith, John K. 1967. *The New Industrial State.* Boston: Houghton Mifflin.

Ghemawat, Pankaj. 2007. *Redefining Global Strategy: Crossing Borders in a World Where Differences Still Matter*. Boston: Harvard Business School Press.

Goldstein, A., and C. Harrison. 2002. "International Firms Monitor Security Threats." *Dallas Morning News*, May 31.

Gopalakrishnan, Kris. 2008. "The Best Advice I Ever Got." *Harvard Business Review*, March 2008, 28.

Gordon, Robert J. 1999. "Has the 'New Economy' Rendered the Productivity Slowdown Obsolete?" Manuscript, Northwestern University, June 12.

———. 2004. "Why Was Europe Left at the Station When America's Productivity Locomotive Departed?" CEPR Working Paper. http://faculty-web.at.northwestern.edu/economics/gordon.

———. 2006. "Issues in the Comparison of Welfare between Europe and the United States." Paper prepared for the Center on Capitalism and Society/CESifo joint conference, Venice, July 21–22.

Greenspan, Alan. 2007. *The Age of Turbulence: Adventures in a New World*. New York: Penguin.

Griliches, Zvi. 1994. "Productivity, R&D, and the Data Constraint." *American Economic Review* 84:1–23.

Grimm, R. E. 1973. "The Autobiography of Leonardo Pisano." *Fibonacci Quarterly* 11, no. 1 (February): 99–104.

Grossman, G., and E. Rossi-Hansberg. 2006. "The Rise of Offshoring: It's Not Wine for Cloth Anymore." Paper presented at Kansas Federal Reserve's Jackson Hole Conference for Central Bankers, July. http://www.kc.frb.org/.

Hamel, G. 1999. "Bringing Silicon Valley Inside." *Harvard Business Review*, September-October.

Hanson, Gordon H., Raymond J. Mataloni Jr., and Matthew J. Slaughter. 2005. "Vertical Production Networks in Multinational Firms." *Review of Economics and Statistics* 87:664–78.

Harris Corporation. 1996. "Founding Dates of the 1994 'Fortune 500' U.S. Companies." *Business History Review* 70, no. 1 (Spring): 69–90.

Hausman, J. A. 1997. "Valuation of New Goods under Perfect and Imperfect Competition." In *The Economics of New Goods*, ed. Timothy F. Bresnahan and Robert J. Gordon, 209–48. Chicago: University of Chicago Press.

Haxel, Stefanie. 2007. "German Students' Free Ride Ends as Universities Charge Tuition." *Bloomberg News*, February 19. http://www.bloomberg.com/apps/news?pid=20601109&sid=aDeKoxxwNkyY&refer=home.

Hayek, Friedrich A. 1945. "The Use of Knowledge in Society." *American Economic Review* 35:519–30.

Henderson, R. M., and K. B. Clark. 1990. "Architectural Innovation: The Reconfiguration of Existing Product Technologies and the Failure of Established Firms." *Administrative Science Quarterly* 35, no. 1, special issue "Technology, Organizations, and Innovation" (March): 9–30.

Herzlinger, R. 2007. "Where Are the Innovators in Health Care?" *Wall Street Journal*, July 19, A15.

Hitt, G. 2007. "Patent System's Revamp Hits Wall." *Wall Street Journal*, August 27, A3.

Holland, C. P., and B. Light. 1999. "A Critical Success Factors Model for ERP Implementation." *IEEE Software*, May–June, 30–35.

Howard, E. 2005. "Introduction to the Proceedings of the 3rd Asia-Pacific Retail Conference, 2005." In *Full Proceedings of the Third Asia Pacific Retail Conference: Retail-Supplier Relationships in Asia-Pacific*, ed. E. Howard and C. Cuthbertson. Oxford: Templeton College.

Howe, Peter J. 2000. "Messaging Is the Medium." *Boston Globe*, December 4, C1.

Hurst, Erik, and Annamaria Lusardi. 2004. "Liquidity Constraints, Household Wealth and Business Ownership." *Journal of Political Economy* 112:319–47.

Immigration and Naturalization Service. 2002. "Report on Characteristics of Specialty Occupation Workers. H-1B: Fiscal Year 2000." April.

Indian Ministry of Finance. 2003. *Economic Survey, 2002–2003*. New Delhi. http://indiabudget.nic.in.

Jaffe, Adam B., and Josh Lerner. 2004. *Innovation and Its Discontents: How Our Broken Patent System Is Endangering Innovation and Progress, and What to Do about It*. Princeton: Princeton University Press.

Jorgenson, D. W., and K. J. Stiroh. 2000. "Raising the Speed Limit: U.S. Economic Growth in the Information Age." OECD Economics Department Working Paper No. 261.

Kapur D., and P. B. Mehta. 2004. "Indian Higher Education Reform: From Half-Baked Socialism to Half-Baked Capitalism." CID Working Paper No. 108.

Karmarkar, U. S. 2004. "Will You Survive the Services Revolution?" *Harvard Business Review*, June, 1–9.

Kaul, Rekha. 1993. *Caste, Class, and Education: Politics of the Capitation Fee Phenomenon in Karnataka*. New Delhi: Sage.

Kawamoto, D. 2003. "Segway Sales Fall Short." CNet News.com, September 29. http://news.zdnet.co.uk/hardware/0,1000000091,39116739,00.htm. December 7, 2003.

Keynes, John Maynard. 1971–73. "Economic Possibilities for Our Grandchildren." In *Collected Writings*, vol. 9, *Essays in Persuasion* (1930). London: St. Martin's Press.

Kirkegaard, Jacob F. 2005. "Outsourcing and Skill Imports: Foreign High-Skilled Workers on H-1B and L-1 Visas in the United States." Institute for International Economics Working Paper 05–15, December.

——— 2006. "Offshoring and Offshore Outsourcing: Extent and Impact of Labour Markets in Origin and Recipient Countries." Institute for International Economics, Washington, DC.

Knight, Frank H. 1921. *Risk, Uncertainty, and Profit*. Chicago: University of Chicago Press.

Koch, Christopher. N.d. "The ABCs of ERP." *CIO Magazine*. http://www.cio.com/research/erp/edit/erpbasics.html. Accessed January 10, 2006.

Kortum, Samuel S, and J. Lerner. 2000. "Assessing the Contribution of Venture Capital to Innovation." *RAND Journal of Economics* 31:674–92.

Kronholz, J. 2006. "Under a Cloud: For Dr. Sengupta, Long-Term Visa Is a Long Way Off." *Wall Street Journal*, June 27, A1.

Krugman, Paul. 1994. "Competitiveness: A Dangerous Obsession." *Foreign Affairs* 73, no. 2 (March–April): 28–44.

———. 1995. "Growing World Trade: Causes and Consequences." *Brookings Papers on Economic Activity* 1995:327–77.

Lamoreaux, Naomi R., and Kenneth L. Sokoloff. 1996. "Long-Term Change in the Organization of Inventive Activity." *Proceedings of the National Academy of Science* 93:12686–92.

———. 1997. "Location and Technological Change in the American Glass Industry during the Late Nineteenth and Early Twentieth Centuries." NBER Working Paper No. 5938, February.

Landler, M. 2006. "Wal-Mart Decides to Pull Out of Germany." *New York Times*, July 28.

Leamer, E. 2004. "Who's Afraid of Global Trade." October 28. http://www.international.ucla.edu/cms/files/progess.pdf.

———. 2006. "A Flat World, a Level Playing Field, a Small World after All, or None of the Above?" *Journal of Economic Literature* 45, no. 1 (March): 83–126.

Leslie K., with C. H. Deutsch. 2000. "Montgomery Ward to Close Its Doors." *New York Times*, December 29.

Lohr, S. 2004. "High-End Technology Work Not Immune to Outsourcing." *New York Times*, June 16.

———. 2008. "I.B.M. to Introduce a Notably Improved Mainframe." *New York Times*, February 26.

Lucas, Henry C., Jr. 1999. *Information Technology and the Productivity Paradox: The Search for Value.* New York: Oxford University Press.

Maddison, Angus. 1971. *Class Structure and Economic Growth: India and Pakistan since the Moghuls.* London: Allen and Unwin.

———. 1995. *Monitoring the World Economy, 1820–1992.* Paris: OECD Development Centre.

———. 1997. "Causal Influences on Productivity Performance 1820–1992: A Global Perspective." *Journal of Productivity Analysis* 8, no. 4 (November): 325–60.

Malone, M. S. 2007. "iGenius." *Wall Street Journal*, January 11, A15.

Mann, Catherine L. 2003. "Globalization of IT Services and White Collar Jobs: The Next Wave of Productivity Growth." Institute of International Economics, International Economics Policy Briefs 3–11, December.

Mann, Catherine L., with Jacob Funk Kirkegaard. 2006. *Accelerating the Globalization of America: The Role for Information Technology.* Washington, DC: Institute for International Economics.

Mansfield, E., J. Rapoport, A. Romeo, S. Wagner, and G. Beardsley. 1977. "Social and Private Rates of Return from Industrial Innovations." *Quarterly Journal of Economics* 91, no. 2 (May): 221–40.

Mariani, M. 2001. Next to Production or to Technological Clusters? The Economics and Management of R&D Location." *Journal of Management and Governance* 6, no. 2: 131–52.

Markus, M. L., S. Axline, D. Petrie, and C. Tanis. 2003. "Learning from Adopters' Experiences with ERP: Problems Encountered and Successes Achieved." In *Second*

Wave Enterprise Resource Planning Systems: Implementing for Effectiveness, ed. Graeme Shanks, Peter B. Seddon, and Leslie P. Willcocks. Cambridge: Cambridge University Press.

McCary, J. 2007. "House Committee Explores Effect of Outsourcing on the Economy." *New York Times*, June 12.

McCraw, Thomas K. 1997. "American Capitalism." In *Creating Modern Capitalism: How Entrepreneurs, Companies, and Countries Triumphed in Three Industrial Revolutions*, ed. Thomas K. McCraw. Cambridge: Harvard University Press.

McCraw, Thomas K., and R. S. Tedlow. 1997. "Henry Ford, Alfred Sloan, and the Three Phases of Marketing." In *Creating Modern Capitalism: How Entrepreneurs, Companies, and Countries Triumphed in Three Industrial Revolutions*, ed. Thomas K. McCraw. Cambridge: Harvard University Press.

McGettigan, P., J. Golden, J. Fryer, R. Chan, and J. Feely. 2001. "Prescribers Prefer People: The Sources of Information Used by Doctors for Prescribing Suggest That the Medium Is More Important Than the Message." *British Journal of Clinical Pharmacology* 51 (February): 184–89.

McKinsey & Co. 2005. *The Emerging Global Labor Market*. http://www.mckinsey.com/mgi/publications/emerginggloballabormarket/.

Messina, Julián. 2004. "Institutions and Service Employment: A Panel Study for OECD Countries." ECB Working Paper No. 320, March.

Mindlin, A. 2007. "Cellphone-Only Homes Hit a Milestone." *New York Times*, August 27.

Ministry of Economic Affairs, Netherlands, McKinsey & Co. 2004. *Fostering Excellence: Challenges for Productivity Growth in Europe*. Background document for the Informal Competitiveness Council, Maastricht, July 1–3. http://www.ggdc.net/pub/fostering_excellence.pdf.

Mishra, B. B. 1961. *The Indian Middle Classes: Their Growth in Modern Times*. London: Oxford University Press.

Mitchell, J. 1987. "TI's Pulse: Worldwide Computers, Satellites Keep 77,000 Employees, Clientele Connected." *Dallas Morning News*, July 28, 1A.

Mitchell, Neil J. 1991. "Review: Foreign Money & American Politics." *Polity* 24, no. 2 (Winter): 337–52.

Mokyr, Joel. 1990. *The Lever of Riches: Technological Creativity and Economic Progress*. New York: Oxford University Press.

Moore, Gordon E. 1996. "Some Personal Perspectives on Research in the Semiconductor Industry." In *Engines of Innovation: U.S. Industrial Research at the End of an Era*, ed. Richard S. Rosenbloom and William J. Spencer. Boston: Harvard Business School Press.

Mueller, W. F. 1962. "The Origins of the Basic Inventions Underlying DuPont's Major Product and Process Innovations, 1920–1950." In *The Rate and Direction of Inventive Activity: Social Factors*. NBER Conference Series No. 13. Princeton: Princeton University Press.

Murray, C. 2007. "What's Wrong with Vocational School?" *Wall Street Journal*, January 17, A19.

National Academies Committee on Prospering in the Global Economy of the 21st Century. 2005. *Rising Above the Gathering Storm: Energizing and Employing America for a Brighter Economic Future.* Washington, DC: National Academies Press.

National Science Foundation. 2002. *Science and Engineering Indicators—2002.* www.nsf.gov/statistics/seind02.

———. 2006. *Science and Engineering Indicators—2006.* www.nsf.gov/statistics/seind06.

Nelson, Richard R. 1993. *National Innovation Systems: A Comparative Analysis.* New York: Oxford University Press.

———. 2006. "What Makes an Economy Productive and Progressive? What Are the Needed Institutions?" LEM Working Paper Series 2006/24, September. http://ideas.repec.org/p/ssa/lemwps/2006-24.html.

Nelson, Richard R., and Edmund S. Phelps. 1966. "Investment in Humans, Technological Diffusion, and Economic Growth." *American Economic Review* 56, no. 2: 69–75.

Nelson, Richard R., and Sidney G. Winter. 1982. *An Evolutionary Theory of Economic Change.* Cambridge: Belknap Press of Harvard University Press.

———. 1992. "The Rise and Rise and Fall of American Technological Leadership: The Postwar Era in Historical Perspective." *Journal of Economic Literature* 30 (December): 1931–64.

Nichols, N. 1994. "Medicine, Management and Mergers: An Interview with Merck's P. Roy Vagelos." *Harvard Business Review* 72, no. 1 (November–December): 104–14.

Nordhaus, W. D. 1997. "Do Real-Output and Real-Wage Measures Capture Reality? The History of Lighting Suggests Not." In *The Economics of New Goods,* ed. Timothy F. Bresnahan and Robert J. Gordon, 29–66. Chicago: University of Chicago Press.

Norges Bank. 2007. "Developments in Productivity Growth." *Monetary Policy Report* 2/2007, 44–47. http://www.norges-bank.no/Upload/62887/B4_developments_in_productivity_growth.pdf.

O'Connor, H. J. 2002. "*Helicobacter pylori* and Dyspepsia: Physicians' Attitudes, Clinical Practice, and Prescribing Habits." *Alimentary Pharmacology & Therapeutics* 16, no. 3 (March): 487–96.

Ohkawa, Kazushi, and Henry Rosovsky. 1973. *Japanese Economic Growth: Trend Acceleration in the Twentieth Century.* Stanford: Stanford University Press.

Olegario, R. 1997. "IBM and the Two Thomas J. Watsons." In *Creating Modern Capitalism: How Entrepreneurs, Companies, and Countries Triumphed in Three Industrial Revolutions,* ed. Thomas K. McCraw. Cambridge: Harvard University Press.

Olson, M. 1997. "Why Are Differences in Per Capita Incomes So Large and Persistent." In *Chinese Technology Transfer in the 1990s: Current Experiences, Historical Problems, and International Perspectives,* ed. Charles Feinstein and Christopher Howe, 193–222. Lyme, NH: Edward Elgar.

O'Mahony, Mary, and Bart van Ark, eds. 2003. *EU Productivity and Competitiveness: An Industry Perspective; Can Europe Resume the Catching-up Process?* Luxembourg: Office for Official Publications of the European Communities.

Organisation for Economic Co-operation and Development (OECD). *Oslo Manual.* http://www.oecd.org/dataoecd/35/61/2367580.pdf.

———— 2005. *Innovation Policy and Performance: A Cross-Country Comparison*. ISBN 92-64-00672-9. Paris: OECD.

————. 2007. *Economic Survey of Norway, 2007*. Policy brief, January. http://www.oecd.org/dataoecd/52/55/38001508.pdf.

Osterweil, N. 2005. "Medical Research Spending Doubled over Past Decade." *MedPage Today*, September 20.

Ostry, Sylvia, and Richard R. Nelson. 1995. *Techno-Nationalism and Techno-Globalism: Conflict and Cooperation*. Washington, DC: Brookings Institution Press.

Packard, David. 1996. *The HP Way: How Bill Hewlett and I Built Our Company*. Ed. D. Kirby with Karen Lewis. New York: HarperBusiness.

Parente, S. L., and E. C. Prescott. 1994. "Barriers to Technology Adoption and Development." *Journal of Political Economy* 2, no. 2: 298–32.

Peri, Giovanni. 2005. "Skill and Talent of Immigrants: A Comparison between the European Union and the United States." Working paper, July.

Petroski, Henry. 1990. *The Pencil: A History of Design and Circumstance*. New York: Alfred A. Knopf.

Pettus, A. 2005. "Overseas Insourcing." *Harvard Magazine*, November–December, 15.

Phelps, Edmund S. 2007. "Macroeconomics for a Modern Economy." *American Economic Review* 97:543–61.

Pilat, Dirk. 2001. "Innovation and Productivity in Services: State of the Art." In *Innovation and Productivity in Services*. Paris: OECD.

Plant, R., and Leslie P. Willcocks. 2006. "Critical Success Factors in International ERP Implementations: A Case Research Approach." London School of Economics and Political Science Working Paper, May.

Pogue, D. 2007. "Apple Waves Its Wand at the Phone." *New York Times*, January 11.

Polanyi, Michael. 1964. *Personal Knowledge: Towards a Post-critical Philosophy*. London: Routledge.

Popkin, Joel, and Kathryn Kobe. 2006. "U.S. Manufacturing Innovation at Risk." Report issued by the Manufacturing Institute and the Council of Manufacturing Associations. February. www.nam.org/future.

Porter, E. 2006. "The More You Pay, the Better the Care? Think Twice." *New York Times*, December 17.

Postrel, V. 2005. "In Silicon Valley, Job Hopping Contributes to Innovation." *New York Times*, December 1.

Prestowitz, C. 1988. *Trading Places: How We Allowed Japan to Take the Lead*. New York: Basic Books.

————. 2005. *Three Billion New Capitalists: The Great Shift of Wealth and Power to the East*. New York: Basic Books.

————. 2006a. *America's Technology Future at Risk: Broadband and Investment Strategies to Refire Innovation*. Washington, DC: Economic Strategy Institute.

————. 2006b. "The World Is Tilted." *Newsweek*, special issue "Issues 2006."

Pugh, Emerson W. 1995. *Building IBM: Shaping and Industry and Its Technology*. Cambridge: MIT Press.

Rae, John. 1895. *Life of Adam Smith*. London: Macmillan.

Richardson, G. 1972. "The Organization of Industry." *Economic Journal* 84:883–96.

Roach, S. 1988. "White Collar Productivity: A Glimmer of Hope?" Special economic study, Morgan Stanley, September 16.

Roberts, E. 2004. "Here Be Dragons: The Economics of Enterprise Software Systems." Letter to Members of the Faculty Senate, Stanford University, May 27.

Rodgers, T. J. 1990. "No Excuses Management." *Harvard Business Review*, July–August, 84–98. Reprint 90409.

Rodgers, T. J, William Taylor, and Rick Foreman. 1993. *No-Excuses Management: Proven Systems for Starting Fast, Growing Quickly, and Surviving Hard Times.* New York: Currency/Doubleday.

Roe, Mark J. 2007. "Juries and the Political Economy of Legal Origin." *Journal of Comparative Economics* 35:294–308.

Romer, Paul. 2007. "Economic Growth." In *The Concise Encyclopedia of Economics*, ed. David R. Henderson. Indianapolis: Liberty Fund.

Rosenberg, Nathan. 1976. *Perspectives on Technology.* New York: Cambridge University Press.

———. 1982. "Learning by Using." In *Inside the Black Box: Technology and Economics.* New York: Cambridge University Press.

Rosenberg Nathan, and L. E. Birdzell Jr. 1986. *How the West Grew Rich: The Economic Transformation of the Industrial World.* New York: Basic Books.

Rucker, T. Donald 1976. "Drug Information for Prescribers and Dispensers: Toward a Model System." *Med Care* 14, no. 2 (February): 156–65.

Ruff, J. 1996. "The Globalization of a Food Processor." *Food and Drug Law Journal* 51, no. 4: 727–34.

Rundle, R. L. 2004. "Eye Doctor to Elite Blazes New Trail in Selling Surgery." *Wall Street Journal*, October 26, A1.

Sahlman, W. H. 1990. "The Structure and Governance of Venture-Capital Organizations." *Journal of Financial Economics* 27:473–521.

Samuelson, P. A. 2004. "Where Ricardo and Mill Rebut and Confirm Arguments of Mainstream Economists Supporting Globalization." *Journal of Economic Perspectives* 18, no. 3 (Summer): 135–46.

Samuelson, R. J. 2005. "Sputnik Scare, Updated." *Washington Post*, August 10.

Saxenian, A. 1994. *Regional Advantage: Culture and Competition in Silicon Valley and Route 128.* Cambridge: Harvard University Press.

Scaffidi, Chris, M. Shaw, and B. Myers. 2005. "Estimating the Numbers of End Users and End User Programmers." *Proceedings of the 2005 IEEE Symposium on Visual Languages and Human-Centric Computing.* VL/HCC'05. 1–8. http://ieeexplore.ieee.org/Xplore/login.jsp?url=/iel5/10093/32326/01509505.pdf?arnumber=1509505.

Schmidley, D. 2001. *Profile of the Foreign Born Population in the United States: 2000.* Washington, DC: U.S. Census Bureau.

Schumpeter, Joseph. A. 1934. *The Theory of Economic Development* (1911). Cambridge: Harvard University Press.

———. 1961. *Capitalism, Socialism, and Democracy* (1942). London: George Allen and Unwin.

Severson, K. 2007. "The World's Best Candy Bars? English, of Course." *New York Times*, July 11.

Sharma, A. 2006. "Frank Gehry: The Architect." *Wall Street Journal*, December 23, A8.

Silvestrini, Marc. 2002. "Wallingford, Conn., High-Tech Firm Gets Attention from Venture Capitalists." *Waterbury Republican-American*, July 8.

Smart, T. 1996. "Jack Welch's Encore." *BusinessWeek*, October 28.

Smith, Adam. 1776. *An Inquiry into the Nature and Causes of the Wealth of Nations*. Modern Library edition. New York: Random House, 1937.

Solow, Robert M. 1956. "A Contribution to the Theory of Economic Growth." *Quarterly Journal of Economics* 70:65–94.

———. 1957. "Technical Change and the Aggregate Production Function." *Review of Economics and Statistics* 39, no. 3 (August): 312–20.

———. 1987. "We'd Better Watch Out." *New York Times*, July 12, 36.

———. 2006. "Comments on Papers by Saint-Paul, Aghion, and Bhidé." *Capitalism and Society* 1, no. 1, article 3.

Somers, T. M., and K. Nelson. 2001. "The Impact of Critical Success Factors across the Stages of Enterprise Resource Planning Implementations." *Proceedings of the 34th Hawaii International Conference on System Sciences (HICSS-3)*, Maui, Hawaii, January 3–6. CD-ROM.

Stefano Scarpetta, S., P. Hemmings, T. Tressel, and J. Woo. 2002. "The Role of Policy and Institutions for Productivity and Firm Dynamics: Evidence from Micro and Industry Data." OECD Economics Department Working Paper No. 329, April.

Stiglitz, Joseph. 1990. "Comments: Some Retrospective Views on Growth Theory." *Growth, Productivity, Unemployment: Essays to Celebrate Bob Solow's Birthday*, ed. Peter Diamond. Cambridge: MIT Press.

Sutthiphisal, D. 2006. "The Geography of Invention in High- and Low-Technology Industries: Evidence from the Second Industrial Revolution." Dissertation summary. *Journal of Economic History* 66, no. 2 (June): 492–96.

Tedlow, Richard S. 2001. *Giants of Enterprise: Seven Business Innovators and the Empires They Built*. New York: HarperBusiness.

———. 2003. *The Watson Dynasty: The Fiery Reign and Troubled Legacy of IBM's Founding Father and Son*. New York: HarperBusiness.

Teresi, Dick. 2004. "Foreign Policy, Flemish Painters, and Pharoah Placement: The Many Purposes of Science." *In Character*, Fall, 36–43.

Tomlinson, B. R. 1993. *The Economy of Modern India, 1860–1970*. Vol. 3 of *The New Cambridge History of India*. Cambridge: Cambridge University Press.

Trajtenberg, M. 1989. "The Welfare Analysis of Product Innovations, with an Application to Computed Tomography Scanners." *Journal of Political Economy* 97: 444–79.

Triplett, J. E., and B. Bosworth. 2004. *Productivity in the U.S. Services Sector: New Sources of Economic Growth*. Washington, DC: Brookings Institution Press.

U.S. Department of Commerce. 1998. *The Emerging Digital Economy*. Washington, DC: U.S. Department of Commerce.

Van Ark, Bart. 2006. "Mind the Gap! A Comparison of Services Productivity in Europe and the United States." Presentation at Services and Innovation Conference, October 10–11, Helsinki.

Van Ark, Bart, Robert Inklaar, and Robert H. McGuckin. 2002. " 'Changing Gear': Productivity, ICT and Service Industries; Europe and the United States." Research Memorandum GD-60, University of Groningen, Groningen Growth and Development Centre.

Van Biema, M., and B. Greenwald. 1997. "Understanding Productivity in the Service Sector." Columbia Business School Working Paper, January 9.

Van Riper, T. 2007. "GE, at Your Service." Forbes.com, May 18.

Varian, H. R. 2005. "Technology Levels the Business Playing Field." *New York Times*, August 25.

Varma, Subodh. 2007. "NRIs Send Most Money Back Home." *Times of India*, October 21. http://timesofindia.indiatimes.com/articleshow/2477713.cms.

Vedder, R. 2004. *Going Broke by Degree: Why College Costs Too Much*. Washington, DC: AEI Press.

von Hippel, Eric. 1976. "The Dominant Role of Users in the Scientific Instrument Innovation Process." *Research Policy* 5, no. 3: 212–39.

———. 1988. *The Sources of Innovation*. New York: Oxford University Press.

———. 2005. *Democratizing Innovation*. Cambridge: MIT Press.

Von Tunzelmann, N. 1997. "The Transfer of Process Technologies in Comparative Perspective." In *Chinese Technology Transfer in the 1990s: Current Experiences, Historical Problems, and International Perspectives*, ed. Charles Feinstein and Christopher Howe, 203–34. Lyme, NH: Edward Elgar.

Wadhwa, Vivek, Guillermina Jasso, Ben Rissing, Gary Gereffi, and Richard B. Freeman. 2007. "Intellectual Property, the Immigration Backlog, and a Reverse Brain-Drain: America's New Immigrant Entrepreneurs, Part III." August 22. http://ssrn.com/abstract=1008366.

Wadhwa, Vivek, AnnaLee Saxenian, Ben Rissing, and Gary Gereffi. 2007. "America's New Immigrant Entrepreneurs." http://memp.pratt.duke.edu/downloads/americas_new_immigrant_entrepreneurs.pdf.

Wall, N. M. 2005. "Stealing from the Poor to Care for the Rich." *New York Times*, December 14.

Walters, Robert, Tim Stapleton, and Richard Andrews. 2007. *India's Services Sector: Unlocking Opportunity*. Australian Government, Department of Foreign Affairs and Trade, Economic Analytical Unit. http://dfat.ausinfoshop.com/redirector.1351/2534.

Welch, Jack, with John A. Byrne. 2001. *Straight from the Gut*. New York: Warner Books.

Wölfl, Anita. 2003. "Productivity Growth in Service Industries: An Assessment of Recent Patterns and the Role of Measurement." STI Working Paper 2003/7.

World Health Organization. 2006. *The World Health Report 2006: Working Together for Health*. Geneva: World Health Organization.

Yoffie, D. B., T. D. Merrill, and M. Slind. 2006. "iPod vs. Cell Phone: A Mobile Music Revolution?" Harvard Business School Case No. 707–419.

■ Index

The letters *b*, *f*, *n*, and *t* refer to boxes, figures, notes, and tables on the pages indicated. The number following an *n* refers to the note number on that page. The symbols * and † refer to footnotes.